Irregular Migration, Refugee Status and the Law

Through an investigation of the protection needs of 'irregularised migrants', this book offers a novel approach to the phenomenon of irregular migration by reframing it as a matter of refugee law.

Thousands of people have died, disappeared and suffered mental and physical harm on their dangerous migratory journeys to Europe. This book addresses an issue which, so far, has been largely omitted from the study of refugee law: the fact that harm experienced during irregular migration is often as serious as harm feared by recognised refugees in their countries of origin. Grundler argues that harm experienced during dangerous journeys can constitute persecution and that a risk of irregular re-migration can form the basis for a claim to refugee status. Drawing insights from a comparative content analysis of trafficked persons' asylum claims, other disciplines such as psychology and sociology and additional case law, this book provides readers with new understandings on the scope of the *refugee* definition, adds new concepts to migration theories and challenges states' migration control policies.

This volume will be an important point of reference for scholars, practitioners, policymakers and students working on refugee and human rights law, (irregular) migration and vulnerability.

Maja Grundler is Lecturer at Northumbria Law School and holds a PhD in Law from Queen Mary University of London. Her research interests include refugee law, irregular migration and human trafficking.

Law and Migration

Series Editor
Satvinder S. Juss
King's College London, UK

Migration and its subsets of refugee and asylum policy are rising up the policy agenda at national and international level. Current controversies underline the need for rational and informed debate of this widely misrepresented and little understood area.

Law and Migration contributes to this debate by establishing a monograph series to encourage discussion and help to inform policy in this area. The series provides a forum for leading new research principally from the Law and Legal Studies area but also from related social sciences. The series is broad in scope, covering a wide range of subjects and perspectives.

Other titles in this series:

Human Rights and The Revision of Refugee Law
Romit Bhandari

Refugees, Democracy and the Law
Political Rights at the Margins of the State
Dana Schmalz

Inside Asylum Appeals
Access, Participation and Procedure in Europe
Nick Gill, Nicole Hoellerer, Jessica Hambly and Daniel Fisher

Protection of Human Life at Sea in International Law
Rescuing Maritime Migrants
Aphrodite Papachristodoulou

Irregular Migration, Refugee Status and the Law
Protection from Dangerous Migratory Journeys
Maja Grundler

For more information about this series, please visit: www.routledge.com/Law-and-Migration/book-series/LAWANDMIG

Irregular Migration, Refugee Status and the Law

Protection from Dangerous Migratory Journeys

Maja Grundler

Routledge
Taylor & Francis Group
LONDON AND NEW YORK

First published 2026
by Routledge
4 Park Square, Milton Park, Abingdon, Oxon OX14 4RN

and by Routledge
605 Third Avenue, New York, NY 10158

Routledge is an imprint of the Taylor & Francis Group, an informa business

British Library Cataloguing-in-Publication Data
A catalogue record for this book is available from the British Library

ISBN: 978-1-032-64174-4 (hbk)
ISBN: 978-1-032-66462-0 (pbk)
ISBN: 978-1-032-66464-4 (ebk)

DOI: 10.4324/9781032664644

Typeset in ITC Galliard Pro
by Apex CoVantage, LLC

Contents

Acknowledgements

The argument in this book – that the risk of undertaking dangerous migratory journeys ought to warrant refugee protection – developed as a result of conversations with asylum seekers in a Berlin refugee shelter where I worked between November 2016 and February 2018. People whose protection claims had been refused, and who anxiously awaited the outcome of their appeals, talked about what they would do if they were to be returned to their countries of origin. Most agreed that they would try again, that they would undertake another perilous journey. This book was written with their stories, courage and determination in mind. I am grateful to every single one of them for sharing their experiences with me and for inspiring this research.

This book draws and builds on my PhD thesis, which I completed at Queen Mary University of London in 2022. First and foremost, I want to thank my supervisors, Professor Elspeth Guild and Professor Violeta Moreno-Lax, for their encouragement, kindness and generosity in sharing their knowledge with me, and for being wonderful colleagues and mentors post-PhD. I also want to thank Dr Niovi Vavoula for her valuable comments on my work. Further, I wish to express my gratitude to Professor Dallal Stevens and Professor Nora Markard, who examined my thesis, for their careful and constructive feedback. Finally, I am grateful to the Leverhulme Trust for funding my PhD research, and to Professor Engin Isin for making this possible and for many inspiring conversations.

I am also grateful to the friends and colleagues who have been a constant source of support and inspiration throughout my PhD journey and beyond. While it is impossible to name everyone without missing someone deserving, please know how much I appreciate each of you. That said, I would like to extend special thanks to Dr Nicolette Busuttil, Dr Kathryn Allinson, Dr Janina Pescinski and Dr Gillian Kane, as well as the Refugee Law Initiative and everyone involved in creating the community and inspiration it provides.

Thank you also to Northumbria Law School and Professor Michael Stockdale, Dr Laura Graham and the Law and Society research group for the time and resources to complete this book.

Finally, thank you to my friends, my family in Germany and the UK and, most of all, my wonderful partner, Matt, for your love and support – you mean everything to me.

Table of Cases

Court of Justice of the European Union

C-175/08, C-176/08, C-178/08 and C-179/08 *Abdulla and Others* [2010] ECLI:EU:C:2010:105
C-179/11 *Cimande and GISTI* [2012] ECLI:EU:C:2012:594
C-268/99 *Jany and Others* [2001] ECLI:EU:C:2001:616
C-465/07 *Elgafaji, Opinion of AG Maduro* [2008] ECLI:EU:C:2008:479
C-465/07 *Elgafaji* [2009] ECLI:EU:C:2009:94
C-542/13 *M'Bodj* [2014] ECLI:EU:C:2014:2452
C-621/21 *WS* [2024] ECLI:EU:C:2024:47
C-79/13 *Saciri and Others* [2014] ECLI:EU:C:2014:103
C-604/12 *HN* [2014] ECLI:EU:C:2014:302

European Commission/European Court of Human Rights

Aydin v Turkey App no 57/1996/676/866 (ECtHR, 25 September 1997)
Banković and Others v Belgium and Others App no 52207/99 (ECtHR, 12 December 2001)
Chahal v The United Kingdom App no 22414/93 (ECtHR, 15 November 1996)
Cyprus v Turkey App no 25781/94 (ECtHR, 10 May 2001)
D v The United Kingdom App no 30240/96 (ECtHR, 2 May 1997)
FG v Sweden App no 43611/11 (ECtHR, 23 March 2016)
Greek Case App nos 3321/67, 3322/67, 3323/67, 3344/67 (European Commission of Human Rights, 5 November 1969)
Hirsi Jamaa and Others v Italy App no 27765/09 (ECtHR, 23 February 2012)
HLR v France App no 24573/94 (ECtHR, 29 April 1997)
Ilias and Ahmed v Hungary App no 47287/15 (ECtHR, 21 November 2019)
Ireland v The United Kingdom App no 5310/71 (ECtHR, 13 December 1977)
JK and Others v Sweden App no 59166/12 (ECtHR, 23 August 2016)
MN and Others v Belgium App no 3599/18 (ECtHR, 5 May 2020)
MSS v Belgium and Greece App no 30696/09 (ECtHR, 21 January 2011)
N v The United Kingdom App no 26565/05 (ECtHR, 27 May 2008)
ND and NT v Spain App nos 8675/15 and 8697/15 (ECtHR, 13 February 2020)

Paposhvili v Belgium App no 41738/10 (ECtHR, 13 December 2016)
SHH v The United Kingdom App no 60367/10 (ECtHR, 29 January 2013)
Soering v United Kingdom App no 14038/88 (ECtHR, 7 July 1989)
Sufi and Elmi v The United Kingdom App nos 8319/07 and 11449/07 (ECtHR, 28 June 2011)
Tarakhel v Switzerland App no 29217/12 (ECtHR, 4 November 2014)
Tyrer v UK App no 5856/72 (ECtHR, 25 April 1978)
X v Finland App no 34806/04 (ECtHR, 3 July 2012)

Germany

Bayerischer Verwaltungsgerichtshof, 13a B 14.30285, 21.11.2014
Bayerischer Verwaltungsgerichtshof, 13a B 17.30030, 23.03.2017
Bayerischer Verwaltungsgerichtshof, 13a B 19.33510, 06.02.2020
Bayerischer Verwaltungsgerichtshof, 13a B 19.34211, 17.12.2020
Bayerischer Verwaltungsgerichtshof, 13a B 20.30347, 29.10.2020
Bayerischer Verwaltungsgerichtshof, 8 ZB 18.31141, 09.08.2018
Bundesgerichtshof, BGH 5 StR 154/14, 16.07.2014
Bundesverwaltungsgericht, 1 B 25.18, 08.08.2018
Bundesverwaltungsgericht, 1 C 10.21, 21.04.2022
Bundesverwaltungsgericht, 6 C 3.96, 26.02.1997
OVG Berlin-Brandenburg, OVG 4 B 8/22, 30.11.2023
OVG Bremen, 1 LB 258/20, 22.09.2020
Verwaltungsgerichtshof Baden-Württemberg, A 11 S 1704/17, 03.11.2017
Verwaltungsgerichtshof Baden-Württemberg, A 11 S 2042/20, 17.12.2020
VG Aachen, 2 K 1712/10.A, 24.05.2012
VG Aachen, 2 K 2224/15.A, 28.12.2017
VG Aachen, 2 K 2514/21 A, 06.06.2023
VG Aachen, 2 K 2521/18.A, 10.11.2020
VG Aachen, 2 K 2738/13.A, 24.08.2015
VG Aachen, 3 K 12/07, 08.05.2007
VG Aachen, 8 K 1220/02.A, 21.01.2004
VG Ansbach, AN 14 K 11.30049, 17.05.2011
VG Augsburg, Au 7 K 12.30184, 18.09.2012
VG Augsburg, Au 7 K 16.31586, 21.07.2017
VG Augsburg, Au 7 K 17.30060, 13.12.2017
VG Berlin, 20 K 666.17 A, 24.03.2022
VG Berlin, 31 K 305/20 A, 17.08.2022
VG Braunschweig, 5 A 317/20, 16.08.2024
VG Bremen, 2 K 610/19, 23.12.2022
VG Bremen, 7 K 2424/21, 29.11.2022
VG Chemnitz, 2 K 322/19.A, 26.08.2022
VG Cottbus, 3 K 633/20.A, 29.05.2020
VG Cottbus, 9 K 1516/18.A, 11.01.2021
VG Darmstadt, 3 K 1022/19.DA.A, 31.01.2024

VG Düsseldorf, 27 K 2264/18.A, 15.12.2020
VG Düsseldorf, 27 K 3867/19.A, 12.12.2022
VG Gelsenkirchen, 17a K 2612/18.A, 04.11.2022
VG Gera, 2 K 968/22 Ge, 05.09.2022
VG Gießen, 18 K 535/22.GI.A, 04.06.2024
VG Göttingen, 3 A 135/21, 03.04.2024
VG Hamburg, 10 A 6516/16, 10.01.2017
VG Hannover, 10 A 6353/18, 09.09.2021
VG Hannover, 5 A 11015/17, 29.10.2020
VG Hannover, 5 A 2783/17, 30.09.2020
VG Hannover, 5 A 8988/17, 04.01.2021
VG Karlsruhe, A 18 K 5065/18, 02.06.2021
VG Karlsruhe, A 5 K 4693/23, 28.05.2024
VG Kassel, 4 K 1583/18.KS.A, 30.03.2022
VG Koblenz, 1 K 1013/08.KO, 12.11.2008
VG Köln, 2 K 5595/18.A, 28.05.2019
VG Köln, 8 K 4355/18 A, 29.02.2024
VG Leipzig, 7 K 153/18.A, 28.04.2021
VG Lüneburg, 6 A 350/19, 10.06.2021
VG Lüneburg, 6 A 7/20, 22.02.2021
VG Magdeburg, 6 A 40/19, 28.01.2020
VG Minden, 3 K 1476/19.A, 28.01.2022
VG München, M 10 K 16.30286, 17.11.2016
VG München, M 10 K 23.32418, 31.05.2024
VG München, M 11 K 06.51323, 11.09.2007
VG München, M 11 K 19.30060, 04.10.2023
VG München, M 13 K 21.30776, 21.06.2022
VG München, M 21 K 11.30680, 28.04.2014
VG München, M 23 K 11.30389, 30.09.2013
VG München, M 24 K 07.50603, 06.11.2007
VG Münster, 5 K 3492/21 A, 22.08.2022
VG Oldenburg, 3 A 710/23, 09.02.2024
VG Regensburg, 15 K 21.31190, 16.12.2021
VG Regensburg, RN 5 K 16.30603, 19.10.2016
VG Regensburg, RO 15 K 20.30871, 26.04.2021
VG Saarland, 3 K 1408/20, 01.06.2021
VG Saarland, 5 K 741/20, 23.02.2022
VG Sigmaringen, A 7 K 4913–20, 15.02.2023
VG Stuttgart, A 1 K 8819/18, 5770443, 16.11.2020
VG Stuttgart, A 7 K 1405/12, 16.05.2014
VG Wiesbaden, 3 K 1465/09.WI.A, 14.03.2011
VG Wiesbaden, 3 K 264/19.WI.A, 08.06.2022
VG Würzburg, W 8 K 04.30919, 19.09.2005
VG Würzburg, W 4 K 09.30232, 29.07.2011
VG Würzburg, W 2 K 14.30213, 17.11.2015
VG Würzburg, W 10 K 18.31682, 21.12.2018

VG Würzburg, W 10 K 19.50275, 26.01.2019
VG Würzburg, W 8 K 20 31251, 20.05.2022

Human Rights Committee

Human Rights Committee, *Ioane Teitiota v New Zealand*, UN doc CCPR/C/127/D/2728/2016 (24 October 2019)
Human Rights Committee, *Lopez Burgos v Uruguay*, Comm 52/1979 (29 July 1981)
Human Rights Committee, *Vidal Martins v Uruguay*, Comm 57/1979 (23 March 1982)

New Zealand

AC (Eritrea) [2023] NZIPT 802201–202
AC (Tuvalu) [2014] NZIPT 800517–520
AF (Kiribati) [2013] NZIPT 800413
AF (Tuvalu) [2015] NZIPT 800859
AI (Tuvalu) [2017] NZIPT 801093–094
AJ (Tuvalu) [2017] NZIPT 801120–123
AV (Tulvalu) [2022] NZIPT 505532
AW (Kiribati) [2022] NZIPT 802085
BG (Fiji) [2012] NZIPT 800091
Refugee Appeal No 72185 [2000] NZRSAA (10 August 2000)
Refugee Appeal No 72186 [2000] NZRSAA 336 (10 August 2000)
Refugee Appeal No 72313 [2000] NZRSAA 491 (19 October 2000)
Refugee Appeal No 72314 [2000] NZRSAA 492 (19 October 2000)
Refugee Appeal No 72315 [2000] NZRSAA 493 (19 October 2000)
Refugee Appeal No 72316 [2000] NZRSAA 464 (19 October 2000)
Refugee Appeal Nos 72179–72181 [2000] NZRSAA 385 (31 August 2000)
Refugee Appeal Nos 72189–72195 [2000] NZRSAA 355 (17 August 2000)

United Kingdom

AB v SSHD [2018] UKUT (IAC) AA/10878/2015
Ainte (material deprivation – Art 3 – AM (Zimbabwe) [2021] UKUT 00203 (IAC)
AM and BM (Trafficked women) Albania CG [2010] UKUT 80 (IAC)
AMM and Others v SSHD [2011] UKUT 00445 (IAC), [2011] 7 WLUK 464
AN v SSHD [2017] UKUT (IAC) PA/04137/2016
AS (Albania) v SSHD [2024] UKUT (IAC) UI-2024–000611
AZ (Trafficked women) Thailand CG [2010] UKUT 118 (IAC)
BA (Returns to Baghdad) Iraq CG [2017] UKUT 18 (IAC)
BA v SSHD [2014] UKUT (IAC) AA/03923/2013
BT v SSHD [2019] UKUT (IAC) PA/07306/2017
DH (Particular Social Group: Mental Health) Afghanistan [2020] UKUT 223 (IAC), [2020] 6 WLUK 523

DK v SSHD [2024] UKUT (IAC) UI-2023-003379
EK (Article 4 ECHR: Anti-Trafficking Convention) Tanzania v SSHD [2013] UKUT 00313 (IAC)
EMAP (Gang violence, Convention Reason) (CG) [2022] UKUT (IAC) 00335
ES (s82 NIA 2002, Negative NRM) [2018] UKUT 335 (IAC)
FK v SSHD [2015] UKUT (IAC) AA/08453/2014
FT v SSHD [2022] UKUT (IAC) PA/03526/2020
HC & RC (Trafficked Women) China v SSHD CG [2009] UKAIT 00027
HC v SSHD [2021] UKUT (IAC) PA/05060/2019
HD (Trafficked women) Nigeria CG [2016] UKUT 00454 (IAC)
HD v SSHD [2022] UKUT (IAC) PA/10137/2019
HG v SSHD [2019] UKUT (IAC) PA/10947/2018
Horvath v SSHD [2000] UKHL 37, [2000] Imm AR 552
HQB v SSHD [2019] UKUT (IAC) PA/10410/2018
HVT v SSHD [2018] UKUT (IAC) PA/03104/2017
IR v SSHD [2013] UKUT (IAC) IA178072010
JA v SSHD [2020] UKUT (IAC) PA/13132/2018
Januzi v SSHD [2006] UKHL 5, [2006] 2 WLR 397
JFK v SSHD [2018] UKUT (IAC) PA/06854/2016
JO (internal relocation – no risk of re-trafficking) Nigeria [2004] UKIAT 00251
JV v SSHD [2024] UKUT (IAC) UI-2024-001176
K v SSHD, Fornah v SSHD [2006] UKHL 46, [2006] 3 WLR 733
Kamara v SSHD [2016] EWCA Civ 813, [2016] 8 WLUK 174
Karanakaran v SSHD [2000] EWCA Civ 11, [2000] Imm AR 271
KF v SSHD [2024] UKUT (IAC) UI-2023-003705
Lowe v SSHD [2021] EWCA Civ 62, [2021] 1 WLUK 248
LTD v SSHD [2015] UKUT (IAC) AA/13630/2011
MD v SSHD [2021] UKUT (IAC) PA/12142/2019
MHK v SSHD [2023] UKUT (IAC) UI-2022-005774
MI v SSHD [2020] UKUT (IAC) PA/10163/2018
MP (Trafficking – Sufficiency of Protection) Romania [2005] UKIAT 00086
MS (Pakistan) v SSHD [2020] UKSC 9, [2020] Imm AR 967
MS v SSHD [2020] UKUT (IAC) PA/07803/2016
MZ (Hospital order: whether a 'foreign criminal') Pakistan [2020] UKUT 00225 (IAC)
NP v SSHD [2020] UKUT (IAC) PA/05297/2018
NX v SSHD [2014] UKUT (IAC) AA/01621/2013
OA (Somalia) Somalia CG [2022] UKUT 00033 (IAC)
Parveen v SSHD [2018] EWCA Civ 932, [2018] 4 WLUK 429
PG v SSHD [2022] UKUT (IAC) PA/00229/2020
PO (Trafficked Women) Nigeria CG [2009] UKAIT 00046
PQ v SSHD [2017] UKUT (IAC) PA/01480/2015
R (MN) v Secretary of State for the Home Department [2018] EWHC 3268 (QB), [2018] 11 WLUK 495
R v SSHD, ex p Sivakumaran [1987] UKHL 1, [1988] Imm AR 147
RK v SSHD [2023] UKUT (IAC) UI-2022-006079

SB (PSG – Protection Regulations – Reg 6) Moldova CG [2008] UKAIT 00002
SC (Jamaica) v SSHD [2022] UKSC 15, [2022] 6 WLUK 110
Sepet v SSHD [2003] UKHL 15, [2003] 3 WLUK 555
Shah v SSHD [2022] UKUT (IAC) HU/02664/2020
SHL (Tracing obligation/Trafficking) Afghanistan v SSHD [2013] UKUT 00312 (IAC)
SS v SSHD [2022] UKUT (IAC) PA/00677/2020
SSHD v Bodun [2016] UKUT (IAC) IA/10292/2015
SSHD v ES [2023] UKUT (IAC) UI-2023-000934
SSHD v HK and JS [2018] UKUT (IAC) HU/13283/2016 and HU/13292/2016
SSHD v Ismail Mohamoud Ali [2024] UKUT (IAC) UI-2024–000166
SSHD v Joachim Cardos [2023] UKUT (IAC) UI-2022–004930
SSHD v Kapinga [2016] UKUT (IAC) IA/07269/2015
SSHD v NAMT [2023] UKUT (IAC) UI-2023–002124
SSHD v Rakeshkumar and Hetal [2016] UKUT (IAC) IA/14784/2015 and IA/14788/2015
SSHD v Said [2016] EWCA Civ 442, [2016] 5 WLUK 88
SSHD v ZY [2015] UKUT (IAC) IA/18670/2014
TAN v SSHD [2016] UKUT (IAC) AA/05644/2014
TD and AD (trafficked women) CG [2016] UKUT 92
TDL v SSHD [2021] UKUT (IAC) PA/00358/2020
TSN v SSHD [2019] UKUT (IAC) PA/07665/2017
TVD v SSHD [2022] UKUT (IAC) PA/00252/2020
TVP v SSHD [2018] UKUT (IAC) PA/02997/2018
VD (Trafficking) Albania CG [2004] UKIAT 00115
Veintimilla v SSHD [2024] UKUT (IAC) UI-2024–002985
Wright v SSHD [2024] UKUT (IAC) UI-2023–005380
YT v SSHD [2020] UKUT (IAC) PA/02930/2019

Table of Legislation

International Instruments

Convention on the Elimination of All Forms of Discrimination against Women (adopted 18 December 1979, entered into force 3 September 1981) 1249 UNTS 13 (CEDAW)

Convention on the Rights of the Child (adopted 20 November 1989, entered into force 2 September 1990) 1577 UNTS 3 (CRC)

Convention Relating to the Status of Refugees (adopted 28 July 1951, entered into force 22 April 1954) 189 UNTS 137 (Refugee Convention)

Council of Europe Convention on Action against Trafficking in Human Beings (adopted 16 May 2005, entered into force 1 February 2008) ETS 197 (ECAT)

European Convention for the Protection of Human Rights and Fundamental Freedoms Rights, as Amended (adopted 4 November 1950, entered into force 3 September 1953) CETS No 005 (ECHR)

Global Compact on Refugees (UNGA, 2 August 2018) UN doc A/73/12 (Part II)

International Covenant on Civil and Political Rights (adopted 16 December 1966, entered into force 23 March 1976) 999 UNTS 171 (ICCPR)

International Covenant on Economic, Social and Cultural Rights (adopted 16 December 1966, entered into force 3 January 1976) 993 UNTS 3 (ICESCR)

Protocol against the Smuggling of Migrants by Land, Sea and Air, Supplementing the United Nations Convention against Transnational Crime (adopted 15 November 2000, entered into force 28 January 2004) 2241 UNTS 480 (Smuggling Protocol)

Protocol Relating to the Status of Refugees (adopted 31 January 1967, entered into force 4 October 1967) 606 UNTS 267 (1967 Protocol)

Protocol to Prevent, Suppress and Punish Trafficking in Persons, Especially Women and Children, Supplementing the United Nations Convention against Transnational Organized Crime (adopted 15 November 2000, entered into force 25 December 2003) 2237 UNTS 319 (Trafficking Protocol)

United Nations Convention against Torture and Other Cruel, Inhuman or Degrading Treatment or Punishment (adopted 10 December 1984, entered into force 26 June 1987) 1465 UNTS 85 (CAT)

United Nations Convention against Transnational Organized Crime (adopted 15 November 2000, entered into force 29 September 2003) 2225 UNTS 209 (UNTOC)

Vienna Convention on Consular Relations (adopted 24 April 1963, entered into force 19 March 1967) 596 UNTS 261 (VCCR)

Vienna Convention on the Law of Treaties (adopted 23 May 1969, entered into force on 27 January 1980) 1155 UNTS 331 (VCLT)

European Union Law

Charter of Fundamental Rights of the European Union [2012] OJ C 326 (EUCFR)

Consolidated Version of the Treaty on the Functioning of the European Union [2012] OJ C 326 (TFEU)

Convention Implementing the Schengen Agreement of 14 June 1985 between the Governments of the States of the Benelux Economic Union, the Federal Republic of Germany and the French Republic on the Gradual Abolition of Checks at Their Common Borders [2000] OJ L 239 (CISA)

Council Directive 2002/90/EC of 28 November 2002 Defining the Facilitation of Unauthorised Entry, Transit and Residence [2002] OJ L 328 (Facilitation Directive)

Council Directive 2003/86/EC of 22 September 2003 on the Right to Family Reunification [2003] OJ L 251 (Family Reunification Directive)

Council Directive 2004/81/EC of 29 April 2004 on the Residence Permit Issued to Third-Country Nationals Who Are Victims of Trafficking in Human Beings or Who Have Been the Subject of an Action to Facilitate Illegal Immigration, Who Cooperate with the Competent Authorities [2004] OJ L 261 (Residence Permit Directive)

Council Directive 2004/83/EC of 29 April 2004 on Minimum Standards for the Qualification and Status of Third-Country Nationals or Stateless Persons as Refugees or as Persons Who Otherwise Need International Protection and the Content of the Protection Granted [2004] OJ L304/12 (Qualification Directive)

Council Framework Decision of 28 November 2002 on the Strengthening of the Penal Framework to Prevent the Facilitation of Unauthorised Entry, Transit and Residence [2002] OJ L 328 (Framework Decision)

Directive (EU) 2024/1346 of the European Parliament and of the Council of 14 May 2024 Laying Down Standards for the Reception of Applicants for International Protection [2024] OJ L 2024/134 (Reception Conditions Directive)

Directive (EU) 2024/1712 of the European Parliament and of the Council of 13 June 2024 Amending Directive 2011/36/EU on Preventing and Combating Trafficking in Human Beings and Protecting Its Victims [2024] OJ L 2024/1712 (Trafficking Amendment Directive)

Directive 2008/115/EC of the European Parliament and of the Council of 16 December 2008 on Common Standards and Procedures in Member States for Returning Illegally Staying Third-Country Nationals [2008] OJ L 348 (Return Directive)

Directive 2011/36/EU of the European Parliament and of the Council of 5 April 2011 on Preventing and Combating Trafficking in Human Beings and Protecting Its Victims, and Replacing Council Framework Decision 2002/629/JHA [2011] OJ L 101/1 (Trafficking Directive)

Directive 2011/95/EU of the European Parliament and of the Council of 13 December 2011 on Standards for the Qualification of Third-Country Nationals or Stateless Persons as Beneficiaries of International Protection, for a Uniform Status for Refugees or for Persons Eligible for Subsidiary Protection and for the Content of the Protection Granted (recast) [2011] OJ L337/9 (recast Qualification Directive)

Directive 2012/29/EU of the European Parliament and of the Council of 25 October 2012 Establishing Minimum Standards on the Rights, Support and Protection of Victims of Crime, and Replacing Council Framework Decision 2001/220/JHA [2012] OJ L 315 (Victim Protection Directive)

Directive 2013/32/EU of the European Parliament and of the Council of 26 June 2013 on Common Procedures for Granting and Withdrawing International Protection [2013] OJ L 180 (Asylum Procedures Directive)

Regulation (EC) No 810/2009 of the European Parliament and of the Council of 13 July 2009 Establishing a Community Code on Visas [2009] OJ L 243 (Visa Code)

Regulation (EU) 2016/399 of the European Parliament and of the Council of 9 March 2016 on a Union Code on the Rules Governing the Movement of Persons across Borders [2016] OJ L 77 (Schengen Borders Code)

Regulation (EU) 2018/1240 of the European Parliament and of the Council of 12 September 2018 Establishing a European Travel Information and Authorisation System (ETIAS) and Amending Regulations (EU) No 1077/2011, (EU) No 515/2014, (EU) 2016/399, (EU) 2016/1624 and (EU) 2017/2226 (ETIAS Regulation)

Regulation (EU) 2018/1806 of the European Parliament and of the Council of 14 November 2018 Listing the Third Countries Whose Nationals Must Be in Possession of Visas When Crossing the External Borders and Those Whose Nationals Are Exempt from That Requirement [2018] OJ L 303 (Visa Regulation)

Regulation (EU) 2024/1347 of the European Parliament and of the Council of 14 May 2024 on Standards for the Qualification of Third-Country Nationals or Stateless Persons as Beneficiaries of International Protection, for a Uniform Status for Refugees or for Persons Eligible for Subsidiary Protection and for the Content of the Protection Granted, Amending Council Directive 2003/109/EC and Repealing Directive 2011/95/EU of the European Parliament and of the Council (Qualification Regulation)

United Kingdom

Nationality and Borders Act 2022
Immigration Rules (HC 395)
Nationality, Immigration and Asylum Act 2002

Germany

Asylgesetz (AsylG) 2 September 2008 (BGBl. I S. 1798) (Asylum Act)
Gesetz über den Aufenthalt, die Erwerbstätigkeit und die Integration von Ausländern im Bundesgebiet (Aufenthaltsgesetz – AufenthG) 25 February 2008 (BGBl. I S. 162) (Residence Act)
Strafgesetzbuch (StGB) 13 November 1998 (BGBl. I S. 3322) (Criminal Code)

Abbreviations

AC	administrative court
CAT	Convention against Torture
CEDAW	Convention on the Elimination of All Forms of Discrimination against Women
CJEU	Court of Justice of the European Union
CRC	Convention on the Rights of the Child
ECAT	Council of Europe Convention on Action against Trafficking in Human Beings
ECHR	European Convention on Human Rights
ECtHR	European Court of Human Rights
EU	European Union
EUCFR	EU Charter of Fundamental Rights
FTT	First-Tier Tribunal
HRC	Human Rights Committee
ICCPR	International Covenant on Civil and Political Rights
ICESCR	International Covenant on Economic, Social and Cultural Rights
IOM	International Organization for Migration
IPA	Internal Protection Alternative
LGBTIQA	lesbian, gay, bisexual, transgender, intersex, queer and/or questioning and asexual
NGO	non-governmental organisation
NZIPT	New Zealand Immigration and Protection Tribunal
OHCHR	Office of the High Commissioner for Human Rights
PSG	particular social group
PTSD	post-traumatic stress disorder
RSAA	Refugee Status Appeals Authority
RSD	refugee status determination
SSHD	Secretary of State for the Home Department
TFEU	Treaty on the Functioning of the European Union
UK	United Kingdom
UN	United Nations

UNHCR	United Nations High Commissioner for Refugees
UNODC	United Nations Office on Drugs and Crime
UNTOC	UN Convention against Transnational Organised Crime
UT	Upper Tribunal
VCCR	Vienna Convention on Consular Relations
VCLT	Vienna Convention on the Law of Treaties
VG	*Verwaltungsgericht* (Administrative Court)

1 Introduction

1.1 Protection From Dangerous Migratory Journeys

1.1.1 Irregular Migration as a Protection Issue

Irregular migration is extremely dangerous. Persons travelling irregularly face serious harm, such as physical and sexual violence, deprivation of liberty, forced labour or even death.[1] Many go missing, and their fate is never known.[2] Further, people who live in host countries without documents are frequently exposed to abuse and exploitation.[3] For the purpose of this book, I will use the term 'dangerous migratory journeys' to encompass both irregular travel and undocumented stay. Despite the dangers inherent in dangerous migratory journeys, irregular migration is seen as a policy problem which must be prevented, as a crime which must be fought but not normally as a protection issue. This book offers a novel approach to the phenomenon of irregular migration by treating it as a protection issue for the purpose of refugee law. It argues that harm experienced during dangerous journeys can constitute persecution, and that a risk of irregular re-migration can form the basis for a claim to refugee status. The arguments in this book are derived from empirical evidence: an in-depth analysis of trafficked persons' asylum claims. It is well accepted that trafficked persons – many of whom are irregular migrants – may be eligible for refugee status due to a risk of re-trafficking. In this chapter, I explain why trafficked persons' asylum claims have implications for other irregular migrants. I consider the legal and policy categories irregular migrants are grouped into, the assumptions about their protection needs attached to those categories and

1 UNHCR, 'On This Journey, No One Cares If You Live or Die: Abuse, Protection and Justice Along Routes between East and West Africa and Africa's Mediterranean Coast: A Route-based Perspective on Key Risks' vol 2 (March 2024) <www.unhcr.org/media/journey-no-one-cares-if-you-live-or-die-abuse-protection-and-justice-along-routes-between-1> accessed 19 August 2024.

2 IOM, 'Missing Migrants Project' <https://missingmigrants.iom.int> accessed 25 August 2024.

3 Sarah Spencer and Anna Triandafyllidou, 'Irregular Migration' in Peter Scholten (ed), *Introduction to Migration Studies: An Interactive Guide to the Literatures on Migration and Diversity* (Springer 2022).

DOI: 10.4324/9781032664644-1

how disengaging from those categories and assumptions allows for a progressive interpretation of refugee law which conceives of irregular re-migration as a risk potentially warranting refugee status.

The International Organization for Migration (IOM) defines 'irregular migration' as 'movement of persons that takes place outside the laws, regulations, or international agreements governing the entry into or exit from the State of origin, transit or destination'.[4] While there is no universally accepted definition of 'irregular migration', the IOM definition reflects the widespread tendency to approach the issue from the perspective of the state. States see migration as governable, and irregular migration as a contravention of their immigration rules, which challenges their sovereignty.[5] As a result, irregular migration is exercised in the face of a wide range of measures designed to prevent movement.[6] Extraterritorial border control measures include visa restrictions, carrier sanctions and 'contactless' control measures, implemented in cooperation with third countries, which prevent migrants from leaving, for example, through pullbacks and detention.[7] Extraterritorial border controls prevent persons subject to visa requirements from travelling by regular transport. Because carrier sanctions oblige carriers, such as airline companies, to check passports and visas before departure and to impose penalties for transporting persons without the correct documents,[8] individuals not in possession of such documents cannot simply board a plane to their destination state. Thus, these individuals are forced to travel through irregular routes, made ever more dangerous by the need to evade detection on the way. In practice, as Last explains, this involves 'stowing away on regular transport (ferries, busses, lorries) or . . . taking irregular transport (walking, swimming, jumping fences, or using "migrant boats")'.[9]

4 IOM, 'Key Migration Terms' <www.iom.int/key-migration-terms> accessed 25 September 2024.

5 Elspeth Guild, *Security and Migration in the 21st Century* (Polity 2009).

6 Elspeth Guild, 'The Legal Framework: Who Is Entitled to Move?' in Didier Bigo and Elspeth Guild (eds), *Controlling Frontiers: Free Movement into and within Europe* (Ashgate 2005); Thomas Gammeltoft-Hansen, *Access to Asylum: International Refugee Law and the Globalisation of Migration Control* (CUP 2011); Maarten den Heijer, *Europe and Extraterritorial Asylum* (Hart Publishing 2012); Thomas Gammeltoft-Hansen and James C Hathaway, 'Non-refoulement in World of Cooperative Deterrence' (2015) 53(2) Columbia Journal of Transnational Law 235; Violeta Moreno-Lax, *Accessing Asylum in Europe: Extraterritorial Border Controls and Refugee Rights under EU Law* (OUP 2017); Mariagiulia Giuffré and Violeta Moreno-Lax, 'The Rise of Contactless Containment: From "Contactless Control" to "Contactless Responsibility" for Migratory Flows' in Satvinder Singh Juss (ed), *Research Handbook on International Refugee Law* (Edward Elgar Publishing 2019).

7 Giuffré and Moreno-Lax (n 6).

8 Convention Implementing the Schengen Agreement of 14 June 1985 between the Governments of the States of the Benelux Economic Union, the Federal Republic of Germany and the French Republic on the Gradual Abolition of Checks at Their Common Borders [2000] OJ L 239, arts 26(1)(b) and 26(2).

9 Tamara Last, 'Who Is the "Boat Migrant"? Challenging the Anonymity of Death at Border-Sea' in Violeta Moreno-Lax and Efthymios Papastavridis (eds), *"Boat Refugees" and Migrants at Sea: A Comprehensive Approach* (Brill 2016) 85.

While some individuals migrate by their own means, most rely on facilitators, such as traffickers and smugglers.[10] This, in turn, is used by states in the Global North to justify ever more extensive and sophisticated border control measures. This is done, one the one hand, in the name of fighting the 'crimes' of trafficking and smuggling;[11] on the other hand, and paradoxically, states claim that protecting borders also protects irregular migrants.[12] Thus, facilitation of irregular migration in the form of 'trafficking in persons' and 'smuggling of migrants' has been criminalised in international law.[13] Irregular entry and stay, meanwhile, are criminal offences in states across the globe.[14] By focusing on the 'crime' of (facilitation of) irregular migration, states in the Global North divert attention away from the question of why people undertake dangerous journeys to begin with.[15] They conveniently ignore colonial legacies and their ongoing effects, which not only produce violence, conflict and inequality in countries of origin but also continue to racialise and regulate mobility.[16] They also ignore the fact that their own deterrence measures create irregular migration in the first place.[17]

Europe is a prominent example of a region practising both deterrence and criminalisation. Mitsilegas explains that, particularly since the so-called refugee crisis of 2015, the European Union (EU) and its member states have put an 'increasing emphasis on prevention by hindering and halting movement

10 According to Frontex, 88% of irregular arrivals use the help of facilitators; see Frontex, 'Risk Analysis for 2018' (2018) <www.statewatch.org/media/documents/news/2018/mar/eu-frontex-report-risk-analysis-2018.pdf> accessed 16 September 2021, 35.

11 Anne T Gallagher and Fiona David, *The International Law of Migrant Smuggling* (CUP 2014) 12.

12 Violeta Moreno-Lax, 'The EU Humanitarian Border and the Securitization of Human Rights: The "Rescue-Through-Interdiction/Rescue-Without-Protection' Paradigm"' (2018) 56(1) Journal of Common Market Studies 119 <https://doi.org/10.1111/jcms.12651>.

13 Protocol to Prevent, Suppress and Punish Trafficking in Persons, Especially Women and Children, Supplementing the United Nations Convention against Transnational Organized Crime (adopted 15 November 2000, entered into force 25 December 2003) 2237 UNTS 319 (Trafficking Protocol) art 3(a); Protocol against the Smuggling of Migrants by Land, Sea and Air, Supplementing the United Nations Convention against Transnational Crime (adopted 15 November 2000, entered into force 28 January 2004) 2241 UNTS 480 (Smuggling Protocol) art 3(a).

14 Law Library of Congress, 'Criminalization of Illegal Entry Around the World' (2019) <www.loc.gov/item/2019685473/> accessed 22 June 2022; European Union Agency for Fundamental Rights (FRA), 'Criminalisation of Migrants in an Irregular Situation and of Persons Engaging with Them' (2014) <https://fra.europa.eu/sites/default/files/fra-2014-criminalisation-of-migrants_en.pdf> accessed 22 January 2023.

15 Vicki Squire and others, *Reclaiming Migration: Voices from Europe's 'Migrant Crisis'* (Manchester UP 2021) 23.

16 E Tendayi Achiume, 'Migration as Decolonization' (2019) 71 Stanford Law Review 1509.

17 Mathias Czaika and Mogens Hobolth, 'Do Restrictive Asylum and Visa Policies Increase Irregular Migration into Europe?' (2016) 17(3) European Union Politics 345 <https://doi.org/10.1177/1465116516633299>; Julien Brachet, 'Manufacturing Smugglers: From Irregular to Clandestine Mobility in the Sahara' (2018) 676(1) The Annals of the American Academy of Political and Social Science 16.

through extraterritorial controls'.[18] Indeed, the EU has been described as a 'world leader' in externalisation policy.[19] The EU also criminalises human trafficking and migrant smuggling[20] and prioritises the return of 'illegally staying' third-country nationals,[21] who are frequently subject to administrative measures reminiscent of criminal law penalties.[22]

This book is situated in the context of EU and European policy on irregular migration and asks what effect such deterrence measures have on irregular migrants. More specifically, it is concerned with persons arriving in Europe irregularly, despite all deterrence efforts, and the question of whether these persons need protection. Thus, rather than taking a state-centric perspective on irregular migration, the book approaches the issue from the perspective of individuals undertaking dangerous migratory journeys. Despite its focus on irregular migration towards Europe, this book is relevant beyond the EU/European context since restrictive border control measures are employed by states in the Global North generally.

States in the Global North do not differentiate between refugees and other migrants when it comes to visa requirements and other border control measures.[23] In 2018, it was estimated that 'up to 90% of the total population of subsequently recognised refugees and beneficiaries of subsidiary protection in the EU reach the territory of the member states irregularly and, often, through life-threating routes'.[24] While statistics like these show that border

18 Valsamis Mitsilegas, Violeta Moreno-Lax and Niovi Vavoula, 'Introduction' in Valsamis Mitsilegas, Violeta Moreno-Lax and Niovi Vavoula (eds), *Securitising Asylum Flows: Deflection, Criminalisation and Challenges for Human Rights* (Brill Nijhoff 2020) 1.

19 T Spijkerboer, 'Migration Management Clientelism: Europe's Migration Funds as a Global Political Project' (2022) 48(12) Journal of Ethnic and Migration Studies 2892, 2902 <https://doi.org/10.1080/1369183X.2021.1972567>.

20 Directive 2011/36/EU of the European Parliament and of the Council of 5 April 2011 on Preventing and Combating Trafficking in Human Beings and Protecting Its Victims, and Replacing Council Framework Decision 2002/629/JHA [2011] OJ L 101/1 (Trafficking Directive), as Amended by Directive (EU) 2024/1712 of the European Parliament and of the Council of 13 June 2024 Amending Directive 2011/36/EU on Preventing and Combating Trafficking in Human Beings and Protecting Its Victims [2024] OJ L 2024/1712 (Trafficking Amendment Directive); Council Directive 2002/90/EC of 28 November 2002 Defining the Facilitation of Unauthorised Entry, Transit and Residence [2002] OJ L 328 (Facilitation Directive).

21 Directive 2008/115/EC of the European Parliament and of the Council of 16 December 2008 on Common Standards and Procedures in Member States for Returning Illegally Staying Third-Country Nationals [2008] OJ L 348 (Return Directive).

22 Lorenzo Bernardini, 'Administrative Immigration Detention as a Punitive Measure: Is It Time for a New Standpoint?' in Angela Di Stasi Rossana Palladino and Angela Festa (eds), *Migrations, Rule of Law and European Values* (Editoriale Scientifica 2023).

23 Moreno-Lax (n 6) 100.

24 European Parliament, 'Humanitarian Visas: European Added Value Assessment Accompanying the European Parliament's Legislative Own-initiative Report (Rapporteur: Juan Fernando López Aguilar)' (22 October 2018) <www.europarl.europa.eu/RegData/etudes/STUD/2018/621823/EPRS_STU(2018)621823_EN.pdf> accessed 4 November 2020, 28.

control measures have a disproportionate impact on refugees because refugees have no choice but to take life-threating routes to escape persecution, they also suggest that those who are not 'recognised refugees' undertake the same journey in the absence of a comparable risk. Indeed, the view persists that irregular arrivals move in 'mixed migratory flows' which consist of people with different motivations for moving, and therefore different protection needs.[25] Thus, although the distinction between 'forced' and 'voluntary' migration is difficult, if not impossible, to make,[26] 'voluntary' migrants are perceived as having 'no legitimate reason for seeking protection'.[27] Indeed, the perception that an individual has 'voluntarily' embarked on a dangerous migratory journey may lead to the rejection of that person's protection claim.[28] Even the European Court of Human Rights (ECtHR) has justified the collective expulsion of migrants who allegedly 'chose' to enter the EU irregularly with reference to their 'own conduct'.[29]

The main distinction underlying the mixed migration paradigm is what Hamlin calls the 'migrant/refugee binary', which is sustained by the assumptions that migrants' movement is 'voluntary' while refugees' movement is 'forced', that refugees are in need of protection but migrants are not and that 'refugees are rare'.[30] As Hamlin explains, 'the label "irregular migrant" seems almost designed to proclaim the "non-refugeeness" of arrivals'.[31] In summary, irregular migration, which is created by states' immigration policies in the first place, is used not only to justify further border controls but also to portray irregular arrivals as voluntary migrants not in need of protection, with refugees representing the exception to the rule.

In this book, I will challenge the migrant/refugee binary and the notion that persons migrating irregularly are not in need of protection. Starting from the premise that harm experienced during dangerous migratory journeys is extremely serious, this book argues that there is such a thing as a risk of irregular re-migration and that this risk can form the basis for a claim to refugee

25 Nick Van Hear, 'Mixed Migration: Policy Challenges' (*The Migration Observatory Policy Primer*, 2011) 2 <https://migrationobservatory.ox.ac.uk/wp-content/uploads/2016/04/PolicyPrimer-Mixed_Migration.pdf> accessed 19 March 2021.

26 Aristide R Zolberg, Astri Suhrke and Sergio Aguayo, *Escape from Violence: Conflict and the Refugee Crisis in the Developing World* (OUP 1989) 30–31; Anthony H Richmond, *Global Apartheid: Refugees, Racism, and the New World Order* (OUP 1994) 58; David Turton, 'Conceptualising Forced Migration' (2003) RSC Working Paper 12 <www.rsc.ox.ac.uk/files/files-1/wp12-conceptualising-forced-migration-2003.pdf> accessed 9 March 2020, 11.

27 Michelle Foster, *International Refugee Law and Socio-Economic Rights: Refuge from Deprivation* (CUP 2007) 6.

28 ibid 238.

29 *ND and NT v Spain* App nos 8675/15 and 8697/15 (ECtHR, 13 February 2020) para 242.

30 Rebecca Hamlin, *Crossing: How We Label and React to People on the Move* (Stanford UP 2021) 9–18.

31 ibid 158.

status under the 1951 Convention Relating to the Status of Refugees (hereinafter 'Refugee Convention').[32]

1.1.2 *Irregularised Migrants*

Based on how refugee law is currently interpreted, irregular migrants *qua* irregular migrants would not be recognised as refugees. The Refugee Convention, as amended by its 1967 Protocol,[33] defines a *refugee* as any person who

> owing to well-founded fear of being persecuted for reasons of race, religion, nationality, membership of a particular social group or political opinion, is outside the country of his nationality and is unable or, owing to such fear, is unwilling to avail himself of the protection of that country; or who, not having a nationality and being outside the country of his former habitual residence, is unable or, owing to such fear, is unwilling to return to it.[34]

The predominant view amongst refugee law scholars is that 'the basic inquiry into the existence of a well-founded fear [of being persecuted] focuses squarely on the risks faced *in the country of which the individual is a citizen*'.[35] As a result, asylum seekers' claims will be assessed based on the circumstances in their country of origin, and if they are not found to be at risk of persecution (or serious harm for the purpose of human rights law) there, they will be returned. Once returned, however, they may re-migrate irregularly, undertaking another dangerous journey.

It is this scenario of persons re-migrating irregularly that this book is concerned with. I will refer to these persons as 'irregularised migrants' to describe people who undertake dangerous migratory journeys due to a lack of legal migration pathways, who are unable to obtain refugee protection based on harm feared in their country of origin and who, if returned, may re-migrate irregularly. The possibility of re-migration is significant because, as outlined earlier, irregular migration is extremely dangerous. Indeed, it may entail harm similar in type and degree to harm experienced or feared by recognised refugees in their countries of origin.[36] While states have the sovereign right to

32 Convention Relating to the Status of Refugees (adopted 28 July 1951, entered into force 22 April 1954) 189 UNTS 137 (Refugee Convention).

33 Protocol Relating to the Status of Refugees (adopted 31 January 1967, entered into force 4 October 1967) 606 UNTS 267 (1967 Protocol) art 1(2).

34 Refugee Convention (n 32) art 1A(2).

35 James C Hathaway and Michelle Foster, *The Law of Refugee Status* (2nd edn, CUP 2014) 50; emphasis added. See also Guy S Goodwin-Gill and Jane McAdam, *The Refugee in International Law* (4th edn, OUP 2021) 92.

36 See Chapters 2 and 4.

control entry into and stay within their territory, such control is subject to their obligations under refugee and human rights law.[37] Thus, if harm experienced during dangerous journeys *outside* an applicant's country of origin could be taken into account in deciding who is entitled to refugee protection, irregularised migrants may be reconceptualised as refugees.

This is what this book seeks to do. The book will examine whether irregularised migrants should be eligible for refugee status. To do so, the book makes three main claims: First, that, rather than constituting a 'voluntary' choice, irregular re-migration is a risk certain individuals, and especially those with previous experiences of irregular migration, are exposed to. This risk can be established by identifying a range of intersecting vulnerabilities which make it difficult for individuals to earn a livelihood in the country of origin and cause them to respond to the resulting socio-economic deprivation through irregular re-migration. The second claim of the book is that the concept of persecution in the Refugee Convention is not limited to the territory of the country of origin. This book will draw on the cumulative nature of persecution to argue that harm experienced during a (future) dangerous migratory journey can be taken into account during refugee status determination (RSD). I argue that irregularised migrants are escaping two sequential harms, one in the country of origin and one *en route*, with the country of origin's failure to protect against the former causing the latter to manifest. As such, irregularised migrants are refugees *sur place* in that they were not refugees when they left their countries of origin for the first time but become refugees later on.[38] Third, the book argues that as members of the PSG 'persons in vulnerable situations' and as persons whose nationality contributes to the risk of undertaking dangerous journeys, irregularised migrants can establish a nexus between the risk of irregular re-migration and Refugee Convention grounds.

These three main claims of the book are not simply theoretical considerations regarding the scope of the Refugee Convention's *refugee* definition; rather, they are derived from existing case law, more specifically, from trafficking-based asylum claims from the United Kingdom (UK) and Germany. The following section explains why these asylum claims serve as a point of departure for considering whether irregularised migrants may be able to claim asylum based on a fear of a future dangerous migratory journey.

37 Refugee Convention (n 32) art 33; Declaration on the Human Rights of Individuals Who Are Not Nationals of the Country in Which They Live (adopted 3 December 1985) UNGA Res 40/144, art 2(1). See also, for example, *N v The United Kingdom* App no 26565/05 (ECtHR, 27 May 2008) para 30; *Ilias and Ahmed v Hungary* App no 47287/15 (ECtHR, 21 November 2019) para 125; *MN and Others v Belgium* App no 3599/18 (ECtHR, 5 May 2020) para 124.

38 UNHCR, 'Handbook on Procedures and Criteria for Determining Refugee Status and Guidelines on International Protection Under the 1951 Convention and the 1967 Protocol Relating to the Status of Refugees' HCR/1P/4/ENG/REV.4 (1979, reissued 2019) (UNHCR Handbook) para 94.

1.1.3 Employing the Concept of Human Trafficking in Refugee Law

While the argument in this book is based on case law detailing the experiences of trafficked persons, it is important to clarify that irregularised migrants cannot be equated with trafficked persons. Trafficking in persons is a crime in international law, so that trafficked persons – the 'victims' of this crime – are identifiable with reference to the relevant legal definition.[39] Further, they are protected by a specialist legal regime,[40] which includes (temporary) protection from removal. What is more, and as this book will show, trafficked persons are often able to obtain refugee status based on their trafficking experience and future fear related thereto. Irregularised migrants, on the other hand, are not similarly protected; indeed, based on how the law is currently applied, they are unable to obtain refugee status. Nevertheless, trafficked persons whose claims to refugee status fail may be able to argue that they are irregularised migrants. Both groups have a range of commonalities which allow for arguing that irregularised migrants ought to be able to meet the elements of the *refugee* definition in a similar way to trafficked persons.

First, both trafficked persons and irregularised migrants may experience harm outside their countries of origin. Significantly, despite the predominant view that the 'locus of persecution' is a refugee's country of origin,[41] in trafficked persons' asylum claims, fearing harm which would manifest largely outside the country of origin is no obstacle to claiming refugee protection.[42] Second, and relatedly, based on these experiences and other similarities,[43] it is difficult to distinguish between irregularised migrants and trafficked persons. To illustrate this with an example, consider the following scenario: A young man decides to leave his country of origin, China; enters the UK irregularly; works there without authorisation and eventually claims asylum.[44] Initially, his claim is refused by the Home Office, and later, on appeal, also by the First-Tier Tribunal, on the basis that he consented to leaving China and is a 'voluntary

39 Trafficking Protocol (n 13) art 3(a); Smuggling Protocol (n 13) art 3(a).

40 On an international level, this includes the Trafficking Protocol (n 13), while in the EU/European context, two legal instruments are of particular relevance: the Trafficking Directive (n 20) and the Council of Europe Convention on Action against Trafficking in Human Beings (adopted 16 May 2005, entered into force 1 February 2008) ETS 197 (ECAT).

41 Goodwin-Gill and McAdam (n 35) 92.

42 The UNHCR Trafficking Guidelines state that 'even where the exploitation experienced by a victim of trafficking occurs mainly outside the country of origin, this does not preclude the existence of a well-founded fear of persecution in the individual's own country'; see UNHCR, 'Guidelines on International Protection: The Application of Article 1A(2) of the 1951 Convention and/or 1967 Protocol Relating to the Status of Refugees to Victims of Trafficking and Persons at Risk of Being Trafficked' (2006) HCR/GIP/06/07 (UNHCR Trafficking Guidelines) para 27.

43 See Chapters 2 and 3.

44 *JFK v SSHD* [2018] UKUT (IAC) PA/06854/2016.

economic migrant'.[45] At this point, the claimant may be said to be an irregularised migrant – a person who has travelled irregularly, is denied protection but may re-migrate if returned. This is the case of *JFK v Secretary of State for the Home Department* (SSHD), decided by the UK Upper Tribunal (UT) in 2018. While risk of irregular re-migration, as such, was not considered during the case, the UT found that the claimant in *JFK* was a trafficked person, at risk of re-trafficking, and a refugee for the purpose of the Refugee Convention. At this point, the claimant was no longer an irregularised migrant but someone whose status had been regularised as a trafficked person and a refugee.

As this case illustrates, one and the same experience can be characterised in different terms with real consequences under refugee law. The re-categorisation of the claimant from 'voluntary economic migrant' to 'trafficked person' is accompanied by a shift from characterising his migration as a choice to finding that 'the fact that he consented to come to the United Kingdom [was] not relevant'.[46] The case of *JFK*, like other trafficking-based asylum claims, raises questions about the future risk analysis in refugee law, the relevance of migration motivations for this enquiry and, more generally, the value of distinguishing between irregular(ised) migrants and trafficked persons.

Against this background, the question I seek to answer in this book is as follows: What are the effects and implications of employing the concept of human trafficking in refugee law? In asking about the effects of employing the concept of human trafficking in refugee law, I seek to observe under what circumstances trafficking-based asylum claims succeed, aiming to describe patterns in decision-making. In asking about the implications, I question binary migration law categories and their underlying assumptions. This part of the research question seeks to apply the findings from the trafficking context to the factual situation of irregularised migrants in order to infer whether the factors determining the success of trafficking-based asylum claims are also present for irregularised migrants.

In summary, the asylum claims analysed in this book serve as a point of departure for understanding under what circumstances (a future fear of) harm experienced outside the country of origin and during irregular migration is seen to warrant refugee protection. They also serve as a comparison between the experiences of trafficked persons and irregularised migrants. As such, the book questions the distinction between refugee/migrant, human trafficking/migrant smuggling and forced/voluntary migration. Disengaging from these categories and assumptions has effects on the application of refugee law to members of these groups. Thus, while this book conducts a doctrinal examination of the scope of the *refugee* definition, it also has real-life implications for irregularised migrants.

45 ibid [7].
46 ibid [33].

1.2 Trafficking, Smuggling and Asylum

1.2.1 A Note on Terminology

A book which aims to challenge migration law categories might be expected to eschew using such categories. Yet to an extent, categorisation is useful in order to refer to people with similar experiences and protection needs. In fact, I use the category 'irregularised migrants' to collectively refer to a group of people at risk of irregular re-migration. I use 'irregularised migrant' rather than 'irregular migrant' to draw attention to the role of states in creating irregular migration. The term refers to migrants who are being irregularised, that is, made irregular, by states and their border regimes.[47] As such, the passive 'irregularised' points to 'a condition that is *produced* through various processes of (ir)regularization'.[48] In this book, I will argue that this irregular status contributes to the risk of irregular re-migration.

In addition, I use existing migration law categories. While challenging the migrant/refugee binary, I nevertheless rely on 'refugee' as a category to refer to persons who fall within the personal scope of Article 1A(2) of the Refugee Convention. The aim of this book is not to do away with the refugee category; on the contrary, recognising that the refugee label not only affords comprehensive protection to non-nationals[49] but also refers to a category of persons towards whom states have reaffirmed their protection obligations,[50] I seek to include persons who would otherwise be thought of as 'migrants' within the *refugee* definition. Thus, I simultaneously challenge the refugee/migrant binary and acknowledge that only by being recognised as the former will the latter be able to obtain protection.

The final two migration law categories I continue to use, while simultaneously challenging them, are 'trafficked person' and 'smuggled person'. Since this book is concerned with the protection needs of persons undertaking dangerous migratory journeys, the terms 'irregularised migrant' and 'smuggled person' can, to an extent, be used interchangeably. Yet as this book will show, the category of 'irregularised migrants' is broader than that of 'smuggled persons', with the former encompassing persons who have travelled regularly but who live undocumented in countries of destination. Further, as explained earlier, not every irregularised migrant need necessarily to have been smuggled, although most irregular arrivals do rely on facilitators. The category

47 Yolande Jansen, Robin Celikates and Joost de Bloois (eds), *The Irregularization of Migration in Contemporary Europe: Detention, Deportation, Drowning* (Rowman & Littlefield 2014); Catherine Dauvergne, *Making People Illegal: What Globalization Means for Migration and Law* (CUP 2008).

48 Vicki Squire, 'The Contested Politics of Mobility: Politicising Mobility, Mobilising Politics' in Vicki Squire (ed), *The Contested Politics of Mobility: Borderzones and Irregularity* (Routledge 2011) 5; emphasis in original.

49 See Section 1.2.3.1.

50 Global Compact on Refugees (UNGA, 2 August 2018) UN doc A/73/12 (Part II) para 5.

'smuggled person' reflects states' attitudes towards irregularised migrants in that persons moving across borders (and staying in countries of destination) irregularly are perceived as moving 'voluntarily' and as not being in need of protection.[51] As such, this category is useful as a juxtaposition to 'trafficked person', a legal category entitled to protection under criminal, human rights and refugee law. 'Trafficked person', then, is used throughout this book to highlight (and question) the distinction made in law between trafficked and smuggled persons – and, by extension, irregularised migrants – and between both groups' migration motivations and protection needs.

Nevertheless, these categories – and, indeed, a number of terms often used to describe individuals deemed to fit within them, such as 'victim' and 'forced', 'voluntary' or 'economic' migrant – are problematic since, as explained earlier, they perpetuate unhelpful assumptions about these individuals. As a consequence, throughout this book, I put terms such as 'victim', but also adjectives like 'vulnerable', in quotation marks.

1.2.2 *The Smuggled/Trafficked and Migrant/Refugee Binaries*

Despite the problematic nature of the terms themselves, both the smuggled/trafficked and the migrant/refugee binaries are at the heart of this book. *JFK* and other cases like it highlight the impact of migration law categories and binaries and their underlying assumptions. Not only are trafficking and smuggling two distinct crimes in international law,[52] as Serughetti notes, the labels 'trafficked person' and 'smuggled person' are also 'used to separate between those deemed as deserving protection and others to be deported', much like the categories 'refugee' and '(irregular) migrant'.[53] Thus, the migrant/refugee binary is reflected in the smuggled/trafficked binary. As such, challenging the latter binary also challenges the former.

In this book, this challenge consists of investigating whether, like trafficked persons, smuggled persons should be able to claim asylum based on (a future fear related to) their smuggling experience. Investigations of trafficked persons' eligibility for refugee status, or *non-refoulement* more generally, already exist.[54]

51 See Chapter 2, Section 2.3.2.

52 Trafficking Protocol (n 13) art 3(a); Smuggling Protocol (n 13) art 3(a).

53 Giorgia Serughetti, 'Smuggled or Trafficked? Refugee or Job Seeker? Deconstructing Rigid Classifications by Rethinking Women's Vulnerability' (2018) 11 Anti-Trafficking Review 16, 18 <https://doi.org/10.14197/atr.201218112>.

54 Kaori Saito, 'International Protection for Trafficked Persons and Those Who Fear Being Trafficked' (2007) UNHCR Research Paper No 149 <www.unhcr.org/sites/default/files/legacy-pdf/476652742.pdf> accessed 2 February 2019; Anna Dorevitch and Michelle Foster, 'Obstacles on the Road to Protection: Assessing the Treatment of Sex-Trafficking Victims under Australia's Migration and Refugee Law' (2008) 9(1) Melbourne Journal of International Law 1; Martina Pomeroy, 'Left Out in the Cold: Trafficking Victims, Gender, and Misinterpretation of the Refugee Convention's "Nexus" Requirement' (2010) 16(2) Michigan Journal of Gender and Law 453; Udara Jayasinghe and Sasha Baglay, 'Protecting Victims of Human

In addition, it has been recognised that smuggling of migrants, too, raises human rights issues, and that the distinction between trafficking and smuggling 'undermine[s] the protection of the human rights of those smuggled'.[55] This book contributes to the existing literature by examining the similarities between trafficked and smuggled persons' experiences and considering smuggled persons' eligibility for refugee status.

To date, those who have considered 'smuggled persons',[56] 'vulnerable irregular migrants'[57] or 'extremely vulnerable people'[58] as possible beneficiaries of protection either envision their inclusion via long-term residence permits,[59] under a soft law framework similar to that governing internally displaced persons,[60] or as beneficiaries of humanitarian protection.[61] The assumption in these studies is that the persons concerned 'fall outside the framework of the

---

Trafficking within a "Non-Refoulement" Framework: Is Complementary Protection an Effective Alternative in Canada and Australia?' (2011) 23(3) International Journal of Refugee Law 489 <https://doi.org/10.1093/ijrl/eer022>; Susan Kneebone, 'Protecting Trafficked Persons from Refoulement: Re-examining the Nexus' in Satvinder S Juss and Colin Harvey (eds), *Contemporary Issues in Refugee Law* (Edward Elgar Publishing 2013); Jean-Pierre Gauci, 'Trafficked Persons as Refugees' (PhD thesis, King's College London 2013) <https://kclpure.kcl.ac.uk/ws/portalfiles/portal/44864641/2014_Gauci_Jean_Pierre_1034261_ethesis.pdf> accessed 5 February 2019; Idil Atak and James C Simeon, 'Human Trafficking: Mapping the Legal Boundaries of International Refugee Law and Criminal Justice' (2014) 12(5) Journal of International Criminal Justice 1019 <https://doi.org/10.1093/jicj/mqu093>; Christine Köhler, *Opferschutz im Bereich des Menschenhandels* (Duncker & Humblot 2016) ch 3; Nula Frei, *Menschenhandel und Asyl: Die Umsetzung der völkerrechtlichen Verpflichtungen zum Opferschutz im schweizerischen Asylverfahren* (Nomos 2018); Noemi Magugliani, '(In) Vulnerable Masculinities and Human Trafficking: Men, Victimhood, and Access to Protection in the United Kingdom' (2022) 44(2) Journal of Human Rights Practice 726 <https://doi.org/10.1093/jhuman/huac001>; Noemi Magugliani, 'Trafficked Adult Males as (Un) Gendered Protection Seekers: Between Presumption of Invulnerability and Exclusion from Membership of a Particular Social Group' (2022) 34(3–4) International Journal of Refugee Law 353 <https://doi.org/10.1093/ijrl/eeac030>.

55 Tom Obokata, 'Smuggling of Human Beings from a Human Rights Perspective: Obligations of Non-State and State Actors under International Human Rights Law' (2005) 17(2) International Journal of Refugee Law 394, 396 <https://doi.org/10.1093/ijrl/eei013>.

56 Matilde Ventrella, *The Control of People Smuggling and Trafficking in the EU: Experiences from the UK and Italy* (Routledge 2010).

57 Alexander Betts, 'Towards a "Soft Law" Framework for the Protection of Vulnerable Irregular Migrants' (2010) 22(2) International Journal of Refugee Law 209 <https://doi.org/10.1093/ijrl/eeq018>.

58 Kinga Janik, 'A Human Rights Approach to Extremely Vulnerable People: Challenges and Feasibility in Assessing Smuggled Migrants' in Valsamis Mitsilegas, Violeta Moreno-Lax and Niovi Vavoula (eds), *Securitising Asylum Flows: Deflection, Criminalisation and Challenges for Human Rights* (Brill Nijhoff 2020) 58.

59 Ventrella (n 56) 146ff; 201ff.

60 Betts (n 57) 215. See also Betts's concept of 'survival migration' in Alexander Betts, *Survival Migration: Failed Governance and the Crisis of Displacement* (Cornell UP 2013).

61 Janik (n 58) 75.

refugee regime'.[62] This book, however, argues that the Refugee Convention is the appropriate protection instrument.

1.2.3 Protection Under the Refugee Convention

1.2.3.1 The Focus on the Refugee Convention

This book focuses on the Refugee Convention, and thus on eligibility for refugee status, rather than on eligibility for human rights protection;[63] regional complementary protection regimes, such as subsidiary protection under EU law;[64] or domestic forms of complementary protection. The book discusses the scope of the Refugee Convention's *refugee* definition in the context of the relevant regional (EU and European) and national (case) law.[65] The focus on the Refugee Convention is justified, first of all, by the fact that where trafficked persons' protection claims analysed in this book succeed, most do so under the Refugee Convention, or as I will show in subsequent chapters, it can be argued that they should have succeeded under this instrument. Indeed, as this book will demonstrate, the Refugee Convention's *refugee* definition allows for a step-by-step investigation of an individual applicant's circumstances, so that its structure and the questions raised by its individual elements are particularly useful to challenging preconceived notions about risk and protection needs.

62 Betts (n 60) 5.

63 Conferred, for example, under provisions of the European Convention for the Protection of Human Rights and Fundamental Freedoms Rights, as amended (adopted 4 November 1950, entered into force 3 September 1953) CETS No 005 (ECHR); the International Covenant on Civil and Political Rights (adopted 16 December 1966, entered into force 23 March 1976) 999 UNTS 171 (ICCPR); the Convention on the Elimination of All Forms of Discrimination against Women (adopted 18 December 1979, entered into force 3 September 1981) 1249 UNTS 13 (CEDAW); or the Convention on the Rights of the Child (adopted 20 November 1989, entered into force 2 September 1990) 1577 UNTS 3 (CRC).

64 *Subsidiary protection* is a protection status introduced by Article 15 of the 2004 EU Qualification Directive; see Council Directive 2004/83/EC of 29 April 2004 on Minimum Standards for the Qualification and Status of Third-Country Nationals or Stateless Persons as Refugees or as Persons Who Otherwise Need International Protection and the Content of the Protection Granted [2004] OJ L304/12 (Qualification Directive); The 2004 Directive was recast in 2011: Directive 2011/95/EU of the European Parliament and of the Council of 13 December 2011 on Standards for the Qualification of Third-Country Nationals or Stateless Persons as Beneficiaries of International Protection, for a Uniform Status for Refugees or for Persons Eligible for Subsidiary Protection, and for the Content of the Protection Granted (recast) [2011] OJ L337/9 (recast Qualification Directive). The recast Qualification Directive was replaced in 2024 by Regulation (EU) 2024/1347 of the European Parliament and of the Council of 14 May 2024 on Standards for the Qualification of Third-Country Nationals or Stateless Persons as Beneficiaries of International Protection, for a Uniform Status for Refugees or for Persons Eligible for Subsidiary Protection and for the Content of the Protection Granted, Amending Council Directive 2003/109/EC and Repealing Directive 2011/95/EU of the European Parliament and of the Council [2024] OJ L 2024/1347 (Qualification Regulation).

65 See following Section 3 on methodology.

The focus on the Refugee Convention is also justified by the fact that states continue to affirm their commitment to the Convention as the 'core' of the principle of *non-refoulement*,[66] the fundamental principle in international law protecting individuals against being returned to countries where they would experience 'persecution, torture, or other serious ill-treatment'.[67] Indeed, EU asylum law must be compatible with the Refugee Convention,[68] with the latter taking precedence over the former,[69] and eligibility for refugee status is the first point of departure for assessing protection claims.[70] It is important to note, however, that the *non-refoulement* principle is also expressed in international and regional human rights law, either explicitly, for example, in the United Nations (UN) Convention against Torture and Other Cruel, Inhuman or Degrading Treatment or Punishment (CAT),[71] or as 'an implied aspect of [a range of human] rights, in particular, but not restricted to, the right to life and the prohibition of torture, cruel, inhuman and degrading treatment'.[72] Further, *non-refoulement* may be said to constitute customary international

66 Global Compact on Refugees (n 50) para 5. See also UNHCR, 'Declaration of States Parties to the 1951 Convention and/or its 1967 Protocol Relating to the Status of Refugees' (16 January 2002) UN Doc HCR/MMSP/2001/09; cf Refugee Convention (n 32) art 33(1).

67 Goodwin-Gill and McAdam (n 35) 241.

68 Consolidated Version of the Treaty on the Functioning of the European Union [2012] OJ C 326 (TFEU) art 78; Charter of Fundamental Rights of the European Union [2012] OJ C 326 (EUCFR) art 18.

69 TFEU ibid art 351.

70 C-604/12 *HN* [2014] ECLI:EU:C:2014:302, para 35: '[A]n application for subsidiary protection should not, in principle, be considered before the competent authority has reached the conclusion that the person seeking international protection does not qualify for refugee status'. See also the EU Qualification Regulation (n 64) where provisions on granting refugee status (Chapter IV) precede 'Qualification for subsidiary protection' (Chapter V) and which specifies that '"person eligible for subsidiary protection" means a third-country national or a stateless person *who does not qualify as a refugee*' (see Article 3(6); emphasis added), while clarifying that '[s]ubsidiary protection should be complementary and additional to the refugee protection enshrined in the Geneva Convention' (Recital 48). Further, the EU Asylum Procedures Directive clarifies that '[w]hen examining applications for international protection, the determining authority shall first determine whether the applicants qualify as refugees and, if not, determine whether the applicants are eligible for subsidiary protection'; see Directive 2013/32/EU of the European Parliament and of the Council of 26 June 2013 on Common Procedures for Granting and Withdrawing International Protection [2013] OJ L 180 (Asylum Procedures Directive) art 10(2); cf Steve Peers and others (eds), *EU Immigration and Asylum Law (Text and Commentary): Second Revised Edition: Volume 3: EU Asylum Law* (Brill 2015) 133–34. See further Hathaway and Foster (n 35) 2.

71 United Nations Convention against Torture and Other Cruel, Inhuman or Degrading Treatment or Punishment (adopted 10 December 1984, entered into force 26 June 1987) 1465 UNTS 85 (CAT) art 3(1).

72 Başak Çalı, Cathryn Costello and Stewart Cunningham, 'Hard Protection through Soft Courts? *Non-Refoulement* before the United Nations Treaty Bodies' (2020) 21(3) German Law Journal 355 <https://doi.org/10.1017/glj.2020.28>; This is the case, for example, under the ECHR (n 63); cf *Soering v United Kingdom* App no 14038/88 (ECtHR, 7 July 1989); *JK and Others v Sweden* App no 59166/12 (ECtHR, 23 August 2016) paras 77–105.

law.[73] Nevertheless, the outcome of the *non-refoulement* enquiry differs under refugee law on the one hand and human rights law on the other in terms of the protection status granted. Refugee status is the most beneficial protection status available since, as opposed to some complementary forms of protection, the Refugee Convention 'confers a range of civil and political and socio-economic rights on those recognized as refugees',[74] and thus provides the most comprehensive form of protection. While some complementary forms of protection do come with a catalogue of rights, for example, in case of subsidiary protection status under EU law, there are a number of important differences.[75] As such, eligibility for the most beneficial protection status available should be considered first, rather than risking, as Costello puts it, 'siphon[ing] off those who warrant recognition as Convention refugees into [a] lesser status'.[76]

While it has been argued that complementary protection regimes are more inclusive than the Refugee Convention because they do not limit the personal scope of those eligible for protection by reference to Refugee Convention grounds, do not exclude certain categories of persons from protection[77] and are therefore 'applicable to everyone',[78] in this book I will show that the Refugee Convention is particularly well-suited to protecting trafficked persons and irregularised migrants.

Yet when focusing on the Refugee Convention, particularly in the context of protection for trafficked persons and irregularised migrants, a caveat to the utility of this instrument must be mentioned. In arguing for an application of the Refugee Convention which (to an extent) addresses the predicament of

73 Penelope Mathew, '*Non-refoulement*' in Cathryn Costello, Michelle Foster and Jane McAdam (eds), *The Oxford Handbook of International Refugee Law* (OUP 2021) 904.

74 Foster (n 27) 353. For a detailed discussion of these rights, see James C Hathaway, *The Rights of Refugees under International Law* (2nd edn, CUP 2021).

75 For example, beneficiaries of refugee status receive resident permits initially valid for at least three years, while beneficiaries of subsidiary receive residence permits initially valid for at least one year. See Qualification Regulation (n 64) art 24(4). In addition, for beneficiaries of subsidiary protection, access to social assistance can be limited to core benefits. See Qualification Regulation (n 64) art 31(2). Further, the EU Family Reunification Directive – and its favourable provisions foreseen for refugees – does not apply to beneficiaries of subsidiary protection. See Council Directive 2003/86/EC of 22 September 2003 on the Right to Family Reunification [2003] OJ L 251 (Family Reunification Directive) art 3(2)(c). See also Minos Mouzourakis, 'Refugee Rights Subsiding? Europe's Two-Tier Protection Regime and Its Effect on the Rights of Beneficiaries' (*ECRE*, 2016) 15–23 <www.refworld.org/reference/regionalreport/ecre/2016/en/116217> accessed 21 July 2021. See further Jane McAdam, 'Complementary Protection' in Cathryn Costello, Michelle Foster and Jane McAdam (eds), *The Oxford Handbook of International Refugee Law* (OUP 2021) 670–71.

76 Cathryn Costello, *The Human Rights of Migrants and Refugees in European Law* (OUP 2016) 200.

77 Jane McAdam, *Complementary Protection in International Refugee Law* (OUP 2007) 15.

78 Vincent Chetail, 'Moving towards an Integrated Approach of Refugee Law and Human Rights Law' in Cathryn Costello, Michelle Foster and Jane McAdam (eds), *The Oxford Handbook of International Refugee Law* (OUP 2021) 205.

persons experiencing harm during irregular migration, one cannot ignore the fact that the Convention itself is complicit in states parties' migration control agenda.[79] Arguing that certain persons should be granted refugee status (even if it is a broad class of persons) implies that others will not be granted this status and thus perpetuates the idea 'that sovereign states have a right to exclude, but that certain political strangers warrant discretionary admission and inclusion because some terrible event creates exceptional circumstances'.[80] Indeed, the argument advanced in this book only benefits those who have already reached countries of protection, rather than those yet to undertake, or in the process of undertaking, dangerous journeys; and it only benefits those who can meet the *refugee* definition in the manner suggested over the coming chapters. As such, there is a limit to the creative interpretation of the Refugee Convention.

1.2.3.2 Re-Migration as the Relevant Risk Under the Refugee Convention

Nonetheless, a creative interpretation of the Refugee Convention's *refugee* definition opens up new avenues for protection by extending the Convention's prohibition of *refoulement* in Article 33 (and the other rights contained in the Convention) to new beneficiaries. As an exception to states' otherwise largely sovereign decision on who can enter and remain in their territory,[81] the *non-refoulement* principle, and therefore the Refugee Convention, is a popular starting point for legal academics seeking to challenge states' migration control prerogative. Existing studies in this area can be divided into two approaches: first, those concerned with persons outside the destination state's territory and, second, those concerned with persons already inside the territory.

The former group argues that states' border control systems are incompatible with their obligations under refugee and human rights law.[82] This includes

79 James C Hathaway, 'A Reconsideration of the Underlying Premise of Refugee Law' (1990) 31(1) Harvard International Law Journal 129; Patricia Tuitt, *False Images: Law's Construction of the Refugee* (Pluto Press 1996); BS Chimni, 'The Geopolitics of Refugee Studies: A View from the South' (1998) 11(4) Journal of Refugee Studies 350 <https://doi.org/10.1093/jrs/11.4.350-a>; Nevzat Soguk, *States and Strangers: Refugees and Displacements of Statecraft* (University of Minnesota Press 1999); BS Chimni, 'The Birth of a "Discipline": From Refugee to Forced Migration Studies' (2009) 22(1) Journal of Refugee Studies 11 <https://doi.org/10.1093/jrs/fen051>; Simon Behrman, 'Refugee Law as a Means of Control' (2019) 32(1) Journal of Refugee Studies 43 <https://doi.org/10.1093/jrs/fey016>; Nadine El-Enany, *(B)ordering Britain: Law, Race and Empire* (Manchester UP 2020) ch 4.

80 Achiume (n 16) 1532.

81 Guild notes that in the EU context, in addition to exceptions introduced by refugee and human rights law, the right of member states to expel non-nationals is circumscribed with respect to EU citizens, as well as third-country nationals who are long-term legal residents. See Guild (n 5) 55–60.

82 Examples of this type of study include: Gammeltoft-Hansen (n 6); Den Heijer (n 6); Gammeltoft-Hansen and Hathaway (n 6); Moreno-Lax (n 6); Giuffré and Moreno-Lax (n 6); Vladislava Stoyanova, 'The Right to Life Under the EU Charter and Cooperation with Third

the right to *non-refoulement*, but also other human rights, such as the right to life; the right to leave any country, or, as Moreno-Lax puts it, the 'right to flee';[83] as well as socio-economic rights of migrants contained within third countries. These approaches are concerned with irregular migration in that they advocate for solutions for persons still outside the destination state's territory. Studies in this area focus on human rights violations experienced during irregular migration and tend to argue that, despite states' efforts to absolve themselves of their obligations towards protection seekers through externalised border controls, a jurisdictional link between the state and individual migrants can be established, so that states can be held accountable for rights violations and should provide remedies.

A second approach to challenging states' migration control prerogative seeks to expand the category of persons entitled to *non-refoulement* in order to prevent their removal. Studies in this area are concerned with persons already in the destination state's territory and argue for an expansive reading of the *refugee* definition in order to enable an individual to claim protection and avoid removal. Studies in this area often rely on the nature of the Refugee Convention as a 'living instrument'[84] and its ability to adapt to new refugee claims. Indeed, developments in the interpretation of the Convention ground 'membership of a particular social group' (PSG) have expanded the boundaries of the *refugee* definition to include claims based on persecution due to 'gender, sexual orientation, family, age, and disability'.[85] Indeed, studies in this area have argued for the inclusion within the scope of the *refugee* definition of persons fleeing socio-economic deprivation,[86] armed conflict,[87] climate change and disasters[88] and have examined the application of the definition to

States to Combat Human Smuggling' (2020) 21(3) German Law Journal 436 <https://doi.org/10.1017/glj.2020.22>; Vladislava Stoyanova, 'The Right to Leave Any Country and the Interplay between Jurisdiction and Proportionality in Human Rights Law' (2020) 32(3) International Journal of Refugee Law 403 <https://doi.org/10.1093/ijrl/eeaa030>; Annick Pijnenburg, *At the Frontiers of State Responsibility: Socio-Economic Rights and Cooperation on Migration* (Intersentia 2021).

83 Moreno-Lax (n 6) 341; Violeta Moreno-Lax, 'Intersectionality, Forced Migration, and the Jus-generation of the Right to Flee: Theorising a Composite Entitlement to Leave to Escape Irreversible Harm' in Başak Çalı, Ledi Bianku and Iulia Motoc (eds), *Migration and the European Convention on Human Rights* (OUP 2021).

84 See, for example, *Sepet v SSHD* [2003] UKHL 15, [2003] 3 WLUK 555 [6]. See also UNHCR ExCom, 'Conclusion on the Provision on International Protection Including Through Complementary Forms of Protection' (2005) <www.refworld.org/policy/polcomp/unhcr/2017/en/120301> accessed 13 April 2020, para c.

85 Hathaway and Foster (n 35) 363.

86 Foster (n 27).

87 Nora Markard, *Kriegsflüchtlinge: Gewalt gegen Zivilpersonen in bewaffneten Konflikten als Herausforderung für das Flüchtlingsrecht und den subsidiären Schutz* (Mohr Siebeck 2012); Christel Querton, *Conflict Refugees: European Union Law and Practice* (CUP 2023).

88 Matthew Scott, *Climate Change, Disasters and the Refugee Convention* (CUP 2020).

children[89] and to persons with disabilities.[90] Irregular migration as such plays no role in these types of studies; instead, the focus is on allowing persons who are already in the territory to stay by (creatively) interpreting the *refugee* definition in their favour.

In this book, I combine the two approaches described previously, taking elements from each yet offering a new perspective. Like the first group of authors, I look at experiences during irregular migration and at human rights violations experienced in this context. However, rather than focusing on irregular migrants still outside destination states' territory and seeking to establish state responsibility for human rights violations, I follow the second group of authors in adopting a living instrument approach to the Refugee Convention. As such, I am interested in persons who have made it to states of destination despite extraterritorial border controls. I examine whether a future fear of another dangerous journey, and the human rights violations this entails, can form the basis for *non-refoulement* and, more specifically, for refugee status.

A novel aspect of this book, therefore, is its focus on irregular *re*-migration as the relevant risk. In the existing studies described in the preceding text, migratory journeys are usually represented as having a beginning and an end point. They are conceived of either as linear, from the country of origin to countries of protection; as circuitous, from the country of origin to a transit country and back to the country of origin; or as aborted, where migrants are unable to leave their countries of origin in the first place, become stranded in transit countries or do not survive the journey. By contrast, I approach irregular migration as a continuous phenomenon, with emphasis on the importance of irregular re-migration after the return to the country of origin. Nonetheless, as this book will show (see, in particular, Chapter 7), claims of persons at risk of irregular migration, rather than irregular *re*-migration, should also be considered. The risk of irregular re-migration is derived from the risk of re-trafficking. In both instances, there will be individuals at risk of being trafficked or of migrating irregularly for the first time. The focus on irregular *re*-migration in this book is therefore not intented to preclude protection claims from persons with no prior trafficking or irregular migration experience. Instead, focusing on irregular re-migration shows how such an experience contributes to a heightened future risk.

While irregular re-migration has been researched from the perspective of sociology,[91] there is, to date, no assessment of the legal implications of

89 Jason M Pobjoy, *The Child in International Refugee Law* (CUP 2017).

90 Stephanie Motz, *The Refugee Status of Persons with Disabilities* (Brill 2021).

91 Liza Schuster and Nassim Majidi, 'What Happens Post-Deportation? The Experience of Deported Afghans' (2013) 1(2) Migration Studies 221 <https://doi.org/10.1093/migration/mns011>; Nauja Kleist, 'Life after Deportation and Migration Crisis: The Challenges of Involuntary Return' (*DIIS Policy Brief*, 2013) <www.researchgate.net/publication/279449121_Life_after_Deportation_and_Migration_Crisis_the_Challenges_of_Involuntary_Return> accessed 9 April 2021; Liza Schuster and Nassim Majidi, 'Deportation Stigma

irregular re-migration as a protection issue. With this book I seek to close this gap in the literature and direct attention to those irregular migrants who would not be recognised as refugees based on a future fear of harm related to the situation in their country of origin alone, but who have experienced serious harm during the dangerous migratory journey and who may be at risk of experiencing such harm once again.

1.2.3.3 Questions Raised by Irregularised Migrants' Claims to Refugee Protection

A number of questions arise in attempting to bring irregularised migrants within the scope of the Refugee Convention's *refugee* definition. Besides the requirement of alienage, there are three main elements to this definition: The first is the requirement of a well-founded fear, that is, a future risk of harm; harm which, second, must amount to persecution, a concept which has been interpreted to encompass a failure on the part of the country of origin to provide protection; and finally, there must be a connection between the persecution feared and at least one of the five Refugee Convention grounds – race, religion, nationality, membership of a PSG or political opinion.[92] Each of these elements raises questions with regard to claims by irregularised migrants.

First, there is the question of future fear of harm. It may be suggested that, in the absence of irregularised migrants' well-founded fear of being persecuted *in* their country of origin, any renewed dangerous journey they undertake will necessarily be 'voluntary'. Thus, the question is whether there can be said to be a *risk* of irregular re-migration. Second, do persons who experience serious harm outside their country of origin experience persecution? The harm they experience may be serious, but seeing as it is transit and destination states which prevent migrants from travelling regularly through their migration control policies and in which the actual harm is experienced, can migrants' countries of origin be said to fail to protect them? Finally, even if a future risk of persecution can be established, can this be said to be for reasons of one of the five Convention grounds? I will answer these questions over the course of the book, coming to the conclusion that irregularised migrants may, indeed, be able to meet the *refugee* definition.

1.3 Methodology

I come to this conclusion based on an examination of empirical data. I analyse UK and German trafficking-based asylum claims in order to form a hypothesis

---

and Re-migration' (2015) 41(4) Journal of Ethnic and Migration Studies 635 <https://doi.org/10.1080/1369183X.2014.957174>; Nauja Kleist, 'Disrupted Migration Projects: The Moral Economy of Involuntary Return to Ghana from Libya' (2017) 87(2) Africa 322 <https://doi.org/10.1017/S000197201600098X>.

92 Hathaway and Foster (n 35) chs 1–5; Goodwin-Gill and McAdam (n 35) ch 3.

about the scope and meaning of the *refugee* definition in relation to trafficked persons. The testing of this hypothesis is undertaken through the comparative and empirical aspects of the research. Finally, the theory derived from this concerns the application of the *refugee* definition to irregularised migrants.

The main norm interpreted in this book is Article 1A(2) of the Refugee Convention through reliance on the general rule of treaty interpretation as stipulated in the Vienna Convention on the Law of Treaties (VCLT), which requires interpretation 'in good faith in accordance with the ordinary meaning to be given to the terms of the treaty in their context and in the light of its object and purpose'.[93] The Refugee Convention's object and purpose is the protection of refugees, and its Preamble calls for 'the widest possible exercise' of the fundamental rights and freedoms laid down in the Convention and other human rights treaties. Based on this, a good faith interpretation justifies an expansive reading of the Refugee Convention's *refugee* definition. Only such a reading can take account of the changing nature of refugees' protection needs and thus uphold the status of the Convention as a living instrument.

Refugees' protection needs can be gauged by studying case law on a particular topic, and thus, such case law will play an important role in this book. Indeed, comparing state practice in applying the Refugee Convention can inform arguments about the Convention's meaning and scope.[94] In this context, it should be noted that even though I approach the different elements of the *refugee* definition separately and after one another, these elements are part of a whole, and 'a unitary process' is required to interpret the *refugee* definition.[95] Nevertheless, while, as Foster notes, 'there is a certain element of artificiality in analysing the various elements of the Refugee Convention definition separately',[96] doing so is necessary when adopting a 'methodical approach',[97] which allows determining the 'key issues in each element' and how these play out in irregularised migrants' protection claims.[98] Of course, the elements of the *refugee* definition do not stand alone but are assessed in the context of each individual claimant's particular circumstances. Thus, issues such as an applicant's credibility, or the existence of an internal protection alternative (IPA),[99] play an important role in the process. However, these elements are not part of

93 Vienna Convention on the Law of Treaties (adopted 23 May 1969, entered into force on 27 January 1980) 1155 UNTS 331 (VCLT) art 31(1).

94 Markard (n 87) 20.

95 *Karanakaran v SSHD* [2000] EWCA Civ 11, [2000] Imm AR 271 [Sedley LJ at 19].

96 Foster (n 27) 25.

97 *Karanakaran* (n 95) [Sedley LJ at 12].

98 Foster (n 27) 25.

99 The IPA concept precludes refugee protection where an applicant can safely move to, and remain in, a region in the country of origin where he or she is either not at risk of persecution or where state protection is available, in which case that applicant will not be entitled to refugee status. See Qualification Regulation (n 64) art 8.

the *refugee* definition as such,[100] and thus, while they do come up in the discussion, they are not examined separately.

For the purpose of the present research, case law illustrates the effects of employing a particular concept – human trafficking – in the context of refugee law. As such, I am adopting the functional method of comparative law, which 'focuses not only on rules, but on their effects, not on doctrinal structures and arguments alone, but on the consequences they bring about'.[101] I compare case law on trafficking-based asylum claims from two different jurisdictions in order to highlight trends and problems in the case law. As Lundmark notes, one of the purposes of comparative law is 'the search for universal commonalities and, of course, differences'.[102]

The relevant comparison, then, is one between case law from the UK and that from Germany.[103] There are compelling methodological reasons to compare these two jurisdictions. Both operate(d) under the same overarching legal framework, both with regard to EU asylum law and the EU and European legal framework on human trafficking and smuggling.[104] This includes EU

100 Schultz notes that although the Refugee Convention does not explicitly mention the IPA concept, this concept may nevertheless be implied in the text of the treaty. See Jessica Schultz, *The Internal Protection Alternative in Refugee Law: Treaty Basis and Scope of Application under the 1951 Convention relating to the Status of Refugees and Its 1967 Protocol* (Brill Nijhoff 2019).

101 Ralf Michaels, 'The Functional Method' in Mathias Reimann and Reinhard Zimmermann (eds), *The Oxford Handbook of Comparative Law* (2nd edn, OUP 2019) 347.

102 Thomas Lundmark, *Charting the Divide between Common and Civil Law* (OUP 2012) 12.

103 In Germany, only decisions the courts deem 'worthy of publication' are published. See Bundesverwaltungsgericht, 6 C 3.96, 26.02.1997; cf Lundmark (n 102) 364. Similarly, while in the UK decisions of higher courts will be reported, not all tribunal decisions are. First-tier tribunal decisions are not reported at all, and therefore not publicly available, and only a selection of Upper Tribunal (UT) decisions is reported, though unreported UT decisions are nevertheless available. The process for selecting decisions for reporting has been criticised. See Gina Clayton, *Textbook on Immigration and Asylum Law* (8th edn, OUP 2018) 37. I include unreported UT decisions in my analysis to expand its scope to particular issues and examples which reported cases do not cover. For example, reported cases focus overwhelmingly on the experiences of female trafficked persons, while unreported cases serve to illustrate the experiences of male claimants. Further, unreported cases consider risk of trafficking for persons without a prior experience of trafficking. In addition, unreported cases expand the geographical scope of the analysis to countries of origin of trafficked persons not covered by reported cases. Generally, these cases add detail and nuance to the analysis.

104 Even though EU law ceased to apply in the UK on 31 January 2020 (with the exception of retained EU law) – the day of its exit from the EU – most of the case law discussed in this book was decided before that date. Even after exit day, however, the UK remained bound by international and European law and continued to apply EU standards on the qualification for refugee status through the Refugee or Person in Need of International Protection (Qualification) Regulations. These Regulations transposed the 2004 EU Qualification Directive (n 64), with the UK having opted out of the 2011 version. The Nationality and Borders Act 2022 codified parts of the Qualification Directive, in particular in sections 31 and 33–35 of the Act. In Germany, the Refugee Convention's *refugee* definition is codified in s 3(1) of the Asylum Act [Asylgesetz (AsylG) 2 September 2008 (BGBl. I S. 1798) (Asylum Act)], while s 60(1)

asylum law in the form of the Qualification Regulation,[105] as well as judgments by the Court of Justice of the European Union (CJEU) and the ECtHR. In this sense, this comparison is a variation of the 'most similar case design' which is useful for 'evaluating whether similar legal frameworks are used in the same way, or produce similar effects, across contexts'.[106] As such, comparing case law from the UK and from Germany serves to uncover approaches to trafficking-based asylum claims which the two jurisdictions have in common. At the same time, the comparison serves to highlight where the two countries diverge in their approach. As Markesinis notes, '[t]he full benefit of comparing systems comes . . . when one compares factually equivalent litigated circumstances'.[107] Thus, both the commonalities of and differences between the two jurisdictions constitute the basis for forming a hypothesis on the scope and meaning of the *refugee* definition in relation to trafficked persons.

The case law discussed in this book was obtained through a Boolean search of terms around 'human trafficking' and 'asylum' in several databases.[108] The time frame spanned by the decisions found is 2004 to 2024. It is important to note here that the case law I am using as my primary legal source material often draws on gender stereotypes or colonial tropes to justify why a particular individual is in need of refugee protection while another is not. In this book, I seek to unpack assumptions underlying judicial reasoning, and while I rely on the broader legal arguments made in the case law, I do not agree with either the restrictive application of the law to different groups of protection seekers or the, at times, essentialising language used in the judgments.[109]

---

of the Residence Act codifies art 33(1) Refugee Convention, the prohibition of *refoulement* [Gesetz über den Aufenthalt, die Erwerbstätigkeit und die Integration von Ausländern im Bundesgebiet (Aufenthaltsgesetz – AufenthG) 25 February 2008 (BGBl. I S. 162) (Residence Act)]. German law has transposed the provisions of the 2011 Qualification Directive (n 64) pertaining to interpreting the *refugee* definition. Of particular relevance are arts 6–10 of the Directive, which are transposed in arts 31–3e Asylum Act.

105 Qualification Regulation (n 64); NB, throughout this book I will refer to the provisions of the Qualification Regulation, though in the time frame covered by the case law discussed in the book, the UK and Germany applied the Qualification Directive (the UK opted out of recast 2011 Directive and, until Brexit, continued to apply the 2004 version).

106 Katerina Linos and Melissa Carlson, 'Qualitative Methods for Law Review Writing' (2017) 84(1) The University of Chicago Law Review 213.

107 Basil Markesinis, 'Judicial Style and Judicial Reasoning in England and Germany' (2000) 59(2) The Cambridge Law Journal 294 <https://doi.org/10.1017/S0008197300000131>.

108 UK cases were obtained from LexisNexis, Westlaw, BAILII, Refworld and the UK IAT Database (available at: https://tribunalsdecisions.service.gov.uk/utiac), and German cases from Beck Online, Juris and openJur (available at: https://openjur.de).

109 *Essentialism* is 'the thesis that certain of an object's properties are necessary to it', for example, 'the thesis of gender essentialism holds that there is some property (or properties) necessary to . . . being a woman, like being nurturing, or being oppressed, or having a uterus'. See Charlotte Witt, 'Anti-Essentialism in Feminist Theory' (1995) 23(2) Philosophical Topics 321, 321–22.

The case law has been analysed through qualitative content analysis with the aim to uncover 'broad patterns in the case law', which works best for an analysis of 'a larger group of similarly weighted' cases.[110] Thus, this method is appropriate for my sample of cases, the majority of which in the UK context were decided by the UT's Immigration and Asylum Chamber (or its predecessor, the Asylum and Immigration Tribunal), and in the German context by the administrative courts (ACs – *Verwaltungsgerichte*). In my analysis, I seek to uncover patterns in each of the two bodies of case law and then compare UK and German case law to see whether patterns across the two jurisdictions emerge.

Finally, in order to develop a hypothesis as to the applicability of the *refugee* definition to irregularised migrants, I compare the circumstances of trafficked persons and irregularised migrants to draw 'analogies . . . based upon the similarities between the facts of two cases'.[111] Thus, by drawing analogies between trafficked persons and irregularised migrants, I seek to assess the facts of the latter's cases in the context of the same rule which the former succeeded under – Article 1A(2) Refugee Convention. This involves incorporating research from other disciplines to illustrate the relevant facts. In order to fill the elements of the *refugee* definition with concrete meaning in a particular context, it is necessary to draw on other disciplines which give insight into the factual circumstances underlying the relevant context.[112] This helps avoid drawing premature conclusions regarding who is a refugee, based on stereotypical assumptions.[113] Thus, the *refugee* definition can only meaningfully be applied when informed by factual information.

1.4 Structure of the Book and Outline of the Argument

In this book, I aim to foreground the experiences of trafficked persons and smuggled persons, or irregularised migrants. I compare the two groups, asking under which circumstances they are, or ought to be, eligible for refugee status. The remainder of this book is divided into six chapters addressing different aspects of this enquiry, as well as a conclusion.

Chapter 2 sets the scene for the enquiry by analysing the distinction in international law between two categories of irregular migrants: trafficked and smuggled persons. The chapter shows that due to the way *trafficking* and *smuggling* are defined in international law, there is a presumption that *trafficked persons* are forced migrants, who are in need of protection, whereas *smuggled persons* are deemed to be voluntary migrants, who do not need protection.

110 Mark A Hall and Ronald F Wright, 'Systematic Content Analysis of Judicial Opinions' 2008 96(1) California Law Review 63, 66.

111 Grant Lamond, 'Analogical Reasoning in the Common Law' (2014) 34(3) Oxford Journal of Legal Studies 567, 571 <https://doi.org/10.1093/ojls/gqu014>.

112 Markard (n 87) 12.

113 ibid 11–12.

The chapter shows that despite this framing, trafficked and smuggled persons have very similar experiences with regard to their reasons for migrating, the journeys they undertake and the harm experienced during those journeys. The criminal law framework, however, does not look at those experiences and focuses instead on the actions and intentions of traffickers and smugglers, so that smuggled persons' protection needs are not captured in international law. As a result, to investigate these protection needs, it is necessary to turn to a protection framework which is primarily concerned with individual experiences – the refugee law framework. The chapter sets out how the investigation into trafficked and smuggled persons' need for refugee protection will proceed, while taking care not to import the assumptions generated by the criminal law definitions into this enquiry.

Chapter 3 explores how the concept of vulnerability informs the future risk analysis in refugee law for trafficked persons and irregularised migrants. It begins with an analysis of trafficked persons' asylum claims, showing that courts rely on so-called vulnerability indicators in establishing the risk of re-trafficking. The chapter then discusses the meaning of 'vulnerability' in anti-trafficking legislation and examines legal and feminist theory on the concept of vulnerability. These theoretical considerations form the foundation for transposing the vulnerability reasoning from the trafficking to the irregular re-migration context. Thus, the chapter seeks to establish irregular re-migration as a risk paralleling the risk of re-trafficking and considers whether irregularised migrants can meet the well-founded fear element of the *refugee* definition. Moving away from the simplistic view that 'root causes' lead to re-migration, the chapter explores 'route causes' of irregular re-migration, which puts the focus on irregularised migrants' experiences during displacement and the effect these experiences have on inducing future migratory journeys. The chapter concludes by finding that, just like trafficked persons may be at risk of re-trafficking, irregularised migrants may be at risk of re-migrating irregularly and can therefore meet the well-founded fear element of the *refugee* definition.

Chapter 4 focuses on the question of persecution. The chapter shows that trafficked persons and irregularised migrants experience similar types of harm during migration, such as physical and sexual violence, deprivation of liberty and forced labour. The chapter then considers whether this harm amounts to persecution for the purpose of refugee law, seeing as it takes place largely outside the individual's country of origin. The chapter argues that trafficked persons and irregularised migrants experience two cumulative and sequential harms. This entails, first, socio-economic deprivation in the country of origin, which, in itself, is unlikely to be considered to constitute serious harm, and, second, violations of civil and political rights experienced outside the country of origin as a result of individuals trying to respond to the lack of livelihood options through irregular migration. The chapter argues that since persecution can be considered to be cumulative under refugee law, in conjunction, these two harms amount to persecution, with the country of origin's failure to protect against the former causing the latter to manifest.

Chapter 5 analyses the nexus element of the *refugee* definition and considers how trafficked and smuggled persons may meet this requirement. In the case law analysed, a nexus is usually established based on the Convention ground membership of a PSG, either the PSG 'women' or the PSG 'trafficked persons'. The chapter, however, considers whether there are nexus grounds which better explain the predicament of both trafficked persons and irregularised migrants. It argues that the PSG 'persons in vulnerable situations' best explains why both groups are at a disproportionately high risk of re-migrating irregularly. Thus, the chapter returns to the vulnerability indicators from the future risk analysis and argues that these identify 'vulnerable' individuals as a PSG and explain why they will re-migrate irregularly. The chapter also considers the Convention ground nationality, showing that this explains why an individual's journeys will be irregular, with nationality determining migrants' (in)ability to travel legally and safely.

Chapter 6 considers evidence for the fact that individuals who could benefit from the argument made in this book already submit protection claims. These claims are not based on a risk of irregular re-migration and do not focus on the Refugee Convention but succeed under complementary protection regimes because the applicants fear destitution or obstacles to integration in their countries of origin. As such, these cases are based on socio-economic deprivation and an inability to reintegrate – factors familiar from trafficking-based asylum claims and relevant to establishing a risk of irregular re-migration. The chapter posits that these claimants may be identified as irregularised migrants 'hidden' in existing case law and that, by shifting the focus of the protection enquiry onto the assessment of a risk of irregular re-migration, they may be found to be eligible for refugee status rather than complementary protection. Further, the chapter shows that because establishing a risk of destitution or 'very significant' obstacles to integration entails a high threshold, individuals unable to meet this threshold, and therefore refused protection, may nevertheless be able to show that the factors underlying their claim are material to the risk of trafficking or irregular re-migration, and thus to the question of persecution.

Chapter 7 applies the argument made in this book to a group of persons who, so far, remain unprotected under the Refugee Convention. Persons affected by climate change and disasters are currently unable to meet the *refugee* definition. However, they may be able to argue that they are irregularised migrants, and thus in need of refugee protection, based on a risk of irregular (re-)migration. The chapter analyses case law from the UK, New Zealand and Germany to show that many protection claims made against the background of climate change and disasters revolve around a risk of socio-economic deprivation. Based on the premise that this is an indicator for the risk or irregular (re-)migration, the chapter outlines how such a risk can be established in the disaster context. It considers what a risk of irregular (re-)migration entails in the context of migration in response to climate change and disasters, examining, in particular, risks resulting from becoming undocumented in the process of adapting to climate change through migration. Further, it shows how a risk of irregular (re-)migration can be established by considering the effects of disasters and individual vulnerabilities on a sliding scale of risk.

In Chapter 8, the book concludes by summarising its main contributions. It begins by outlining how the analysis of trafficking-based asylum claims and the drawing of analogies to irregularised migrants lead to the latter being reconceptualised as refugees. The chapter then shows how the argument made in this book informs and develops refugee law doctrine, in particular by proposing a novel approach to the scope of the concept of persecution, by contributing new insights on the Convention ground 'membership of a PSG' and the Convention ground 'nationality', and by exploring the *refugee* definition's relationship with vulnerability theory. Noting that such a progressive interpretation of refugee law doctrine broadens the scope of the *refugee* definition, the chapter outlines who may benefit from the argument made in this book and anticipates criticism and the possible negative consequences of making this argument. Based on this, the chapter then considers the argument's implications for migration policy, showing that conceiving of irregularised migrants as refugees implies a need for a shift away from states' restrictive border control measures.

References

Achiume ET, 'Migration as Decolonization' (2019) 71 Stanford Law Review 1509

Asylgesetz (AsylG) 2 September 2008 (BGBl. I S. 1798) (Asylum Act)

Atak I and James C Simeon, 'Human Trafficking: Mapping the Legal Boundaries of International Refugee Law and Criminal Justice' (2014) 12(5) Journal of International Criminal Justice 1019 <https://doi.org/10.1093/jicj/mqu093>

Behrman S, 'Refugee Law as a Means of Control' (2019) 32(1) Journal of Refugee Studies 43 <https://doi.org/10.1093/jrs/fey016>

Bernardini L, 'Administrative Immigration Detention as a Punitive Measure: Is It Time for a New Standpoint?' in Angela Di Stasi, Rossana Palladino and Angela Festa (eds), *Migrations, Rule of Law and European Values* (Editoriale Scientifica 2023)

Betts A, *Survival Migration: Failed Governance and the Crisis of Displacement* (Cornell UP 2013)

Betts A, 'Towards a "Soft Law" Framework for the Protection of Vulnerable Irregular Migrants' (2010) 22(2) International Journal of Refugee Law 209 <https://doi.org/10.1093/ijrl/eeq018>

Brachet J, 'Manufacturing Smugglers: From Irregular to Clandestine Mobility in the Sahara' (2018) 676(1) The Annals of the American Academy of Political and Social Science 16

Bundesverwaltungsgericht, 6 C 3.96, 26.02.1997

C-604/12 *HN* [2014] ECLI:EU:C:2014:302

Çalı B, Cathryn Costello and Stewart Cunningham, 'Hard Protection through Soft Courts? *Non-Refoulement* before the United Nations Treaty Bodies' (2020) 21(3) German Law Journal 355 <https://doi.org/10.1017/glj.2020.28>

Charter of Fundamental Rights of the European Union [2012] OJ C 326 (EUCFR)

Chetail V, 'Moving Towards an Integrated Approach of Refugee Law and Human Rights Law' in Cathryn Costello, Michelle Foster and Jane McAdam (eds), *The Oxford Handbook of International Refugee Law* (OUP 2021)

Chimni BS, 'The Birth of a "Discipline": From Refugee to Forced Migration Studies' (2009) 22(1) Journal of Refugee Studies 11 <https://doi.org/10.1093/jrs/fen051>

Chimni BS, 'The Geopolitics of Refugee Studies: A View from the South' (1998) 11(4) Journal of Refugee Studies 350 <https://doi.org/10.1093/jrs/11.4.350-a>
Clayton G, *Textbook on Immigration and Asylum Law* (8th edn, OUP 2018)
Consolidated Version of the Treaty on the Functioning of the European Union [2012] OJ C 326 (TFEU)
Convention Implementing the Schengen Agreement of 14 June 1985 between the Governments of the States of the Benelux Economic Union, the Federal Republic of Germany and the French Republic on the Gradual Abolition of Checks at Their Common Borders [2000] OJ L 239
Convention on the Elimination of All Forms of Discrimination against Women (adopted 18 December 1979, entered into force 3 September 1981) 1249 UNTS 13 (CEDAW)
Convention on the Rights of the Child (adopted 20 November 1989, entered into force 2 September 1990) 1577 UNTS 3 (CRC)
Convention Relating to the Status of Refugees (adopted 28 July 1951, entered into force 22 April 1954) 189 UNTS 137 (Refugee Convention)
Costello C, *The Human Rights of Migrants and Refugees in European Law* (OUP 2016)
Council Directive 2002/90/EC of 28 November 2002 Defining the Facilitation of Unauthorised Entry, Transit and Residence [2002] OJ L 328 (Facilitation Directive)
Council Directive 2003/86/EC of 22 September 2003 on the Right to Family Reunification [2003] OJ L 251 (Family Reunification Directive)
Council Directive 2004/83/EC of 29 April 2004 on Minimum Standards for the Qualification and Status of Third-Country Nationals or Stateless Persons as Refugees or as Persons Who Otherwise Need International Protection and the Content of the Protection Granted [2004] OJ L304/12 (Qualification Directive)
Council of Europe Convention on Action against Trafficking in Human Beings (adopted 16 May 2005, entered into force 1 February 2008) ETS 197 (ECAT)
Czaika M and Mogens Hobolth, 'Do Restrictive Asylum and Visa Policies Increase Irregular Migration into Europe?' (2016) 17(3) European Union Politics 345 <https://doi.org/10.1177/1465116516633299>
Dauvergne C, *Making People Illegal: What Globalization Means for Migration and Law* (CUP 2008)
Declaration on the Human Rights of Individuals Who Are Not Nationals of the Country in Which They Live (adopted 3 December 1985) UNGA Res 40/144
Den Heijer M, *Europe and Extraterritorial Asylum* (Hart Publishing 2012)
Directive (EU) 2024/1712 of the European Parliament and of the Council of 13 June 2024 Amending Directive 2011/36/EU on Preventing and Combating Trafficking in Human Beings and Protecting Its Victims [2024] OJ L 2024/1712 (Trafficking Amendment Directive)
Directive 2008/115/EC of the European Parliament and of the Council of 16 December 2008 on Common Standards and Procedures in Member States for Returning Illegally Staying Third-Country Nationals [2008] OJ L 348 (Return Directive)
Directive 2011/36/EU of the European Parliament and of the Council of 5 April 2011 on Preventing and Combating Trafficking in Human Beings and Protecting Its Victims, and Replacing Council Framework Decision 2002/629/JHA [2011] OJ L 101/1 (Trafficking Directive)
Directive 2011/95/EU of the European Parliament and of the Council of 13 December 2011 on Standards for the Qualification of Third-Country Nationals or Stateless Persons as Beneficiaries of International Protection, for a Uniform Status for Refugees or for Persons Eligible for Subsidiary Protection, and for the Content of the Protection Granted (recast) [2011] OJ L337/9 (recast Qualification Directive)
Directive 2013/32/EU of the European Parliament and of the Council of 26 June 2013 on Common Procedures for Granting and Withdrawing International Protection [2013] OJ L 180 (Asylum Procedures Directive)

Dorevitch A and Michelle Foster, 'Obstacles on the Road to Protection: Assessing the Treatment of Sex-Trafficking Victims under Australia's Migration and Refugee Law' (2008) 9(1) Melbourne Journal of International Law 1

El-Enany N, *(B)ordering Britain: Law, Race and Empire* (Manchester UP 2020)

European Convention for the Protection of Human Rights and Fundamental Freedoms Rights, as Amended (adopted 4 November 1950, entered into force 3 September 1953) CETS No 005 (ECHR)

European Parliament, 'Humanitarian Visas: European Added Value Assessment Accompanying the European Parliament's Legislative Own-initiative Report (Rapporteur: Juan Fernando López Aguilar)' (22 October 2018) <www.europarl.europa.eu/RegData/etudes/STUD/2018/621823/EPRS_STU(2018)621823_EN.pdf> accessed 4 November 2020

European Union Agency for Fundamental Rights (FRA), 'Criminalisation of Migrants in an Irregular Situation and of Persons Engaging with Them' (2014) <https://fra.europa.eu/sites/default/files/fra-2014-criminalisation-of-migrants_en.pdf> accessed 22 January 2023

Foster M, *International Refugee Law and Socio-Economic Rights: Refuge from Deprivation* (CUP 2007)

Frei N, *Menschenhandel und Asyl: Die Umsetzung der völkerrechtlichen Verpflichtungen zum Opferschutz im schweizerischen Asylverfahren* (Nomos 2018)

Frontex, 'Risk Analysis for 2018' (2018) <www.statewatch.org/media/documents/news/2018/mar/eu-frontex-report-risk-analysis-2018.pdf> accessed 16 September 2021

Gallagher AT and Fiona David, *The International Law of Migrant Smuggling* (CUP 2014)

Gammeltoft-Hansen T, *Access to Asylum: International Refugee Law and the Globalisation of Migration Control* (CUP 2011)

Gammeltoft-Hansen T and James C Hathaway, 'Non-refoulement in World of Cooperative Deterrence' (2015) 53(2) Columbia Journal of Transnational Law 235

Gauci JP, 'Trafficked Persons as Refugees' (PhD thesis, King's College London 2013) <https://kclpure.kcl.ac.uk/ws/portalfiles/portal/44864641/2014_Gauci_Jean_Pierre_1034261_ethesis.pdf> accessed 5 February 2019

Gesetz über den Aufenthalt, die Erwerbstätigkeit und die Integration von Ausländern im Bundesgebiet (Aufenthaltsgesetz – AufenthG) 25 February 2008 (BGBl. I S. 162) (Residence Act)

Giuffré M and Violeta Moreno-Lax, 'The Rise of Contactless Containment: From "Contactless Control" to "Contactless Responsibility" for Migratory Flows' in Satvinder Singh Juss (ed), *Research Handbook on International Refugee Law* (Edward Elgar Publishing 2019)

Goodwin-Gill GS and Jane McAdam, *The Refugee in International Law* (4th edn, OUP 2021)

Guild E, 'The Legal Framework: Who Is Entitled to Move?' in Didier Bigo and Elspeth Guild (eds), *Controlling Frontiers: Free Movement into and within Europe* (Ashgate 2005)

Guild E, *Security and Migration in the 21st Century* (Polity 2009)

Hall MA and Ronald F Wright, 'Systematic Content Analysis of Judicial Opinions' (2008) 96(1) California Law Review 63

Hamlin R, *Crossing: How We Label and React to People on the Move* (Stanford UP 2021)

Hathaway JC, 'A Reconsideration of the Underlying Premise of Refugee Law' (1990) 31(1) Harvard International Law Journal 129

Hathaway JC, *The Rights of Refugees under International Law* (2nd edn, CUP 2021)

Hathaway JC and Michelle Foster, *The Law of Refugee Status* (2nd edn, CUP 2014)

Hirsi Jamaa and Others v Italy App no 27765/09 (ECtHR, 23 February 2012)

Ilias and Ahmed v Hungary App no 47287/15 (ECtHR, 21 November 2019)

International Covenant on Civil and Political Rights (adopted 16 December 1966, entered into force 23 March 1976) 999 UNTS 171 (ICCPR)
IOM, 'Key Migration Terms' <www.iom.int/key-migration-terms> accessed 25 September 2024
IOM, 'Missing Migrants Project' <https://missingmigrants.iom.int> accessed 25 August 2024
Janik K, 'A Human Rights Approach to Extremely Vulnerable People: Challenges and Feasibility in Assessing Smuggled Migrants' in Valsamis Mitsilegas, Violeta Moreno-Lax and Niovi Vavoula (eds), *Securitising Asylum Flows: Deflection, Criminalisation and Challenges for Human Rights* (Brill Nijhoff 2020)
Jansen Y, Robin Celikates and Joost de Bloois (eds), *The Irregularization of Migration in Contemporary Europe: Detention, Deportation, Drowning* (Rowman & Littlefield 2014)
Jayasinghe U and Sasha Baglay, 'Protecting Victims of Human Trafficking within a "Non-Refoulement" Framework: Is Complementary Protection an Effective Alternative in Canada and Australia?' (2011) 23(3) International Journal of Refugee Law 489 <https://doi.org/10.1093/ijrl/eer022>
JFK v SSHD [2018] UKUT (IAC) PA/06854/2016
JK and Others v Sweden App no 59166/12 (ECtHR, 23 August 2016)
Karanakaran v SSHD [2000] EWCA Civ 11, [2000] Imm AR 271
Kleist N, 'Disrupted Migration Projects: The Moral Economy of Involuntary Return to Ghana from Libya' (2017) 87(2) Africa 322 <https://doi.org/10.1017/S000197201600098X>
Kleist N, 'Life after Deportation and Migration Crisis: The Challenges of Involuntary Return' (*DIIS Policy Brief*, 2013) <www.researchgate.net/publication/279449121_Life_after_Deportation_and_Migration_Crisis_the_Challenges_of_Involuntary_Return> accessed 9 April 2021
Kneebone S, 'Protecting Trafficked Persons from Refoulement: Re-examining the Nexus' in Satvinder S Juss and Colin Harvey (eds), *Contemporary Issues in Refugee Law* (Elgar 2013)
Köhler C, *Opferschutz im Bereich des Menschenhandels* (Duncker & Humblot 2016)
Lamond G, 'Analogical Reasoning in the Common Law' (2014) 34(3) Oxford Journal of Legal Studies 567 <https://doi.org/10.1093/ojls/gqu014>
Last T, 'Who Is the "Boat Migrant"? Challenging the Anonymity of Death at Border-Sea' in Violeta Moreno-Lax and Efthymios Papastavridis (eds), *"Boat Refugees" and Migrants at Sea: A Comprehensive Approach* (Brill 2016)
Law Library of Congress, 'Criminalization of Illegal Entry around the World' (2019) <www.loc.gov/item/2019685473/> accessed 22 June 2022
Linos K and Melissa Carlson, 'Qualitative Methods for Law Review Writing' (2017) 84(1) The University of Chicago Law Review 213
Lundmark T, *Charting the Divide between Common and Civil Law* (OUP 2012)
Magugliani N, '(In)Vulnerable Masculinities and Human Trafficking: Men, Victimhood, and Access to Protection in the United Kingdom' (2022) 44(2) Journal of Human Rights Practice 726 <https://doi.org/10.1093/jhuman/huac001>
Magugliani N, 'Trafficked Adult Males as (Un)Gendered Protection Seekers: Between Presumption of Invulnerability and Exclusion from Membership of a Particular Social Group' (2022) 34(3–4) International Journal of Refugee Law 353 <https://doi.org/10.1093/ijrl/eeac030>
Markard N, *Kriegsflüchtlinge: Gewalt gegen Zivilpersonen in bewaffneten Konflikten als Herausforderung für das Flüchtlingsrecht und den subsidiären Schutz* (Mohr Siebeck 2012)
Markesinis B, 'Judicial Style and Judicial Reasoning in England and Germany' (2000) 59(2) The Cambridge Law Journal 294 <https://doi.org/10.1017/S0008197300000131>

Mathew P, '*Non-refoulement*' in Cathryn Costello, Michelle Foster and Jane McAdam (eds), *The Oxford Handbook of International Refugee Law* (OUP 2021)
McAdam J, 'Complementary Protection' in Cathryn Costello, Michelle Foster and Jane McAdam (eds), *The Oxford Handbook of International Refugee Law* (OUP 2021)
McAdam J, *Complementary Protection in International Refugee Law* (OUP 2007)
Michaels R, 'The Functional Method' in Mathias Reimann and Reinhard Zimmermann (eds), *The Oxford Handbook of Comparative Law* (2nd edn, OUP 2019)
Mitsilegas V, Violeta Moreno-Lax and Niovi Vavoula, 'Introduction' in Valsamis Mitsilegas, Violeta Moreno-Lax, Niovi Vavoula (eds), *Securitising Asylum Flows: Deflection, Criminalisation and Challenges for Human Rights* (Brill Nijhoff 2020)
MN and Others v Belgium App no 3599/18 (ECtHR, 5 May 2020)
Moreno-Lax V, *Accessing Asylum in Europe: Extraterritorial Border Controls and Refugee Rights under EU Law* (OUP 2017)
Moreno-Lax V, 'The EU Humanitarian Border and the Securitization of Human Rights: The "Rescue-Through-Interdiction/Rescue-Without-Protection' Paradigm"' (2018) 56(1) Journal of Common Market Studies 119 <https://doi.org/10.1111/jcms.12651>
Moreno-Lax V, 'Intersectionality, Forced Migration, and the Jus-generation of the Right to Flee: Theorising a Composite Entitlement to Leave to Escape Irreversible Harm' in Başak Çalı, Ledi Bianku and Iulia Motoc (eds), *Migration and the European Convention on Human Rights* (OUP 2021)
Motz S, *The Refugee Status of Persons with Disabilities* (Brill 2021)
Mouzourakis M, 'Refugee Rights Subsiding? Europe's Two-Tier Protection Regime and Its Effect on the Rights of Beneficiaries' (2016) ECRE <www.refworld.org/reference/regionalreport/ecre/2016/en/116217> accessed 21 July 2021
N v The United Kingdom App no 26565/05 (ECtHR, 27 May 2008)
Nationality and Borders Act 2022
ND and NT v Spain App nos 8675/15 and 8697/15 (ECtHR, 13 February 2020)
Obokata T, 'Smuggling of Human Beings from a Human Rights Perspective: Obligations of Non-State and State Actors under International Human Rights Law' (2005) 17(2) International Journal of Refugee Law 394 <https://doi.org/10.1093/ijrl/eei013>
Peers S, Violeta Moreno-Lax, Madeline Garlick and Elspeth Guild (eds), *EU Immigration and Asylum Law (Text and Commentary): Second Revised Edition: Volume 3: EU Asylum Law* (Brill 2015)
Pijnenburg A, *At the Frontiers of State Responsibility: Socio-Economic Rights and Cooperation on Migration* (Intersentia 2021)
Pobjoy JM, *The Child in International Refugee Law* (CUP 2017)
Pomeroy M, 'Left Out in the Cold: Trafficking Victims, Gender, and Misinterpretation of the Refugee Convention's "Nexus" Requirement' (2010) 16(2) Michigan Journal of Gender and Law 453
Protocol against the Smuggling of Migrants by Land, Sea and Air, Supplementing the United Nations Convention against Transnational Crime (adopted 15 November 2000, entered into force 28 January 2004) 2241 UNTS 480 (Smuggling Protocol)
Protocol Relating to the Status of Refugees (adopted 31 January 1967, entered into force 4 October 1967) 606 UNTS 267 (1967 Protocol)
Protocol to Prevent, Suppress and Punish Trafficking in Persons, Especially Women and Children, Supplementing the United Nations Convention against Transnational Organized Crime (adopted 15 November 2000, entered into force 25 December 2003) 2237 UNTS 319 (Trafficking Protocol)
Querton C, *Conflict Refugees: European Union Law and Practice* (CUP 2023)
RefMig, 'Refugees are Migrants: Refugee Mobility, Recognition and Rights' (2021) <www.refmig.org> accessed 18 September 2021

Refugee or Person in Need of International Protection (Qualification) Regulations
Regulation (EU) 2024/1347 of the European Parliament and of the Council of 14 May 2024 on Standards for the Qualification of Third-Country Nationals or Stateless Persons as Beneficiaries of International Protection, for a Uniform Status for Refugees or for Persons Eligible for Subsidiary Protection and for the Content of the Protection Granted, Amending Council Directive 2003/109/EC and Repealing Directive 2011/95/EU of the European Parliament and of the Council (Qualification Regulation)

Richmond AH, *Global Apartheid: Refugees, Racism, and the New World Order* (OUP 1994)

Saito K, 'International Protection for Trafficked Persons and Those Who Fear Being Trafficked' (2007) UNHCR Research Paper No 149 <www.unhcr.org/sites/default/files/legacy-pdf/476652742.pdf> accessed 2 February 2019

Schultz J, *The Internal Protection Alternative in Refugee Law: Treaty Basis and Scope of Application under the 1951 Convention relating to the Status of Refugees and Its 1967 Protocol* (Brill Nijhoff 2019)

Schuster L and Nassim Majidi, 'Deportation Stigma and Re-migration' (2015) 41(4) Journal of Ethnic and Migration Studies 635 <https://doi.org/10.1080/1369183X.2014.957174>

Schuster L and Nassim Majidi, 'What Happens Post-Deportation? The Experience of Deported Afghans' (2013) 1(2) Migration Studies 221 <https://doi.org/10.1093/migration/mns011>

Scott M, *Climate Change, Disasters and the Refugee Convention* (CUP 2020)

Sepet v SSHD [2003] UKHL 15, [2003] 3 WLUK 555

Serughetti G, 'Smuggled or Trafficked? Refugee or Job Seeker? Deconstructing Rigid Classifications by Rethinking Women's Vulnerability' (2018) 11 Anti-Trafficking Review 16 <https://doi.org/10.14197/atr.201218112>

Soering v United Kingdom App no 14038/88 (ECtHR, 7 July 1989)

Soguk N, *States and Strangers: Refugees and Displacements of Statecraft* (University of Minnesota Press 1999)

Spencer S and Anna Triandafyllidou, 'Irregular Migration' in Peter Scholten (ed), *Introduction to Migration Studies: An Interactive Guide to the Literatures on Migration and Diversity* (Springer 2022)

Spijkerboer T, 'Migration Management Clientelism: Europe's Migration Funds as a Global Political Project' (2022) 48(12) Journal of Ethnic and Migration Studies 2892 <https://doi.org/10.1080/1369183X.2021.1972567>

Squire V, 'The Contested Politics of Mobility: Politicising Mobility, Mobilising Politics' in Vicki Squire (ed), *The Contested Politics of Mobility: Borderzones and Irregularity* (Routledge 2011)

Squire V, Nina Perkowski, Dallal Stevens and Nick Vaughan-Williams, *Reclaiming Migration: Voices from Europe's 'Migrant Crisis'* (Manchester UP 2021)

Stoyanova V, 'The Right to Leave Any Country and the Interplay between Jurisdiction and Proportionality in Human Rights Law' (2020) 32(3) International Journal of Refugee Law 403 <https://doi.org/10.1093/ijrl/eeaa030>

Stoyanova V, 'The Right to Life under the EU Charter and Cooperation with Third States to Combat Human Smuggling' (2020) 21(3) German Law Journal 436 <https://doi.org/10.1017/glj.2020.22>

Tuitt P, *False Images: Law's Construction of the Refugee* (Pluto Press 1996)

Turton D, 'Conceptualising Forced Migration' (2003) RSC Working Paper 12 <www.rsc.ox.ac.uk/files/files-1/wp12-conceptualising-forced-migration-2003.pdf> accessed 9 March 2020

UNGA, 'Global Compact on Refugees' (2 August 2018) UN Doc A/73/12 (Part II)

UNHCR, 'Declaration of States Parties to the 1951 Convention and/or Its 1967 Protocol Relating to the Status of Refugees' (16 January 2002) UN Doc HCR/MMSP/2001/09

UNHCR, 'Guidelines on International Protection: The Application of Article 1A(2) of the 1951 Convention and/or 1967 Protocol Relating to the Status of Refugees to Victims of Trafficking and Persons at Risk of Being Trafficked' (2006) HCR/GIP/06/07 (UNHCR Trafficking Guidelines)

UNHCR, 'Handbook on Procedures and Criteria for Determining Refugee Status and Guidelines on International Protection Under the 1951 Convention and the 1967 Protocol Relating to the Status of Refugees' HCR/1P/4/ENG/REV.4 (1979, reissued 2019) (UNHCR Handbook)

UNHCR, 'On This Journey, No One Cares If You Live or Die: Abuse, Protection and Justice Along Routes between East and West Africa and Africa's Mediterranean Coast: A Route-based Perspective on Key Risks' vol 2 (March 2024) <www.unhcr.org/media/journey-no-one-cares-if-you-live-or-die-abuse-protection-and-justice-along-routes-between-1> accessed 19 August 2024

UNHCR ExCom, 'Conclusion on the Provision on International Protection Including through Complementary Forms of Protection' (2005) <www.refworld.org/policy/polcomp/unhcr/2017/en/120301> accessed 13 April 2020

United Nations Convention against Torture and Other Cruel, Inhuman or Degrading Treatment or Punishment (adopted 10 December 1984, entered into force 26 June 1987) 1465 UNTS 85 (CAT)

Van Hear N, 'Mixed Migration: Policy Challenges' (2011) The Migration Observatory Policy Primer <https://migrationobservatory.ox.ac.uk/wp-content/uploads/2016/04/PolicyPrimer-Mixed_Migration.pdf> accessed 19 March 2021

Ventrella M, *The Control of People Smuggling and Trafficking in the EU: Experiences from the UK and Italy* (Routledge 2010)

Vienna Convention on the Law of Treaties (adopted 23 May 1969, entered into force on 27 January 1980) 1155 UNTS 331 (VCLT)

Witt C, 'Anti-Essentialism in Feminist Theory' (1995) 23(2) Philosophical Topics 321

Zolberg AR, Astri Suhrke and Sergio Aguayo, *Escape from Violence: Conflict and the Refugee Crisis in the Developing World* (OUP 1989)

2 'Trafficking in Persons' and 'Smuggling of Migrants'

Different Concepts, Similar Experiences

2.1 Introduction

Reconceptualising harm experienced during irregular migration as a protection issue starts with examining assumptions about the protection needs ascribed to different categories of irregular migrants. International criminal law relies on two binary categories to describe individuals who move across international borders irregularly: trafficked persons and smuggled persons. Although 'trafficking in persons' and 'smuggling of migrants' are two separate concepts in international law, this chapter will show that trafficked and smuggled persons' experiences are, in fact, extremely similar. These experiences, however, are not acknowledged in international law, which instead focuses on the actions and intentions of perpetrators – of traffickers and smugglers. These perpetrator-centric criminal law definitions, in turn, lead to a skewed perception of irregular migrants' protection needs. While *trafficked persons* are perceived as 'forced migrants', who are in need of protection, *smuggled persons* are considered to be 'voluntary migrants', without protection needs. When considering both groups' entitlement to refugee protection, however – which this book will do over the coming chapters – it is necessary to focus on trafficked and smuggled persons' actual experiences. The chapter begins to do this by comparing trafficked and smuggled persons' situation in their countries of origin and during their journeys. The chapter lays the foundation for analysing trafficked persons' asylum claims in the coming chapters and for understanding their implications for irregularised migrants' protection needs.

2.2 Defining Trafficking and Smuggling

'Trafficking in persons' and 'smuggling of migrants' are criminal law concepts, first defined in international law in two Protocols supplementing the UN Convention against Transnational Organized Crime (UNTOC).[1] Both

1 United Nations Convention against Transnational Organized Crime (adopted 15 November 2000, entered into force 29 September 2003) 2225 UNTS 209 (UNTOC).

DOI: 10.4324/9781032664644-2

the Trafficking Protocol[2] and the Smuggling Protocol[3] must be interpreted together with the Convention. The UNTOC's purpose 'is to promote cooperation to prevent and combat transnational organized crime more effectively'.[4] Among other things, it defines what an organised criminal group is, criminalises participation in such a group, and suggests that such groups operate across borders. Thus, in international law, both trafficking and smuggling are conceived of as crimes committed by organised groups and across borders.

Since 'trafficking in persons' and 'smuggling of migrants' are dealt with in two different Protocols supplementing the UNTOC, they are presented as two distinct, yet related, concepts. Thus, a distinction is also made between the 'victims' of both crimes. Indeed, the legal definitions introduce a number of assumptions about trafficked and smuggled persons, which shape states' responses towards both groups. As Letschert and Rijken note, 'the attention for specific groups of victims [of crime] might generate a hierarchy between groups of victims and fragmentation of the rights given'.[5] As explained in what follows, such a hierarchy is clearly visible between trafficked persons on the one hand and smuggled persons on the other.

*2.2.1 **Human Trafficking***

The Trafficking Protocol defines 'trafficking in persons' as

> the recruitment, transportation, transfer, harbouring or receipt of persons, by means of the threat or use of force or other forms of coercion, of abduction, of fraud, of deception, of the abuse of power or of a position of vulnerability or of the giving or receiving of payments or benefits to achieve the consent of a person having control over another person, for the purpose of exploitation. Exploitation shall include, at a minimum, the exploitation of the prostitution of others or other forms of sexual exploitation, forced labour or services, slavery or practices similar to slavery, servitude or the removal of organs.[6]

2 Protocol to Prevent, Suppress and Punish Trafficking in Persons, Especially Women and Children, Supplementing the United Nations Convention against Transnational Organized Crime (adopted 15 November 2000, entered into force 25 December 2003) 2237 UNTS 319 (Trafficking Protocol) art 1(1).

3 Protocol against the Smuggling of Migrants by Land, Sea and Air, Supplementing the United Nations Convention against Transnational Crime (adopted 15 November 2000, entered into force 28 January 2004) 2241 UNTS 480 (Smuggling Protocol) art 1(1).

4 UNTOC (n 1) art 1.

5 Rianne Letschert and Conny Rijken, 'Rights of Victims of Crime: Tensions between an Integrated Approach and a Limited Legal Basis for Harmonisation' (2013) 4(3) New Journal of European Criminal Law 226, 229 <https://doi.org/10.1177/203228441300400306>.

6 Trafficking Protocol (n 2) art 3(a).

This definition contains three separate elements: an action element, a means element and a purpose element.[7] The *action* is the 'recruitment, transportation, transfer, harbouring or receipt of persons'; the *means* the 'threat or use of force or other forms of coercion, of abduction, of fraud, of deception, of the abuse of power or of a position of vulnerability or of the giving or receiving payments or benefits to achieve the consent of a person having control over another person'; and the purpose is exploitation.[8] The 'action' and 'means' elements constitute the *actus reus* – the criminal act – and the 'purpose' element constitutes the *mens rea* – the criminal intent behind the action.[9] The definition of *human trafficking* in Article 3(a) of the Trafficking Protocol is followed by additional provisions, in Article 3(b)–(d), clarifying that a trafficked person's consent to the intended exploitation is rendered irrelevant where any of the means described have been used, adding that no such means need to be shown to have been employed where the trafficked person is a child, that is, under the age of 18.

While at first glance the 'action, means and purpose' structure of the trafficking definition seems fairly straightforward, Stoyanova has highlighted that there are a number of 'uncertainties' in the *trafficking* definition's elements.[10] These include the required *mens rea* of the perpetrator (intent, knowledge or negligence?),[11] the point in time at which coercion or deception takes place (during recruitment, during transportation or when the person is already working in the country of destination?), as well as the threshold of deception or coercion required (does this relate to the nature of the work promised or the working conditions?).[12] Further uncertainties arise in the context of the concept of 'exploitation', which is not defined, only illustrated with a number of examples.[13] Some of the practices listed under the exploitation element remain undefined too; especially, the notions of 'prostitution' and 'sexual exploitation', for which there are no existing definitions in international law, create uncertainty since it is left up to signatory states' domestic law to define these terms.[14]

The Trafficking Protocol's definition of *trafficking*, and with it the uncertainties described, is reproduced (almost) verbatim in European and European Union (EU) anti-trafficking instruments. The 2005 Council of Europe Convention on Action against Trafficking in Human Beings (ECAT) adopts

7 Anne T Gallagher, *The International Law of Human Trafficking* (CUP 2010) 29.

8 ibid.

9 ibid 31–34.

10 Vladislava Stoyanova, *Human Trafficking and Slavery Reconsidered: Conceptual Limits and States' Positive Obligations in European Law* (CUP 2017) 33.

11 ibid 43ff.

12 ibid 50ff.

13 ibid 59.

14 ibid 57–60.

the Trafficking Protocol's definition word for word.[15] However, in contrast to the Trafficking Protocol, which conceives of *trafficking* as 'transnational in nature',[16] carried out by an organised criminal group operating across international borders, the ECAT conceptualises *trafficking* as 'national or transnational, whether or not connected with organised crime'.[17] Meanwhile, the 2011 EU Trafficking Directive adds 'the exchange or transfer of control over . . . persons'[18] to the action element, as well as 'begging' and 'the exploitation of criminal activities' to the list of examples of exploitation.[19] The 2024 amendment of the Directive further adds 'exploitation of surrogacy, of forced marriage, or of illegal adoption' as types of exploitation.[20]

'Victims' of the offence of trafficking, then, according to the legal definition, have been forced, deceived or coerced into being trafficked and are likely to experience harm in the process. As we will see in what follows, this conceptualisation of trafficked persons is radically different from that of smuggled persons.

2.2.2 Migrant Smuggling

The Smuggling Protocol states that

> '[s]muggling of migrants' shall mean the procurement, in order to obtain, directly or indirectly, a financial or other material benefit, of the illegal entry of a person into a State Party of which the person is not a national or a permanent resident.[21]

Like the *trafficking* definition, this definition has different elements: an action element, that is, the procurement of illegal entry, and a purpose element, that is, the smuggler's financial or material benefit.[22] As such, the *smuggling* definition is more straightforward than the *trafficking* definition and does not

15 Council of Europe Convention on Action against Trafficking in Human Beings (adopted 16 May 2005, entered into force 1 February 2008) ETS 197 (ECAT) art 4(a).

16 Trafficking Protocol (n 2) art 4.

17 ECAT (n 15) art 2.

18 Directive 2011/36/EU of the European Parliament and of the Council of 5 April 2011 on Preventing and Combating Trafficking in Human Beings and Protecting Its Victims, and Replacing Council Framework Decision 2002/629/JHA [2011] OJ L 101/1 (Trafficking Directive) art 2(1).

19 ibid art 2(3).

20 Directive (EU) 2024/1712 of the European Parliament and of the Council of 13 June 2024 Amending Directive 2011/36/EU on Preventing and Combating Trafficking in Human Beings and Protecting Its Victims [2024] OJ L 2024/1712 (Trafficking Amendment Directive) art 1(1)(a).

21 Smuggling Protocol (n 3) art 3(a).

22 Anne T Gallagher and Fiona David, *The International Law of Migrant Smuggling* (CUP 2014) 47.

contain the same uncertainties as the latter. Yet difficulties arise in EU law on smuggling, which omits the purpose element contained in the Smuggling Protocol's definition. The EU Facilitation Directive obliges EU member states to criminalise intentionally assisting 'a person who is not a national of a Member State to enter, or transit across, the territory of a Member State in breach of the laws of the State concerned on the entry or transit of aliens'.[23] This has led to legal uncertainty regarding the distinction 'between criminal and legitimate acts of assistance to migrants',[24] as well as overcriminalisation at odds with fundamental rights.[25]

Moving away from the criminal law meaning of 'smuggling of migrants' and considering what the definition tells us about these migrants themselves, a *smuggled person* is described essentially as a customer who pays for a service. Smuggled persons appear to choose to pay a smuggler in order to enter a country irregularly. There is no mention of any form of coercion, deception, etc., nor of exploitation.

2.2.3 *Assumptions About Trafficked and Smuggled Persons*

Thus, international law describes trafficked and smuggled persons as having very different experiences. Yet this apparent difference stems from a number of assumptions introduced by the relevant legal definitions. First, as opposed to the *trafficking* definition, the *smuggling* definition does not contain a 'means' element. Since in the *trafficking* definition the means element gives the impression that trafficked persons have been forced, coerced or deceived into migrating, its absence in the *smuggling* definition introduces the assumption that smuggled persons embark on their journeys voluntarily. While the Trafficking Protocol states that '[t]he consent of a victim of trafficking in persons to the intended exploitation . . . shall be irrelevant',[26] for smuggled persons, consent to the smuggling process (and anything this may entail) is assumed. In this context, the choice of words in speaking of trafficking in *persons* but smuggling of *migrants* is also noteworthy. Of course, everyone who is trafficked or smuggled is a person, but the choice of the word 'migrants' in the *smuggling* definition – a term usually describing individuals moving

23 Council Directive 2002/90/EC of 28 November 2002 Defining the Facilitation of Unauthorised Entry, Transit and Residence [2002] OJ L 328 (Facilitation Directive) art 1(1)(a).

24 Chiara Maria Ricci, 'Criminalising Solidarity? Smugglers, Migrants and Rescuers in the Reform of the "Facilitators' Package"' in Valsamis Mitsilegas, Violeta Moreno-Lax and Niovi Vavoula (eds), *Securitising Asylum Flows: Deflection, Criminalisation and Challenges for Human Rights* (Brill 2020) 46.

25 Stefano Zirulia, 'Is That a Smuggler? The Blurring Line between Facilitating Illegal Immigration and Providing Humanitarian Assistance at the European Border' in Gian Luigi Gatta, Valsamis Mitsilegas and Stefano Zirulia (eds), *Controlling Immigration through Criminal Law: European and Comparative Perspectives on "Crimmigration"* (Hart Publishing 2021).

26 Trafficking Protocol (n 2) art 3(b).

voluntarily – reinforces the impression that those smuggled migrate of their own free will. The assumption that trafficking is forced while smuggling is voluntary can also be found in case law. For example, in *PO (trafficked women) Nigeria*, the UK Upper Tribunal (UT) stated that 'it is important to distinguish between human smuggling, where the trafficked [sic] individual is a willing participant and human trafficking, where those who are trafficked are trafficked for the purpose of exploitation, often against their will'.[27]

This forced/voluntary binary is also connected to assumptions about the gender of trafficked and smuggled persons and related notions of agency. The very title of the 'Protocol to Prevent, Suppress and Punish Trafficking in Persons, Especially Women and Children' fuels the idea that trafficked persons are more likely to be female. As Buckland notes, there is a 'preconception that smuggled "criminals" are men, while trafficked "victims" are women'.[28] De Angelis shows that this 'victim' narrative paints trafficked women as 'inherently passive, action-less and incapable of making choices'.[29] Thus, by stating that trafficked persons have been coerced into trafficking and that their consent is irrelevant, the *trafficking* definition denies their 'capacity for self-directed and purposeful action'[30] – it denies their agency. Yet it is well-known that women do exercise agency in the trafficking context, making the informed choice to be trafficked in order to be able to migrate to another country.[31] Nevertheless, the trafficked woman is imagined as an 'ideal victim'[32] – who, as Haverkamp explains, is believed to be 'innocent, helpless, not complicit in the offence and [with] no personal direct or indirect connections to the crimes or their perpetrators'.[33]

27 *PO (Trafficked Women) Nigeria* CG [2009] UKAIT 00046 [196].

28 Benjamin S Buckland, 'Human Trafficking & Smuggling: Crossover & Overlap' in Cornelius Friesendorf (ed), *Strategies against Human Trafficking: The Role of the Security Sector* (National Defence Academy and Austrian Ministry of Defence and Sports 2009) 155. See also Jayashri Srikantiah, 'Perfect Victims and Real Survivors: The Iconic Victim in Domestic Human Trafficking Law' (2007) 87 Boston University Law Review 157, 187; Anne T Gallagher, 'Human Rights and Human Trafficking: Quagmire or Firm Ground – A Response to James Hathaway' (2009) 49(4) Virginia Journal of International Law 789, 792.

29 Maria De Angelis, *Human Trafficking: Women's Stories of Agency* (Cambridge Scholars Publishing 2016) 45.

30 ibid 2.

31 Rutvica Andrijasevic, 'The Difference Borders Make: (Il)legality, Migration and Trafficking in Italy among Eastern European Women in Prostitution' in Sara Ahmed and others (eds), *Uprootings/Regroundings: Questions of Home and Migration* (Routledge 2003); Nandita Sharma, 'Anti-Trafficking Rhetoric and the Making of a Global Apartheid' (2005) 17(3) NWSA Journal 88, 95; Rutvica Andrijasevic, *Migration, Agency and Citizenship in Sex Trafficking* (Palgrave Macmillan 2010); Kyunghee Kook, '"I Want to Be Trafficked So I Can Migrate!": Cross-Border Movement of North Koreans into China through Brokerage and Smuggling Networks' (2018) 676(1) The Annals of the American Academy of Political and Social Science 114 <https://doi.org/10.1177/0002716217748591>.

32 Nils Christie, 'The Ideal Victim' in Ezzat A Fattah (ed), *From Crime Policy to Victim Policy: Reorienting the Justice System* (Macmillan 1986).

33 Rita Haverkamp, 'Victims of Human Trafficking: Considerations from a Crime Prevention Perspective' in Rita Haverkamp, Ester Herlin-Karnell and Claes Lernstedt (eds), *What Is Wrong with Human Trafficking? Critical Perspectives on the Law* (Hart Publishing 2019) 55.

Haverkamp also notes that the '"ideal victim" bias . . . means that other victims are overlooked'.[34] First, the focus on female 'victims' of trafficking has the effect of excluding trafficked men from the protective scope of the trafficking legal framework,[35] as well as from refugee protection based on a future risk related to the trafficking experience.[36] Second, based on the construction of a 'victim' as a (female) trafficked person, smuggled persons are not perceived as such 'victims' and, therefore, are assumed not to be in need of protection.

This is also reflected in the fact that the *smuggling* definition makes no reference to exploitation. As Gallagher puts it, since the *smuggling* definition 'remove[s] the "exploitation" element from the concept of migrant smuggling', it 'shift[s] the focus of the definition on to the action of migrant smuggling rather than its impact on those who are smuggled'.[37] While the *trafficking* definition does not reveal much about trafficked persons' experiences, it does show that besides deception, coercion, etc., harm in the form of 'use of force', and (possibly) exploitation, can be part of the trafficking experience. In contrast, by not mentioning similar elements, the *smuggling* definition seems to suggest that smuggled persons do not experience any harm. Indeed, it is not the smuggled person, but the state which that person enters irregularly, which is considered to be the 'victim' of smuggling.[38] This is evident from the fact that the Smuggling Protocol speaks of 'activities of organized criminal groups in smuggling of migrants . . . , which bring *great harm to the States concerned*'.[39]

In summary, the criminal law definitions of 'trafficking in persons' and 'smuggling of migrants' and their interplay create two main assumptions: that trafficked persons are forced into trafficking while smuggled persons migrate voluntarily, and that the former experience harm in the process, and therefore need protection, while the latter do not experience harm and thus need not be

34 ibid 69.

35 William Shankley, 'Gender, Modern Slavery and Labour Exploitation: Experiences of Male Polish Migrants in England' (2023) 49(5) Journal of Ethnic and Migration Studies 1274 <http://dx.doi.org/10.1080/1369183x.2021.2000853>; Sharma (n 31) 93.

36 Noemi Magugliani, '(In)Vulnerable Masculinities and Human Trafficking: Men, Victimhood, and Access to Protection in the United Kingdom' (2022) 44(2) Journal of Human Rights Practice 726 <https://doi.org/10.1093/jhuman/huac001>; Noemi Magugliani, 'Trafficked Adult Males as (Un)Gendered Protection Seekers: Between Presumption of Invulnerability and Exclusion from Membership of a Particular Social Group' (2022) 34(3–4) International Journal of Refugee Law 353 <https://doi.org/10.1093/ijrl/eeac030>.

37 Gallagher and David (n 22) 44.

38 Elspeth Guild, 'Conclusions: The Variable Political and Legal Geography of People Smuggling and Trafficking in Europe' in Elspeth Guild and Paul Minderhoud (eds), *Immigration and Criminal Law in the European Union: The Legal Measures and Social Consequences of Criminal Law in Member States on Trafficking and Smuggling in Human Beings* (Martinus Nijhoff 2006) 411; Paolo Campana and Federico Varese, 'Exploitation in Human Trafficking and Smuggling' (2016) 22 European Journal on Criminal Policy and Research 89, 93 <https://doi.org/10.1007/s10610-015-9286-6>.

39 Smuggling Protocol (n 3) Preamble; emphasis added.

protected. Thus, criminal law constructs a binary between trafficked persons as 'victims' and smuggled persons as '"illegals" who are considered less deserving of protection and support than trafficked victims because of their original motive – their decision to choose to migrate illegally'.[40] As a result, states respond very differently to trafficked persons on the one hand and smuggled persons on the other with regard to the protection extended to each group.

2.3 State Responses to Trafficked and Smuggled Persons

'Trafficking in persons' and 'smuggling of migrants' are criminal law definitions seeking to define offences and thus focus on the actions and intentions of perpetrators. Distinguishing between the two offences makes sense from a criminal law perspective. Arguably, it makes a difference whether an offender merely helps another person violate a state's immigration laws or whether this offender also harms, or intends to harm, that person. However, in drawing a distinction between traffickers and smugglers, the definitions also automatically create a binary between trafficked persons and smuggled persons. What is more, the assumptions made in the legal definitions about the two groups shape states' responses towards them.

States have binding obligations towards trafficking 'victims', resulting in a range of assistance measures, a (short-term) right to remain in the territory and (longer-term) residence permits issued at the discretion of the state. In contrast, states have no such obligations towards smuggled persons, although under EU law, they can choose to extend assistance measures to them.

2.3.1 Protection for Trafficked Persons

Gallagher shows that the Trafficking Protocol imposes 'very little in the way of "hard" or detailed obligation[s]' on states with respect to protecting trafficked persons.[41] The Protocol's protection provisions begin by stipulating how trafficked persons shall be treated in the context of criminal proceedings, which includes protection of their privacy and access to information.[42] Further, states 'shall consider' providing recovery measures, such as housing and medical care;[43] 'shall endeavour' to ensure trafficked persons' physical safety;[44] and 'shall ensure' that trafficked persons are able to claim compensation. As such, the Trafficking Protocol sees trafficked persons mainly as victims of crime who are likely to take part in criminal proceedings, may claim compensation and

40 International Council on Human Rights Policy (ICHRP), 'Irregular Migration, Migrant Smuggling and Human Rights: Towards Coherence' (2010) 72 <https://imumi.org/documentos/Irregular_Migration_and_Smuggling_2010.pdf> accessed 5 May 2020.

41 Gallagher (n 7) 82.

42 Trafficking Protocol (n 2) art 6(1)–6(2).

43 ibid art 6(3).

44 ibid art 6(5).

should be kept safe during the process – for their own sake and because they constitute key witnesses whose testimony is crucial for the successful prosecution of the crimes concerned. The Protocol also reflects the assumption that trafficked persons have experienced harm, which they need to recover from. For these purposes, states 'shall consider' allowing trafficked persons to remain in the territory of the state 'temporarily or permanently'.[45] This provision stems from the conceptualisation of trafficking as a transnational crime, which assumes that trafficked persons will be foreign nationals. However, the Trafficking Protocol clarifies that, ultimately, trafficked persons shall be returned to their countries of origin.[46] Thus, it does not create a right to remain in the country the person was trafficked to.

The ECAT and the EU Trafficking Directive follow a similar logic as the Trafficking Protocol. However, while the latter 'does not impose binding identification, assistance and protection obligations',[47] the ECAT's and the Directive's provisions are binding and somewhat more extensive. Importantly, both instruments introduce a requirement to identify 'victims'.[48] Being identified as a trafficked person is extremely important, because only those who are identified can then benefit from assistance measures under the relevant instruments. However, as Stoyanova notes with regard to the ECAT, states parties still have 'considerable discretion as to how they organize their victim identification procedures'.[49] Further, due to the complexities and uncertainties of the trafficking definition, '[i]t might be hard to make the definition of human trafficking workable in the context of criminal law and for the purpose of identifying migrants who need to be protected and assisted'.[50] Nevertheless, once there are 'reasonable grounds to believe' that a person has been trafficked, an entitlement to assistance is triggered.[51] The ECAT also stipulates that an individual for whom there are reasonable grounds to believe that he or she has been trafficked shall not be removed until the identification process has been completed.[52] The Trafficking Directive, meanwhile, stipulates that EU member states shall 'ensure that assistance and support for a victim are not made conditional on the victim's willingness to cooperate in the criminal investigation'.[53]

In terms of assistance measures for trafficked persons, the provisions of the ECAT and the Directive are fairly similar to those provided in the Trafficking Protocol. Both instruments specify that, among other things, states *shall* provide access to information, safe accommodation, material assistance and

45 ibid art 7(1).
46 ibid art 8(1).
47 Stoyanova (n 10) 87.
48 ECAT (n 15) art 10(1)–10(2); Trafficking Directive (n 18) art 11(4).
49 Stoyanova (n 10) 90.
50 ibid 72.
51 ECAT (n 15) art 10(2); Trafficking Directive (n 18) art 11(2).
52 ECAT (n 15) art 10(2).
53 Trafficking Directive (n 18) art 11(3).

medical treatment[54] and *shall* ensure that trafficked persons are able to claim compensation.[55] In addition, trafficked persons are entitled to a recovery and reflection period, during which they cannot be removed from the territory.[56] The ECAT specifies that this shall be a period of at least 30 days, while EU law leaves it up to member states to determine the duration, though, since all EU member states are also members of the Council of Europe, 30 days will be the minimum. During this period, trafficked persons are expected to recover from their experience, escape the influence of the traffickers and think about whether they want to cooperate in the criminal investigation of their trafficking.[57] The decision whether or not to cooperate with law enforcement authorities may then be relevant in the context of being granted a residence permit. In this context, it should be noted that under the ECAT, no residence permit needs to be issued for the duration of the recovery and reflection period.[58]

Under the ECAT, residence permits shall be issued either where 'the competent authority considers that [trafficked persons'] stay is necessary owing to their personal situation'[59] or where 'the competent authority considers that their stay is necessary for the purpose of their cooperation with the competent authorities in investigation or criminal proceedings'.[60] Although the provision states that residence permits *shall* be issued, it leaves considerable discretion to states by leaving it up to them to decide whether such a permit is *necessary*. Under EU law, residence permits are firmly linked to cooperation in criminal proceedings. Such permits are granted under the Residence Permit Directive,[61] whose purpose is 'to define the conditions for granting residence permits of limited duration, linked to the length of the relevant national proceedings, to third-country nationals who cooperate in the fight against trafficking in human beings or against action to facilitate illegal immigration'.[62] Thus, member states 'shall consider' issuing trafficked persons with residence permits, but only where such persons intend to cooperate in the criminal investigation and have severed all ties with their traffickers.[63] In this sense, EU law is more

54 ECAT (n 15) art 12(1); Trafficking Directive (n 18) art 11(5).
55 ECAT (n 15) art 15; Trafficking Directive (n 18) art 17.
56 ECAT (n 15) art 13(1); Council Directive 2004/81/EC of 29 April 2004 on the Residence Permit Issued to Third-Country Nationals Who Are Victims of Trafficking in Human Beings or Who Have Been the Subject of an Action to Facilitate Illegal Immigration, Who Cooperate with the Competent Authorities [2004] OJ L 261 (Residence Permit Directive) art 6(1)–(2).
57 Helmut Sax, 'Article 13: Recovery and Reflection Period' in Julia Planitzer and Helmut Sax (eds), *A Commentary on the Council of Europe Convention on Action against Trafficking in Human Beings* (Edward Elgar Publishing 2020) para 13.02.
58 ibid para 13.26.
59 ECAT (n 15) art 14(1)(a).
60 ibid art 14(1)(b).
61 Residence Permit Directive (n 56).
62 ibid art 1.
63 ibid art 8(1).

restrictive than the Trafficking Protocol and the ECAT, because not only does it give discretion to states whether or not to issue residence permits; it also specifies under what conditions this discretion may be exercised.

Those trafficked persons who manage to obtain a residence permit under the ECAT and are therefore lawfully resident are entitled to additional assistance measures, such as access to regular medical care, rather than just emergency care, and access to the labour market, to vocational training and education.[64] Residence permits under the Residence Permit Directive, too, come with additional entitlements, such as access to 'necessary' medical care for trafficked persons with special needs, 'such as pregnant women, the disabled or victims of sexual violence or other forms of violence'.[65] Residence permits lead to access to the labour market, to vocational training and education, though it is up to individual member states to define the rules for access.[66] Despite the possibility of obtaining a residence permit, like the Trafficking Protocol, European and EU law ultimately aim to return trafficked persons to their countries of origin.[67] Although 'voluntary' return is preferred, 'in the absence of some international protection obligation or other basis for remaining in the destination country, the trafficked victim, as an alien, has no right to remain . . . and may be removed, if necessary by force'.[68] Thus, as Stoyanova explains, 'identification as a victim of human trafficking is not a channel for non-removal *per se* and an avenue for remaining in the host country'.[69] Indeed, none of the legal instruments discussed in the preceding passages provide 'an individual entitlement to a [residence] permit'.[70]

In summary, the status of 'victim' of human trafficking leads to 'limited entitlements' under international, European and EU law.[71] The main purpose of trafficking instruments is to prevent trafficking and prosecute traffickers, while assistance to trafficked persons is only secondary and limited.[72] Thus, states' responses to trafficked persons consist of treating them as victims entitled to some assistance based on their past experiences of harm. Beyond this, trafficked persons are conceived of as participants in criminal proceedings who

64 ECAT (n 15) arts 12(3) and 12(4).
65 Residence Permit Directive (n 56) art 9(2).
66 ibid art 11.
67 ECAT (n 15) art 16; Residence Permit Directive (n 56) art 12(1).
68 Ryszard Piotrowicz and Conny Rijken, 'Article 16: Repatriation and Return of Victims' in Julia Planitzer and Helmut Sax (eds), *A Commentary on the Council of Europe Convention on Action against Trafficking in Human Beings* (Edward Elgar Publishing 2020) para 16.01.
69 Stoyanova (n 10) 133.
70 ibid 136.
71 ibid 183.
72 James C Hathaway, 'The Human Rights Quagmire of Human Trafficking' (2008) 49(1) Virginia Journal of International Law 1; Susan Kneebone, 'The Refugee–Trafficking Nexus: Making Good (the) Connections' (2010) 29(1) Refugee Survey Quarterly 137 <https://doi.org/10.1093/rsq/hdq011>; Idil Atak and James C Simeon, 'Human Trafficking: Mapping the Legal Boundaries of International Refugee Law and Criminal Justice' (2014) 12(5) Journal of International Criminal Justice 1019 <https://doi.org/10.1093/jicj/mqu093>.

should return to their countries of origin once those proceedings have concluded and they have sufficiently recovered.

2.3.2 *Protection for Smuggled Persons*

Even though protection and assistance measures for trafficked persons are limited, those for smuggled persons are even less extensive. The Smuggling Protocol contains one article on protection and assistance measures, which, essentially, obliges states to protect smuggled persons' right to life and freedom from torture and inhuman and degrading treatment.[73] Thus, the provision simply duplicates existing human rights law provisions but says nothing about the point in time at which states should act to guarantee those rights, or the exact measures to be taken to ensure them. The Smuggling Protocol does recognise that smuggling can endanger peoples' lives or entail inhuman or degrading treatment,[74] but no concrete protection obligations are foreseen to address the consequences of such treatment. Instead, like the Trafficking Protocol, the Smuggling Protocol clarifies that smuggled persons should be returned to their countries of origin,[75] but as opposed to the Trafficking Protocol, states are not obliged to consider allowing smuggled persons to remain in their territory.

Meanwhile, EU law on smuggling, or 'facilitation', which is the term used in the relevant legal instruments, does not contain any provision on protection at all.[76] In this context, it should be noted, however, that the EU Residence Permit Directive gives EU member states the option to extend its provisions to 'third-country nationals who have been the subject of an action to facilitate illegal immigration',[77] that is, to smuggled persons. Thus, the victim protection provisions of the Residence Permit Directive *may* be applied to smuggled persons, so that they, too, may be able to benefit from, *inter alia*, a recovery and reflection period, medical treatment (but only where the individual concerned has insufficient means and special needs), as well as access to the labour market (the conditions and procedures for this are defined by member states).[78] It must be kept in mind, however, that the main purpose of the Residence Permit Directive is not the protection of irregular migrants but to 'combat illegal immigration'[79] and to incentivise irregular migrants to cooperate in criminal

73 Smuggling Protocol (n 3) art 16(1).
74 ibid arts 6(3) and 16(1).
75 ibid art 18.
76 Facilitation Directive (n 23); Council Framework Decision of 28 November 2002 on the Strengthening of the Penal Framework to Prevent the Facilitation of Unauthorised Entry, Transit and Residence [2002] OJ L 328 (Framework Decision).
77 Residence Permit Directive (n 56) art 3(2).
78 ibid arts 6; 9(2); 11.
79 ibid Recitals 1 and 2.

proceedings against those who facilitate such migration.[80] In addition, as for trafficked persons, these protections, if applied to smuggled persons, will be 'limited in terms of both time and substance'.[81]

Nonetheless, since trafficking and smuggling are framed as crimes, it is conceivable that trafficked and smuggled persons could also benefit from the provisions of the EU Victim Protection Directive.[82] This Directive acknowledges that a victim of crime will have 'suffered harm, including physical, mental or emotional harm or economic loss',[83] which is relevant in the trafficking and the smuggling context, and can be a 'family member . . . of a person whose death was directly caused by a criminal offence and who have suffered harm as a result of that person's death',[84] which is mainly relevant in the smuggling context. However, the Victim Protection Directive does not offer protection as such but is more concerned with providing access to information about available support,[85] as well as the right to access victim support services, which, in turn, are to provide, among other things, additional advice, psychological support and access to shelters.[86] In addition, the Directive makes it clear that '[r]eporting a crime and participating in criminal proceedings' does 'not create any rights regarding the residence status of the victim'.[87]

Overall, as Gallagher and David note, 'the status of "smuggled migrant" has not been elevated to a legal category to which any special or additional rights are attached'.[88] Even though both trafficking and smuggling are crimes in international and regional law, only trafficked persons are perceived as victims of crime who need (admittedly limited) assistance measures, while smuggled persons are not normally perceived as 'victims', a status which may be extended to them on a discretionary basis if they are perceived to be useful in criminal proceedings. As a result, state responses to trafficked and smuggled persons differ in that trafficking 'victims' are given the opportunity to recover and to remain in the host state's territory for a certain

80 ibid Recital 9.

81 Valsamis Mitsilegas and Niovi Vavoula, 'Criminal Law: Institutional Rebalancing and Judicialisation as Drivers of Policy Change' in Florian Trauner and Ariadna Ripoll Servent (eds), *Policy Change in the Area of Freedom, Security and Justice: How EU Institutions Matter* (Routledge 2015) 142.

82 Directive 2012/29/EU of the European Parliament and of the Council of 25 October 2012 Establishing Minimum Standards on the Rights, Support and Protection of Victims of Crime, and Replacing Council Framework Decision 2001/220/JHA [2012] OJ L 315 (Victim Protection Directive).

83 ibid art 2(1)(a)(i).

84 ibid art 2(1)(a)(ii).

85 ibid art 4.

86 ibid art 8.

87 ibid Recital 10.

88 Gallagher and David (n 22) 553.

time. Smuggled persons, on the other hand, are 'assumed to be in substantially less need of protection'.[89] As such, the *trafficking* and *smuggling* definitions' assumptions about protection needs are reflected in the protection provisions of the relevant legal instruments. This framing of some irregular migrants as more worthy of protection than others, in turn, helps the EU justify its migration policies.[90]

2.4 Trafficked and Smuggled Persons' Experiences: Challenging Assumptions

As evident from the earlier discussion, being identified as either a trafficked or a smuggled person has real consequences in terms of protection, assistance and the right to remain in the territory of the state a person was trafficked or smuggled to. In this context, the focus on perpetrators in the *trafficking* and *smuggling* definitions and the assumptions introduced about trafficked and smuggled persons become problematic. Trafficked and smuggled persons are identified based on the (alleged) actions and intentions of traffickers and smugglers and do or do not receive protection on this basis, rather than based on their actual experiences of harm. In this context, it is worth noting that, since only intent to exploit must be shown to meet the *trafficking* definition, a trafficked person whose trafficker intends to sexually exploit him or her but who escapes before any exploitation takes place will be entitled to protection under the anti-trafficking legal framework, but a smuggled person who was raped on his or her journey will not be entitled to protection. Thus, the relevant legal instruments engage with trafficked and smuggled persons' experiences only selectively and in order to reinforce the distinction between the two, rather than depicting the complexities of trafficking and smuggling. The following discussion seeks to challenge the assumption that smuggled persons are voluntary migrants not in need of protection by contrasting the legal framing of trafficked and smuggled persons with their *actual* experiences.

2.4.1 Migration Motivations

Like all migrants, trafficked and smuggled persons have varied motivations for moving, and both groups exercise agency in making the decision to migrate. As Buckland notes, 'both trafficked and smuggled people most often choose to leave their homes, whether as economic migrants, asylum seekers, or to be

89 Buckland (n 28) 141.

90 Maja Grundler, 'Who Is the "Vulnerable" Victim? Trafficked and Smuggled Persons as Victims of Crime under EU Law' in Lilian Tsourdi, Valsamis Mitsilegas and Niovi Vavoula (eds), *Intertwining Criminal Justice and Immigration Control in the EU: Theoretical, Interdisciplinary, and Practical Perspectives* (Routledge 2025).

reunited with their families (among many other reasons)'.[91] It is not within the scope of this section to explore all possible motivations trafficked and smuggled persons might have for migrating; instead, the focus will be on their migration motivations as presented in the Trafficking and the Smuggling Protocols. The section will show that the same underlying motivations can be framed differently in order to argue that they indicate either 'forced' or 'voluntary' movement.

The Trafficking and the Smuggling Protocols suggest that there is a socio-economic dimension underlying both practices. The Trafficking Protocol requires states to 'take or strengthen measures . . . to alleviate the factors that make persons, especially women and children, vulnerable to trafficking, such as poverty, underdevelopment and lack of equal opportunity'.[92] Similarly, the Smuggling Protocol requires states to 'combat the root socio-economic causes of the smuggling of migrants, such as poverty and underdevelopment'.[93] 'Root causes' of irregular migration and the distinction between forced and voluntary migration are discussed in more detail in the next chapter. For now, it suffices to note that it is normally assumed that economic motives for migrating can be equated with voluntary movement.[94]

However, in the Trafficking Protocol, socio-economic deprivation, which is seen as an underlying cause of trafficking, stands in the context of both the means element as well as a provision stating that the consent of a trafficked person to the intended exploitation is irrelevant where such means are used. The means element includes the 'abuse of a position of vulnerability'. The concept of vulnerability in the context of trafficking, and irregular migration more generally, is discussed in detail in the next chapter. For present purposes, it is sufficient to note that 'abuse of a position of vulnerability' 'can encompass a very broad range of situations', such as 'poverty, hunger, illness, lack of education and displacement'.[95] Accordingly, a trafficked person can consent to being trafficked in order to escape socio-economic deprivation and will still be considered a 'forced migrant' because his or her position of vulnerability was abused so that his or her consent is rendered irrelevant. In the absence of a means element in the *smuggling* definition, however, a smuggled person cannot claim that his or her position of vulnerability was abused by the smuggler. His or her escape from socio-economic deprivation will be considered to be voluntarily.

91 Buckland (n 28) 143; On agency of presumed smuggling or trafficking 'victims' see also Kook (n 31); see further Andrijasevic, *Migration* (n 31).
92 Trafficking Protocol (n 2) art 9(4).
93 Smuggling Protocol (n 3) art 15(3).
94 Idil Atak and Francois Crépau, 'Refugees as Migrants' in Cathryn Costello, Michelle Foster and Jane McAdam (eds), *The Oxford Handbook of International Refugee Law* (OUP 2021) 136.
95 ICHRP (n 40) 77.

Thus, the Trafficking and the Smuggling Protocols acknowledge that trafficked and smuggled persons have similar experiences in terms of reasons for migrating yet frame these experiences as a form of coercion for the former and a voluntary choice for the latter. However, the Protocols' very suggestion that the underlying motive for moving is the same for both groups calls into question the distinction they seek to draw between forced and voluntary movement.

2.4.2 Migration Routes

The similarities between trafficked and smuggled persons do not end with their motivations for migrating; instead, the two groups are also, literally, in the same boat with regard to the migration routes they travel on. As Dimitriadi shows, 'smugglers and traffickers often adopt the same routes and transportation'.[96] As mentioned in the Introduction to this book, extraterritorial border controls prevent irregular migrants from travelling to states of destination legally and safely. The fact that the vast majority of asylum seekers who come to the EU, many of whom are later recognised as refugees, have to rely on the services of smugglers to reach EU territory points to the fact that, in many instances, neither the departure nor the means of transport was chosen freely.[97] Thus, traffickers and smugglers use the same routes and means of transportation because travelling regularly is difficult.[98] In the EU, the Visa Regulation divides third counties into 'whitelisted' countries, whose nationals do not need a visa to enter the EU, and 'blacklisted' countries, whose nationals do need a visa.[99] Meanwhile, the Schengen

96 Angeliki Dimitriadi, 'The Interrelationship between Trafficking and Irregular Migration' in Sergio Carrera and Elspeth Guild (eds), *Irregular Migration, Trafficking and Smuggling of Human Beings: Policy Dilemmas in the EU* (CEPS, 2016) 67 <www.ceps.eu/wp-content/uploads/2016/02/Irregular%20Migration,%20Trafficking%20and%20SmugglingwithCovers.pdf> accessed 4 April 2019.

97 European Parliament, 'Resolution of 11 December 2018 with Recommendations to the Commission on Humanitarian Visas' (11 December 2018) 2018/2271(INL) <www.europarl.europa.eu/doceo/document/TA-8-2018-0494_EN.html#title1> accessed 14 February 2020, Recital E.

98 Sharma (n 31) 91.

99 Regulation (EU) 2018/1806 of the European Parliament and of the Council of 14 November 2018 Listing the Third Countries Whose Nationals Must Be in Possession of Visas When Crossing the External Borders and Those Whose Nationals Are Exempt from That Requirement [2018] OJ L 303 (Visa Regulation) Annex I and Annex II; cf Henk Van Houtum, 'Human Blacklisting: The Global Apartheid of the EU's External Border Regime' (2010) 28(6) Environment and Planning D: Society and Space 957 <https://doi.org/10.1068/d1909>. For blacklisting procedures and criteria, see Violeta Moreno-Lax, *Accessing Asylum in Europe: Extraterritorial Border Controls and Refugee Rights under EU Law* (OUP 2017) 87ff.

Borders Code sets out the rules for regular entry in the EU.[100] In order to obtain a Schengen visa to enter the EU, applicants must meet a number of entry conditions,[101] hold travel medical insurance and pay a visa fee.[102] These financial requirements alone make visa applications difficult for some people; women especially may be less able to obtain visas due to their 'globally disadvantaged socio-economic position'.[103]

There are a number of legal migration schemes to the EU besides Schengen visas, such as visas for highly skilled and seasonal workers, students and family reunification.[104] In practice, however, these visas have little utility for many of those who migrate irregularly. The main beneficiaries of visas for highly skilled migrants, for example, are citizens of developed countries.[105] Meanwhile, 'low-skilled workers have limited opportunities to migrate legally to the European Union, though seasonal migration is an important exception'.[106] Further, obstacles to obtaining family reunification visas include the requirement that a family member must already be lawfully resident in an EU member state,[107] and that only certain family members qualify for reunification.[108] Thus, not only are visas difficult to obtain, but EU member states also do not have diplomatic representations everywhere in the world, and thus, for some people, it is impossible to apply for a visa, even if they wish to do so.[109] Especially in regions where the security situation is unstable, embassies and consulates may close down. What is more, even persons who, in theory, have good prospects

100 Regulation (EU) 2016/399 of the European Parliament and of the Council of 9 March 2016 on a Union Code on the Rules Governing the Movement of Persons across Borders [2016] OJ L 77 (Schengen Borders Code).

101 ibid art 6(1)(a)-(c). As per Annex I of the Schengen Borders Code, a range of documents can be requested to verify the fulfilment of these entry conditions.

102 Regulation (EC) No 810/2009 of the European Parliament and of the Council of 13 July 2009 Establishing a Community Code on Visas [2009] OJ L 243 (Visa Code) arts 15 and 16.

103 Thomas Spijkerboer, 'The Global Mobility Infrastructure: Reconceptualising the Externalisation of Migration Control' (2018) 20 European Journal of Migration and Law 452, 468 <https://doi.org/10.1163/15718166-12340038>.

104 European Parliamentary Research Service, 'Briefing: Legal Migration to the EU' (*European Parliament*, 2019) 2 <www.europarl.europa.eu/RegData/etudes/BRIE/2019/635559/EPRS_BRI(2019)635559_EN.pdf> accessed 29 May 2020.

105 ibid 5.

106 Kate Hooper and Camille Le Coz, 'Seasonal Worker Programmes in Europe: Promising Practices and Ongoing Challenges' (*MPI Europe*, 2020) 2 <www.migrationpolicy.org/research/seasonal-worker-programs-europe> accessed 22 January 2021.

107 Council Directive 2003/86/EC of 22 September 2003 on the Right to Family Reunification [2003] OJ L 251 (Family Reunification Directive) art 1.

108 ibid art 4.

109 Moreno-Lax (n 99) 115.

of obtaining a visa often decide to migrate irregularly because the visa process takes too long.[110]

Without a visa, it is almost impossible to travel by regular transport. As Moreno-Lax shows, visa requirements and carrier sanctions 'have driven asylum flows underground, "irregularizing" movement towards the EU, and leaving protection seekers with no alternative but to rely on smuggling services (or fall prey to traffickers) to reach safety'.[111] Both trafficked and smuggled migrants are likely to travel irregularly, not because they wish to do so, but because regular migration pathways are closed to them. They are likely to risk more and more dangerous routes in order not to be apprehended before reaching their destination. In light of this, it is difficult to uphold the claim that relying on smugglers is voluntary while trafficking is coerced. Irregular migrants are forced to rely on traffickers and smugglers because these facilitators are their best hope of making it to their destination alive.[112]

2.4.3 Harm During Migratory Journeys

So far, we have seen that trafficked and smuggled persons may have the same underlying reasons for migrating and use the same dangerous migratory routes due to a lack of safe options. In addition, trafficked and smuggled persons' experiences during their migratory journeys are extremely similar. As explained earlier, attributes normally associated with smuggled persons, especially agency, are also held by trafficked persons. While it is often assumed that trafficked persons 'have had no meaningful control over their decision to migrate',[113] in reality, as Stoyanova notes, trafficked persons may 'seek avenues to migrate and desire to be recruited'.[114] Conversely, many elements normally associated with trafficking are also present in the smuggling experience. For example, Dimitriadi explains that '[r]ecruitment is a common first step to both trafficking and smuggling'.[115] Further, as Buckland shows, '[b]oth trafficked

110 Friederike Stahlmann, 'Erfahrungen und Perspektiven abgeschobener Afghanen im Kontext Aktueller Politischer und Wirtschaftlicher Entwicklungen Afghanistans' (*Diakonie Deutschland, Brot für die Welt, Diakonie Hessen*, June 2021) 4 <www.fluechtlingsrat-mv.de/wp-content/uploads/2021/06/AFG_Monitoring-Studie_FINAL.pdf> accessed 28 August 2024.

111 Moreno-Lax (n 99) 119.

112 Khalid Koser, 'Asylum Policies, Trafficking and Vulnerability' (2000) 38(3) International Migration 91 <https://doi.org/10.1111/1468-2435.00116> 103; Luigi Achilli, '"The Good Smuggler": The Ethics and Morals of Human Smuggling among Syrians' (2018) 676(1) The Annals of the American Academy of Political and Social Science 77 <https://doi.org/10.1177/0002716217746641>; Tekalign Ayalew Mengiste, 'Refugee Protections from Below: Smuggling in the Eritrea-Ethiopia Context' (2018) 676(1) The Annals of the American Academy of Political and Social Science 57 <https://doi.org/10.1177/0002716217743944>.

113 ICHRP (n 40) 71–72.

114 Stoyanova (n 10) 34.

115 Dimitriadi (n 96) 66.

and smuggled people . . . are coerced',[116] and smugglers, too, deceive people through 'misinformation'.[117] In addition, even though only trafficked persons are thought to experience exploitation, trafficked and smuggled persons are also difficult to distinguish with reference to the harm experienced.

The UNHCR Trafficking Guidelines provide a useful summary of possible experiences in the trafficking context. These can include 'abduction, incarceration, rape, sexual enslavement, enforced prostitution, forced labour, removal of organs, physical beatings, starvation [and] the deprivation of medical treatment'.[118] While some of these harms may be inferred from the trafficking definition, consulting additional sources provides a more comprehensive picture of trafficked persons' experiences.

This is even more the case for smuggled persons, whose experiences of harm are almost entirely omitted in anti-smuggling legislation. UNHCR also details experiences of smuggled persons. Types of harm encountered by individuals on the Mediterranean and Western Balkans routes to Europe include 'abuse and violence by smugglers' as well as kidnappings, 'sexual violence and torture' and forced labour.[119] With regard to routes between East and West Africa and Africa's Mediterranean Coast, UNHCR has compiled a 'non-exhaustive list of "unimaginable horrors"', which includes 'death, SGBV [sexual and gender-based violence], torture and physical violence, kidnapping for ransom, trafficking in persons, robbery, arbitrary detention, collective expulsions and refoulement'.[120] One of the most detailed accounts of harm experienced during dangerous journeys comes from journalist Sally Hayden, who has documented the experiences of African migrants en route to the Mediterranean Sea: pullbacks, arbitrary detention in inhumane conditions, torture, violence, rape, forced labour and forced recruitment, starvation and even death at the hands of smugglers, EU-funded militias, detention centre guards and sometimes locals or other migrants.[121] As Stoyanova notes – and as the aforementioned

116 Buckland (n 28) 147.

117 UNODC, 'Global Study on Smuggling of Migrants 2018' (2018) 6 <https://www.unodc.org/documents/data-and-analysis/glosom/GLOSOM_2018_web_small.pdf> accessed 9 January 2024.

118 UNHCR, 'Guidelines on International Protection: The Application of Article 1A(2) of the 1951 Convention and/or 1967 Protocol Relating to the Status of Refugees to Victims of Trafficking and Persons at Risk of Being Trafficked' (2006) HCR/GIP/06/07 (UNHCR Trafficking Guidelines) para 15.

119 UNHCR, 'Desperate Journeys: Refugees and Migrants Entering and Crossing Europe via the Mediterranean and Western Balkans Routes' (February 2017) <www.unhcr.org/uk/news/updates/2017/2/58b449f54/desperate-journeys-refugees-migrants-entering-crossing-europe-via-mediterranean.html> accessed 11 September 2022.

120 UNHCR, 'On This Journey, No One Cares If You Live Or Die: Abuse, Protection and Justice along Routes between East and West Africa and Africa's Mediterranean Coast: A Route-based Perspective on Key Risks' vol 2 (March 2024) xi–xii <www.unhcr.org/media/journey-no-one-cares-if-you-live-or-die-abuse-protection-and-justice-along-routes-between-1> accessed 19 August 2024.

121 Sally Hayden, *My Fourth Time, We Drowned: Seeking Refuge on the World's Deadliest Migration Route* (4th Estate 2022).

sources illustrate – being smuggled 'can involve truly traumatic experiences, including physical violence, rape, loss of family members etc., and can be even more traumatic than being deceived and forced to migrate to the EU for the purpose of exploitation'.[122]

Further, just like trafficked persons, smuggled persons may continue to experience harm once they reach the country of destination. Whereas 'trafficking [is] considered an ongoing and relational process that violate[s] rights', the relationship between smuggler and smuggled person is thought to end with entry into the country of destination.[123] However, as Brolan explains, smuggled persons 'may be forced into drug pushing, prostitution, begging, or theft' once in the country of destination in order to 'repay smuggling debts'.[124] These similarities are not reflected in the *trafficking* and *smuggling* definitions. When examining trafficked and smuggled persons' actual experiences, the distinction between both practices and the claim that the former need protection while the latter do not appear extremely questionable.

2.5 Trafficked and Smuggled Persons Under the Refugee Law Framework

In light of the fact that both trafficked and smuggled persons may face serious types of harm during dangerous journeys, an enquiry into their protection needs must focus on those experiences of harm, rather than on the assumptions created by the definitions of *trafficking* and *smuggling* and their interplay. Refugee law and human rights law, which explicitly examine individuals' experiences,[125] are better placed than the criminal law framework to assess both trafficked and smuggled persons' protection needs. As explained in the Introduction to this book, the analysis in the coming chapters will focus on the refugee law framework, which requires that the relevant fear be forward-looking.[126] Nevertheless, the question remains what role identification as a trafficked person should play in the context of examining trafficked and smuggled persons' eligibility for refugee status and whether the assumptions

122 Vladislava Stoyanova, 'Victims of Human Trafficking: A Legal Analysis of the Guarantees for "Vulnerable Persons" under the Second Phase of the EU Asylum Legislation' in Céline Bauloz and others (eds), *Seeking Asylum in the European Union: Selected Protection Issues Raised by the Second Phase of the Common European Asylum System* (Brill Nijhoff 2015) 77.

123 ICHRP (n 40) 80.

124 Claire Brolan, 'An Analysis of the Human Smuggling Trade and the Protocol Against the Smuggling of Migrants by Land, Air and Sea (2000) from a Refugee Protection Perspective' (2002) 14(4) International Journal of Refugee Law 561, 578–79 <https://doi.org/10.1093/ijrl/14.4.561>.

125 James C Hathaway and Michelle Foster, *The Law of Refugee Status* (2nd edn, CUP 2014) 121–28. Under human rights law, an *ex nunc* assessment of an applicant's individual circumstances must be conducted. See, for example, *FG v Sweden* App no 43611/11 (ECtHR, 23 March 2016) para 115.

126 Hathaway and Foster (n 125) 105.

introduced by the trafficked/smuggled binary will hinder an assessment of trafficked and smuggled persons' need for refugee protection.

2.5.1 *The Role of the Status of 'Victim of Trafficking'*

Based on the obvious similarities between trafficked and smuggled persons, it could be argued that the *trafficking* definition should be interpreted more broadly in order to cover those currently categorised as 'smuggled persons', so that they can either obtain protection under the trafficking legal framework and/or more easily claim refugee status; after all, currently, only trafficked persons can claim asylum based on their trafficking experience and future fear related thereto, while smuggled persons can make no such claim based on their experience of smuggling.

However, despite the similarities between trafficked and smuggled persons, the three-tier structure of the trafficking definition makes it difficult to characterise their experience as 'trafficking'. As Stoyanova has shown, a person can be recruited, transported, etc. for the purpose of exploitation; however, if the person cannot show that he or she was coerced or deceived, he or she will fall outside the trafficking definition.[127] Further, where it cannot be proven that a trafficker has 'recruited, transported, etc. [a person] by deception or coercion with the *specific intention of exploitation*',[128] this means that this person cannot be said to have been trafficked. Although trafficked persons are identified 'on the balance of probabilities',[129] while the standard to proof to convict a trafficker is 'beyond reasonable doubt', the uncertainties in the elements of the trafficking definition will make the correct identification of trafficked persons even more challenging.

As such, arguing for the inclusion of smuggled persons under the *trafficking* definition will not necessarily result in appropriate protection, either because individuals will be unable to prove that they were trafficked or because, as described earlier, protection for trafficked persons *qua* trafficked persons is very limited. While advocating for ensuring that all irregular migrants who have experienced harm during migration receive appropriate protection and assistance is important, it is doubtful whether the trafficking legal framework is best suited to do so.

In the context of assessing eligibility for refugee protection, the finding that an individual is a trafficked person, or the finding that he or she is a smuggled person, will be relevant in refugee law insofar as past experiences of harm are

127 Stoyanova (n 10) 35. NB trafficked children are an exception here since the means elements need not be present, where they have been recruited, etc., for the purpose of exploitation.

128 ibid 47; emphasis in original.

129 *R (MN) v Secretary of State for the Home Department* [2018] EWHC 3268 (QB), [2018] 11 WLUK 495 [68].

indicators for future risk.[130] However, 'past persecution is neither a sufficient nor a mandatory means of showing a well-founded fear of being persecuted'.[131] Thus, it is important not to immediately dismiss a claim where the individual is not recognised as having been trafficked or smuggled. This is illustrated by the case of *EL*,[132] concerning a woman the UK competent authority incorrectly identified as not having been trafficked. The claimant's ex-partner obtained forged documents for them to enter the UK and forced her to become a sex worker to pay off the debt incurred for obtaining the documents. In reviewing the negative trafficking decision, the High Court remarked that the claimant's 'application for asylum was refused . . . , no doubt, in large part, because of the negative [trafficking] decision'.[133]

It should be noted that, in the UK, the problem of negative trafficking decisions defeating asylum claims has since been addressed in the case of *ES*.[134] This case concerned an Albanian woman forced into sex work in Albania and Italy. She eventually escaped to the UK but received a negative trafficking decision. The UT decided that, in determining the appeal, it must 'not just rely on the decision reached by the Competent Authority',[135] which uses 'balance of probabilities as the appropriate standard of proof' but make its own findings regarding the trafficking issue, applying 'the far lower standard of proof applicable in Refugee Convention decisions',[136] namely, 'that of a reasonable degree of likelihood or a serious possibility'.[137] The claimant was granted refugee status.

As such, courts and tribunals assessing whether there is a future risk of re-trafficking (or of irregular re-migration, as I will argue in subsequent chapters) for the purpose of refugee law must make their own assessment of this risk (on the correct standard of proof).[138] While decisions as to the status of 'trafficked person'

130 Hathaway and Foster (n 125) 165; see also Atle Grahl-Madsen, *The Status of Refugees in International Law*, vol I (A W Sijthoff 1966) 176–77; Regulation (EU) 2024/1347 of the European Parliament and of the Council of 14 May 2024 on Standards for the Qualification of Third-Country Nationals or Stateless Persons as Beneficiaries of International Protection, for a Uniform Status for Refugees or for Persons Eligible for Subsidiary Protection and for the Content of the Protection Granted, Amending Council Directive 2003/109/EC and Repealing Directive 2011/95/EU of the European Parliament and of the Council [2024] OJ L 2024/1347 (Qualification Regulation) art 4(4).

131 Hathaway and Foster (n 125) 169.

132 *The Queen (on the application of EL) v SSHD* [2018] EWHC 968 (Admin), [2018] 4 WLUK 483.

133 ibid [1].

134 *ES (s82 NIA 2002, Negative NRM)* [2018] UKUT 335 (IAC) [3].

135 ibid [35].

136 ibid [33].

137 ibid [35].

138 Since the introduction of the Nationality and Borders Act 2022, however, according to s 32, decision-makers in the UK must first decide, on the balance of probabilities, whether an applicant fears persecution for reasons of a Convention ground and, if so, whether there is a reasonable likelihood of persecution.

under criminal law can inform that assessment, they are not decisive, because the only legal definition claimants have to meet during refugee status determination (RSD) is that of 'refugee' in Article 1A(2) Refugee Convention.

2.5.2 Employing the Trafficking and Smuggling Concepts in Refugee Law

In aiming to examine trafficked and smuggled persons' protection needs, the question arises whether employing the trafficking and smuggling concepts in refugee law would not import the problems and assumptions inherent in the *trafficking* and *smuggling* definitions into RSD. An analysis in refugee law which, for example, assumes that trafficked women are victims without any agency, that men are unlikely to be trafficked and that smuggled persons do not need protection, risks reproducing damaging assumptions to the detriment of applicants. The following chapters will show that assumptions like these have been, or are still being, made in refugee law. At the same time, these assumptions are being challenged, and this book will contribute to doing so.

In order to prevent criminal law definitions from introducing assumptions about certain claimants into refugee law, it is important to be aware of the relationship between criminal law and refugee law more generally. These two branches of law have different purposes. As noted already, criminal law primarily aims to identify and prosecute perpetrators; in the trafficking context, it also identifies victims of crime for the purpose of providing them with limited assistance. Refugee law, on the other hand, aims to identify persons who are in need of (often long-term) protection from *refoulement*. Thus, as Stoyanova notes, while the criminal law trafficking framework is aimed at eventually returning trafficked persons to their countries of origin, refugee law identifies 'migrants who cannot be returned'.[139] To do so, refugee law engages in a forward-looking enquiry, whereas identifying trafficked persons entails an 'assessment of past events and past harm'.[140] Stoyanova also contrasts the 'limited entitlements' envisioned for trafficked persons with the more extensive ones granted to refugees.[141] I would add that the strong emphasis on the acts and intentions of the traffickers, that is, the persecutors, is incompatible with the Refugee Convention, since the 'goal of the Convention is not to prosecute those responsible for persecution, but to provide surrogate protection to those at risk of being persecuted'.[142]

Further, it should be noted that certain terms and concepts used in both branches of law have different meanings. Thus, in the context of irregular migration, 'harm' means something different in criminal law on the one hand

139 Stoyanova (n 10) 141.
140 ibid.
141 ibid.
142 Hathaway and Foster (n 125) 378. See also Michelle Foster, *International Refugee Law and Socio-Economic Rights: Refuge from Deprivation* (CUP 2007) 58.

and in refugee (and human rights) law on the other. As mentioned earlier, in criminal law, irregular migration is, first and foremost, seen as causing harm to the state and its borders, and to individuals only where they are the 'victims' of traffickers, rather than of states' border regimes. In refugee law, however, harm experienced or feared by a person is a reason for protecting this individual.[143] This book posits that experiences during irregular migration constitute such harm. In contrast, conceiving of 'harm' primarily as harm to the state would have detrimental effects on the protection of irregularised migrants. As such, throughout this book, 'harm' in the context of irregular migration denotes human rights violations experienced by trafficked and smuggled persons,[144] rather than violations of the integrity of states' borders.[145]

As Stoyanova notes in relation to differences between criminal law and human rights law, because 'these two bodies of law have different purposes, the transplantation of concepts and case law from human rights to criminal law and vice versa should not be endorsed uncritically'.[146] The same is true for criminal law on the one hand and refugee law on the other. By being aware of the differences between both branches of law, and by actively questioning assumptions introduced about trafficked and smuggled persons in criminal law, it is possible to ensure that these factors will not hinder an assessment of trafficked and smuggled persons' need for refugee protection.

2.6 Conclusion

Since smuggled persons have similar experiences to trafficked persons, they may have similar protection needs. Trafficked and smuggled persons travel on the same routes and experience similar types of harm in this context, so that, in theory, they should be entitled to the same kind of protection in countries of destination. Yet due to assumptions about trafficked and smuggled persons created by the legal definitions of 'trafficking in persons' and 'smuggling of migrants', only the anti-trafficking legal framework provides (some) protection. Smuggled persons, by contrast, are considered to be undeserving of protection and are thus excluded from the protective scope of the anti-trafficking legal framework. This framework, in turn, determines protection needs based on a legal definition which not only focuses on perpetrators of an offence rather than its 'victims' but also contains uncertainties, so that

143 Guy S Goodwin-Gill and Jane McAdam, *The Refugee in International Law* (4th edn, OUP 2021) 78.

144 This is discussed in detail in Chapter 4.

145 In this context, it should be noted that the idea that irregular migration constitutes a harm to the receiving state or its citizens has been challenged. See, for example, Alessandro Spena, 'A Just Criminalization of Irregular Immigration: Is It Possible?' (2017) 11 Criminal Law and Philosophie 351 <https://doi.org/10.1007/s11572-015-9375-0>.

146 Stoyanova (n 10) 334.

it is questionable whether it is able to reliably identify 'trafficked persons' for the purpose of protecting them. Even if one is identified as a trafficked person, however, the protection provided by anti-trafficking instruments is limited, both in terms of assistance measures and in terms of the right to remain in the territory of the state the individual in question was trafficked to.

In addition to receiving this limited protection under the anti-trafficking legal framework, some trafficked persons are able to secure more comprehensive protection under refugee law based on a fear of future harm related to their trafficking experience. Under the refugee law framework, the status of 'trafficked person' is not (or should not be) decisive for receiving protection; what matters is that an individual meets the definition of 'refugee' in Article 1A(2) Refugee Convention. As opposed to the legal definitions of *trafficking* and *smuggling*, the *refugee* definition pays special attention to individual experiences. As such, the refugee law framework is more suited to determining the protection needs of both trafficked and smuggled persons.

The similarities between trafficked and smuggled persons' experiences justify a comparison between the two. In the coming chapters, trafficked persons' experiences will serve as a point of departure for assessing the protection needs of smuggled persons – and of irregularised migrants more broadly – under the refugee law regime. This will be done by analysing case law. Trafficked persons have taken to the courts to claim their rights, as a result of which it is possible to analyse trafficking-based asylum claims. This analysis will serve to understand the circumstances under which trafficked persons are seen to be in need of refugee protection and whether these circumstances apply to irregularised migrants as well.

References

Achilli L, '"The Good Smuggler": The Ethics and Morals of Human Smuggling among Syrians' (2018) 676(1) The ANNALS of the American Academy of Political and Social Science 77 <https://doi.org/10.1177/0002716217746641>

Andrijasevic R, 'The Difference Borders Make: (Il)legality, Migration and Trafficking in Italy among Eastern European Women in Prostitution' in Sara Ahmed and others (eds), *Uprootings/Regroundings: Questions of Home and Migration* (Routledge 2003)

Andrijasevic R, *Migration, Agency and Citizenship in Sex Trafficking* (Palgrave Macmillan 2010)

Atak I and Francois Crépau, 'Refugees as Migrants' in Cathryn Costello, Michelle Foster and Jane McAdam (eds), *The Oxford Handbook of International Refugee Law* (OUP 2021)

Atak I and James C Simeon, 'Human Trafficking: Mapping the Legal Boundaries of International Refugee Law and Criminal Justice' (2014) 12(5) Journal of International Criminal Justice 1019 <https://doi.org/10.1093/jicj/mqu093>

Brolan C, 'An Analysis of the Human Smuggling Trade and the Protocol Against the Smuggling of Migrants by Land, Air and Sea (2000) from a Refugee Protection Perspective' (2002) 14(4) International Journal of Refugee Law 561 <https://doi.org/10.1093/ijrl/14.4.561>

Buckland BS, 'Human Trafficking & Smuggling: Crossover & Overlap' in Cornelius Friesendorf (ed), *Strategies Against Human Trafficking: The Role of the Security Sector* (National Defence Academy and Austrian Ministry of Defence and Sports 2009)
Campana P and Federico Varese, 'Exploitation in Human Trafficking and Smuggling' (2016) 22 European Journal on Criminal Policy and Research 89 <https://doi.org/10.1007/s10610-015-9286-6>
Christie N, 'The Ideal Victim' in Ezzat A Fattah (ed), *From Crime Policy to Victim Policy: Reorienting the Justice System* (MacMillan 1986)
Council Directive 2002/90/EC of 28 November 2002 Defining the Facilitation of Unauthorised Entry, Transit and Residence [2002] OJ L 328 (Facilitation Directive)
Council Directive 2003/86/EC of 22 September 2003 on the Right to Family Reunification [2003] OJ L 251 (Family Reunification Directive)
Council Directive 2004/81/EC of 29 April 2004 on the Residence Permit Issued to Third-Country Nationals Who Are Victims of Trafficking in Human Beings or Who Have Been the Subject of an Action to Facilitate Illegal Immigration, Who Cooperate with the Competent Authorities [2004] OJ L 261 (Residence Permit Directive)
Council Framework Decision of 28 November 2002 on the Strengthening of the Penal Framework to Prevent the Facilitation of Unauthorised Entry, Transit and Residence [2002] OJ L 328 (Framework Decision)
Council of Europe Convention on Action against Trafficking in Human Beings (adopted 16 May 2005, entered into force 1 February 2008) ETS 197 (ECAT)
De Angelis M, *Human Trafficking: Women's Stories of Agency* (Cambridge Scholars Publishing 2016)
Dimitriadi A, 'The Interrelationship between Trafficking and Irregular Migration' in Sergio Carrera and Elspeth Guild (eds), *Irregular Migration, Trafficking and Smuggling of Human Beings: Policy Dilemmas in the EU* (*CEPS*, 2016) <www.ceps.eu/wp-content/uploads/2016/02/Irregular%20Migration,%20Trafficking%20and%20SmugglingwithCovers.pdf> accessed 4 April 2019
Directive 2011/36/EU of the European Parliament and of the Council of 5 April 2011 on Preventing and Combating Trafficking in Human Beings and Protecting Its Victims, and Replacing Council Framework Decision 2002/629/JHA [2011] OJ L 101/1 (Trafficking Directive)
Directive 2012/29/EU of the European Parliament and of the Council of 25 October 2012 Establishing Minimum Standards on the Rights, Support and Protection of Victims of Crime, and Replacing Council Framework Decision 2001/220/JHA [2012] OJ L 315 (Victim Protection Directive)
Directive (EU) 2024/1712 of the European Parliament and of the Council of 13 June 2024 Amending Directive 2011/36/EU on Preventing and Combating Trafficking in Human Beings and Protecting Its Victims [2024] OJ L 2024/1712 (Trafficking Amendment Directive)
ES (s82 NIA 2002, Negative NRM) [2018] UKUT 335 (IAC)
European Parliament, 'Resolution of 11 December 2018 with Recommendations to the Commission on Humanitarian Visas' (11 December 2018, 2018/2271(INL)) <www.europarl.europa.eu/doceo/document/TA-8-2018-0494_EN.html#title1> accessed 14 February 2020
European Parliamentary Research Service, *Briefing: Legal Migration to the EU* (European Parliament 2019) <www.europarl.europa.eu/RegData/etudes/BRIE/2019/635559/EPRS_BRI(2019)635559_EN.pdf> accessed 29 May 2020
FG v Sweden App no 43611/11 (ECtHR, 23 March 2016)
Foster M, *International Refugee Law and Socio-Economic Rights: Refuge from Deprivation* (CUP 2007)
Gallagher AT, 'Human Rights and Human Trafficking: Quagmire or Firm Ground – a Response to James Hathaway' (2009) 49(4) Virginia Journal of International Law 789
Gallagher AT, *The International Law of Human Trafficking* (CUP 2010)

Gallagher AT and Fiona David, *The International Law of Migrant Smuggling* (CUP 2014)

Goodwin-Gill GS and Jane McAdam, *The Refugee in International Law*, (4th edn, OUP 2021)

Grahl-Madsen A, *The Status of Refugees in International Law*, vol I (A W Sijthoff 1966)

Grundler M, 'Who is the "Vulnerable" Victim? Trafficked and Smuggled Persons as Victims of Crime under EU Law' in Lilian Tsourdi, Valsamis Mitsilegas and Niovi Vavoula (eds), *Intertwining Criminal Justice and Immigration Control in the EU: Theoretical, Interdisciplinary, and Practical Perspectives* (Routledge 2025)

Guild E, 'Conclusions: The Variable Political and Legal Geography of People Smuggling and Trafficking in Europe' in Elspeth Guild and Paul Minderhoud (eds), *Immigration and Criminal Law in the European Union: The Legal Measures and Social Consequences of Criminal Law in Member States on Trafficking and Smuggling in Human Beings* (Martinus Nijhoff 2006)

Hathaway JC, 'The Human Rights Quagmire of Human Trafficking' (2008) 49(1) Virginia Journal of International Law 1

Hathaway JC and Michelle Foster, *The Law of Refugee Status* (2nd edn, CUP 2014)

Haverkamp R, 'Victims of Human Trafficking: Considerations from a Crime Prevention Perspective' in Rita Haverkamp, Ester Herlin-Karnell and Claes Lernstedt (eds), *What is Wrong with Human Trafficking? Critical Perspectives on the Law* (Hart 2019)

Hayden S, *My Fourth Time, We Drowned: Seeking Refuge on the World's Deadliest Migration Route* (4th Estate 2022)

Hooper K and Camille Le Coz, *Seasonal Worker Programmes in Europe: Promising Practices and Ongoing Challenges* (*MPI Europe*, 2020) <www.migrationpolicy.org/research/seasonal-worker-programs-europe> accessed 22 January 2021

International Council on Human Rights Policy (ICHRP), 'Irregular Migration, Migrant Smuggling and Human Rights: Towards Coherence' (2010) <https://imumi.org/documentos/Irregular_Migration_and_Smuggling_2010.pdf> accessed 5 May 2020

Kneebone S, 'The Refugee–Trafficking Nexus: Making Good (the) Connections' (2010) 29(1) Refugee Survey Quarterly 137 <https://doi.org/10.1093/rsq/hdq011>

Kook K, '"I Want to Be Trafficked So I Can Migrate!": Cross-Border Movement of North Koreans into China through Brokerage and Smuggling Networks' (2018) 676(1) The ANNALS of the American Academy of Political and Social Science 114 <https://doi.org/10.1177/0002716217748591>

Koser K, 'Asylum Policies, Trafficking and Vulnerability' (2000) 1 International Migration 91 <https://doi.org/10.1111/1468-2435.00116>

Letschert R and Conny Rijken, 'Rights of Victims of Crime: Tensions Between an Integrated Approach and a Limited Legal Basis for Harmonisation' (2013) 4(3) New Journal of European Criminal Law 226 <https://doi.org/10.1177/203228441300400306>

Magugliani N, '(In)Vulnerable Masculinities and Human Trafficking: Men, Victimhood, and Access to Protection in the United Kingdom' (2022) 44(2) Journal of Human Rights Practice 726 <https://doi.org/10.1093/jhuman/huac001>

Magugliani N, 'Trafficked Adult Males as (Un)Gendered Protection Seekers: Between Presumption of Invulnerability and Exclusion from Membership of a Particular Social Group' (2022) 34(3–4) International Journal of Refugee Law 353 <https://doi.org/10.1093/ijrl/eeac030>

Mengiste TA, 'Refugee Protections from Below: Smuggling in the Eritrea-Ethiopia Context' (2018) 676(1) The ANNALS of the American Academy of Political and Social Science 57 <https://doi.org/10.1177/0002716217743944>

Mitsilegas V and Niovi Vavoula, 'Criminal Law: Institutional Rebalancing and Judicialisation as Drivers of Policy Change' in Florian Trauner and Ariadna Ripoll Servent (eds), *Policy Change in the Area of Freedom, Security and Justice: How EU Institutions Matter* (Routledge 2015)

Piotrowicz R and Conny Rijken, 'Article 16: Repatriation and Return of Victims' in Julia Planitzer and Helmut Sax (eds), *A Commentary on the Council of Europe Convention on Action against Trafficking in Human Beings* (Edward Elgar Publishing 2020)

PO (Trafficked Women) Nigeria CG [2009] UKAIT 00046

Protocol against the Smuggling of Migrants by Land, Sea and Air, Supplementing the United Nations Convention against Transnational Crime (adopted 15 November 2000, entered into force 28 January 2004) 2241 UNTS 480 (Smuggling Protocol)

Protocol to Prevent, Suppress and Punish Trafficking in Persons, Especially Women and Children, Supplementing the United Nations Convention against Transnational Organized Crime (adopted 15 November 2000, entered into force 25 December 2003) 2237 UNTS 319 (Trafficking Protocol)

The Queen (on the Application of EL) v SSHD [2018] EWHC 968 (Admin), [2018] 4 WLUK 483

R (MN) v Secretary of State for the Home Department [2018] EWHC 3268 (QB), [2018] 11 WLUK 495

Regulation (EC) No 810/2009 of the European Parliament and of the Council of 13 July 2009 Establishing a Community Code on Visas [2009] OJ L 243 (Visa Code)

Regulation (EU) 2016/399 of the European Parliament and of the Council of 9 March 2016 on a Union Code on the Rules Governing the Movement of Persons across Borders [2016] OJ L 77 (Schengen Borders Code)

Regulation (EU) 2018/1806 of the European Parliament and of the Council of 14 November 2018 Listing the Third Countries Whose Nationals Must Be in Possession of Visas When Crossing the External Borders and Those Whose Nationals Are Exempt from That Requirement [2018] OJ L 303 (Visa Regulation)

Regulation (EU) 2024/1347 of the European Parliament and of the Council of 14 May 2024 on Standards for the Qualification of Third-Country Nationals or Stateless Persons as Beneficiaries of International Protection, for a Uniform Status for Refugees or for Persons Eligible for Subsidiary Protection and for the Content of the Protection Granted, Amending Council Directive 2003/109/EC and Repealing Directive 2011/95/EU of the European Parliament and of the Council [2024] OJ L 2024/1347 (Qualification Regulation)

Ricci CM, 'Criminalising Solidarity? Smugglers, Migrants and Rescuers in the Reform of the "Facilitators' Package"' in Valsamis Mitsilegas, Violeta Moreno-Lax and Niovi Vavoula (eds), *Securitising Asylum Flows: Deflection, Criminalisation and Challenges for Human Rights* (Brill 2020)

Sax H, 'Article 13: Recovery and Reflection Period' in Julia Planitzer and Helmut Sax (eds), *A Commentary on the Council of Europe Convention on Action against Trafficking in Human Beings* (Edward Elgar Publishing 2020)

Shankley W, 'Gender, Modern Slavery and Labour Exploitation: Experiences of Male Polish Migrants in England' (2023) 49(5) Journal of Ethnic and Migration Studies 1274 <http://dx.doi.org/10.1080/1369183x.2021.2000853>

Sharma N, 'Anti-Trafficking Rhetoric and the Making of a Global Apartheid' (2005) 17(3) NWSA Journal 88

Spena A, 'A Just Criminalization of Irregular Immigration: Is It Possible?' (2017) 11 Criminal Law and Philosophie 351 <https://doi.org/10.1007/s11572-015-9375-0>

Spijkerboer T, 'The Global Mobility Infrastructure: Reconceptualising the Externalisation of Migration Control' (2018) 20 European Journal of Migration and Law 452 <https://doi.org/10.1163/15718166-12340038>

Srikantiah J, 'Perfect Victims and Real Survivors: The Iconic Victim in Domestic Human Trafficking Law' (2007) 87 Boston University Law Review 157

Stahlmann F, 'Erfahrungen und Perspektiven abgeschobener Afghanen im Kontext Aktueller Politischer und Wirtschaftlicher Entwicklungen Afghanistans' (*Diakonie Deutschland, Brot für die Welt, Diakonie Hessen*, June 2021) <www.fluechtlingsrat-mv.de/wp-content/uploads/2021/06/AFG_Monitoring-Studie_FINAL.pdf> accessed 28 August 2024

Stoyanova V, *Human Trafficking and Slavery Reconsidered: Conceptual Limits and States' Positive Obligations in European Law* (CUP 2017)

Stoyanova V, 'Victims of Human Trafficking: A Legal Analysis of the Guarantees for "Vulnerable Persons" under the Second Phase of the EU Asylum Legislation' in Céline Bauloz and others (eds), *Seeking Asylum in the European Union: Selected Protection Issues Raised by the Second Phase of the Common European Asylum System* (Brill Nijhoff 2015)

UNHCR, 'Desperate Journeys: Refugees and Migrants Entering and Crossing Europe via the Mediterranean and Western Balkans Routes' (February 2017) <www.unhcr.org/uk/news/updates/2017/2/58b449f54/desperate-journeys-refugees-migrants-entering-crossing-europe-via-mediterranean.html> accessed 11 September 2022

UNHCR, 'Guidelines on International Protection: The Application of Article 1A(2) of the 1951 Convention and/or 1967 Protocol Relating to the Status of Refugees to Victims of Trafficking and Persons at Risk of Being Trafficked' (2006) HCR/GIP/06/07 (UNHCR Trafficking Guidelines)

UNHCR, 'On this Journey, No One Cares If You Live or Die: Abuse, Protection and Justice Along Routes between East and West Africa and Africa's Mediterranean Coast: A Route-Based Perspective on Key Risks', vol 2 (March 2024) <www.unhcr.org/media/journey-no-one-cares-if-you-live-or-die-abuse-protection-and-justice-along-routes-between-1> accessed 19 August 2024

United Nations Convention against Transnational Organized Crime (adopted 15 November 2000, entered into force 29 September 2003) 2225 UNTS 209 (UNTOC)

UNODC, 'Global Study on Smuggling of Migrants 2018' (2018) <https://www.unodc.org/documents/data-and-analysis/glosom/GLOSOM_2018_web_small.pdf> accessed 9 January 2024

Van Houtum H, 'Human Blacklisting: The Global Apartheid of the EU's External Border Regime' (2010) 28(6) Environment and Planning D: Society and Space 957 <https://doi.org/10.1068/d1909>

Zirulia S, 'Is that a Smuggler? The Blurring Line between Facilitating Illegal Immigration and Providing Humanitarian Assistance at the European Border' in Gian Luigi Gatta, Valsamis Mitsilegas and Stefano Zirulia (eds), *Controlling Immigration through Criminal Law: European and Comparative Perspectives on "Crimmigration"* (Hart 2021)

3 'Route Causes' of Irregular Re-Migration

Vulnerability Indicators for Future Risk

3.1 Introduction

Having set the scene for a comparison between trafficked and smuggled persons in the previous chapter, in this chapter, I begin to analyse under what circumstances trafficked persons' asylum claims succeed and whether the relevant factors can be applied to the situation of smuggled persons and irregularised migrants more broadly. More specifically, this chapter is concerned with the way future risk is established in trafficking-based asylum claims and considers whether such a risk may exist for irregularised migrants as well.[1]

As explained in the Introduction to this book, a well-founded fear, or future risk, of harm is one of the main elements of the *refugee* definition. Future risk in the trafficking context manifests mainly in two ways: first, the risk of experiencing reprisals from those traffickers who originally trafficked the applicant; second, experiencing re-trafficking either at the hands of the original traffickers or through other traffickers. Since this book is concerned with the question of whether harm experienced outside the country of origin and in the context of irregular migration can form the basis of an asylum claim, this chapter focuses on the risk of re-trafficking and, by analogy, the risk of irregular re-migration. In both UK and German case law, risk of re-trafficking is established based on the applicant's 'vulnerabilities'. This chapter explores whether these vulnerabilities can also function as an indicator for the risk of irregular re-migration.

In order to gain a better understanding of the vulnerability concept, the chapter discusses the meaning of 'vulnerability' in anti-trafficking legislation and examines legal and feminist theory on the concept of vulnerability. These theoretical considerations form the foundation for applying the vulnerability reasoning from the trafficking context to the situation of irregularised migrants. Thus, the chapter seeks to establish irregular re-migration as a risk paralleling the risk of re-trafficking and considers whether irregularised

1 Parts of the analysis in this chapter have appeared in Maja Grundler, '"Route Causes" and Consequences of Irregular (Re-)Migration: Vulnerability as an Indicator of Future Risk in Refugee Law' (2024) 20(1) International Journal of Law in Context 35 <https://doi.org/10.1017/S1744552323000344>.

DOI: 10.4324/9781032664644-3

migrants can meet the well-founded fear element of the *refugee* definition. Moving away from the simplistic view that 'root causes' lead to re-migration, the chapter explores 'route causes' of irregular re-migration, which puts the focus on the experiences of irregularised migrants during displacement and the effect these experiences have on inducing future migratory journeys.

The chapter concludes by finding that, just like trafficked persons may be at risk of re-trafficking, irregularised migrants may be at risk of re-migrating irregularly and can therefore meet the well-founded fear element of the *refugee* definition.

3.2 Vulnerability as an Indicator of Future Risk in Trafficking-Based Asylum Claims

As explained in the previous chapter, the *trafficking* definition assumes that traffickers make use of certain means to recruit, transport, etc. a person. One of these means is the abuse of a person's 'position of vulnerability'. The *trafficking* definition therefore introduces the idea that trafficked persons are 'vulnerable'. This, in turn, is also reflected in refugee law. In both UK and German case laws, the vulnerability concept plays an important role in establishing a future risk of re-trafficking.

3.2.1 Vulnerability Indicators in UK Case Law

In the UK, reliance on the concept of vulnerability developed over time, as courts and tribunals grappled with questions of agency and knowledge of trafficked persons, shifting from the view that trafficked persons who have been trafficked before would not be deceived into a similar experience again, to an understanding that a previous trafficking experience contributes to trafficked persons' vulnerability to re-trafficking.

Thus, in the 2005 case of *MP*, concerning a Romanian woman who was kidnapped and forced into sex work in Romania, escaped but was found by her traffickers and then trafficked to Italy, the Immigration and Asylum Tribunal, as it was at the time, found that

> [T]he vast majority of those who are trafficked go willingly, hoping for a better job and a better life in a different country. They are deceived as to what will happen to them. The Appellant has not suggested that she could be deceived in this way. She was not deceived in the past and, knowing what she knows now, it is inconceivable that she could be duped in the same way as most victims of traffickers.[2]

2 *MP (Trafficking – Sufficiency of Protection) Romania* [2005] UKIAT 00086 [98].

Despite the fact that the appellant in this case was kidnapped and re-captured, the tribunal notes that most trafficked persons go 'willingly'.[3] At the same time, the tribunal speculates that 'the traffickers targeted [the appellant] because they knew she was a single woman living on her own and perhaps also a person who had lived in an orphanage and was not likely to have close family'.[4] As we will see in what follows, this case would perhaps be decided differently today, as lack of family support is seen as a risk factor for re-trafficking. In 2005, however, the tribunal focused on the appellant's willingness to avoid re-trafficking, rather than her ability to do so.

Similarly, in the 2009 case of *HC & RC*, the tribunal, in assessing the risk of re-trafficking, noted that the 'appellant is not somebody who has exhibited any signs of willingness to act as a prostitute' and 'is now fully aware of the dangers in considering employment which offers to pay a considerable amount of money'.[5] The case concerned a Chinese woman – a minor at the time of trafficking – who was first forced into sex work in China, where she was allowed to keep some of her earnings. She then approached an agent to take her out of the country, who forced her into sex work anew.[6] The same type of reasoning was employed as recently as 2022 in the case of *HD*, concerning a Vietnamese man trafficked for forced labour (cannabis cultivation).[7] The Upper Tribunal (UT) stated that the applicant would

> clearly [be] aware if approached by unknown individuals offering him the opportunity to travel to the UK by way of provision of a loan agreement, that this may result in his falling into the type of situation he has experienced in the past.[8]

In these cases, knowledge of the trafficking process is treated as something that will prevent individuals from 'choosing' to put themselves in a similar situation again. Applying a 'fool me once, shame on you; fool me twice, shame on me' type of reasoning, the means element of the *trafficking* definition is used to shift blame to trafficked persons, to claim that re-trafficking will be something they could only enter into willingly and therefore avoid.

However, the 2008 case of *SB* heralded a shift in the assessment of future risk for trafficked persons.[9] This case concerned a Moldovan woman who was trafficked to the UK for sex work and gave evidence against her trafficker, which resulted in a successful prosecution. The trafficker had served his prison term, and she feared that he or his associates would re-traffic her or subject her to other reprisals if she was returned to Moldova. Although the case mainly

3 ibid [65] and [98].
4 ibid [98].
5 *HC & RC (Trafficked Women) China v SSHD CG* [2009] UKAIT 00027 [84].
6 ibid [5].
7 *HD v SSHD* [2022] UKUT (IAC) PA/10137/2019.
8 ibid [43].
9 *SB (PSG – Protection Regulations – Reg 6) Moldova CG* [2008] UKAIT 00002.

dealt with the question of whether the appellant was a member of a particular social group (see Chapter 5), it also briefly considered questions of future risk. Rather than rejecting the possibility that the appellant would be re-trafficked based on her knowledge of the experience, the tribunal first considered the structural issues underlying human trafficking:

> [T]he fact that Moldova is Europe's poorest nation taken in conjunction with other factors (such as family relations, lack of employment, lack of awareness of the dangers of being trafficked as well as corruption which enables traffickers to operate) go some way towards explaining the reasons why individuals are pressurised to, or feel compelled to, enter into arrangements which result in their being trafficked.[10]

The tribunal then considered how a previous trafficking experience affects a trafficked person's ability to reintegrate in the country of origin and how this relates to risk of re-trafficking, highlighting the impact of

> social stigmatisation of victims of trafficking for sexual exploitation and the fact that victims of trafficking for sexual exploitation rarely avail . . . themselves of follow-up assistance because of concerns about members of their home communities learning about their experience. Social stigmatisation is mentioned as one of the difficulties faced in any reintegration process, as well as one of the reasons for the phenomena of re-trafficking, described as a 'prominent' issue in Moldova.[11]

Thus, the tribunal took into account both structural factors and the appellant's personal circumstances in assessing the risk of re-trafficking and granted her refugee status. This marks a departure from the cases in which re-trafficking is seen as something freely chosen by trafficked persons. This approach to establishing risk in the trafficking context was strengthened further in the 2010 case of *AZ*, which concerned a Thai woman who was forced into sex work in the UK and also granted refugee status.[12] The UT acknowledged that mere knowledge of the trafficking process does not protect trafficked persons from being re-trafficked. The tribunal found that

> [i]t could be said that having been trafficked once, [the appellant] would be wiser the next time round. However, the evidence indicates the opposite is the case and that former victims of trafficking are even more *vulnerable* to re-trafficking because they have already been through the business and know how to be compliant.[13]

10 ibid [105].
11 ibid.
12 *AZ (Trafficked Women) Thailand CG* [2010] UKUT 118 (IAC).
13 ibid [150]; emphasis added.

This is exactly the opposite approach to claiming that a former trafficking experience protects against re-trafficking due to knowledge of the process, introducing, instead, the idea of 'vulnerability' to re-trafficking. Significantly, from *AZ* onwards, the majority of UK case law acknowledges that coercion in the trafficking context need not necessarily take the form of abduction or deception but can also be the result of a person's general circumstances, or 'vulnerabilities'.

In *AZ*, the tribunal held further that the risk of re-trafficking depends on 'the age, marital status, domestic background, educational level, qualifications and work experience of the appellant' and that the 'availability of employment and a familial or other support network will also be significant factors'.[14] With reference to the appellant herself, the UT noted that she was 'a particularly vulnerable young woman' and that 'it would be very difficult for her to reintegrate into Thai society and support herself without falling back into the hands of traffickers because her fragility would inevitably attract the wrong kind of attention'.[15] While it is questionable whether this stereotypical representation of a 'fragile' 'victim' is helpful for the future risk analysis, the reference to problems in reintegrating and the different factors causing these problems are useful. The tribunal uses the term 'vulnerable' and connects it to the applicant's mental health, as well as her having 'no family support, no home and limited education'.[16] The UT also noted that

> for the appellant it would be difficult to reintegrate into her home community because of the fact that she would be unable to adequately explain her long absence and her return without funds and with a clearly fragile state of mind.[17]

In addition, the UT found that it was 'likely that the appellant would be forced by economic necessity to seek out work in the tourist industry . . . where traffickers operate'.[18] Thus, the tribunal identifies a number of different factors which may contribute to a risk of re-trafficking. Although these factors are not presented in a particularly organised way, there is a visible shift in the case law away from asserting that trafficked persons can choose not to be re-trafficked towards assessing the applicant's personal characteristics and circumstances, and how these impact both the prospects of reintegrating and the risk of re-trafficking.

The reasons for re-trafficking are also explored in two country guidance decisions for Albania, the 2010 case of *AM and BM*[19] and the 2016 case of

14 ibid [Headnote 2].
15 ibid [146].
16 ibid.
17 ibid [148].
18 ibid [149].
19 *AM and BM (Trafficked Women) Albania CG* [2010] UKUT 80 (IAC).

TD and AD.[20] *AM and BM* dealt with two Albanian women trafficked for sex work and granted refugee status. The case deals with causes of trafficking and questions of agency, stating thus:

> Those that *see themselves outside society*, for example, *divorced or abandoned women*, or others who wish to live abroad, may seek out traffickers in order to facilitate their departure from Albania and their establishment in prostitution abroad. Although such women are not 'trafficked women' in the sense that they have not been abducted against their will, there is likely to be considerable violence within the relationships and the *psychological affect* of that violence may lead to a situation where the pressures which they are under and the lack of freedom they are under means that such women should be treated as trafficked women.[21]

This paragraph points to societal stigma experienced by 'divorced or abandoned women' as a reason why trafficked persons may 'choose' to be trafficked but also emphasises the violence experienced in trafficking situations and its effect on these women's mental health. Thus, while the judgment recognises trafficked persons' agency in making the decision to be trafficked, it also acknowledges that a trafficked person's choices in this context are constrained. More specifically, the UT found that, in considering the risk of re-trafficking, the appellant's individual characteristics have to be taken into account, 'includ[ing] her age, her social, economic and educational background, the network of support which she might have, whether or not she has an illegitimate child and the way in which she has been trafficked in the past'.[22]

In *TD and AD*, the tribunal made similar findings regarding trafficked persons' agency in the decision to be re-trafficked. The case, again, concerned two Albanian women forced into sex work. Regarding the degree of choice the appellants had in leaving Albania, the judgment states:

> Some women are lured to leave Albania with false promises of relationships or work. Others may seek out traffickers in order to facilitate their departure from Albania and their establishment in prostitution abroad. Although such women cannot be said to have left Albania against their will, where they have fallen under the control of traffickers for the purpose of exploitation there is likely to be considerable violence within the relationships and a lack of freedom: such women are victims of trafficking.[23]

20 *TD and AD (Trafficked Women) CG* [2016] UKUT 92.
21 *AM and BM* (n 19) [Headnote d]; emphasis added.
22 ibid [182].
23 *TD and AD* (n 20) [Headnote c)].

The judgment states further:

> Re-trafficking is a reality. Whether that risk exists for an individual claimant will turn in part on the factors that led to the initial trafficking, and on her personal circumstances, including her background, age, and her willingness and ability to seek help from the authorities. For a proportion of victims of trafficking, their situations may mean that they are especially ***vulnerable to re-trafficking***, or being forced into other exploitative situations.[24]

Thus, with regard to the initial departure, the UT focused on the control of the trafficker over the 'victim' and the intention to exploit, while acknowledging that women may actively seek out traffickers. However, with regard to a risk of *re*-trafficking, the tribunal finds it necessary to consider an applicant's individual characteristics which make her ***vulnerable*** to re-trafficking. Further, the tribunal considered that returning trafficked persons may face 'stigma, isolation, financial hardship and uncertainty, a sense of physical insecurity and the subjective fear of being found either by their families or former traffickers', which makes reintegration into the home society difficult, especially for persons with 'mental illness or psychological scarring'.[25]

The relationship between what the UT has termed 'indicators of vulnerability' and risk of re-trafficking is made explicit in *HD*, another 2016 case resulting in refugee status.[26] This case concerned a Nigerian woman who was trafficked for domestic servitude, first within Nigeria, and then to the UK. She was able to escape but was then sexually abused by different men with whom she stayed in the UK. In this case, the UT lists a number of 'indicators that [show that a trafficked person returning to Nigeria] is at enhanced real risk of being trafficked', including 'the original indicators that resulted in her being identified and trafficked originally'; '[r]ejection by her family'; 'being psychologically damaged subsequent to the serious harm she has sustained during the period she was trafficked', which 'may render her less able to find work or access employment and result in her being at enhanced risk of destitution'; '[b]eing stigmatised and ostracised'; '[h]aving been subjected to sexual abuse/exploitation during domestic servitude'; experiencing destitution or poverty as well as 'pressure from her family . . . to provide an income from sexual exploitation'.[27]

Importantly, the case law shows that men, too, can be vulnerable to re-trafficking. An example is the 2016 case of *TAN*, in which a male minor trafficked for sexual exploitation was found to be vulnerable to re-trafficking

24 ibid [Headnote g)]; emphasis added.
25 ibid [Headnote f)].
26 *HD (Trafficked Women) Nigeria CG* [2016] UKUT 00454 (IAC) [169].
27 ibid [168].

based on the stigma he would experience, a lack of family support and lack of maturity – he was granted refugee status.[28] In 2018, in the case of *JFK*, a Chinese man trafficked for labour exploitation was found to be 'vulnerable to re-trafficking' due to his 'history of trauma, debt and . . . exploitation' and was also granted refugee status.[29] Likewise, the claimant in the 2019 case of *BT*, a Vietnamese man trafficked for forced labour, was found to be vulnerable to re-trafficking and granted refugee status.[30] The tribunal found that '[t]he trafficking came about because of his *extreme vulnerability* which was brought about by poverty, loss of land, mental health problems and family responsibilities to name but a few of the circumstances'.[31] Similarly, in the 2022 case of *TVD*,[32] the appeal of a gay man trafficked for sexual exploitation was allowed on asylum grounds, with the First-Tier Tribunal having found him to have a range of vulnerability indicators, such as post-traumatic stress disorder (PTSD), no support network in Vietnam, limited practical skills, stigma and lack of access to material or financial support. Further, in the 2024 case of *DK*, concerning a male minor trafficked for forced labour and sexual exploitation, the applicant was found to be vulnerable to re-trafficking due to mental health issues, poverty, lack of family support and stigma.[33] In *JV*, another 2024 case, a male applicant from Albania who was trafficked within Albania for labour exploitation was found to be a 'vulnerable young man' at risk of re-trafficking due to a lack of education, employment experience and family support, as well as his mental health issues.[34]

What is more, men trafficked within the UK may be vulnerable to re-trafficking on return to their country of origin. This was held to be the case for the applicant in the 2023 case of *MHK*, concerning a Somali man who came to the UK as a child and had been granted refugee status on grounds of being a member of a minority clan.[35] The Home Office sought to revoke this status, and the tribunal found that it was indeed no longer made out. However, the applicant was found to have been trafficked within the UK, as he had been forced to deal drugs to pay off a debt. The UT found that the applicant would be at risk of re-trafficking if returned to Somalia due to his mental and physical health issues (a learning disability and eye problems), lack of a family network in Somalia, limited employment opportunities, as well as difficulties in accessing social and community links via his minority clan; he was granted refugee status. Finally, a risk of trafficking can be established based on the applicant's vulnerabilities, even if that applicant has no prior experience

28 *TAN v SSHD* [2016] UKUT (IAC) AA/05644/2014.
29 *JFK v SSHD* [2018] UKUT (IAC) PA/06854/2016 [37] and [40].
30 *BT v SSHD* [2019] UKUT (IAC) PA/07306/2017.
31 ibid [38]; emphasis added.
32 *TVD v SSHD* [2022] UKUT (IAC) PA/00252/2020.
33 *DK v SSHD* [2024] UKUT (IAC) UI-2023–003379.
34 *JV v SSHD* [2024] UKUT (IAC) UI-2024–001176 [18].
35 *MHK v SSHD* [2023] UKUT (IAC) UI-2022–005774.

of having been trafficked. This is evident from the 2021 case of *TDL*, which concerned an autistic Vietnamese man whose mother sent him to school in the UK because he was being discriminated against in Vietnam due to his autism.[36] The UT found that due to his mental health issues, lack of a support network in Vietnam, poverty and lack of education and vocational skills, the applicant was at risk of being trafficked if returned to Vietnam. Likewise, in the 2024 case of *AS*, an Albanian man who had come to the UK as a minor was found to be at risk of trafficking on return due to his lack of education, employment experience and family support, his mental health issues and the discrimination he would experience due to his Roma ethnicity, 'all of which would impact on his ability to integrate' in Albania.[37] As such, it would be more accurate to speak of a 'risk of (re-)trafficking', rather than 're-trafficking' in this chapter. For reasons of readability, however, I will continue to use 're-trafficking', while keeping in mind that persons without prior trafficking experience may also be at risk.

Even though the case law clearly shows that men can be vulnerable to re-trafficking, male gender has been treated as a factor countering vulnerability. Indeed, as Magugliani has shown, UK decision-makers systematically denied men's vulnerabilities and protection needs in decisions issued only a few years before the cases mentioned in the preceding discussion.[38]

Nevertheless, the case law shows that a risk of re-trafficking can be established by way of vulnerability indicators for both male and female applicants. In addition, the relevant indicators of vulnerability preclude reintegration in a region other than the applicant's region of origin; that is, they preclude an internal protection alternative (IPA). Although the IPA concept is not explicitly part of the *refugee* definition, in state practice, and indeed in EU and UK law, where applicants can safely move to, and remain in, a region in their home country where they are not at risk of persecution or other serious harm, they will not be entitled to refugee status.[39]

As evident from the case law, however, trafficked persons' vulnerabilities may preclude them from reintegrating in the entirety of the country of origin,

36 *TDL v SSHD* [2021] UKUT (IAC) PA/00358/2020.

37 *AS (Albania) v SSHD* [2024] UKUT (IAC) UI-2024–000611 [10].

38 Noemi Magugliani, 'Trafficked Adult Males as (Un)Gendered Protection Seekers: Between Presumption of Invulnerability and Exclusion from Membership of a Particular Social Group' (2022) 34(3–4) International Journal of Refugee Law 353 <https://doi.org/10.1093/ijrl/eeac030>.

39 Regulation (EU) 2024/1347 of the European Parliament and of the Council of 14 May 2024 on Standards for the Qualification of Third-Country Nationals or Stateless Persons as Beneficiaries of International Protection, for a Uniform Status for Refugees or for Persons Eligible for Subsidiary Protection and for the Content of the Protection Granted, Amending Council Directive 2003/109/EC and Repealing Directive 2011/95/EU of the European Parliament and of the Council [2024] OJ L 2024/1347 (Qualification Regulation) art 8; Nationality and Borders Act 2022, s 35; cf Jessica Schultz, *The Internal Protection Alternative in Refugee Law: Treaty Basis and Scope of Application under the 1951 Convention relating to the Status of Refugees and Its 1967 Protocol* (Brill Nijhoff 2019).

so that a risk of persecution can be assumed to exist country-wide. This is evident from *TD and AD*, though the focus in this case was on the impact of having children out of wedlock, and the resulting stigma, on the ability to reintegrate and relocate.[40] Similar findings were made in the case of *ES*, which concerned an Albanian woman forced into sex work.[41] The applicant had mental health issues and an 'illegitimate' child, both of which were seen as precluding reintegration throughout Albania.[42] In addition, there are cases which explain in more detail why (other) vulnerabilities also preclude relocation. Thus, in the case of *IR*, which concerned a Sri Lankan woman trafficked for domestic servitude and granted refugee status, the tribunal stated that, due to her vulnerabilities, the applicant was at risk of re-trafficking 'whether she lived in her home area or in another area in Sri Lanka', since 'the risks are said to be the same'.[43] Further, the cases of *HC*[44] and *LVC*,[45] both resulting in refugee status for the claimants, show that this reasoning also applies to male applicants. *HC* concerned a man trafficked from Vietnam to Serbia, where he performed forced labour in a factory. The UT found that he had 'no family support, few educational or vocational skills' and experienced trauma, all of which would not only put him at risk of re-trafficking but also prelude an IPA.[46] *LVC* concerned another Vietnamese man, who was trafficked for cannabis cultivation. The tribunal found that he 'faced a real risk of trafficking *wherever* he lived in Vietnam . . . because the cumulative impact of his personal characteristics rendered him especially vulnerable', mentioning, in particular, lack of family support, education and employment prospects, as well as his poor mental health.[47]

Based on the aforementioned cases, it can be concluded that future risk of re-trafficking is seen as being connected to the presence of 'vulnerability indicators'. These exacerbate one another and ultimately converge to impact a person's livelihood options, make it difficult for them to reintegrate in their country of origin and result in socio-economic deprivation and, ultimately, re-trafficking. As the UT put it in the case of *IR*, '[p]re-existing vulnerabilities of those who have been trafficked . . . are exacerbated by the trafficking experience and makes [sic] them even more vulnerable to further exploitation'.[48] As such, the case law acknowledges that, under certain circumstances, a person may have no choice but to 'consent' to being re-trafficked in order to ensure their economic survival. The vulnerability indicators for risk of re-trafficking

40 *TD and AD* (n 20) [Headnote b].
41 *ES (s82 NIA 2002, Negative NRM)* [2018] UKUT 335 (IAC).
42 ibid [67]–[75].
43 *IR v SSHD* [2013] UKUT (IAC) IA178072010 [133].
44 *HC v SSHD* [2021] UKUT (IAC) PA/05060/2019.
45 *SSHD v LVC* [2021] UKUT (IAC) PA/06804/2019.
46 *HC* (n 44) [42]–[43] and [48].
47 *LVC* (n 45) [8]; emphasis in original. See also *JV* (n 34) [27].
48 *IR* (n 43).

identified from UK case law can be summed up as young age, poverty, lack of employment opportunities and experience, having little education, having no family or other support networks in the country of origin or experiencing pressure from the family to earn money, having mental health issues, experiencing stigmatisation and having 'illegitimate' children. Where (some of) these vulnerabilities are present, they generally indicate a risk of re-trafficking. Interestingly, similar vulnerability indicators to those relied upon in UK case law can be identified in German case law as well.

3.2.2 Vulnerability Indicators in German Case Law

German case law on trafficking-based asylum claims also mentions the term 'vulnerability' in future risk analysis, although this is not always immediately obvious.[49] In a number of cases, the courts mention the term *Zwangslage*, which can be translated as 'predicament' and which stems from the codification of part of the *trafficking* definition's means element in the German Criminal Code. There, 'abuse of a position of vulnerability' roughly translates as 'abuse of a personal or economic predicament, or of helplessness, which is related to the sojourn in a foreign country'.[50] The meaning of *Zwangslage* is discussed in greater detail later in Section 3.3.1 in the context of looking at the meaning of vulnerability in anti-trafficking legislation. In addition to the use of this term, German courts' reliance on the vulnerability concept is obvious from the fact that the vulnerability indicators identifiable in UK case law are also present in German case law. Even though German courts do not employ the term 'vulnerability indicators', I will continue to use it throughout this section in order to highlight similarities between UK and German case law.

German case law relying on vulnerabilities to establish a risk of re-trafficking is sparser than its UK equivalent. This is because some German courts focus on the immediate effects of the relevant vulnerabilities, that is, socio-economic

49 In German-language versions of the relevant EU and European legal instruments speaking of 'vulnerability', the term has been translated in a number of different ways. Both 'endangerment' (*Gefährdung*) and 'need for protection' (*Schutzbedürftigkeit*), as well as the adjectives *schutzbefürftig* ('in need of protection') and *schutzwürdig* ('worthy of protection'), are used in the EU Trafficking Directive. See Richtlinie 2011/36/EU des Europäischen Parlaments und des Rates vom 5. April 2011 zur Verhütung und Bekämpfung des Menschenhandels und zum Schutz seiner Opfer sowie zur Ersetzung des Rahmenbeschlusses 2002/629/JI des Rates, OJ L 101 (Menschenhandelsrichtlinie) Recitals 2, 8, 12, 22 and 23; art 2(1), art (2)(2), art 4(2)(a). 'Helplessness' (*Hilflosigkeit*) is used in the official translation of the ECAT. See Gesetz zu dem Übereinkommen des Europarats vom 16. Mai 2005 zur Bekämpfung des Menschenhandels, 17 October 2012 (BGBl. II, Nr. 31, S. 1089) art 1. None of these terms are employed in the relevant case law discussed here; however, the term *vulnerabel* ('vulnerable') is used in case law related to Dublin returns of trafficked persons. See, for example, VG Würzburg, W 10 K 19.50275, 26.01.2019.

50 Strafgesetzbuch (StGB) 13 November 1998 (BGBl. I S. 3322) (Criminal Code) s 232: *Ausnutzung ihrer persönlichen oder wirtschaftlichen Zwangslage oder ihrer Hilflosigkeit, die mit dem Aufenthalt in einem fremden Land verbunden ist* (my translation).

deprivation, and grant applicants complementary protection on this basis (see Chapter 6) instead of considering the long-term effects of vulnerabilities and the risk of re-trafficking. Nevertheless, German courts showed an awareness of the connection between vulnerability indicators and risk of re-trafficking as early as 2005, in the case of a Ukrainian woman who was taken to the Czech Republic believing she would be able to work there but who was instead forced into sex work.[51] The administrative court (AC) Würzburg recognised that it was her and her son's socio-economic need that had put her at risk of trafficking, and the applicant was granted refugee status.

Later judgments explicitly link vulnerabilities and risk of re-trafficking. Thus, in 2014, the AC Stuttgart, in deciding the case of a Nigerian applicant who had been taken to Italy to become a sex worker, found that she would be at risk of having to return to this arrangement due to a lack of education and the general economic situation in Nigeria, which, coupled with stigmatisation and rejection by her family, would leave her no other choice.[52] Similarly, in a 2020 judgment, the AC Magdeburg found that the applicant was at increased risk of re-trafficking due to her poverty, lack of education and family support and mental health issues (PTSD).[53] The applicant in question, who was granted refugee status, was a Nigerian woman who was brought to Germany and forced into sex work. In another 2020 judgment, the AC Stuttgart granted refugee status to a Nigerian woman trafficked to Europe for sexual exploitation based on a risk of re-trafficking due to being a single mother with outstanding debts to the traffickers, who had no family support, little education and little employment experience, and who would be ostracised.[54] In a 2024 judgment by the AC Göttingen, concerning a Zambian woman who was trafficked to France for labour exploitation, and then to Germany for sexual exploitation, the court found that the applicant was at risk of re-trafficking due to her mental health issues, the fact that she had an 'illegitimate' child, her lack of family support and because she would be stigmatised upon return.[55] The applicant was granted refugee status.

As in UK case law, in German case law, vulnerability indicators are also considered to preclude an IPA. Thus, in 2011, the AC Wiesbaden found that a Nigerian woman had no IPA due to a lack of family support and lack of livelihood options.[56] The appellant had been taken to Germany to work as a sex worker, feared both reprisals from her traffickers and re-trafficking and was granted refugee status. Similarly, in 2015, the AC Würzburg found that a Nigerian woman trafficked to Italy for sex work had no feasible IPA due to a lack of education and family support, as well as the stigma she would

51 VG Würzburg, W 8 K 04.30919, 19.09.2005.
52 VG Stuttgart, A 7 K 1405/12, 16.05.2014.
53 VG Magdeburg, 6 A 40/19, 28.01.2020.
54 VG Stuttgart, A 1 K 8819/18, 5770443, 16.11.2020.
55 VG Göttingen, 3 A 135/21, 03.04.2024.
56 VG Wiesbaden, 3 K 1465/09.WI.A, 14.03.2011.

experience.[57] This woman, too, feared reprisals and re-trafficking and was granted refugee status. Further, in 2019, the AC Cologne, in considering whether a Nigerian woman who feared reprisals from the woman who had trafficked her could avail herself of an IPA, took into account the applicant's vulnerabilities.[58] Since she was a single mother of two small children with no family support, who had not completed her education to become a hairdresser and who would be at risk of destitution, it was held that there was no IPA and that she was entitled to refugee status. Similarly, in a 2021 case concerning a Nigerian woman trafficked to France and Italy for sexual exploitation, the applicant was granted refugee status, with the AC Hannover finding that she had little education and employment experience and would face stigma and a lack of family support if she were to relocate.[59] Likewise, in a 2022 case heard by the AC Munich, a Nigerian woman trafficked to Spain for sexual exploitation was found not to be able to relocate due to risk of destitution and insufficient mental healthcare.[60]

Clearly, vulnerability indicators are considered when establishing a risk of re-trafficking in both the UK and Germany. In this context, it is important to highlight that all applicants who are found to be vulnerable and thus at risk of re-trafficking in German case law are female, while male applicants are often not seen as equally vulnerable. This is evident from a 2012 case in which the AC Augsburg found that a Nigerian man who was trafficked to Germany for sex work was not entitled to protection.[61] The appellant was forced to have sex with clients but was not paid and was also denied medical treatment for anal bleeding caused by penetration. Despite the facts of the judgment showing that the applicant faced socio-economic deprivation and possibly stigmatisation on return to Nigeria, and that he had little education, as well as health issues, he was not seen as being vulnerable, with the court suggesting that he could avoid destitution by working in the construction sector.

As discussed in Chapter 2, vulnerability to re-trafficking is strongly associated with female gender, and evidently, this assumption introduced by trafficking legislation is reproduced in some of the case law discussed here. However, as the next section will show, when theorised and applied carefully, the vulnerability concept has the potential to overcome such assumptions and their exclusionary effects.

3.3 The Concept of Vulnerability in Law

In light of the finding that the concept of vulnerability plays a major role in establishing a risk of re-trafficking, it is necessary to examine this concept in more detail. Courts and tribunals use the concept uncritically and without

57 VG Würzburg, W 2 K 14.30213, 17.11.2015.
58 VG Köln, 2 K 5595/18.A, 28.05.2019.
59 VG Hannover, 10 A 6353/18, 09.09.2021.
60 VG München, M 13 K 21.30776, 21.06.2022.
61 VG Augsburg, Au 7 K 12.30184, 18.09.2012.

theorising it. Yet 'vulnerability' is a contested concept. It is a widely used term in law and other disciplines,[62] yet it is rarely defined and thus has no single agreed meaning.[63] While the vulnerability concept is normally used to identify those most in need of protection and assistance (and to promote their resilience),[64] it may be unsuited to this task due to its vagueness. Indeed, the concept may be 'so broad as to obscure the needs of specific groups and individuals'.[65] Thus, designating an entire group as 'vulnerable' can lead to essentialising and stigmatising members of that group and to overlooking differences within the group.[66] At the same time, it can exclude from protection those who are not part of the relevant group.[67] On the other hand, vulnerability, specifically what Baumgärtel calls 'migratory vulnerability', constitutes a tool for taking 'the lived reality of individual migrant applicants' into account in judicial reasoning.[68]

Certainly, being labelled (not) vulnerable has real consequences for individuals, including in the asylum context. For example, 'vulnerable' persons may be seen to have special reception needs,[69] to be eligible for refugee

62 '[V]ulnerability as an analytical concept first emerged in the environmental sciences in reference to the impact of natural or economic disasters on human populations' and is now also used in 'medicine and public health', as well as many other disciplines, including law; see Elina Virokannas, Suvi Liuski and Marjo Kuronen, 'The Contested Concept of Vulnerability – A Literature Review' (2020) 23(2) European Journal of Social Work 327 <https://doi.org/10.1080/13691457.2018.1508001>.

63 Vera Bergelson, 'Vulnerability, Exploitation and Choice' in Rita Haverkamp, Ester Herlin-Karnell and Claes Lernstedt (eds), *What Is Wrong with Human Trafficking? Critical Perspectives on the Law* (Hart Publishing 2019) 199.

64 Martha Albertson Fineman, 'The Vulnerable Subject: Anchoring Equality in the Human Condition' (2008) 20(1) Yale Journal of Law and Feminism 9; Martha Albertson Fineman, 'Equality, Autonomy, and the Vulnerable Subject in Law and Politics' in Martha Albertson Fineman and Anna Grear (eds), *Vulnerability: Reflections on a New Ethical Foundation for Law and Politics* (Routledge 2016); Francesca Ippolito, *Understanding Vulnerability in International Human Rights Law* (Editoriale Scientifica 2020) 18.

65 Alyson Cole, 'All of Us Are Vulnerable, But Some Are More Vulnerable Than Others: The Political Ambiguity of Vulnerability Studies, an Ambivalent Critique' (2016) 17(2) Critical Horizons 260, 267 <https://doi.org/10.1080/14409917.2016.1153896>.

66 Lourdes Peroni and Alexandra Timmer, 'Vulnerable Groups: The Promise of an Emerging Concept in European Human Rights Convention Law' (2013) 11(4) International Journal of Constitutional Law 1056 <https://doi.org/10.1093/icon/mot042>; Francesca Ippolito and Sara Iglesias Sánchez, 'Introduction' in Francesca Ippolito and Sara Iglesias Sánchez (eds), *Protecting Vulnerable Groups: The European Human Rights Framework* (Hart Publishing 2015).

67 Fineman, 'Equality' (n 64); Ben Hudson, 'Migration in the Mediterranean: Exposing the Limits of Vulnerability at the European Court of Human Rights' (2018) 4 Maritime Safety and Security Law Journal 26; Ben Hudson, 'Asylum Marginalisation Renewed: "Vulnerability Backsliding" at the European Court of Human Rights' (2024) 20(1) International Journal of Law in Context 16 <https://doi.org/10.1017/S1744552323000332>.

68 Moritz Baumgärtel, 'Facing the Challenge of Migratory Vulnerability in the European Court of Human Rights' (2020) 38(1) Netherlands Quarterly of Human Rights 12, 13 <https://doi.org/10.1177/0924051919898127>.

69 Directive (EU) 2024/1346 of the European Parliament and of the Council of 14 May 2024 Laying Down Standards for the Reception of Applicants for International Protection [2024] OJ L 2024/134 (Reception Conditions Directive) Chapter IV.

resettlement[70] and for humanitarian assistance.[71] At the same time, vulnerability carries mainly negative connotations, and the use of the concept can result in a denial of agency, as well as attempts to impose assistance and control the behaviour of 'vulnerable' persons.[72] Thus, rather than simply adopting the term uncritically, this section explores the meanings, functions and potential of the vulnerability concept with the aforementioned criticism in mind. The section focuses on the use of the term in law, specifically in the context of trafficking and refugee law.

3.3.1 Vulnerability in Anti-Trafficking Legislation

Since the present discussion on vulnerability is situated in the context of vulnerability to human trafficking, it is pertinent to begin by examining the meaning of the vulnerability concept in the trafficking context. Indeed, as mentioned already, the concept can be found in the very definition of human trafficking, one of the 'means' employed by traffickers being the 'abuse of a position of vulnerability'. While the UN Trafficking Protocol does not define the concept of vulnerability, the EU Trafficking Directive defines it as 'a situation in which the person concerned has no real or acceptable alternative but to submit to the abuse involved'.[73] The same phrase is used in the Explanatory Report to the Council of Europe Convention on Action against Trafficking in Human Beings (ECAT), which clarifies that

> [b]y abuse of a position of vulnerability is meant abuse of any situation in which the person involved has no real and acceptable alternative to submitting to the abuse. The vulnerability may be of any kind, whether physical, psychological, emotional, family-related, social or economic. The situation might, for example, involve insecurity or illegality of the victim's administrative status, economic dependence or fragile health. In short, the situation can be any state of hardship in which a human being is impelled to accept being exploited.[74]

70 UNHCR, 'UNHCR Resettlement Handbook' (2011) 182 <www.refworld.org/policy/opguidance/unhcr/2011/en/97558> accessed 28 October 2024.

71 Lewis Turner, 'The Politics of Labeling Refugee Men as "Vulnerable"' (2021) 28(1) Social Politics: International Studies in Gender, State & Society 1 <https://doi.org/10.1093/sp/jxz033>.

72 Peroni and Timmer (n 66); Turner (n 71).

73 Directive 2011/36/EU of the European Parliament and of the Council of 5 April 2011 on Preventing and Combating Trafficking in Human Beings and Protecting Its Victims, and Replacing Council Framework Decision 2002/629/JHA [2011] OJ L 101/1 (Trafficking Directive) art 2(2).

74 Council of Europe, 'Explanatory Report to the Council of Europe Convention on Action against Trafficking in Human Beings' (2005) para 83 <https://rm.coe.int/16800d3812> accessed 18 May 2021.

Thus, as also evident from trafficking-based asylum claims, vulnerability is heavily associated with socio-economic deprivation and lack of choice. Indeed, Gallagher and McAdam note that

> [i]n the context of trafficking, 'vulnerability' is typically used to refer to those inherent, environmental or contextual factors that increase the susceptibility of an individual or group to being trafficked. These factors are generally agreed to include human rights violations such as poverty, inequality, discrimination and gender-based violence – all of which contribute to creating economic deprivation and social conditions that limit individual choice and make it easier for traffickers and exploiters to operate.[75]

In this context, it is worth noting that 'factors shaping vulnerability to trafficking tend to impact differently and disproportionately on groups that already lack power and status in society . . . so that a genuine understanding of vulnerability will thereby almost always require a situation-specific analysis'.[76]

Interestingly, German criminal law takes a similar approach to vulnerability. As mentioned earlier, in the Criminal Code, 'abuse of a position of vulnerability' roughly translates as 'abuse of a personal or economic predicament, or of helplessness, which is related to the sojourn in a foreign country'. Thus, German criminal law recognises underlying personal and economic factors which may lead to re-trafficking. The Federal Court of Justice has clarified the meaning of 'predicament' (*Zwangslage*), stating that such a predicament arises where the individual in question lives in precarious socio-economic conditions, which restrict that person's autonomy with respect to making decisions and taking actions, leading to decreased resistance against attacks on that person's sexual self-determination.[77] Thus, German law, too, explicitly recognises that 'vulnerable' persons may have no choice but to submit to re-trafficking. Further, Vogeler, drawing on a range of commentary on the German Criminal Code, explains that the notion of 'predicament' in the Code signifies a personal or economic want which need not necessarily threaten the survival of the person in question.[78] Examples of such predicaments include economic ruin, homelessness, divorce and unemployment.[79] The most common predicament, however, is that of poverty and poor socio-economic conditions in the

75 Anne T Gallagher and Marika McAdam, 'Issue Paper: Abuse of a Position of Vulnerability and other "Means" within the Definition of Trafficking in Persons' (*UNODC*, 2013) 13 <www.unodc.org/documents/human-trafficking/2012/UNODC_2012_Issue_Paper_-_Abuse_of_a_Position_of_Vulnerability.pdf> accessed 5 January 2021.

76 Ippolito (n 64) 87.

77 Bundesgerichtshof, BGH 5 StR 154/14, 16.07.2014; my translation.

78 Lena Vogeler, *Rechtliche Prävention von Menschenhandel zum Zweck der sexuellen Ausbeutung: Ein Rechtsvergleich unter besonderer Berücksichtigung der Prostitutionspolitiken Deutschlands und Schwedens* (Lit Verlag 2018) 179.

79 ibid.

country of origin, combined with an inability to make a living in a way which does not involve submitting to being trafficked.[80]

What can be concluded from the foregoing discussion on vulnerability in anti-trafficking laws is a common understanding at the international, regional and German domestic (and, if taking into account the relevant UK case law discussed earlier, also UK domestic) level of vulnerability to re-trafficking as related to socio-economic deprivation and capacity to act.

3.3.2 Vulnerabilities as the Reasons for Exposure to Harm

The concept of vulnerability is not only used in the anti-trafficking legal framework but also has long played a role in academic and judicial legal thinking. Vulnerability theory was pioneered by Fineman as an alternative to the anti-discrimination framework.[81] Fineman proposes that '[v]ulnerability initially should be understood as arising from [human] embodiment, which carries with it the ever-present possibility of harm, injury, and misfortune from mildly adverse to catastrophically devastating events, whether accidental, intentional, or otherwise'.[82] At the same time, she explains that vulnerability is 'experienced uniquely by each of us'[83] due to differences between individuals, for example, with respect to health and economic or social capital.[84] Thus, Fineman conceives of vulnerability as being both universal and particular. While personal characteristics and a lack of resources can exacerbate a person's vulnerability, such characteristics and resources can also 'provide individuals with "resilience" in the face of vulnerability'.[85] In this context, Fineman mentions health, wealth and education,[86] but also family and other relationships,[87] as well as structural factors, such as the environment in which an individual lives.[88]

These factors are clearly similar to the vulnerability indicators discussed earlier. Further, the vulnerability indicators utilised in the context of trafficking-based asylum claims are also similar to 'indicators of vulnerability' uncovered by Peroni and Timmer while analysing the European Court of Human Rights' (ECtHR) jurisprudence on 'vulnerable groups'.[89] The indicators identified by Peroni and Timmer include '(historical) prejudice and

80 ibid 180.
81 Fineman, 'The Vulnerable Subject' (n 64) 2–5; Fineman, 'Equality' (n 64).
82 Fineman, 'The Vulnerable Subject' (n 64) 9.
83 ibid 10.
84 Fineman, 'Equality' (n 64) 21–22.
85 Fineman, 'The Vulnerable Subject' (n 64) 13.
86 ibid 14.
87 ibid 15.
88 Fineman, 'Equality' (n 64) 23.
89 Peroni and Timmer (n 66) 1070.

stigmatization', as well as 'social disadvantage and material deprivation'.[90] Timmer, in a separate study, identifies factors such as age, gender, mental and physical disability, trauma, experiencing pressure to act a certain way and the applicant's environment as additional vulnerability indicators.[91]

Thus, vulnerability theory, and its applications to concrete cases, is helpful for understanding the content and nuances of the concept. In order to systematise these different vulnerability indicators, Mackenzie *et al.* propose a 'taxonomy of three different sources of vulnerability (i.e., *inherent*, *situational*, and *pathogenic*) and two different states of vulnerability (i.e., *dispositional* and *occurrent*)'.[92] *Inherent vulnerability* broadly corresponds to Fineman's conceptualisation of vulnerability as universal, described by Mackenzie *et al.* as 'intrinsic to the human condition' and related to the state of the physical body, including its age and health.[93] *Situational vulnerability*, on the other hand, is 'context specific' and 'caused or exacerbated by the personal, social, political, economic, or environmental situations of individuals or social groups'.[94] *Pathogenic vulnerability* is 'a subset of situational vulnerability' and arises through 'morally dysfunctional or abusive interpersonal and social relationships and sociopolitical oppression or injustice'.[95] Both forms of vulnerability – inherent and situational – Mackenzie *et al.* argue, can be either dispositional, where there is the potential to experience vulnerability, or occurrent, where, as the term suggests, vulnerability actually occurs.[96] What both Fineman's and Mackenzie *et al.*'s approach to conceptualising vulnerability have in common is an interest in understanding the reason(s) for exposure to harm. This understanding of vulnerability can contribute to a better appreciation of the lived realities of human beings, and thus of their protection needs. It allows for an examination of a person's individual circumstances which put them at risk of harm.

Mackenzie *et al.*'s taxonomy is particularly useful in categorising the vulnerability indicators from the trafficking context. Whereas a trafficked person's age and health are inherent sources of vulnerability to re-trafficking, most sources of vulnerability are situational, such as poverty, lack of employment

90 ibid 1065.

91 Alexandra Timmer, 'A Quiet Revolution: Vulnerability in the European Court of Human Rights' in Martha Albertson Fineman and Anna Grear (eds), *Vulnerability: Reflections on a New Ethical Foundation for Law and Politics* (Routledge 2016) 152–61.

92 Catriona Mackenzie, Wendy Rogers and Susan Dodds, 'Introduction: What Is Vulnerability, and Why Does It Matter for Moral Theory?' in Catriona Mackenzie, Wendy Rogers and Susan Dodds (eds), *Vulnerability: New Essays in Ethics and Feminist Philosophy* (OUP 2014) 7; italics in original.

93 ibid.

94 ibid.

95 ibid 9.

96 ibid 8.

opportunities and experience, having no family or other support networks in the country of origin or experiencing pressure from the family to earn money, having little education, being stigmatised and having 'illegitimate' children. The taxonomy's differentiation between occurrent and dispositional vulnerabilities is also relevant to understanding future risk in the trafficking context. While some of these indicators are likely to have existed at the time of the initial trafficking, others – in particular stigmatisation, mental health issues and 'illegitimate' children – are often only brought about by the trafficking experience itself. Thus, while vulnerability is undoubtedly occurrent both at the time of the initial trafficking and at the time of re-trafficking, those vulnerabilities brought about by the trafficking experience are still dispositional at the time of initial trafficking, so that a person who has been trafficked before will be even more vulnerable to re-trafficking because he or she possesses additional vulnerabilities.

Nevertheless, neither Fineman's nor Mackenzie *et al.*'s vulnerability framework adequately reflects one particularly important aspect of vulnerability which emerges from the analysis of the relevant case law. The different sources and states of vulnerability proposed in Mackenzie *et al.*'s taxonomy do not account for the effect of formerly dispositional vulnerabilities becoming occurrent and interacting with other (occurrent) vulnerabilities. In other words, while the taxonomy foresees vulnerabilities which may come about in the future ('dispositional') and acknowledges that vulnerabilities may result from the individual's personal situation ('situational'), including abusive relationships ('pathogenic'), it lacks a term for vulnerabilities which are created by a particular experience and which increase the risk of being exposed to this same situation again. In the present context, the relevant risk is re-trafficking, and this risk is increased for individuals with a prior experience of trafficking because this experience leads to additional vulnerabilities. Vulnerabilities acquired through trafficking can be inherent or situational; mental health issues, as a health condition, are an example of the former, while stigmatisation, which is created by a social situation, is an example of the latter. While it should be noted that not all trafficked persons will necessarily experience these vulnerabilities and may not see themselves as vulnerable at all,[97] acquiring additional vulnerabilities is a common consequence of trafficking. As Serughetti explains,

> [t]he notion of vulnerability in the international definition of human trafficking is ambiguous and generally interpreted in two main ways: first, *as a condition produced by the experience of trafficking itself*, from which special protection obligations derive for states; and second, as

97 Rutvica Andrijasevic, *Migration, Agency and Citizenship in Sex Trafficking* (Palgrave Macmillan 2010).

> *a characteristic of individuals and their environments* that makes them more exposed than others to the risks of human trafficking.[98]

Thus, Serughetti effectively sums up the three layers of vulnerability which emerge from the trafficking context and are relevant for the future risk enquiry: individual characteristics (universal/inherent vulnerabilities), surrounding circumstances (particular/situational vulnerabilities), and what I call 'consequential vulnerability' – inherent or situational vulnerabilities brought about by the initial trafficking experience. This corresponds to what Timmer calls '*ex-post* vulnerability', describing instances where a person is 'particularly vulnerable after (and because of) suffering [a certain] kind of human rights abuse'.[99] While Timmer does not explore this idea and its implications in any detail, in the trafficking context, the effects of consequential vulnerabilities are obvious and of particular relevance to the future risk analysis.

The UK case of *FT* illustrates this: FT was an Albanian woman who had moved to Italy to find work, where she began a relationship with a man who then forced her into sex work.[100] In the judgment she is described as having been resourceful and independent before her trafficking experience but, as a consequence of this, now suffering with PTSD and hepatitis C, so that in the absence of a family support network, she would find it difficult to support herself.[101]

Thus, the term *consequential vulnerability* conveys the temporal sequence of events which lead to additional vulnerabilities. In this context, it is important to note that different layers of vulnerability are likely to exacerbate one another, so that different vulnerabilities must be considered holistically as reasons for exposure to harm. Timmer, noticing a similar convergence of different vulnerabilities in ECtHR case law, calls this 'compounded vulnerability'.[102]

Understood in this way, the vulnerability concept can make a meaningful contribution to the future risk analysis in refugee law. In particular, the vulnerability analysis explains why past experiences are relevant to the future risk enquiry.[103] Rather than focusing only on the persecutors and their (presumed) intentions to re-victimise the applicant, vulnerability reasoning puts the focus on the effects past persecution has on the applicant and their ability to evade harm in the future. As explained earlier, under the vulnerability analysis, an

98 Giorgia Serughetti, 'Smuggled or Trafficked? Refugee or Job Seeker? Deconstructing Rigid Classifications by Rethinking Women's Vulnerability' (2018) 11 Anti-Trafficking Review 16, 25 <https://doi.org/10.14197/atr.201218112>; emphasis added.

99 Timmer (n 91) 155.

100 *FT v SSHD* [2022] UKUT (IAC) PA/03526/2020.

101 ibid [21]–[26].

102 Timmer (n 91) 161.

103 ibid 165; see also Atle Grahl-Madsen, *The Status of Refugees in International Law*, vol I (A W Sijthoff 1966) 176–77; Qualification Regulation (n 39) art 4(4).

applicant's individual characteristics and their surrounding circumstances are examined, as well as vulnerabilities resulting from prior experiences of harm. Thus, such consequential vulnerabilities explain what effect past persecution has had on the applicant and how these additional vulnerabilities further constrain their choices, putting them at future risk.

This approach is also compatible with the finding that '[e]vidence of individualized past persecution is neither a sufficient nor a mandatory means of showing a well-founded fear of being persecuted'.[104] This is especially relevant 'in the case of an applicant who has not yet experienced persecution'.[105] As the cases of *TDL* and *AS*,[106] discussed in the preceding text, demonstrate, prior victimisation is not necessary to make out a risk of trafficking. Thus, even for trafficking-based asylum claims not involving a claimant with a previous experience of trafficking, an analysis of vulnerability indicators will be useful, since demonstrating a well-founded fear may be based on 'evidence that persons similarly situated to the claimant are at risk in the country of origin'.[107] Thus, an analysis of the vulnerability indicators found in trafficking-based asylum claims could benefit a person making such a claim (or, indeed, a claim based on a risk of irregular re-migration, as argued in Chapters 6 and 7) without having a prior experience of having been trafficked.

In addition, the vulnerability concept can help resolve questions regarding the temporal dimension of the future risk analysis. An issue which continues to be debated is the question of how soon after a hypothetical return to the country of origin a risk would have to manifest in order to be considered 'real'.[108] In the context of asylum claims based on health deterioration and climate change, Anderson *et al.* argue that '[i]f the evidence is strong, an event or occurrence can be foreseeable even if it is not likely to manifest in the short term. A risk can be real notwithstanding the fact that its manifestation is some time away'.[109] Similarly, as Foster *et al.* demonstrate with regard to establishing future risk in the context of armed conflict, 'while a fear of persecution must be current, the ill-treatment feared may occur in the present or the future.

104 James C Hathaway and Michelle Foster, *The Law of Refugee Status* (2nd edn, CUP 2014) 169.

105 ibid 173.

106 See n 36 and n 37.

107 Hathaway and Foster (n 104) 169.

108 Bruce Burson, 'The Concept of Time and the Assessment of Risk in Refugee Status Determination' (Kaldor Centre Annual Conference, Sydney, 18 November 2016) 5 <www.kaldorcentre.unsw.edu.au/sites/default/files/B_Burson_2016_Kaldor_Centre_Annual_Conference.pdf> accessed 8 November 2020.

109 Adrienne Anderson and others, 'Imminence in Refugee and Human Rights Law: A Misplaced Notion for International Protection' (2019) 68(1) International and Comparative Law Quarterly 111, 138 <https://doi.org/10.1017/S0020589318000398>.

The test is whether it is reasonably foreseeable, which necessarily embodies a degree of speculation'.[110]

The vulnerability analysis supports this approach. In *TD and AD*, for example, the UT considered that persons with persisting vulnerabilities, such as 'mental illness or psychological scarring', may still be at risk of re-trafficking after having stayed in a shelter for trafficked persons for up to two years.[111] Further, in a 2020 judgment by the AC Stuttgart, the court found that a woman who was first trafficked from Nigeria to Europe in 2004 would still be at risk of re-trafficking 16 years later due to her vulnerabilities.[112]

In sum, vulnerability is a useful tool to determine risk in the context of refugee law. Refugee law requires an individual determination of risk, and indeed, as evident from the earlier discussion, the vulnerability concept is best suited for analysing a person's individual circumstances. Further, relying on vulnerability in the future risk analysis creates a better understanding of the relationship between past persecution and future risk and shows that, while vulnerabilities are present, risk of harm is present too, thus contributing to resolving contentious questions about imminence of harm. While there are clearly some flaws in courts' application of the concept in the trafficking context – most notably their focus on female claimants' vulnerability and male claimants' alleged lack thereof – when theorised and applied carefully, the vulnerability analysis creates a better understanding of each individual's reasons for exposure to harm, irrespective of gender or other types of group membership. What matters is whether inherent, situational and consequential vulnerabilities are present for an individual applicant and how these vulnerabilities interact.

The next section proposes that the vulnerabilities identified in the trafficking context are also present for irregularised migrants and that these vulnerabilities result in a risk of irregular re-migration.

3.4 'Route Causes' of Irregular Re-Migration

Since the vulnerability-based future risk assessment described in the preceding section is of an individualised nature, this assessment cannot be limited to either the group of 'trafficked persons' who have experienced trafficking in the past or the trafficking context generally. Indeed, the vulnerability indicators identified in trafficking-based asylum claims may apply beyond the trafficking context and to persons who are similarly vulnerable but who have not experienced trafficking, such as the applicants in *TDL* and *AS*, or, indeed, irregularised migrants.

110 Michelle Foster and others, '"Time" in Refugee Status Determination in Australia and the United Kingdom: A Clear and Present Danger from Armed Conflict?' (2022) 34(2) International Journal of Refugee Law 163, 177 <https://doi.org/10.1093/ijrl/eeac033>.

111 *TD and AD* (n 20) [Headnote e) and f)].

112 A 1 K 8819/18, 5770443 (n 54).

Yet arguing that irregularised migrants are *at risk* of irregular re-migration may appear counterintuitive. As per the definition used in this book, irregularised migrants have undertaken a dangerous migratory journey (at least) once before but have been unable to obtain refugee protection based on harm feared in their country of origin. Seeing as they are not at risk of persecution in their country of origin, it seems as though irregularised migrants have no reason to feel compelled to leave for a second time.

Conceiving of irregular re-migration as a response to vulnerabilities, however, calls into question the allegedly voluntary nature of such migration. This section analyses how the vulnerability analysis from the trafficking context serves to reconceptualise irregular re-migration as a risk.

3.4.1 'Vulnerable' Trafficked Persons and 'Vulnerable' Irregularised Migrants

The vulnerability indicators identified in trafficking-based asylum claims are likely to apply beyond the trafficking context and to irregularised migrants. Indeed, it is easily conceivable that irregularised migrants are young and poor; lack education, employment opportunities and experience; and have no family or other support networks in the country of origin. If they do have a family network, they may experience pressure from the family to earn money. They, too, may have 'illegitimate' children (although this is most likely to be the case mainly for women, for example, those who are raped during the migratory journey), develop mental health issues and experience stigmatisation if returned to their country of origin. While it is not within the scope of this chapter to provide evidence for the fact that each of these vulnerability indicators applies beyond the trafficking context, in this section I will briefly look at such evidence with a focus on mental health issues and stigma. Since in trafficking case law vulnerabilities are discussed mainly in relation to female applicants, in this section, I highlight the experiences of men, where possible.

With regard to stigma, Schuster and Majidi's research on (male) irregular migrants deported back to Afghanistan has found that 'the socio-cultural shame of failure and the suspicions of the community' are reasons for re-migration.[113] This stigma results from a 'failed' migration experience, that is, a failure to return with capital to invest in the home community and to repay debts, and failure to enable other family members to migrate, as well as the suspicion that, in order to be deported, an individual must have committed criminal acts.[114]

113 Liza Schuster and Nassim Majidi, 'What Happens Post-Deportation? The Experience of Deported Afghans' (2013) 1(2) Migration Studies 221, 225 <https://doi.org/10.1093/migration/mns011>.

114 Liza Schuster and Nassim Majidi, 'Deportation Stigma and Re-migration' (2015) 41(4) Journal of Ethnic and Migration Studies 635, 640–41 <https://doi.org/10.1080/1369183X.2014.957174>; see also Friederike Stahlmann, 'Erfahrungen und Perspektiven Abgeschobener Afghanen im Kontext Aktueller Politischer und Wirtschaftlicher Entwicklungen Afghanistans' (*Diakonie Deutschland, Brot für die Welt, Diakonie Hessen*, June 2021) 3 <www.

Likewise, Tyldum notes that '[i]n many communities, failed migration experiences with exploitation and abuse are in and of themselves stigmatized'.[115] This may be because the decision to migrate is seen as abandoning the home community, or because 'return [is] seen as a failure or a failure to return with adequate wealth/earnings'.[116] In Sierra Leone, for example, 'returnees are often rejected by relatives and friends', are 'seen as failures' or rejected because they 'stole from their families to pay for their journey'.[117] This is also reflected in the case law. In a 2020 judgment by the AC Stuttgart, for example, the court found that the appellant was likely to be ostracised upon return for not having returned 'successfully'.[118]

Meanwhile, Plambech observes that 'deportees experience cultural estrangement, stigmatisation, high levels of violence, and low access to basic material needs'.[119] She notes that for former Nigerian sex workers returned to Benin, 'deportation appeared to be more embarrassing and stigmatising than sex-work because deportation does not hold the potential or concrete result of upward mobility'.[120] Turnbull, too, looks at the stigmatising effects of deportation, explaining that 'detention and deportation are not typically well understood but still associated with wrongdoing and illegality', and that 'those subject to them are guilty by association', so that the stigma attached to having been deported may 'impact [their] future career prospects'.[121] Thus, it is clear that not only do persons who fall outside the trafficking definition experience stigma on return to the country of origin, but that this experience also has similar effects in that it contributes to the decision to re-migrate.

Further, persons migrating irregularly experience mental health issues, which, in turn, may contribute to irregular re-migration. Ringold notes that displaced persons 'are at high risk for chronic mental health disorders because of the multiple stressors they experience before, during, and after their flight' and 'are at particularly high risk for post-traumatic stress disorder . . . depression, and somatization (emotional trauma or stress experienced as physical

---

fluechtlingsrat-mv.de/wp-content/uploads/2021/06/AFG_Monitoring-Studie_FINAL.pdf> accessed 28 August 2024.

115 Guri Tyldum, 'Limitation in Research on Human Trafficking' (2010) 48(5) International Migration 1, 9 <https://doi.org/10.1111/j.1468-2435.2009.00597.x>.

116 IOM, 'Towards an Integrated Approach to Reintegration in the Context of Return' (2017) 6 <www.iom.int/sites/g/files/tmzbdl486/files/our_work/DMM/AVRR/Towards-an-Integrated-Approach-to-Reintegration.pdf> accessed 20 October 2024.

117 Tim Whewell, '"We Failed to Reach Europe – Now Our Families Disown Us"' (*BBC World Service*, 14 November 2019) <www.bbc.co.uk/news/stories-50391297> accessed 1 May 2020.

118 A 1 K 8819/18, 5770443 (n 54).

119 Sine Plambech, 'Back From "The Other Side": The Post-Deportee Life of Nigerian Migrant Sex Workers' in Shahram Khosravi (ed), *After Deportation: Ethnographic Perspectives* (Palgrave Macmillan 2018) 87.

120 ibid 97.

121 Sarah Turnbull, 'Starting again: Life After Deportation from the UK' in Shahram Khosravi (ed), *After Deportation: Ethnographic Perspectives* (Palgrave Macmillan 2018) 49.

symptoms)'.[122] Further, Arsenijević *et al.* show that mental health problems are by no means limited to female irregular migrants. Their study of male migrants' experiences while travelling alone to Europe shows that 'the majority of male migrants' found their experiences of border crossing traumatic and that these men experienced '[f]eelings of hopelessness, desperation, lack of self-value and self-esteem',[123] as well as 'psychosomatic symptoms', such as 'headaches, tremors and heart palpitations'.[124]

In sum, as these accounts of the experiences of (male) irregular migrants (who were not trafficked) show, consequential vulnerabilities are brought about not only by a past experience of trafficking but also by a past experience of migrating irregularly. Coupled with other inherent and situational vulnerabilities, consequential vulnerabilities do not only indicate a risk of re-trafficking but also may put individuals at risk of irregular re-migration. Schuster and Majidi find that 'the majority of those who are deported want to, will attempt to, and often do leave again'.[125] As in the trafficking context, these vulnerabilities may affect an individual's ability to reintegrate in the country of origin and to make a living, so that irregular re-migration is 'chosen' to address the situation. Conceiving of irregular re-migration as a risk, then, has implications for theories on migration dynamics, particularly the allegedly 'voluntary' nature of re-migration for mainly economic reasons, as discussed in the next subsection.

3.4.2 Movement for Economic Reasons: From 'Voluntary' to 'Forced' Migration

Seeing as vulnerability indicators converge to make reintegration and earning a livelihood in the country of origin very difficult, there is a strong socio-economic dimension to the risk of irregular re-migration. As Schuster and Majidi explain, besides stigma and a lack of local ties, factors such as 'deepening economic opportunity losses and the impossibility of repaying debts incurred by the initial departure' make re-migration more likely.[126]

This observation is important and interesting because, normally, people migrating for mainly economic reasons are not deemed to be in need of refugee

122 Sarah Ringold, 'Refugee Mental Health' (2005) 294(5) The Journal of the American Medical Association 646 <https://doi.org/10.1001/jama.294.5.646>.

123 Jovana Arsenijević and others, '"I Feel Like I Am Less Than Other People": Health-Related Vulnerabilities of Male Migrants Travelling Alone on Their Journey to Europe' (2018) 209 Social Science & Medicine 86, 90–91 <https://doi.org/10.1016/j.socscimed.2018.05.038>.

124 ibid 92.

125 Schuster and Majidi (n 113) 224.

126 ibid 222; see also Nauja Kleist, 'Disrupted Migration Projects: The Moral Economy of Involuntary Return to Ghana from Libya' (2017) 87(2) Africa 322 <https://doi.org/10.1017/S000197201600098X>.

protection.[127] The UNHCR Handbook, for example, states that if a person is 'moved to [leave his country of origin] exclusively by economic considerations, he is an economic migrant not a refugee'.[128] In theory, migration motivations should be irrelevant to the protection enquiry under refugee law. Nothing in the Refugee Convention suggests that leaving one's country of origin 'voluntarily' is detrimental to a refugee claim.[129] Indeed, nothing in the Convention requires a refugee to have *left* his or her country of origin due to a well-founded fear of being persecuted, which is confirmed by the existence of refugees *sur place*.[130] The only requirement is that, at the time of refugee status determination, the prospective refugee is outside the country and is at risk of persecution for reasons of Convention grounds upon return.[131]

Nevertheless, the notion that 'economic migrants' move voluntarily and do not have protection needs persists. Thus, reconceptualising socio-economic deprivation (caused by intersecting vulnerabilities) as a risk factor for irregular re-migration, which entails serious violations of civil and political rights and may amount to persecution,[132] allows people who may normally be dismissed as economic migrants to argue that they are, in fact, refugees.

Indeed, the analysis in this chapter shows that socio-economic deprivation can cause people to move and to be exposed to danger as a result. This is not a novel observation as such, since this is also acknowledged in the context of the IPA enquiry. UNHCR notes that

> [if] the situation [in the proposed area of relocation] is such that the claimant will be unable to earn a living or to access accommodation or where medical care cannot be provided or is clearly inadequate, the area may not be a reasonable alternative.[133]

127 Nonetheless, Foster has shown that a deprivation of socio-economic rights can, under certain circumstances, form the basis of a claim under the Refugee Convention. See Michelle Foster, *International Refugee Law and Socio-Economic Rights: Refuge from Deprivation* (CUP 2007). Violations of socio-economic rights may also lead to an autonomous *non-refoulement* duty under human rights law (independent of violations of civil and political rights). See Mariana Ferolla Vallandro do Valle, 'Fleeing Deprivation: Deducing *Non-Refoulement* Obligations from Economic, Social and Cultural Rights' (2024) 36(4) International Journal of Refugee Law 353 <https://doi.org/10.1093/ijrl/eeae036>.

128 UNHCR, 'Handbook on Procedures and Criteria for Determining Refugee Status and Guidelines on International Protection Under the 1951 Convention and the 1967 Protocol Relating to the Status of Refugees' HCR/1P/4/ENG/REV.4 (1979, reissued 2019) (UNHCR Handbook) 22.

129 Grahl-Madsen (n 103) 173.

130 UNHCR Handbook (n 128) 26.

131 Convention Relating to the Status of Refugees (adopted 28 July 1951, entered into force 22 April 1954) 189 UNTS 137 (Refugee Convention) art 1A(2); cf Grahl-Madsen (n 103) 179.

132 See Chapter 4.

133 UNHCR, 'Guidelines on International Protection: "Internal Flight or Relocation Alternative" within the Context of Article 1A(2) of the 1951 Convention and/or 1967 Protocol relating to the Status of Refugees' (23 July 2003) HCR/GIP/03/04, para 29.

Further:

> [I]f the conditions [in the proposed area of relocation] are such that the claimant may be compelled to go back to the original area of persecution, or indeed to another part of the country where persecution or other forms of serious harm may be a possibility, [an IPA is not viable].[134]

Thus, 'conditions in the IPA may compel the claimant to return to an established risk of persecution'.[135] In other words, in the context of the IPA enquiry, it is accepted that movement for socio-economic reasons cannot be said to be voluntary.

A similar line of reasoning is employed in trafficking-based asylum claims. Trafficked persons respond to socio-economic deprivation by deciding to be re-trafficked in the absence of 'acceptable alternatives'.[136] As such, while trafficked persons exercise agency in deciding to submit to re-trafficking, the 'choice' to be re-trafficked cannot be considered to be voluntary. As Ottonelli and Torresi put it, '[p]eople whose only alternatives to migration involve starvation, destitution, bodily injury, or incapacitating poverty cannot be said to migrate voluntarily'.[137] Essentially, trafficked persons opt for re-trafficking because their vulnerabilities leave them no other choice.

This is illustrated by the case of *JA*, heard by the UT in 2020,[138] in which the tribunal found that under certain circumstances, an appellant may be 'driven to seek work abroad'.[139] The case concerned a Filipino single mother of two children, one of whom had a disability. In order to earn enough money to enable her disabled daughter to visit a special school and have medical treatment, the appellant sought work in the United Arab Emirates, where she was subjected to forced labour and then trafficked to the UK by her employers. The UT accepted that upon return she would be compelled to seek work abroad again because her daughter's condition 'would require the appellant to earn more money than she could earn in the Philippines',[140] and that she would

134 ibid para 21; cf Schultz (n 39) 167; Hathaway and Foster (n 104) 348–49.

135 Schultz (n 39) 167.

136 Council of Europe, 'Explanatory Report to the ECAT' (n 74); Valeria Ottonelli and Tiziana Torresi, 'When Is Migration Voluntary?' (2013) 47(4) The International Migration Review 783, 800 <https://doi.org/10.1111/imre.12048>; see also David Bartram, 'Forced Migration and "Rejected Alternatives": A Conceptual Refinement' (2015) 13(4) Journal of Immigrant & Refugee Studies 439 <https://doi.org/10.1080/15562948.2015.1030489>.

137 Ottonelli and Torresi (n 136) 798; Bartram (n 136) 439; cf Marta Bivand Erdal and Ceri Oeppen, 'Forced to Leave? The Discursive and Analytical Significance of Describing Migration as Forced and Voluntary' (2018) 44(6) Journal of Ethnic and Migration Studies 981 <https://doi.org/10.1080/1369183X.2017.1384149>.

138 *JA v SSHD* [2020] UKUT (IAC) PA/13132/2018, p 9.

139 ibid.

140 ibid p 10.

therefore be at risk of re-trafficking. Thus, even though, based on her motivations, JA is the classic 'economic migrant', it is recognised that working abroad is not something she does truly voluntarily, and thus, the tribunal focused on the risk to the appellant rather than dismissing her claim.

Both trafficking-based asylum claims and the IPA enquiry illustrate that exercising agency in responding to socio-economic deprivation through migration cannot be equated with voluntary movement and a lack of protection needs. In fact, in both contexts, moving to address socio-economic deprivation leads to serious harm, which warrants protection. The same is true for irregularised migrants who move because their vulnerabilities converge to cause socio-economic deprivation.

3.4.3 From 'Root Causes' to 'Route Causes'

While the fact that risk of irregular re-migration is bound up with socio-economic deprivation has the potential to open up the risk enquiry for persons who would normally be deemed to fall outside the scope of the Refugee Convention, a focus on socio-economic deprivation in this enquiry could prove detrimental to potential refugee claims if the risk of irregular re-migration is not theorised carefully.

At first glance, it seems as though, if the risk of irregular re-migration is effectively caused by socio-economic deprivation, this risk can be countered by addressing the so-called 'root causes' of (irregular) migration. Such root causes are thought to include factors 'such as economic underdevelopment, poverty and unemployment', and it is believed that by addressing these causes, migration can be reduced.[141] This type of reasoning is potentially detrimental to irregularised migrants' claims to refugee status because it could be (and has been) suggested that their vulnerability can simply be countered through financial support.[142] Therefore, it is important to consider the risk of irregular re-migration in light of migration theories, and indeed to build upon those theories, to explain the complexities surrounding this idea. In the following, I will explain what sets the risk of irregular re-migration and its reliance on vulnerability reasoning apart from other migration theories by introducing the concept of 'route causes' of irregular re-migration.

Firstly, it is important to note that root causes theory has been shown to be flawed. Indeed, it has been proven, for example, that addressing so-called root causes through development assistance increases, rather than decreases, people's aspirations and ability to migrate.[143] Nevertheless, development assis-

141 Hein de Haas, 'Turning the Tide? Why Development Will Not Stop Migration' (2007) 38(5) Development and Change 819, 828 <https://doi.org/10.1111/j.1467-7660.2007.00435.x>.
142 See Chapter 4.
143 de Haas (n 141) 833.

tance remains a popular migration management tool to address irregular migration.[144] Due to the limitations of root causes theory, there have been attempts to develop more sophisticated models which explain the phenomenon of irregular migration. These include 'push-and-pull' models, which, like the root causes model, think of migration as a one-off event of moving from a country of origin to a country of destination, but consider not only factors which 'push' migrants out of one country but also factors which 'pull' them towards another.[145]

However, the push–pull model has been criticised for being too simplistic and not taking migrants' agency into account.[146] Thus, other migration theories seek to focus on migrant agency and speak of 'drivers' of irregular migration – 'factors that may make up the external structural elements shaping the decision space for those considering migration'.[147] The drivers model, developed by Van Hear *et al.*, comes close to the vulnerability approach discussed earlier in acknowledging that migration decisions are constrained by structural factors.[148] However, despite conceiving of migration as a process, rather than a one-off event, the drivers model does not engage with the phenomenon of (irregular) re-migration in particular, or with the effects of a previous migratory journey on subsequent migration. In this context, another theory which is particularly relevant is Lemberg-Pedersen's concept of border-induced displacement. This conceptualises restrictive border controls as 'a cause of displacement and forced migration in itself'.[149] Lemberg-Pedersen argues that, while there will be an initial cause for the original migratory journey, 'border-induced forced migration' constitutes a 'second-order displacement', which leads to 'people [being] constantly uprooted and transferred between control elements'.[150]

Against this background, I introduce the concept of 'route causes' of irregular re-migration. The underlying premise of this approach is that there are

144 Loren B Landau, 'A Chronotope of Containment Development: Europe's Migrant Crisis and Africa's Reterritorialisation' (2019) 51(1) Antipode 169 <https://doi.org/10.1111/anti.12420>.

145 Everett S Lee, 'A Theory of Migration' (1966) 3(1) Demography 47.

146 Hein de Haas, 'The Determinants of International Migration: Conceptualising Policy, Origin and Destination Effects' (2011) IMI Working Paper No 32 <www.migrationinstitute.org/publications/wp-32-11> accessed 10 May 2021, 8–9.

147 Nicholas Van Hear, Oliver Bakewell and Katy Long, 'Push-Pull Plus: Reconsidering the Drivers of Migration' (2018) 44(6) Journal of Ethnic and Migration Studies 927, 928 <https://doi.org/10.1080/1369183X.2017.1384135>.

148 ibid 930.

149 Martin Lemberg-Pedersen, 'Forcing Flows of Migrants: European Externalization and Border-Induced Displacement' in Dorte Jagetic Andersen, Martin Klatt and Marie Sandberg (eds), *The Border Multiple: The Practicing of Borders between Public Policy and Everyday Life in a Re-scaling Europe* (Routledge 2012) 47.

150 ibid.

factors which cause irregularised migrants to 'choose' a dangerous migratory route (this can include 'root causes', such as socio-economic deprivation, but also other structural factors, such as a lack of legal migration options), while, at the same time, this dangerous route, and the experiences associated with it, *causes* migrants to develop additional vulnerabilities, which, in turn, exacerbate the risk of irregular re-migration. The 'route causes' approach is not concerned with migration generally but with *irregular re*-migration in particular. As such, it relies on the vulnerability approach to establishing risk discussed earlier. The factors which cause irregularised migrants to 'choose' a dangerous migratory route are inherent or situational vulnerabilities already present at the time of migrating irregularly for the first time. Meanwhile, the additional vulnerabilities caused by the initial dangerous journey are the 'consequential vulnerabilities' referred to in Section 3.3.2 earlier. While the effects of these vulnerabilities manifest upon return to the country of origin, they are caused by the initial dangerous journey insofar as they are the result of (experiences encountered during) such journeys.

I conceive of the dangerous route in broad terms to include experiences of irregularity in countries of transit and destination (such as being undocumented while working), so that individuals who have migrated regularly and, for example, overstayed a visa and experienced the adverse effects of irregularity can be included in the analysis.[151] As mentioned already, the vulnerabilities identified in the trafficking context are likely to apply to irregularised migrants as well. This includes structural factors familiar from the trafficking context, such as 'poverty, inequality, discrimination and gender-based violence'.[152] However, to get a fuller picture of 'route causes' of irregular re-migration, it is necessary to look at the broader structural conditions under which irregular migration (whether designated as 'smuggling or 'trafficking') takes place. In this context, Ingram notes the relevance of a wide array of circumstances in the country of origin, including oppression, conflict and environmental degradation.[153] Importantly, he also highlights the coercive impact of the absence of a right to migrate regularly,[154] so that persons with few or no realistic opportunities to migrate regularly should be considered to be more vulnerable to irregular re-migration. To return to Mackenzie *et al.*'s taxonomy of vulnerability discussed earlier, the global visa regime may be regarded as an example of pathogenic vulnerability – a form of socio-political injustice.[155]

151 See Chapter 7.
152 Gallagher and McAdam (n 75).
153 David Ingram, *World Crisis and Underdevelopment: A Critical Theory of Poverty, Agency, and Coercion* (CUP 2018) 126–27.
154 ibid.
155 Henk Van Houtum, 'Human Blacklisting: The Global Apartheid of the EU's External Border Regime' (2010) 28(6) Environment and Planning D: Society and Space 957 <https://doi.org/10.1068/d1909>.

What is more, to understand 'route causes' of irregular re-migration, other inherent, situational and consequential vulnerability indicators not identified in trafficking-based asylum claims may be of relevance.[156] It is therefore important not to regard the factors identified in this chapter as a closed list but to pay attention to each applicant's individual situation.

What thinking on 'route causes' adds to these considerations is an understanding of how experiences during previous irregular migratory journeys add vulnerabilities which further constrain an individual's choices. At the same time, it must be kept in mind that, as in the trafficking context (see the earlier discussion on the applicants in *TDL* and *AS*), persons who do not possess any consequential vulnerabilities because they have not previously undertaken a dangerous migratory journey, but who do have inherent or situational vulnerabilities, may be at risk of irregular migration. However, a previous irregular migration experience, and the consequential vulnerabilities resulting from it, heighten the risk of irregular *re*-migration. Importantly, consequential vulnerabilities may exacerbate and determine one another. In fact, mental health issues can lead to stigmatisation,[157] and *vice versa*.[158] This is important because, while it must be acknowledged that some situational vulnerabilities, such as mental health issues or pregnancy, may be temporary, they can result in new (and more lasting) vulnerabilities, such as stigma. Thus, just like persons with a prior experience of being trafficked are even more vulnerable to re-trafficking, irregularised migrants will be vulnerable to re-migrating irregularly precisely because they have previously undertaken a dangerous migratory journey (including experiencing the adverse effects of being undocumented in countries of transit and destination).

In summary, like the 'border-induced displacement' approach, 'route causes' theory focuses on what happens after the initial displacement. However, while Lemberg-Pedersen focuses on the responsibility of states of destination for inducing displacement, my focus is on the experiences of irregularised migrants during such displacement and the effect these experiences have on inducing future migratory journeys. Thus, the 'route causes'

156 See Chapter 6, where additional vulnerabilities are identified: drug addiction, a long absence from the country of origin, having dependants, lack of financial assets and lack of specialist skills.

157 Particularly in developing countries, stigma surrounding mental health issues can lead to 'restrictions in the rights to work, education, marriage and participation in community or family functions'. See Emmanuel M Ngui and others, 'Mental Disorders, Health Inequalities and Ethics: A Global Perspective' (2010) 22(3) International Review of Psychiatry 235 <https://doi.org/10.3109/09540261.2010.485273>.

158 Christoph Lauber and Wulf Rössler, 'Stigma towards People with Mental Illness in Developing Countries in Asia' (2007) 19(2) International Review of Psychiatry 157 <https://doi.org/10.1080/09540260701278903>; Susanne Spittel, André Maier and Elke Kraus, 'Awareness Challenges of Mental Health Disorder and Dementia Facing Stigmatisation and Discrimination: A Systematic Literature Review from Sub-Sahara Africa' (2019) 9(2) Journal of Global Health 1 <https://doi.org/10.7189/jogh.09.020419>.

approach explains why irregular migration is a continuous phenomenon, that is, why a previous experience of migrating irregularly increases the likelihood of irregular re-migration after return to the country of origin. In this sense, the 'route causes' approach is similar to what Squire *et al.* refer to as 'intersecting drivers and conditions of flight' – conditions encountered during and created by dangerous journeys which result in onward migration.[159] In explaining that intersecting drivers and conditions of flight may mean that individuals on the move never reach safety, Squire *et al.* lament that these conditions are not being taken into account in the refugee status enquiry.[160] Yet it is possible to do precisely that when approaching 'route causes' of irregular re-migration as vulnerabilities which inform the future risk enquiry under refugee law.

At the same time, considering the complex nature of different vulnerabilities intersecting and exacerbating one another to result in a risk of irregular re-migration shows that although these vulnerabilities lead to socio-economic deprivation, attempts to address and counter this risk cannot be reduced to efforts to address socio-economic deprivation in itself. This finding has important implication for the state protection enquiry under refugee law, which is the subject of the next chapter.

3.5 Conclusion

This chapter has examined vulnerabilities as indicators for the future risk of re-trafficking. The vulnerability concept is part of the *trafficking* definition, and it is used in both UK and German case law to explain why trafficked persons were trafficked in the first place, why they will have difficulty reintegrating and making a livelihood in their country of origin and why they are, therefore, at risk of re-trafficking. This understanding chimes with the use of the vulnerability concept in anti-trafficking legislation, where 'vulnerability' is used to indicate socio-economic deprivation and lack of choice.

Examining the vulnerability concept through the lens of legal and feminist theory, however, allows for a more detailed and careful conceptualisation of vulnerabilities as reasons for exposure to harm. In the trafficking context, a range of vulnerabilities – inherent, situational and consequential – interact with and exacerbate one another. When considered holistically, these vulnerabilities show why a particular individual is at risk of exposure to harm. Indeed, the vulnerability analysis allows for an individualised assessment of risk, which, in the context of refugee law, is useful for creating a better understanding of how individual characteristics and experiences impact future risk. For example, consequential vulnerability shows why a person who has experienced past

159 Vicki Squire and others, *Reclaiming Migration: Voices from Europe's 'Migrant Crisis'* (Manchester UP 2021) 112–13.
160 ibid 121–22.

persecution is at risk of future harm. In addition, the vulnerability analysis shows that where vulnerabilities are likely to remain (or to emerge in the future), risk of harm need not be imminent.

Due to the individualised nature of the vulnerability analysis, it cannot be confined to certain groups, such as the group 'trafficked persons'. In fact, irregularised migrants, too, may possess the vulnerability indicators identified in the trafficking context, as well as additional vulnerabilities. These vulnerabilities constitute the 'route causes' of irregular migration – factors which cause irregularised migrants to 'choose' to undertake a dangerous migratory journey in the first place, as well as vulnerabilities caused by that journey, which, in combination, exacerbate the risk of irregular re-migration. Thus, just like trafficked persons are at risk of re-trafficking due to their intersecting vulnerabilities, irregular migrants may be said to be at risk of irregular re-migration. As such, irregularised migrants can meet the first of the three main elements of the *refugee* definition – the well-founded fear requirement.

References

AM and BM (Trafficked Women) Albania CG [2010] UKUT 80 (IAC)

Anderson A and others, 'Imminence in Refugee and Human Rights Law: A Misplaced Notion for International Protection' (2019) 68(1) International and Comparative Law Quarterly 111 <https://doi.org/10.1017/S0020589318000398>

Arsenijević J and others, '"I Feel Like I am Less Than Other People": Health-Related Vulnerabilities of Male Migrants Travelling Alone on Their Journey to Europe' (2018) 209 Social Science & Medicine 86 <https://doi.org/10.1016/j.socscimed.2018.05.038>

Andrijasevic R, *Migration, Agency and Citizenship in Sex Trafficking* (Palgrave Macmillan 2010)

AS (Albania) v SSHD [2024] UKUT (IAC) UI-2024-000611

AZ (Trafficked Women) Thailand CG [2010] UKUT 118 (IAC)

Bartram D, 'Forced Migration and "Rejected Alternatives": A Conceptual Refinement' (2015) 13(4) Journal of Immigrant & Refugee Studies 439 <https://doi.org/10.1080/15562948.2015.1030489>

Baumgärtel M, 'Facing the Challenge of Migratory Vulnerability in the European Court of Human Rights' (2020) 38(1) Netherlands Quarterly of Human Rights 12 <https://doi.org/10.1177/0924051919898127>

Bergelson V, 'Vulnerability, Exploitation and Choice' in Rita Haverkamp, Ester Herlin-Karnell and Claes Lernstedt (eds), *What is Wrong with Human Trafficking? Critical Perspectives on the Law* (Hart 2019)

Bivand Erdal M and Ceri Oeppen, 'Forced to Leave? The Discursive and Analytical Significance of Describing Migration as Forced and Voluntary' (2018) 44(6) Journal of Ethnic and Migration Studies 981 <https://doi.org/10.1080/1369183X.2017.1384149>

BT v SSHD [2019] UKUT (IAC) PA/07306/2017

Bundesgerichtshof, BGH 5 StR 154/14, 16.07.2014

Burson B, 'The Concept of Time and the Assessment of Risk in Refugee Status Determination' (Kaldor Centre Annual Conference, Sydney, 18 November 2016) <www.kaldorcentre.unsw.edu.au/sites/default/files/B_Burson_2016_Kaldor_Centre_Annual_Conference.pdf> accessed 8 November 2020

Cole A, 'All of Us are Vulnerable, But Some are More Vulnerable than Others: The Political Ambiguity of Vulnerability Studies, an Ambivalent Critique' (2016) 17(2) Critical Horizons 260 <https://doi.org/10.1080/14409917.2016.1153896>

Convention Relating to the Status of Refugees (adopted 28 July 1951, entered into force 22 April 1954) 189 UNTS 137 (Refugee Convention)

Council of Europe, 'Explanatory Report to the Council of Europe Convention on Action against Trafficking in Human Beings' (2005) <https://rm.coe.int/16800d3812> accessed 18 May 2021

De Haas H, 'The Determinants of International Migration: Conceptualising Policy, Origin and Destination Effects' (2011) IMI Working Paper No 32 <www.migrationinstitute.org/publications/wp-32-11> accessed 10 May 2021

De Haas H, 'Turning the Tide? Why Development Will Not Stop Migration' (2007) 38(5) Development and Change 819 <https://doi.org/10.1111/j.1467-7660.2007.00435.x>

Directive (EU) 2024/1346 of the European Parliament and of the Council of 14 May 2024 Laying Down Standards for the Reception of Applicants for International Protection [2024] OJ L 2024/134 (Reception Conditions Directive)

Directive 2011/36/EU of the European Parliament and of the Council of 5 April 2011 on Preventing and Combating Trafficking in Human Beings and Protecting its Victims, and Replacing Council Framework Decision 2002/629/JHA [2011] OJ L 101/1 (Trafficking Directive)

DK v SSHD [2024] UKUT (IAC) UI-2023-003379

ES (s82 NIA 2002, Negative NRM) [2018] UKUT 335 (IAC)

Ferolla Vallandro do Valle M, 'Fleeing Deprivation: Deducing *Non-Refoulement* Obligations from Economic, Social and Cultural Rights' (2024) 36(4) International Journal of Refugee Law 353 <https://doi.org/10.1093/ijrl/eeae036>

Fineman AM, 'Equality, Autonomy, and the Vulnerable Subject in Law and Politics' in Martha Albertson Fineman and Anna Grear (eds), *Vulnerability: Reflections on a New Ethical Foundation for Law and Politics* (Routledge 2016)

Fineman AM, 'The Vulnerable Subject: Anchoring Equality in the Human Condition' (2008) 20(1) Yale Journal of Law and Feminism 9

Foster M, *International Refugee Law and Socio-Economic Rights: Refuge from Deprivation* (CUP 2007)

Foster M and others, '"Time" in Refugee Status Determination in Australia and the United Kingdom: A Clear and Present Danger from Armed Conflict?' (2022) 34(2) International Journal of Refugee Law 163 <https://doi.org/10.1093/ijrl/eeac033>

FT v SSHD [2022] UKUT (IAC) PA/03526/2020

Gallagher AT and Marika McAdam, *Issue Paper: Abuse of a Position of Vulnerability and other "Means" within the Definition of Trafficking in Persons* (UNODC 2013) <www.unodc.org/documents/human-trafficking/2012/UNODC_2012_Issue_Paper_-_Abuse_of_a_Position_of_Vulnerability.pdf> accessed 5 January 2021

Gesetz zu dem Übereinkommen des Europarats vom 16. Mai 2005 zur Bekämpfung des Menschenhandels, 17 October 2012 (BGBl. II, Nr. 31, S. 1089)

Grahl-Madsen A, *The Status of Refugees in International Law*, vol I (A W Sijthoff 1966)

Grundler M, '"Route Causes" and Consequences of Irregular (Re-)Migration: Vulnerability as an Indicator of Future Risk in Refugee Law' (2024) 20(1) International Journal of Law in Context 35 <https://doi.org/10.1017/S1744552323000344>

Hathaway JC and Michelle Foster, *The Law of Refugee Status* (2nd edn, CUP 2014)

HC & RC (Trafficked Women) China v SSHD CG [2009] UKAIT 00027

HC v SSHD [2021] UKUT (IAC) PA/05060/2019

HD (Trafficked Women) Nigeria CG [2016] UKUT 00454 (IAC)

HD v SSHD [2022] UKUT (IAC) PA/10137/2019

Hudson B, 'Asylum Marginalisation Renewed: "Vulnerability Backsliding" at the European Court of Human Rights' (2024) 20(1) International Journal of Law in Context 16 <https://doi.org/10.1017/S1744552323000332>

Hudson B, 'Migration in the Mediterranean: Exposing the Limits of Vulnerability at the European Court of Human Rights' (2018) 4 Maritime Safety and Security Law Journal 26

Ingram D, *World Crisis and Underdevelopment: A Critical Theory of Poverty, Agency, and Coercion* (CUP 2018)

IOM, 'Towards an Integrated Approach to Reintegration in the Context of Return' (2017) <www.iom.int/sites/g/files/tmzbdl486/files/our_work/DMM/AVRR/Towards-an-Integrated-Approach-to-Reintegration.pdf> accessed 20 October 2024

Ippolito F, *Understanding Vulnerability in International Human Rights Law* (Editorial Scientifica 2020)

Ippolito F and Sara Iglesias Sánchez, 'Introduction' in Francesca Ippolito and Sara Iglesias Sánchez (eds), *Protecting Vulnerable Groups: The European Human Rights Framework* (Hart 2015)

IR v SSHD [2013] UKUT (IAC) IA178072010

JA v SSHD [2020] UKUT (IAC) PA/13132/2018

JFK v SSHD [2018] UKUT (IAC) PA/06854/2016

Kleist N, 'Disrupted Migration Projects: The Moral Economy of Involuntary Return to Ghana from Libya' (2017) 87(2) Africa 322 <https://doi.org/10.1017/S000197201600098X>

Landau LB, 'A Chronotope of Containment Development: Europe's Migrant Crisis and Africa's Reterritorialisation' (2019) 51(1) Antipode 169 <https://doi.org/10.1111/anti.12420>

Lauber C and Wulf Rössler, 'Stigma Towards People with Mental Illness in Developing Countries in Asia' (2007) 19(2) International Review of Psychiatry 157 <https://doi.org/10.1080/09540260701278903>

Lee ES, 'A Theory of Migration' (1966) 3(1) Demography 47

Lemberg-Pedersen M, 'Forcing Flows of Migrants: European Externalization and Border-Induced Displacement' in Dorte Jagetic Andersen, Martin Klatt and Marie Sandberg (eds), *The Border Multiple: The Practicing of Borders between Public Policy and Everyday Life in a Re-Scaling Europe* (Routledge 2012)

Mackenzie C, Wendy Rogers and Susan Dodds, 'Introduction: What Is Vulnerability, and Why Does It Matter for Moral Theory?' in Catriona Mackenzie, Wendy Rogers and Susan Dodds (eds), *Vulnerability: New Essays in Ethics and Feminist Philosophy* (OUP 2014)

Magugliani N, 'Trafficked Adult Males as (Un)Gendered Protection Seekers: Between Presumption of Invulnerability and Exclusion from Membership of a Particular Social Group' (2022) 34 (3–4) International Journal of Refugee Law 353 <https://doi.org/10.1093/ijrl/eeac030>

MHK v SSHD [2023] UKUT (IAC) UI-2022-005774

MP (Trafficking – Sufficiency of Protection) Romania [2005] UKIAT 00086

Nationality and Borders Act 2022

Ngui EM and others, 'Mental Disorders, Health Inequalities and Ethics: A Global Perspective' (2010) 22(3) International Review of Psychiatry 235 <https://doi.org/10.3109/09540261.2010.485273>

Ottonelli V and Tiziana Torresi, 'When is Migration Voluntary?' (2013) 47(4) The International Migration Review 783 <https://doi.org/10.1111/imre.12048>

Peroni L and Alexandra Timmer, 'Vulnerable Groups: The Promise of an Emerging Concept in European Human Rights Convention Law' (2013) 11(4) International Journal of Constitutional Law 1056 <https://doi.org/10.1093/icon/mot042>

Plambech S, 'Back From "The Other Side": The Post-Deportee Life of Nigerian Migrant Sex Workers' in Shahram Khosravi (ed), *After Deportation: Ethnographic Perspectives* (Palgrave Macmillan 2018)
Regulation (EU) 2024/1347 of the European Parliament and of the Council of 14 May 2024 on Standards for the Qualification of Third-Country Nationals or Stateless Persons as Beneficiaries of International Protection, for a Uniform Status for Refugees or for Persons Eligible for Subsidiary Protection and for the Content of the Protection Granted, Amending Council Directive 2003/109/EC and Repealing Directive 2011/95/EU of the European Parliament and of the Council [2024] OJ L 2024/1347 (Qualification Regulation)
Richtlinie 2011/36/EU des Europäischen Parlaments und des Rates vom 5. April 2011 zur Verhütung und Bekämpfung des Menschenhandels und zum Schutz seiner Opfer sowie zur Ersetzung des Rahmenbeschlusses 2002/629/JI des Rates, OJ L 101 (Menschenhandelsrichtlinie)
Ringold S, 'Refugee Mental Health' (2005) 294(5) The Journal of the American Medical Association 646 <https://doi.org/10.1001/jama.294.5.646>
SB (PSG - Protection Regulations – Reg 6) Moldova CG [2008] UKAIT 00002
Schultz J, *The Internal Protection Alternative in Refugee Law: Treaty Basis and Scope of Application under the 1951 Convention Relating to the Status of Refugees and Its 1967 Protocol* (Brill Nijhoff 2019)
Schuster L and Nassim Majidi, 'Deportation Stigma and Re-migration' (2015) 41(4) Journal of Ethnic and Migration Studies 635 <https://doi.org/10.1080/1369183X.2014.957174>
Schuster L and Nassim Majidi, 'What Happens Post-Deportation? The Experience of Deported Afghans' (2013) 1(2) Migration Studies 221 <https://doi.org/10.1093/migration/mns011>
Serughetti G, 'Smuggled or Trafficked? Refugee or Job Seeker? Deconstructing Rigid Classifications by Rethinking Women's Vulnerability' (2018) 11 Anti-Trafficking Review 16 <https://doi.org/10.14197/atr.201218112>
Spittel S, André Maier and Elke Kraus, 'Awareness Challenges of Mental Health Disorder and Dementia Facing Stigmatisation and Discrimination: A Systematic Literature Review from Sub-Sahara Africa' (2019) 9(2) Journal of Global Health 1 <https://doi.org/10.7189/jogh.09.020419>
Squire V and others, *Reclaiming Migration: Voices from Europe's 'Migrant Crisis'* (Manchester UP 2021)
SSHD v LVC [2021] UKUT (IAC) PA/06804/2019
Stahlmann F, 'Erfahrungen und Perspektiven Abgeschobener Afghanen im Kontext Aktueller Politischer und Wirtschaftlicher Entwicklungen Afghanistans' (*Diakonie Deutschland, Brot für die Welt, Diakonie Hessen*, June 2021) <www.fluechtlingsrat-mv.de/wp-content/uploads/2021/06/AFG_Monitoring-Studie_FINAL.pdf> accessed 28 August 2024
Strafgesetzbuch (StGB) 13 November 1998 (BGBl. I S. 3322) (Criminal Code)
TAN v SSHD [2016] UKUT (IAC) AA/05644/2014
TD and AD (Trafficked Women) CG [2016] UKUT 92
TDL v SSHD [2021] UKUT (IAC) PA/00358/2020
Timmer A, 'A Quiet Revolution: Vulnerability in the European Court of Human Rights' in Martha Albertson Fineman and Anna Grear (eds), *Vulnerability: Reflections on a New Ethical Foundation for Law and Politics* (Routledge 2016)
Turnbull S, 'Starting Again: Life After Deportation from the UK' in Shahram Khosravi (ed), *After Deportation: Ethnographic Perspectives* (Palgrave Macmillan 2018)
Turner L, 'The Politics of Labeling Refugee Men as "Vulnerable"' (2021) 28(1) Social Politics: International Studies in Gender, State & Society 1 <https://doi.org/10.1093/sp/jxz033>

TVD v SSHD [2022] UKUT (IAC) PA/00252/2020
Tyldum G, 'Limitation in Research on Human Trafficking' (2010) 48(5) International Migration 1 <https://doi.org/10.1111/j.1468-2435.2009.00597.x>
UNHCR, 'Guidelines on International Protection: "Internal Flight or Relocation Alternative" within the Context of Article 1A(2) of the 1951 Convention and/or 1967 Protocol relating to the Status of Refugees' (23 July 2003) HCR/GIP/03/04
UNHCR, 'Handbook on Procedures and Criteria for Determining Refugee Status and Guidelines on International Protection Under the 1951 Convention and the 1967 Protocol Relating to the Status of Refugees' HCR/1P/4/ENG/REV.4 (1979, reissued 2019) (UNHCR Handbook)
UNHCR, 'UNHCR Resettlement Handbook' (2011) <www.refworld.org/policy/opguidance/unhcr/2011/en/97558> accessed 28 October 2024
Van Hear N, Oliver Bakewell and Katy Long, 'Push-Pull Plus: Reconsidering the Drivers of Migration' (2018) 44(6) Journal of Ethnic and Migration Studies 927 <https://doi.org/10.1080/1369183X.2017.1384135>
Van Houtum H, 'Human Blacklisting: The Global Apartheid of the EU's External Border Regime' (2010) 28(6) Environment and Planning D: Society and Space 957 <https://doi.org/10.1068/d1909>
VG Augsburg, Au 7 K 12.30184, 18.09.2012
VG Göttingen, 3 A 135/21, 03.04.2024
VG Hannover, 10 A 6353/18, 09.09.2021
VG Köln, 2 K 5595/18.A, 28.05.2019
VG Magdeburg, 6 A 40/19, 28.01.2020
VG München, M 13 K 21.30776, 21.06.2022
VG Sigmaringen, A 7 K 4913-20, 15.02.2023
VG Stuttgart, A 1 K 8819/18, 5770443, 16.11.2020
VG Stuttgart, A 7 K 1405/12, 16.05.2014
VG Wiesbaden, 3 K 1465/09.WI.A, 14.03.2011
VG Würzburg, W 2 K 14.30213, 17.11.2015
VG Würzburg, W 8 K 04.30919, 19.09.2005
VG Würzburg, W 10 K 19.50275, 26.01.2019
Virokannas E, Suvi Liuski and Marjo Kuronen, 'The Contested Concept of Vulnerability – a Literature Review' (2020) 23(2) European Journal of Social Work 327 <https://doi.org/10.1080/13691457.2018.1508001>
Vogeler L, *Rechtliche Prävention von Menschenhandel zum Zweck der sexuellen Ausbeutung: Ein Rechtsvergleich unter besonderer Berücksichtigung der Prostitutionspolitiken Deutschlands und Schwedens* (Lit Verlag 2018)
Whewell T, 'We Failed to Reach Europe – Now Our Families Disown Us' *BBC World Service* (14 November 2019) <www.bbc.co.uk/news/stories-50391297> accessed 1 May 2020

4 Persecutory Harm and Failure of State Protection

Cumulative and Sequential Harms

4.1 Introduction

The *refugee* definition requires a well-founded fear *of being persecuted* for reasons of Refugee Convention grounds. Having established in the previous chapter that there is such a thing as a well-founded fear of irregular re-migration, this chapter considers whether the harm experienced during dangerous journeys amounts to persecution for the purpose of refugee law. While Chapter 3 challenged, and refuted, the first assumption identified in Chapter 2 as an obstacle to arguing that smuggled persons (and irregularised migrants more broadly) are in need of protection – the claim that they move voluntarily – this chapter not only challenges the second assumption – that smuggled persons do not experience harm – but also argues that this harm amounts to persecution.[1]

To this end, the chapter continues to rely on UK and German trafficking-based asylum claims and to draw analogies between experiences of trafficked persons and irregularised migrants. UK and German courts' approach to the persecution enquiry in the trafficking context was summed up neatly by the UK Upper Tribunal (UT) in *HD*: 'It is not generally in dispute that a victim of trafficking . . . will have sustained serious harm',[2] so that 'the key issues . . . are the availability of sufficiency of protection and the option of safe/reasonable internal relocation'.[3] In fact, the case law suggests that, in the absence of state protection, re-trafficking will amount to persecution. This is also the approach taken in a number of other jurisdictions and in (academic) commentary.[4] As such, the assumption that trafficking *per se*

1 Parts of the analysis in this chapter have appeared in Maja Grundler, 'The Locus of Persecution Reconsidered: Risk of Re-Trafficking, Cumulative Harm and Failure of State Protection' (2023) 35(4) International Journal of Refugee Law 441 <https://doi.org/10.1093/ijrl/eeae016>.

2 *HD (Trafficked Women) Nigeria CG* [2016] UKUT 00454 (IAC) [67].

3 ibid [66].

4 Mathilde Crépin, *Persecution, International Refugee Law and Refugees: A Feminist Approach* (Routledge 2020) 134; see also Kaori Saito, 'International Protection for Trafficked Persons

DOI: 10.4324/9781032664644-4

is harmful (and perhaps, by extension, the idea that smuggling is not) has made its way into refugee law jurisprudence. Yet as explained in Chapter 2, the *trafficking* definition describes the intentions and actions of traffickers, rather than the experiences of 'victims', so that it is not at all clear that trafficking *necessarily* entails serious harm.

First and foremost, *trafficking* describes the process of recruiting and transporting a person. None of the actions described in the *trafficking* definition can be said to constitute harm. However, this process may be achieved through certain means which do imply harm – in particular, 'use of force' comes to mind. Nevertheless, this is only one of a number of possible means. Indeed, the sample of case laws analysed for this book suggests that the means most often employed are 'deception' and 'abuse of a position of vulnerability', neither of which implies harming the trafficked person. This, of course, leaves the purpose element of the definition, and it is here that harm, such as sexual exploitation or forced labour, is found. However, as explained in Chapter 2, since the *trafficking* definition is met where intent of exploitation can be shown, no exploitation needs to have, in fact, occurred. Thus, if a trafficked person escapes before any exploitation takes place, his or her entire experience may consist of being recruited and transported by deception. It is doubtful whether this constitutes serious harm, not to mention persecution for the purpose of refugee law. Therefore, transplanting the concept of 'trafficking' into the refugee law context, where one of the main questions is whether there is a future risk of persecution, is unprincipled, because a risk of re-trafficking cannot be assumed to be synonymous with a risk of persecution.

The preceding considerations are not intended to deny that many trafficked persons *do* experience horrific types of harm, are at risk of experiencing such harm again in the future and are very much in need of refugee protection. Indeed, it is important to keep in mind that the trafficking process, if uninterrupted, will result in exploitation and therefore entail serious harm. However, for the purposes of refugee law, it is essential to understand what harm exactly is experienced during trafficking, and at what point in the trafficking process, as this will inform the state protection enquiry. Thus, the preceding discussion serves to question UK and German courts' approach in designating re-trafficking as the relevant harm for the purpose of the persecution enquiry in refugee law. Instead, the focus should be on types of harm actually experienced in the trafficking context, with past experiences of harm serving as an indicator for future risk.[5] Whereas focusing on categories such as 'trafficked'

---

and Those Who Fear Being Trafficked' (2007) UNHCR Research Paper No 149, 9 <www.unhcr.org/sites/default/files/legacy-pdf/476652742.pdf> accessed 2 February 2019.

5 James C Hathaway and Michelle Foster, *The Law of Refugee Status* (2nd edn, CUP 2014) 165; see also Atle Grahl-Madsen, *The Status of Refugees in International Law*, vol I (A W Sijthoff 1966) 176–77; Regulation (EU) 2024/1347 of the European Parliament and of the Council of 14 May 2024 on Standards for the Qualification of Third-Country Nationals or Stateless Persons as Beneficiaries of International Protection, for a Uniform Status for Refugees or for

and 'smuggled' risks reproducing the underlying assumptions about whether or not the individual in question will experience harm, looking at applicants' actual experiences as evidence of past persecution, which informs future risk, allows assessing protection needs irrespective of (criminal law) categories. Doing this is essential when seeking to apply the reasoning from the trafficking context to the situation of irregularised migrants.

Thus, although this chapter is guided by the relevant case law, I will approach the courts' reasoning critically. Questioning the courts' approach to designating re-trafficking as 'harm' raises questions regarding the examination of what the UT in *HD* has termed the 'key issue' in the persecution enquiry: the availability of state protection. The courts' current approach allows us to think of re-trafficking – the persecutory harm – as at least partially taking place in the country of origin, so that that country can potentially offer protection against this while the trafficked person remains in its territory. However, as Dorevitch and Foster note, in the trafficking context, 'harm is inflicted by multiple actors across a temporal and geographical continuum'.[6] The same is true for harm experienced during irregular migration generally. Indeed, trafficked persons and irregularised migrants are likely to experience harm, mainly outside the country of origin. Thus, focusing on the actual harm experienced by trafficked persons and irregularised migrants raises the question of how a state can protect against harm which takes place outside its territory.

This is one of the main questions this chapter seeks to address. More broadly, it will answer the question whether (fear of future) harm experienced as a result of irregular migration can form the basis of an asylum claim. Harm experienced as a result of irregular migration encompasses experiences in the country of origin, as well as experiences during a renewed dangerous journey.

Before outlining the contents of this chapter, I will briefly mention some limitations to its scope. Although the so-called internal protection alternative (IPA) does play a role in the case law discussed in what follows, it is not within the scope of this chapter to discuss this concept in detail. While generally controversial,[7] the IPA is not a concept unique to the trafficking/irregular re-migration context, so that it suffices to say here that, as shown in the previous chapter, an individual's vulnerabilities may preclude reintegration in the entire country of origin and therefore an IPA. Similarly, the chapter cannot

---

Persons Eligible for Subsidiary Protection and for the Content of the Protection Granted, Amending Council Directive 2003/109/EC and Repealing Directive 2011/95/EU of the European Parliament and of the Council [2024] OJ L 2024/1347 (Qualification Regulation) art 4(4).

6 Anna Dorevitch and Michelle Foster, 'Obstacles on the Road to Protection: Assessing the Treatment of Sex-Trafficking Victims under Australia's Migration and Refugee Law' (2008) 9(1) Melbourne Journal of International Law 140.

7 Jessica Schultz, *The Internal Protection Alternative in Refugee Law: Treaty Basis and Scope of Application under the 1951 Convention Relating to the Status of Refugees and Its 1967 Protocol* (Brill Nijhoff 2019) 2–8.

address other issues frequently raised in the context of discussing (state) protection against persecution, such as the use of diplomatic assurances to refuse otherwise strong claims to international protection[8] or reliance on the 'safe third country' concept.[9]

Thus, the chapter discusses the concept of persecution, and in particular its state protection element, in the context of trafficking-based asylum claims and the doctrinal difficulties these claims raise. Section 2 briefly considers the meaning of the persecution concept, settling on conceiving of *persecution* as a combination of serious harm and failure on the part of the country of origin to protect against it. The section also discusses the appropriate standard of such protection. Next, the section raises the issue of the location where harm is feared during irregular re-migration. It illustrates that courts in the trafficking context have, at times, struggled to understand how harm experienced outside the country relates to future risk on return to that country. The fact that this issue is ignored in trafficking-based asylum claim raises difficult doctrinal issues, in particular regarding the question of how the state of origin can be expected to protect against harm taking place outside its territory. Against this background, the section analyses how UK and German case law approaches harm and state protection in the trafficking context, distinguishing between the 'law enforcement' and the 'reception and reintegration' approaches to state protection, while showing that neither approach details what effective protection against re-trafficking looks like. The section argues that it is necessary to go beyond conceptualisations of harm and protection as presented in the case law and to investigate, in particular, the actual types of harm experienced by trafficked persons and irregularised migrants, their sequence, as well as the relationship between state protection taking place within the country of origin and harm taking place largely outside its territory.

This is what Section 3 seeks to do. First, it considers the types of harm trafficked persons and irregularised migrants experience during the migratory journey, showing that these, indeed, amount to serious harm. The section then explores whether, since the relevant harm takes place outside the country of origin, relying on external, rather than internal, state protection would be more appropriate. The section thus considers the role of diplomatic protection and consular assistance, concluding that neither of these constitutes effective protection in the irregular migration context. The section shows that one basic

8 Gregor Noll, 'Diplomatic Assurances and the Silence of Human Rights Law' (2006) 7(1) Melbourne Journal of International Law 104; UNHCR, 'UNHCR Note on Diplomatic Assurances and International Refugee Protection' (2006) <www.refworld.org/policy/legalguidance/unhcr/2006/en/40015> accessed 13 May 2021; Elspeth Guild, 'Asymmetrical Sovereignty and the Refugee: Diplomatic Assurances and the Failure of Due Process, *Agiza v. Sweden* and *Alzery v. Sweden*' in James C Simeon (ed), *Critical Issues in International Refugee Law* (CUP 2010) 128.

9 Mariagiulia Giuffré, *The Readmission of Asylum Seekers under International Law* (Hart Publishing 2020).

requirement for state protection is that the state has jurisdiction over the person it is meant to protect. Next, the section explores how harm taking place outside the country of origin, and the state protection being provided within that country, can be reconciled with the requirement that the state of origin must have jurisdiction over the individual in question. The section draws on the cumulative nature of persecution to argue that that states' failure to protect against initial harm while an individual is still within its territory leads to that individual experiencing additional harm outside the country of origin. The section returns to the 'reception and reintegration' approach to state protection but argues that such an approach has to take the applicant's individual vulnerabilities into account. In the absence of state protection addressing these vulnerabilities, the socio-economic deprivation they bring about and the harm subsequently experienced outside the country of origin, cumulatively, amount to persecution.

The chapter concludes by finding that irregularised migrants can meet not only the well-founded fear element of the *refugee* definition but also the definition's persecution element.

4.2 Persecution and State Protection: State Practice and Doctrinal Difficulties

4.2.1 The Concept of Persecution and the Role of State Protection

There is no internationally accepted definition of the concept of *persecution* used in the Refugee Convention, and indeed, the lack of a definition allows the Convention to respond to new and emerging refugee situations.[10] The concept of persecution has sparked debates as to its meaning and scope, its relationship to human rights law, as well as to other components of the Refugee Convention's *refugee* definition.[11] At the same time, there is some

10 Grahl-Madsen (n 5) 193; BS Chimni, *International Refugee Law: A Reader* (Sage 2000) 3–4; Hathaway and Foster (n 5) 182; Vincent Chetail, 'Are Refugee Rights Human Rights? An Unorthodox Questioning of the Relations between Refugee Law and Human Rights Law' in Ruth Rubio-Marín (ed), *Human Rights and Immigration* (OUP 2014) 26.

11 For example: Grahl-Madsen (n 5) 193; Chimni (n 10) 3–4; Hathaway and Foster (n 5) 182; Chetail (n 10) 26; Matthew Price, 'Persecution Complex: Justifying Asylum Law's Preference for Persecuted People' (2006) 47 Harvard International Law Journal 413; Hugo Storey, 'What Constitutes Persecution? Towards a Working Definition' (2014) 26(2) International Journal of Refugee Law 272 <https://doi.org/10.1093/ijrl/eeu017>; Jaakko Kuosmanen, 'What's So Special about Persecution?' (2014) 17 Ethical Theory and Moral Practice 129 <https://doi.org/10.1007/s10677-013-9425-4>; James C Hathaway and Hugo Storey, 'What Is the Meaning of State Protection in Refugee Law? A Debate' (2016) 28(3) International Journal of Refugee Law 480 <https://doi.org/10.1093/ijrl/eew053>; Crépin (n 4); Pia Zambelli, 'Knowing Persecution When We See It: Non-State Actors and the Measure of State Protection' (2020) 32(1) International Journal of Refugee Law 28 <https://doi.org/10.1093/ijrl/eeaa001>; Guy S Goodwin-Gill and Jane McAdam, *The Refugee in International Law* (4th edn, OUP 2021); Daniel Wilsher, 'Between Martyrdom and Silence: Dissent, Duress, and Persecution as the Suppression of Human Rights under the Refugee Convention' (2021)

agreement as to the main elements of 'persecution'. For example, Hathaway and Foster suggest that it amounts to a 'sustained and systemic denial of basic human rights demonstrative of a failure of state protection.'[12] Goodwin-Gill and McAdam, meanwhile, conceptualise it as measures taken against individuals with Convention ground–related characteristics which harm their human rights,[13] while stating that 'fear of persecution and lack of protection are . . . interrelated elements'.[14] Thus, persecution entails (serious) harm, whose severity can be measured with reference to human rights standards, and implies a failure of (state) protection against such harm.

Indeed, 'harm is at the core of persecution',[15] and such harm has to reach a certain threshold of severity.[16] Relevant types of harm include physical harms, such as 'beatings, sexual abuse, and mutilation'; deprivation of liberty and privacy, including 'arrests, interrogations, imprisonment, and other means of detention'; as well as slavery, economic harms and psychological harm.[17] A similar conceptualisation of harm can be found in the EU Qualification Regulation, which states that an 'act of persecution' must be 'sufficiently serious by its nature or repetition as to constitute a severe violation of basic human rights'.[18] In order to illustrate the concept of persecution, the Regulation refers to a number of articles in the European Convention on Human Rights (ECHR), including Article 2, on the right to life; Article 3, prohibiting torture and inhuman or degrading treatment; and Article 4, on freedom from slavery. It also gives a number of additional examples, such as 'acts of physical or mental violence, including acts of sexual violence'.[19] In addition, persecution can include 'an accumulation of various measures' which, individually, would not reach the threshold of persecutory harm but cumulatively are 'sufficiently severe' to warrant a finding of persecution.[20]

33(1) International Journal of Refugee Law 28 <https://doi.org/10.1093/ijrl/eeab025>; Ciara Smyth, 'The Human Rights Approach to "Persecution" and Its Child Rights Discontents' (2021) 33(2) International Journal of Refugee Law 238 <https://doi.org/10.1093/ijrl/eeab039>.

12 Hathaway and Foster (n 5) 185.

13 Goodwin-Gill and McAdam (n 11) 156.

14 ibid 70.

15 Scott Rempell, 'Defining Persecution' (2013) 1 Utah Law Review 283, 292; Goodwin-Gill and McAdam (n 11) 78.

16 Jean-Yves Carlier, 'The Geneva Refugee Definition and the "Theory of the Three Scales"' in Frances Nicholson and Patrick Twomey (eds), *Refugee Rights and Realities: Evolving International Concepts and Regimes* (CUP 1999) 49–50; Rempell (n 15) 310.

17 Rempell (n 15) 293–97.

18 Qualification Regulation (n 5) art 9(1)(a). For a critical analysis of this provision, see Steve Peers and others (eds), *EU Immigration and Asylum Law (Text and Commentary): Second Revised Edition: Volume 3: EU Asylum Law* (Brill 2015) 105–10.

19 Qualification Regulation (n 5) art 9(2)(a).

20 ibid art 9(1)(b). See also Rebecca Dowd, 'Dissecting Discrimination in Refugee Law: An Analysis of its Meaning and Its Cumulative Effect' (2011) 23(1) International Journal of Refugee Law 28 <https://doi.org/10.1093/ijrl/eeq043>.

The idea that persecution entails a failure of state protection is also endorsed in the Qualification Regulation. It lists 'the State' or 'stable, established non-State authorities . . . which control the State or a substantial part of the territory of the State' as 'actors of protection', adding that such actors must be 'willing and able' to offer protection.[21] What exactly constitutes 'protection' in refugee law continues to be debated,[22] both in terms of the scope and content of protection offered in countries of asylum and in terms of protection in the country of origin. With regard to the latter, Lehmann has dedicated an entire volume to unpacking the term 'protection' in EU asylum law.[23] It is not within the scope of this chapter to examine the notion of protection generally in detail; rather, the focus will be on the apparent disconnect between conceptualising state protection as internal protection by the country of origin[24] and harm during re-trafficking largely taking place outside that country. While it has been argued that the question of availability of state protection in the country of origin is a matter best discussed in the context of the 'well-founded fear' enquiry,[25] for the purpose of this chapter, and based on the approach taken in the case law, I will work from the premise that state protection by the country of origin is indeed a relevant element of the persecution enquiry.

Against this background, a main focus of this chapter will be the standard of state protection and the related question of how protection plays out in practice. The Qualification Regulation requires that protection 'must be *effective* and of a non-temporary nature'.[26] Although the 'effectiveness' of protection

21 Qualification Regulation (n 5) art 7(1). For a critical analysis of the idea that non-state entities can be actors of protection, see Maria O'Sullivan, 'Acting the Part: Can Non-State Entities Provide Protection Under International Refugee Law?' (2012) 24(1) International Journal of Refugee Law 85 <https://doi.org/10.1093/ijrl/ees001>.

22 Dallal Stevens, 'What Do We Mean by Protection' (2013) 20 International Journal on Minority & Group Rights 233 <http://doi.org/10.1163/15718115-02002005>.

23 Julian M Lehmann, *'Protection' in European Union Asylum Law: International and European Law Requirements for Assessing Available Protection as a Criterion for Refugee and Subsidiary Status* (Brill 2020).

24 David James Cantor, 'Defining Refugees: Persecution, Surrogacy and the Human Rights Paradigm' in Bruce Burson and David James Cantor (eds), *Human Rights and the Refugee Definition: Comparative Legal Practice and Theory* (Brill 2016) 354.

25 '[E]vidence of the lack of protection on either the external or internal level may create a presumption as to the likelihood of persecution and the well-foundedness of the fear.' See Goodwin-Gill and McAdam (n 11) 70. 'A fear of persecution is well-founded because the state has failed to ensure a minimum level of security to some of its citizens or inhabitants.' See Schultz (n 7) 123; see also Cantor (n 24) 316. See further Walter Kälin, 'Non-State Agents of Persecution and the Inability of the State to Protect' (2001) 15 Georgetown Immigration Law Journal 415, 428. The CJEU also seems to support this reasoning, stating that a well-founded fear of being persecuted for Convention reasons 'will indicate that the third country does not protect its national against acts of persecution'. See C-175/08, C-176/08, C-178/08 and C-179/08 *Abdulla and Others* [2010] ECLI:EU:C:2010:105, para 58.

26 Qualification Regulation (n 5) art 7(2); emphasis added.

is not further defined in the Regulation, the United Nations High Commissioner for Refugees (UNHCR), in using an almost-identical phrase to describe the required standard of protection, elaborates that protection 'must be provided by an organised and stable authority exercising full control over the territory and population in question'.[27] While the term 'effective protection' has been criticised as shifting meaning, depending on the context in which it is employed,[28] for the purpose of this chapter, I will use it to distinguish measures which, in fact, reduce risk of re-trafficking or irregular re-migration, as opposed to measures which are seen to address the problem of trafficking and smuggling but which, from a 'victim's' perspective, have no actual impact. In this context, it is worth noting that the Qualification Regulation goes on to state that

> protection shall be considered to be provided where [actors of protection] *take reasonable steps* to prevent persecution or the suffering of serious harm, inter alia, by operating an effective legal system for the detection, prosecution and punishment of acts constituting persecution or serious harm, and when the applicant has access to that protection.[29]

Thus, in a single paragraph, the Regulation appears to set two different standards of protection: an effectiveness standard on the one hand and, on the other, a standard that has been referred to as the 'due diligence' test[30] or the 'sufficiency of protection' test.[31] Lehmann argues that this apparent discrepancy can be reconciled by considering that 'the legal obligations of the authorities in the state of nationality are only of evidentiary value, rather than circumscribing what is or is not "effective" in the individual case'.[32] In this context, it is worth looking at the UNHCR Trafficking Guidelines, which state:

> The mere existence of a law prohibiting trafficking in persons will not of itself be sufficient to exclude the possibility of persecution. If the law exists but is not effectively implemented, or if administrative mechanisms are in place to provide protection and assistance to victims, but the individual concerned is unable to gain access to such mechanisms, the State

27 UNHCR, 'Handbook on Procedures and Criteria for Determining Refugee Status and Guidelines on International Protection under the 1951 Convention and the 1967 Protocol Relating to the Status of Refugees' HCR/1P/4/ENG/REV.4 (1979, reissued 2019) (UNHCR Handbook) para 17.

28 Stevens (n 22) 249.

29 Qualification Regulation (n 5) art 7(2); emphasis added.

30 Kay Hailbronner and Daniel Thym (eds), *EU Immigration and Asylum Law: A Commentary* (2nd edn, Beck, Hart, Nomos 2016) 1156.

31 Stevens (n 22) 253; cf *Horvath v SSHD* [2000] UKHL 37, [2000] Imm AR 552.

32 Lehmann (n 23) 105.

may be deemed unable to extend protection to the victim, or potential victim, of trafficking.[33]

As such, *effective protection* is protection which is, in fact, available, that is, accessible and exercisable, both in law and in practice.[34] In this assessment, 'the laws and regulations of the country of origin ***and the manner in which they are applied***' must be taken into account.[35] In short, there must be 'access to such protection'.[36] Markard makes a similar point with reference to the text of the Refugee Convention's *refugee* definition. She argues that since Article 1A(2) speaks of the country of nationality's protection, rather than that country's *efforts* to provide protection, and of the refugee's inability to avail herself of such protection, the protection in question must be *de facto* available.[37]

Since Germany applies the Qualification Regulation, state protection against harm must, indeed, be effective ('*wirksam*').[38] The UK, however, does not require protection to be effective. Instead, it applies the 'reasonableness' standard while also requiring that asylum seekers must be 'able to access the protection'.[39] Yet despite the fact that the 'due diligence' standard for protection emerged from – and continues to be applied in – UK jurisprudence,[40] as explained later, at least in the trafficking context, UK courts have come to question this standard. The same development is evident in German jurisprudence, and indeed, the effectiveness standard has been endorsed in academic commentary.[41]

As mentioned earlier, the location of the harm feared by trafficked persons – and by irregularised migrants – complicates the state protection and effectiveness enquiry. In the next subsection, I therefore begin to explore

33 UNHCR, 'Guidelines on International Protection: The Application of Article 1A(2) of the 1951 Convention and/or 1967 Protocol Relating to the Status of Refugees to Victims of Trafficking and Persons at Risk of Being Trafficked' (2006) HCR/GIP/06/07 (UNHCR Trafficking Guidelines) para 23.

34 cf Violeta Moreno-Lax, *Accessing Asylum in Europe: Extraterritorial Border Controls and Refugee Rights under EU Law* (OUP 2017) 406.

35 *Abdulla and Others* (n 25) para 71; emphasis added.

36 ibid para 70.

37 Nora Markard, *Kriegsflüchtlinge: Gewalt gegen Zivilpersonen in bewaffneten Konflikten als Herausforderung für das Flüchtlingsrecht und den subsidiären Schutz* (Mohr Siebeck 2012) 200.

38 Asylgesetz (AsylG) 2 September 2008 (BGBl. I S. 1798) (Asylum Act) s 3d.

39 Nationality and Borders Act 2022, s 34(2).

40 In *Horvath*, the House of Lords argued that as long as countries of origin have in place 'a system of domestic protection and machinery for the detection, prosecution and punishment of actings [sic] contrary to the purposes which the [Refugee] Convention requires to have protected' and have 'an ability and a readiness to operate that machinery', state protection is established regardless of whether such 'machinery' is effective. See *Horvath* (n 31) as per Clyde LJ, p 18.

41 See, for example, Hathaway and Foster (n 5) 314.

problems posed by harm which will largely take place outside the asylum seeker's country of origin.

4.2.2 The Location of the Harm Feared

Leading treatises on refugee law designate a refugee's country of nationality (or former habitual residence) as the 'locus of persecution',[42] noting that 'the basic inquiry into the existence of a well-founded fear [of being persecuted] focuses squarely on the risks faced in the country of which the individual is a citizen'.[43] Yet trafficking-based asylum claims provide evidence for the fact that harm experienced outside the country of origin can form the basis of an asylum claim. UNHCR notes that 'even where the exploitation experienced by a victim of trafficking occurs mainly outside the country of origin, this does not preclude the existence of a well-founded fear of persecution in the individual's own country'.[44]

Nevertheless, courts have, at times, struggled with cases in which harm was experienced outside the applicant's country of origin. For example, in the 2019 UK case of *HG*, which dealt with an Ethiopian woman who was trafficked to Sudan, Lebanon and France, the UT shows a lack of understanding regarding how trafficking experienced in third countries might relate to risk on return to country of origin.[45] The tribunal states:

> After the appellant left Ethiopia around 2013 she endured almost unimaginable abuse as a domestic slave until she was brought to the UK in November 2016. The abuse she suffered was not in her home country but in Sudan and Lebanon and, finally, in France. The issue in her appeal, however, was whether she is currently at risk of persecution or serious harm in Ethiopia. Even taken at its highest, the evidence does not establish a real risk of persecution or serious harm in Ethiopia.[46]

Thus, the tribunal fails to engage with the vulnerabilities acquired during this first trafficking experience and the possibility of re-trafficking. Similarly, a 2018 decision by the Bavarian higher administrative court (AC) fails to consider re-trafficking risks.[47] The case concerned a request for permission to appeal, also by an Ethiopian woman, who was seeking protection based on having been 'treated like a slave' by her employer in Dubai. Even though the (somewhat scarce) facts of the case suggest that the applicant had been trafficked, the court does not discuss the possibility of re-trafficking or the

42 Goodwin-Gill and McAdam (n 11) 92.
43 Hathaway and Foster (n 5) 50.
44 UNHCR Trafficking Guidelines (n 33) para 27.
45 *HG v SSHD* [2019] UKUT (IAC) PA/10947/2018.
46 ibid [19].
47 Bayerischer Verwaltungsgerichtshof, 8 ZB 18.31141, 09.08.2018.

applicant's circumstances upon return to Ethiopia and their effects. Instead, the court states that 'inhuman treatment outside the country of origin is without relevance for asylum proceedings'.[48]

Despite the aforementioned judgments, successful trafficking-based asylum claims and the UNHCR Trafficking Guidelines show that the fact that (the majority of) the harm feared in the context of re-trafficking will take place outside the country of origin does not pose an obstacle to claiming refugee protection. The more difficult problem, which the courts and the Guidelines do not address, is the question of how states of origin can be expected to provide protection against harm experienced outside their territory.

Since the Refugee Convention operates within a system of territorial sovereignty with all its constraints,[49] the principle of non-intervention limits states' ability to interfere with the way other states treat those within the latter's territory, including where the host state commits human rights violations.[50] Thus, states of destination cannot intervene in the way countries of origin treat their citizens, nor can countries of origin intervene in the treatment encountered by their nationals once they have left the state's territory. Indeed, where a national is outside his or her country of origin, all that the state of origin is realistically able to do is to provide diplomatic protection.[51] However, this is only possible where another state is responsible for the injury of the state of origin's national and where 'all available and effective local legal remedies in the State alleged to be responsible for the injury' have been exhausted.[52] What this means for the context of irregular re-migration is that, unless another state can be held responsible for harm experienced by a migrant on its territory, or within its jurisdiction (and unless that migrant then makes her case in the courts of that state), the state of origin will not be able to provide protection. Discussing the responsibility of states of transit and destination for harm experienced by irregularised migrants is not within the scope of this book. However, for the purpose of the state protection enquiry in refugee law, it should be noted that the diplomatic 'protection' in question would merely entail that the 'protecting State may claim reparation from the respondent State in the form of restitution, compensation or satisfaction',[53] part of which should be 'transfer[red]

48 ibid Headnote; my translation. See also VG Düsseldorf, 27 K 2264/18.A, 15.12.2020 [3].

49 Simon Behrman, 'Refugee Law as a Means of Control' (2019) 32(1) Journal of Refugee Studies 43, 47 <https://doi.org/10.1093/jrs/fey016>.

50 Naeem Inayatullah, 'Beyond the Sovereignty Dilemma: Quasi-States as Social Construct' in Thomas J Biersteker and Cynthia Weber (eds), *State Sovereignty as Social Construct* (CUP 2011) 50.

51 Individual Opinion by Tomuschat in Human Rights Committee, *Lopez Burgos v Uruguay*, Comm 52/1979 (29 July 1981).

52 John Dugard, 'Diplomatic Protection' in James Crawford and others (eds), *The Law of International Responsibility* (OUP 2010) 1061.

53 ibid 1068.

to the injured person . . . subject to any reasonable deductions'.[54] Thus, this is a reparatory, backward-looking form of protection, available only once an injury has already occurred outside the state of origin's territory, and thus unsuitable for addressing future risk under the Refugee Convention.

Trafficked persons' asylum claims raise interesting doctrinal and practical questions with regard to the scope and meaning of 'persecution', specifically with regard to the country of origin's ability to protect against harm taking place outside its territory. Yet UK and German courts ignore these difficulties when deciding trafficking-based asylum claims. As the next section shows, this results in an unsatisfactory approach to the question of what constitutes effective state protection in the trafficking context.

4.2.3 State Protection Against Re-Trafficking

In UK and German case law, states of origin are seen to be able to protect against re-trafficking in two main ways: first, by having anti-trafficking legislation in place and applying this effectively and, second, by offering reception and reintegration measures for returning trafficked persons. This section refers to the former as the 'law enforcement' approach, and to the latter as the 'reception and reintegration' approach, to state protection. It shows that these approaches to the state protection enquiry are unsatisfactory because they fail to engage sufficiently with the underlying reasons for re-trafficking. The section also shows that the same is true for equivalent state protection measures against a possible risk of irregular re-migration.

The law enforcement approach evaluates the state of origin's willingness and ability to implement anti-trafficking legislation, particularly with regard to prevention, investigation and prosecution of trafficking. This approach was adopted, for example, in a 2004 judgment of the AC Aachen, which concerned a Moldovan applicant who claimed to have lost her job due to the political activities of her mother.[55] To make ends meet, she was forced to take out a loan with an organisation that would force her into prostitution if she defaulted on her repayments. The court found that there was sufficient state protection available since 'the Republic of Moldova prosecutes criminal acts of third parties according to its capacity', and the state cannot be said to be unwilling or unable to protect since prosecutions of trafficking in women and forced prostitution are on the rise.[56] UK judgments from around the same time take a similar stance. In *VD*, also a 2004 case, concerning an applicant who was kidnapped for the purpose of being sold into marriage, the court finds a sufficiency of protection despite a need for 'further improvements' with regard

54 United Nations, 'Draft Articles on Diplomatic Protection' (2006) art 19(c) <https://legal.un.org/ilc/texts/instruments/english/draft_articles/9_8_2006.pdf> accessed 12 May 2021.
55 VG Aachen, 8 K 1220/02.A, 21.01.2004.
56 ibid [38]; my translation.

to combatting trafficking.[57] Meanwhile, in *MP*, a 2005 case, which concerned a Romanian woman who was kidnapped and forced into sexual exploitation, the court shows itself satisfied with a similar 'reasonable level of protection', based on the Romanian government's efforts to combat trafficking.[58] Similarly, in its 2010 judgment in *AM and BM,* a case concerning two Albanian women trafficked for sexual exploitation, the UT points to the mere existence, rather than effectiveness, of reintegration programmes, police training and prosecution of traffickers, stating that '[a]lthough we accept that there is little in the way of witness protection that is effective, there is evidence that there have been prosecutions of police involved in trafficking'.[59]

In contrast, the case of *AZ*, a judgment from the same year, emphasises the importance of '*effectiveness*' of protection, which must 'be judged by its ability to deter and/or to prevent the form of persecution of which there was a risk, *not just punishment of it after the event*'.[60] Indeed, courts have come to recognise that the mere fact that a country of origin has outlawed human trafficking and prosecutes traffickers is not enough to establish state protection. In fact, the UT's 2016 judgment in *HD* questions the relationship between anti-trafficking efforts and protection against re-trafficking, stating that

> there was inadequate evidence . . . to support a finding that [the anti-trafficking] measures were having a significant effect either on the number of victims trafficked for the first time or on the risk of returned victims of trafficking being trafficked again.[61]

The judgment states further that '[m]erely because Nigeria is "doing its best" to meet its international obligations to prevent trafficking does not necessarily result in a finding that there is sufficiency of protection for those identified as being at risk of being trafficked'.[62] The same approach is reflected in a 2020 judgment by the AC Magdeburg in which the court found that passing anti-trafficking legislation and prosecuting traffickers is not enough to protect against re-trafficking.[63] In another 2020 judgment, however, the AC Aachen insists on the same reasoning employed in 2004 in discussing the case of a Nigerian woman who was trafficked to Italy for the purpose of prostitution, in the course of which she was locked up and beaten.[64] The court finds that sufficient state protection exists based on Nigeria having passed anti-trafficking legislation and prosecuting traffickers. The court also states that the effectiveness

57 *VD (Trafficking) Albania* CG [2004] UKIAT 00115 [16.3].
58 *MP (Trafficking – Sufficiency of Protection) Romania* [2005] UKIAT 00086 [106].
59 *AM and BM (Trafficked women) Albania* CG [2010] UKUT 80 (IAC) [182].
60 *AZ (Trafficked women) Thailand* CG [2010] UKUT 118 (IAC) [159]; emphasis added.
61 *HD* (n 2) [141].
62 ibid [172].
63 VG Magdeburg, 6 A 40/19, 28.01.2020.
64 VG Aachen, 2 K 2521/18.A, 10.11.2020.

of protection is not put into question by the fact that not all perpetrators are prosecuted or by the fact that women are being discriminated against in Nigeria, including by being victimised rather than helped by police when seeking protection.[65]

As this rather problematic statement shows, because the 'law enforcement' approach to state protection focuses on punishing perpetrators rather than ensuring protection for the individual trafficked person, it is unlikely to be effective. As explained in Chapter 3, trafficked persons seek out traffickers because socio-economic deprivation, brought about by a range of vulnerabilities, leaves them no other choice. It is important to return to the factors leading to re-trafficking in the context of the state protection enquiry because even where trafficking has been outlawed and traffickers are prosecuted, this does not address the underlying reasons driving people to seek them out. Thus, it is more appropriate for state protection to focus on trafficked persons themselves and to aim to reduce their demand for traffickers' 'services'. Rather than focusing only on states' efforts to deter or prosecute persecutors, the question must be what else the state can do to meaningfully protect an individual.

This is done, to an extent, with regard to the second type of state protection discussed in the case law, that is, the provision of reception and reintegration measures for returned trafficked persons. Under this approach, there will be no state protection where there is a lack of rehabilitation and reintegration measures for trafficked persons. In *AM and BM*, the UT noted that such reception and reintegration measures include

> support to returned victims of trafficking . . . by support for shelters . . . [as well as] the rehabilitation of the victims of trafficking [through] the provision of micro loans and procedures to place former victims of trafficking into the job market.[66]

Thus, one aspect of the 'reception and reintegration' approach to state protection for trafficked persons is reception through dedicated shelters. In *PO*, it was held that protection was available in the form of a 'shelter where [the claimant] will be provided with the care and protection she needs'.[67] The AC Munich has made a similar finding in refusing the protection claim of an Albanian appellant who had fled domestic violence and forced marriage by leaving the country with a man who had promised to marry her but, once in Germany, forced her into sex work. The court decided that there was an IPA available to the claimant, since two shelters for trafficked women exist in Albania, one

65 ibid [56]; see also VG Regensburg, RO 15 K 20.30871, 26.04.2021 [41].
66 *AM and BM* (n 59) [180].
67 *PO (Trafficked Women) Nigeria* CG [2009] UKAIT 00046 [201].

run by the state and one by a non-governmental organisation (NGO).[68] Thus, protection in shelters for trafficked persons may take the shape of state protection, where the state itself runs or supports these shelters, or protection from non-state actors, usually NGOs. However, whether NGO-run shelters for trafficked persons should constitute protection against re-trafficking is questionable.[69] Even though both EU and UK law provide for the possibility of protection being delivered by non-state actors, these have to 'control the State or a substantial part of the territory of the State'.[70]

In addition, where protection through shelters is proposed – whether run by the state or non-state actors – it must be assessed in more detail whether an individual will, in fact, be able to obtain a place in a shelter and how long he or she will be able to stay there. Generally, a low number and the poor quality of such shelters are seen as indicative of a failure of state protection,[71] and protection is ineffective if trafficked persons can stay only for a short period of time.[72] Further, it is important to enquire whether the 'care and protection' provided by a shelter, in fact, effectively protects against re-trafficking. The case of *TAN* takes a step in the right direction by outlining that a Vietnamese man trafficked to France and the UK for forced labour, who suffered from mental health issues and lacked family support, education and work experience, would be able to access mental healthcare, legal advice, accommodation and food through a shelter, as well as reintegration support in the shape of training courses outside the shelter.[73] Nevertheless, it must be kept in mind that specific shelters for trafficked persons can cause them to be exposed to harm, as traffickers may try to recruit individuals from these shelters and inhabitants may be stigmatised if it becomes known that they live in such a shelter.[74] It is also worth noting that, since in many countries trafficking is still seen as an issue affecting only women, states may have reception and reintegration measures in place for women, but not for men, and, thus, a lack of state protection may be found for male claimants.[75]

68 VG München, M 11 K 06.51323, 11.09.2007 [35].
69 O'Sullivan (n 21).
70 Nationality and Borders Act 2022, s 34(1)(b); Qualification Regulation (n 5) art 7(1)(b). For a critical analysis of this provision, see Peers and others (n 18) 100–1.
71 VG Stuttgart, A 7 K 1405/12, 16.05.2014, p 13.
72 The UT has noted that 'vulnerability is not . . . reduced following a six week stay in a . . . shelter'. See *HD* (n 2) [141]. Even a two-year stay in a shelter may be insufficient to reduce risk, see *MD v SSHD* [2021] UKUT (IAC) PA/12142/2019 [63]. See also *PG v SSHD* [2022] UKUT (IAC) PA/00229/2020 [16].
73 *TAN v SSHD* [2023] UKUT (IAC) UI-2022-003801 [44]–[45].
74 *AM and BM* (n 59) [42], [63], [97] and [144].
75 See, for example, *BT v SSHD* [2019] UKUT (IAC) PA/07306/2017 [45] and [50]; *TVP v SSHD* [2018] UKUT (IAC) PA/02997/2018 [24]; *HVT v SSHD* [2018] UKUT (IAC) PA/03104/2017 [6]; *HC v SSHD* [2021] UKUT (IAC) PA/05060/2019 [37]; *DK v SSHD* [2024] UKUT (IAC) UI-2023-003379 [44]; *JV v SSHD* [2024] UKUT (IAC) UI-2024-001176 [42].

The second aspect of the 'reception and reintegration' approach to state protection for trafficked persons concerns reintegration support. Although in the case law this issue is often discussed either in the context of future risk or internal relocation, I discuss it here in the context of the state protection enquiry, because where such support is provided by governments of sending states or international organisations, this has the effect of circumventing the requirement that protection against persecution must be provided by the state of origin.

While some cases, like *TAN* or *AM and BM*, mention job training as part of the reintegration process, in other cases, the notion of reintegration assistance is reduced to purely financial support, and it is, at times, not clearly established whether the claimant in question would in fact have access to such support. For example, in 2020, the AC Düsseldorf speculated that a Nigerian woman who had been trafficked to Italy for the purpose of sexual exploitation would be eligible for a number of different government or NGO-run reintegration programmes on return to Nigeria.[76] Even though the court failed to assess whether the appellant would have access to such support *in practice*, she was refused protection. Similarly, the AC Cottbus, in a 2021 judgment, refused protection to a Nigerian couple who had twice been kidnapped for ransom, stating that they would be able to improve their economic situation in Nigeria by returning 'voluntarily' and thus making themselves eligible for reintegration programmes.[77] Another 2021 case, heard by the AC Regensburg, makes a similar claim, listing a number of reintegration assistance programmes but not investigating whether the applicant, who feared re-trafficking, would, in fact, have access to them.[78] The applicant was refused protection. A 2023 judgment by the AC Aachen, too, lists a number of reintegration assistance programmes available to returnees in Nigeria without enquiring whether the applicant, who also feared re-trafficking, would in fact have access to these.[79] This applicant, too, was refused protection. On the other hand, in a 2022 case heard by the AC Munich, a Nigerian woman trafficked to Spain for sexual exploitation was found not to be able to effectively take advantage of reintegration support due to her mental health issues.[80]

Likewise, in a number of UK cases, reintegration support is seen as neutralising the risk of re-trafficking. Thus, in *LTD*, the UT decided that an appellant who was trafficked to France, and later to the UK, could benefit from a UK 'resettlement package', which would reduce the risk of re-trafficking.[81] Similarly, in *NX*, a case concerning a trafficked woman from Albania with an 'illegitimate' child, the appellant's claim failed, since internal relocation was

76 27 K 2264/18.A (n 48) [55]–[60]. See also 2 K 2521/18.A (n 64) [88].

77 VG Cottbus, 9 K 1516/18.A, 11.01.2021 [26]. See also 2 K 2521/18.A (n 64) [90].

78 VG Regensburg, 15 K 21.31190, 16.12.2021, pp 16–18.

79 VG Aachen, 2 K 2514/21 A, 06.06.2023 [55]–[57].

80 VG München, M 13 K 21.30776, 21.06.2022, p 26; see also VG Würzburg, W 8 K 20 31251, 20.05.2022, in which the applicant has mental health issues and a developmental disorder.

81 *LTD v SSHD* [2015] UKUT (IAC) AA/13630/2011 [30]–[33].

found to be feasible, due to a '[reintegration] package provided by the IOM [which] clearly makes provision for individuals being returned with children'.[82] This case references *AM and BM*, the relevant country guidance case at the time, which considers the 'arrangements and facilities available to enable successful re-integration'.[83] However, *AM and BM* does not mention reintegration packages provided by international organisations at any point but focuses on assistance provided by the Albanian government. In the country guidance case of *TD and AD*, which superseded the guidance in *AM and BM*, the IOM package was discussed in detail as it was noted that this had been portrayed by the Home Office as a protection measure, with IOM itself noting that its programme 'cannot, and was never intended to, offer any protection'.[84] In this case, the applicants were found not to be eligible for the IOM package as this was only available to persons returning 'voluntarily'.[85]

Although reintegration support provided either by the UK or an international organisation is discussed in these cases as a possible risk-reducing measure or in the context of the availability of an IPA, these considerations thus overlap with the state protection enquiry. Indeed, in *LTD*, the tribunal notes in the relevant passages that similar 'assistance from Vietnamese sources . . . is not at a high level'.[86] In *NX*, it is noted that the IOM package was established in response to the 'lack of [Albanian] government funding for victims of trafficking'.[87]

Importantly, the 2019 case of *TSN*, a Vietnamese man trafficked to the UK, shows that protection through reintegration support is not a straightforward matter at all.[88] TSN was first trafficked to the UK in 2009 and removed in 2014. By 2015, he was back in the UK, once again having been trafficked.[89] The tribunal found that 'the appellant had received money under the [Facilitated Returns Scheme] on a previous return to Vietnam but this had not assisted him as he had been re-trafficked' and thus found that he was eligible for refugee status.[90] As Kelly notes, the 'lack of any effective re-integration programmes with which to address issues of housing, education, health, employment, substance abuse, and trauma plays an important part in re-trafficking'.[91] Besides the fact that, as the case of *TSN* shows, financial reintegration support,

82 *NX v SSHD* [2014] UKUT (IAC) AA/01621/2013 [45].
83 *AM and BM* (n 59) [Headnote e].
84 *TD and AD (Trafficked Women) CG* [2016] UKUT 92 [18].
85 ibid [148].
86 *LTD* (n 81) [33].
87 *NX* (n 82) [34] and [36].
88 *TSN v SSHD* [2019] UKUT (IAC) PA/07665/2017.
89 ibid [1].
90 ibid [3].
91 Elizabeth Kelly, 'Journeys of Jeopardy: A Review of Research on Trafficking in Women and Children in Europe' (*IOM*, 2002) 39 <https://publications.iom.int/system/files/pdf/mrs_11_2002.pdf> accessed 29 April 2020.

on its own, is unlikely to constitute protection against re-trafficking, where such support is provided by the sending state or an international organisation, it ought not to be considered to constitute protection. By providing financial reintegration support, the sending country effectively acknowledges that there is a failure of state protection in the country of origin (since this country itself does not provide the requisite support). However, rather than granting refugee status based on this finding, sending states seek to provide protection themselves, through a grant of financial assistance. This goes against the principle that protection must be provided by the country of origin (or, according to EU and UK law, authorities controlling a substantial part of its territory),[92] and that it needs to be durable and meaningful in character. Even though the availability of reintegration assistance through sources other than the country of origin is discussed either in the context of future risk or the IPA enquiry, accepting that this can reduce risk for trafficked persons (which, as evident from *TSN*, is questionable) has the effect of circumventing the requirement that protection against persecution must be provided by the state of origin.

Overall, UK and German courts' approaches to state protection against re-trafficking are unsatisfactory. The law enforcement approach is unlikely to reduce the risk below the well-founded fear standard, as it does not address trafficked persons' need to rely on traffickers. While the reception and reintegration approach does (partially) address this need, this approach, too, is ineffective as it fails to acknowledge the complexities underlying the decision to be re-trafficked and fails to investigate in more detail whether shelters for trafficked persons and reintegration assistance can really counter trafficked persons' vulnerabilities. Indeed, despite its prominence in the future risk enquiry, the vulnerability analysis is conspicuously absent from the state protection enquiry. It seems illogical to first identify what factors put a person at risk of re-trafficking, only to then largely disregard those factors when it comes to the question of availability of protection.

I would argue that this discrepancy stems from approaching re-trafficking as such as the relevant harm, for the purpose of the persecution enquiry. Doing so puts the focus on the 'crime' of trafficking and leads courts to consider a 'law enforcement' approach to state protection, which is ineffective for countering the individual's need for protection and concomitant risk of re-trafficking. The 'reception and reintegration' approach, meanwhile, is reductive. It focuses either on (often only female) 'victims' and their ability to access shelters but does not enquire which services are, in fact, available in those shelters, and whether these address trafficked persons' vulnerabilities. Alternatively, it reduces vulnerability to re-trafficking to socio-economic deprivation and seeks to address this through financial reintegration support (often provided by NGOs or the sending country, rather than the country

92 Qualification Regulation (n 5) art 7(1)(b); Nationality and Borders Act 2022, s 34(1)(b).

of origin). As explained in Chapter 3, the risk of re-trafficking (and irregular re-migration) is caused by a range of intersecting vulnerabilities. While these do lead to socio-economic deprivation, it is the vulnerabilities and their interplay which must be addressed to effectively counter the risk of re-trafficking, so that such efforts cannot be reduced to countering socio-economic deprivation alone.

As a result, existing approaches to state protection are ill-suited to reducing risk for trafficked persons. The same would be true if similar approaches were taken to protect against a risk of irregular re-migration. First, a 'law enforcement' approach to smuggling is unlikely to significantly reduce the availability of smuggling services and does not address the reasons irregularised migrants approach smugglers in the first place. As Squire *et al.* note, 'anti-smuggling measures are unlikely to prevent migration via criminal networks, and fail to protect people on the move from danger and harm'.[93] Second, with regard to protection in shelters, seeing as such protection is normally only available for trafficked women (and often with great shortcomings), it is unlikely that dedicated shelters capable of furnishing comprehensive protection and support will exist for other (male) returnees. Finally, mere financial reintegration support is also unlikely to protect irregularised migrants from irregular re-migration since, just as in the trafficking context, it does not address their intersecting vulnerabilities. Indeed, Stahlmann, through qualitative research with Afghan returnees, has shown that for those few persons who can access financial reintegration support, the money they receive only covers their expenses for a couple of days.[94]

However, when thinking about the effectiveness, or lack thereof, of applying the same types of state protection identified in the trafficking context to the risk of irregular re-migration, an important question is whether courts would even consider claims of irregularised migrants as equivalent to those of trafficked persons. Even if it were accepted that, as established in the previous chapter, there is such a thing as a risk of irregular re-migration, the idea that smuggled persons do not experience harm continues to prevail. Thus, it is probable that, unlike re-trafficking, irregular re-migration would not be perceived as amounting to serious harm in itself.

Therefore, in order to explore whether irregularised migrants, too, ought to be able to claim refugee status, it will be necessary to examine the harm

93 Vicki Squire and others, 'Crossing the Mediterranean Sea by Boat: Mapping and Documenting Migratory Journeys and Experiences' (*University of Warwick*, 2017) 77 <https://warwick.ac.uk/fac/soc/pais/research/projects/crossingthemed/ctm_final_report_4may2017.pdf> accessed 6 August 2021.

94 Friederike Stahlmann, 'Erfahrungen und Perspektiven Abgeschobener Afghanen im Kontext Aktueller Politischer und Wirtschaftlicher Entwicklungen Afghanistans' (*Diakonie Deutschland, Brot für die Welt, Diakonie Hessen*, June 2021) 78 <www.fluechtlingsrat-mv.de/wp-content/uploads/2021/06/AFG_Monitoring-Studie_FINAL.pdf> accessed 28 August 2024.

experienced by this group in more detail, and to consider what state protection in this context could look like. In light of the unsatisfactory approaches to state protection in the trafficking context, such an enquiry will also be relevant to trafficking-based asylum claims, as a better understanding of what types of harm trafficking and irregular migration actually entail will lead to a better conceptualisation of the types of state action that could protect against both. In particular, as the next section will show, it is necessary to reconsider the locus of persecution, that is, engaging with the fact that much of the harm experienced will take place outside the country of origin. In this context, it is necessary to pay attention to the sequence and interplay of different types of harm.

4.3 The Locus of Persecution Reconsidered

The risk of re-trafficking or of irregular re-migration is brought about by socio-economic deprivation, caused by intersecting vulnerabilities. As such, trafficked persons and irregularised migrants experience a sequence of harms: first, socio-economic deprivation in the country of origin (which will only rarely amount to persecution for the purpose of refugee law)[95] and, second, harm outside the country of origin, which, as this section will show, constitutes serious harm.

As explained previously, UK and German courts conceive of re-trafficking as a harm in itself and, based on the 'law enforcement' approach described earlier, seem to understand it as a harm that begins in the country of origin, so that law enforcement activities within that country are considered to be able to protect against it. However, neither trafficking nor smuggling necessarily begins in the country of origin. Smuggling and trafficking exist along a spectrum, and the former can turn into the latter.[96] Further, some people migrate by own means at first and are only trafficked or smuggled later. The United Nations Office on Drugs and Crime (UNODC), for example, notes:

> The routes that lead West Africans to Europe . . . normally involve regular international bus travel from the migrants' country of origin towards a transit country in the Sahel, followed by smuggling by land into North Africa, and from there, smuggling to Europe by sea.[97]

95 Michelle Foster, *International Refugee Law and Socio-Economic Rights: Refuge from Deprivation* (CUP 2007).

96 Angeliki Dimitriadi, 'The Interrelationship between Trafficking and Irregular Migration' in Sergio Carrera and Elspeth Guild (eds), *Irregular Migration, Trafficking and Smuggling of Human Beings: Policy Dilemmas in the EU* (*CEPS*, 2016) 66 <www.ceps.eu/wp-content/uploads/2016/02/Irregular%20Migration,%20Trafficking%20and%20SmugglingwithCovers.pdf> accessed 18 August 2022.

97 UNODC, 'Global Study on Smuggling of Migrants 2018' (2018) 27 <www.unodc.org/documents/data-and-analysis/glosom/GLOSOM_2018_web_small.pdf> accessed 5 June 2020.

Treating re-trafficking as a harm in itself obscures trafficked persons' actual experiences and thus leads to courts paying insufficient attention to the question of what effective state protection might look like. Similarly, viewing irregular re-migration as a harm in itself would be counterproductive. Designating irregular re-migration as a 'harm' risks sanctioning 'protective' measures which, in fact, do more damage than good. For example, it may be argued that an 'effective' way of protecting against irregular re-migration would be prevention of exit. This, however, would infringe the right to leave any country, including one's own.[98] While this right is not absolute,[99] current state practice shows that in enforcing prohibitions of exit, states are likely to use measures which breach other human rights. For example, in the Eritrean context, those caught attempting to leave without an exit visa may be shot at the border, be abused by border guards or face prison terms and/or fines.[100]

Thus, rather than conceiving of re-trafficking and irregular re-migration as harms in themselves, this section explores what exactly happens to trafficked persons and irregularised migrants, the sequence and concurrence of different types of harm, as well as options for effective state protection.

4.3.1 Harm Experienced Outside the Country of Origin

Harm experienced in the trafficking context is likely to take place mainly outside the country of origin and goes beyond the examples of exploitation listed in the trafficking definition. UK and German courts do detail the harm experienced by applicants, which includes sexual exploitation in the majority

98 International Covenant on Civil and Political Rights (adopted 16 December 1966, entered into force 23 March 1976) 999 UNTS 171 (ICCPR) art 12(2); European Convention for the Protection of Human Rights and Fundamental Freedoms Rights, as amended (adopted 4 November 1950, entered into force 3 September 1953) CETS No 005 (ECHR) Protocol 4, art 2(2); cf Vladislava Stoyanova, 'The Right to Leave Any Country and the Interplay between Jurisdiction and Proportionality in Human Rights Law' (2020) 32(3) International Journal of Refugee Law 403 <https://doi.org/10.1093/ijrl/eeaa030>; Violeta Moreno-Lax, 'Intersectionality, Forced Migration, and the Jus-generation of the Right to Flee: Theorising a Composite Entitlement to Leave to Escape Irreversible Harm' in Başak Çalı, Ledi Bianku and Iulia Motoc (eds), *Migration and the European Convention on Human Rights* (OUP 2021).

99 According to the ICCPR, restrictions on the right to leave must be 'provided by law, . . . necessary to protect national security, public order (ordre public), public health or morals or the rights and freedoms of others, and [must be] consistent with the other rights recognized in [the ICCPR]'. See ICCPR (n 98) art 12(3). The ECHR adds 'the prevention of crime' to the reasons for which states may derogate from the right to leave. See ECHR (n 98) Protocol 4, art 2(3).

100 Immigration and Refugee Board of Canada, 'Eritrea: Situation of People Returning to the Country after They Either Spent Time Abroad, Claimed Refugee Status, or Were Seeking Asylum (September 2014–June 2015)' (2015) <www.refworld.org/docid/577b6d024.html> accessed 3 June 2020.

of cases,[101] but also abduction, beatings and rape,[102] deprivation of liberty,[103] starvation and forced injection of drugs,[104] deprivation of medical treatment[105] and forced labour or domestic servitude.[106] A human rights analysis of these harms shows that they are indeed serious. Rape,[107] beatings[108] and starvation[109] violate the right not to be subjected to torture, inhuman or degrading treatment.[110] The deprivation of medical treatment may violate the right to life[111] or may amount to inhuman or degrading treatment.[112] Forced injection of drugs can constitute a violation of the right to private and family life.[113] Deprivation of liberty,[114] as well as forced labour,[115] are human rights violations in themselves.

While the case law takes it for granted that re-trafficking entails serious harm, the same cannot be said for irregular re-migration. However, as explained

101 This applies to women as well as men. For example, in *FK v SSHD* [2015] UKUT (IAC) AA/08453/2014, a male Albanian minor was trafficked to Italy for sexual exploitation.

102 See, for example, *AM and BM* (n 59) [7] and [22]; *AZ* (n 60) [5]; *ES (s82 NIA 2002, Negative NRM)* [2018] UKUT 335 (IAC) [3]; *MP* (n 58) [6]; VG Aachen, 2 K 2224/15.A, 28.12.2017 [9]; VG Augsburg, Au 7 K 17.30060, 13.12.2017 [18]; VG München, M 23 K 11.30389, 30.09.2013 [2].

103 See, for example, *AM and BM* (n 59) [7] and [22]; *AZ* (n 60) [5]; *ES* (n 102) [3]; *MP* (n 58) [6].

104 See, for example, *AZ* (n 60) [5].

105 See, for example, *EK (Article 4 ECHR: Anti-Trafficking Convention) Tanzania v SSHD* [2013] UKUT 00313 (IAC) [27]; VG Augsburg, Au 7 K 12.30184, 18.09.2012, p 3.

106 See, for example, *MS (Pakistan) v SSHD* [2020] UKSC 9, [2020] Imm AR 967 [4]; *EK* (n 105) [59]; *HD* (n 2) [206]; *TT (Vietnam)* [2019] EWCA Civ 248, [2019] 2 WLUK 401 [6]; VG München, M 10 K 16.30286, 17.11.2016 [7]; M 23 K 11.30389 (n 102) [2]. For a discussion on how forced labour is distinguished from servitude and other related concepts, such as slavery, see Vladislava Stoyanova, *Human Trafficking and Slavery Reconsidered: Conceptual Limits and States' Positive Obligations in European Law* (CUP 2017) 218–91.

107 Rape of an applicant in detention can amount to torture; see *Aydin v Turkey* App no 57/1996/676/866 (ECtHR, 25 September 1997) para 86.

108 Article 3 ECHR protects 'a person's dignity and physical integrity'. See *Tyrer v UK* App no 5856/72 (ECtHR, 25 April 1978) para 33. The European Commission of Human Rights, as it was at the time, held that 'inhuman treatment covers at least such treatment as deliberately causing severe suffering, mental or physical, which, in a particular situation, is unjustifiable'. See *Greek Case* App nos 3321/67, 3322/67, 3323/67, 3344/67 (European Commission of Human Rights, 5 November 1969) p 186.

109 Deprivation of food and drink, in combination with other 'interrogation techniques', can amount to inhuman or degrading treatment. See *Ireland v The United Kingdom* App no 5310/71 (ECtHR, 13 December 1977) [167].

110 ECHR (n 98) art 3.

111 In *Cyprus v Turkey*, the ECtHR held that this is the case 'where it is shown that the authorities of a Contracting State put an individual's life at risk through the denial of health care which they have undertaken to make available to the population generally'. See *Cyprus v Turkey* App no 25781/94 (ECtHR, 10 May 2001) [219].

112 *Paposhvili v Belgium* App no 41738/10 (ECtHR, 13 December 2016) para 206.

113 *X v Finland* App no 34806/04 (ECtHR, 3 July 2012) para 222.

114 ICCPR (n 98) art 9(1); ECHR (n 98) art 5.

115 ICCPR (n 98) art 8(3)(a); ECHR (n 98) art 4.

in Chapter 2, the assumption that irregular migration does not entail serious harm is incorrect. Before exploring the types of harm experienced during dangerous journeys in more detail, it should be noted that conceptualising smuggling as inherently violent is dangerous because doing so functions as a justification for states to criminalise both smugglers and smuggled persons.[116] Sanchez shows that 'the most extreme acts of violence in smuggling are not necessarily performed by smuggler facilitators themselves' but by other actors who, rather than facilitating migrants' movement, will kidnap them, hold them captive and abuse them to extort money from their families.[117] Indeed, 'criminal gangs are perceived as the main perpetrators [of harm experienced during irregular migration] followed by armed groups, smugglers, State entities, other migrants, people from local communities and family members.'[118] In addition, it is important to note states' role in exposing irregular migrants to danger through their restrictive immigration policies.[119]

Overall, it is the irregular nature of the journey and migrants' irregular status in transit or destination countries which put them at risk of harm. It is well known that many migrants have died trying to cross the Mediterranean, and that 'twice as many migrants die crossing Africa as crossing the Mediterranean', due to 'transportation accidents, dehydration, violence, starvation and illness'.[120] In addition, smuggled persons may experience harms very similar to those experienced by trafficked persons, such as physical and sexual violence, rape, torture, kidnapping, deprivation of liberty and forced labour.[121] If these experiences amount to serious harm in the trafficking context, this will also be true in the smuggling context. While the experiences of irregularised migrants are varied and cannot be generalised, some prominent examples can shed further light on the types of harm which a large number of irregularised migrants are likely to experience. One such example is the situation in Libya. There are 'well documented patterns of abuse against migrants and refugees by smugglers and traffickers and [a] frequent recovery, across Libya, of bodies of unidentified Sub-Saharan migrants and refugees bearing gunshot wounds,

116 Gabriella Sanchez, *Human Smuggling and Border Crossings* (Routledge 2015) 117–18.

117 ibid 114–17.

118 UNHCR, 'On This Journey, No One Cares If You Live or Die: Abuse, Protection and Justice Along Routes between East and West Africa and Africa's Mediterranean Coast: A Route-based Perspective on Key Risks' vol 2 (March 2024) 43 <www.unhcr.org/media/journey-no-one-cares-if-you-live-or-die-abuse-protection-and-justice-along-routes-between-1> accessed 19 August 2024.

119 Sanchez (n 116) 123.

120 Deutsche Welle, 'Land Migration in Africa Twice as Deadly as Mediterranean, Says UNHCR' (3 November 2019) <www.dw.com/en/land-migration-in-africa-twice-as-deadly-as-mediterranean-says-unhcr/a-51096086> accessed 1 May 2020.

121 UNHCR, 'Desperate Journeys: Refugees and Migrants Entering and Crossing Europe via the Mediterranean and Western Balkans Routes' (February 2017) <www.unhcr.org/uk/news/updates/2017/2/58b449f54/desperate-journeys-refugees-migrants-entering-crossing-europe-via-mediterranean.html> accessed 11 September 2022; UNHCR (n 118).

torture and burn marks'.[122] Migrants face 'mandatory and indefinite arbitrary detention' for their irregular entry and presence.[123] Abuse experienced by migrants in Libya includes 'killings, extreme violence, torture, rape, and forced labour by smugglers or traffickers', 'being systematically held captive in abusive conditions with the aim of extorting money from [migrants'] families', as well as being '"sold" from one criminal gang to another'.[124] In light of the finding in Chapter 3 that men may have difficulties showing that they, too, are 'vulnerable', it is worth noting that men have been reported to experience types of harm usually associated with being female; sexual violence against men is commonplace in Libya, but also in countries of origin and during transit.[125]

The conditions migrants face in Libya have also come to the attention of the International Criminal Court (ICC) Prosecutor, who has stated

> that crimes including torture, unlawful imprisonment, rape and enslavement are committed against migrants throughout their journeys and in both official and unofficial detention centres. The evidence implicates individuals, militias and State actors in the migrant smuggling and trafficking business in many parts of Libya.[126]

The ICC Prosecutor has stated further that '[m]igrants' – without qualification – 'represent a highly vulnerable population in Libya'.[127] While it is not the aim of refugee law to prosecute perpetrators of serious harm,[128] the statement by the ICC Prosecutor highlights the seriousness of the situation. The reference to trafficking ***and smuggling*** networks calls into question the distinction usually made between 'victims' of the two practices. While the situation for migrants in Libya is particularly dire, it is by far not the only example. In Morocco, sub-Saharan migrants are under an 'ever present threat of violence, abuse and exploitation at the hands of security forces, criminal gangs including human smuggling and human trafficking networks, bandits

122 OHCHR, 'Desperate and Dangerous: Report on the Human Rights Situation of Migrants and Refugees in Libya' (2018) 26 <https://reliefweb.int/report/libya/desperate-and-dangerous-report-human-rights-situation-migrants-and-refugees-libya> accessed 29 October 2024.

123 ibid 5.

124 ibid 26.

125 Women's Refugee Commission, '"More Than One Million Pains": Sexual Violence against Men and Boys on the Central Mediterranean Route to Italy' (March 2019) 19ff <www.womensrefugeecommission.org/wp-content/uploads/2020/04/Libya-Italy-Report-03-2019.pdf> accessed 19 September 2020.

126 International Criminal Court, 'Statement to the United Nations Security Council on the Situation in Libya, pursuant to UNSCR 1970 (2011)' (8 May 2019) para 22 <www.icc-cpi.int/Pages/item.aspx?name=180508-otp-statement-libya-UNSC> accessed 3 October 2020.

127 ibid para 21.

128 Hathaway and Foster (n 5) 378.

and, at times, the civilian population'.[129] Further, Algeria is known to have expelled migrants by forcing them to walk across the Sahara Desert to Nigeria, without any food or water – a journey many do not survive.[130] The Special Rapporteur on extrajudicial, summary or arbitrary executions and the Special Rapporteur on torture and other cruel, inhuman or degrading treatment or punishment have reported on the treatment of migrants and refugees during flight generally, citing similar abuses.[131] Notably, once irregular migrants have arrived in Europe, they may still be subject to abuses, including physical violence and pushbacks.[132]

In summary, harm experienced by trafficked persons and irregularised migrants is, indeed, serious. Since the majority of this harm takes place outside the country of origin, the next section considers whether that country is expected to, and can, provide protection outside its territory.

4.3.2 State Protection Outside the Country of Origin?

Even though the general consensus among refugee law scholars is that the enquiry into a well-founded fear of being persecuted focuses on risks in the state of origin,[133] persecution *can* take place with the individual in question located outside his or her country of origin. While the Qualification Regulation in Article 15(b) explicitly excludes this possibility by stating that the provision only applies to situations of 'torture or inhuman or degrading treatment or punishment of an applicant *in the country of origin*',[134] the Refugee Convention is not limited in a similar way. Hathaway and Foster note that though 'the basic inquiry into the existence of a well-founded fear [of being persecuted] focuses squarely on the risks faced *in the country of which the individual is a citizen*',[135] there is 'no need to find that the harm feared is one that would actually take place *inside* the home state, but simply that the risk of being persecuted *accounts* for the inability to return there'.[136] In this context, they give

129 MSF, 'Violence, Vulnerability and Migration: Trapped at the Gates of Europe – A Report on the Situation of Sub-Saharan Migrants in an Irregular Situation in Morocco' (2013) 9 <www.msf.org/violence-vulnerability-and-migration-trapped-gates-europe> accessed 2 May 2020.

130 Sertan Sanderson, 'Left to Die: How Algeria Deports Migrants to Niger' (*INFOMIGRANTS*, 5 May 2019) <www.infomigrants.net/en/post/16148/left-to-die-how-algeria-deports-migrants-to-niger> accessed 1 May 2020.

131 OHCHR, 'Report of the Special Rapporteur on Torture and Other Cruel, Inhuman or Degrading Treatment or Punishment' (26 February 2018) A/HRC/37/50; UNGA, 'Unlawful Death of Refugees and Migrants' A/72/335 (15 August 2017).

132 Border Violence Monitoring Network, 'The Black Book of Pushbacks' vols I and II (2020) <https://left.eu/issues/publications/black-book-of-pushbacks-volumes-i-ii/> accessed 9 September 2021; see also Chapter 7 of this book.

133 Grahl-Madsen (n 5) 192; Hathaway and Foster (n 5) 50; Goodwin-Gill and McAdam (n 11) 92.

134 Qualification Regulation (n 5) art 15(b).

135 Hathaway and Foster (n 5) 50; emphasis added.

136 ibid 250.

the example of the prohibition of re-entry, a 'denial of the right to freedom of movement and thus a serious harm',[137] which would take place with the person in question outside the country of origin.

The prohibition of re-entry example is relevant to better understanding the relationship between the location of the individual and the (protective) role of the state. If the prohibition of re-entry can be linked to a Convention ground, the individual in question will be a refugee *sur place*. While, as detailed earlier, in the context of irregular re-migration, the persecutors are non-state actors, where a state prohibits a national's re-entry, the state itself is the persecutor. As such, failure of state protection is automatically established. Nevertheless, the prohibition of re-entry example is useful for understanding state protection in the context of irregular migration because it illustrates that the state, which has the capacity to persecute or protect the individual, has this capacity only because it retains jurisdiction over the individual who is located outside its territory and whose re-entry is denied.[138]

State protection against harm experienced in the context of irregular migration, then, would require a link to a state of origin's jurisdiction. More specifically, it would require jurisdiction in the public international law sense of the term, since a state would have to be able to enforce its domestic law with regard to its national.[139] The state has jurisdiction to do this within its territory, but extraterritorially only in exceptional circumstances, for example, on diplomatic premises, or on board 'craft and vessels registered in, or flying the flag of, that State'.[140] Thus, persons who are already outside their country of origin and who are experiencing harm are normally only able to bring themselves under their state of origin's jurisdiction by approaching one of its embassies or consular representations. In this context, it has been suggested that 'unwilling[ness] to avail [one]self of the protection of [one's] country [of nationality]' in the Refugee Convention's *refugee* definition should be interpreted as an unwillingness to take advantage of that country's diplomatic protection.[141] Fortin argues that 'the very wording of the definition clearly indicates that the protection that it alludes to is that exercised *outside*

137 ibid 249.

138 The Human Rights Committee has established that issuing a passport to citizens is 'clearly a matter within the jurisdiction' of a state, and refusal to do so interferes with the right to leave any country, including one's own. See, for example, Human Rights Committee, *Vidal Martins v Uruguay*, Comm 57/1979 (23 March 1982) para 7. By analogy, this reasoning may also be applied to cancelling an individual's passport, thus preventing re-entry and the right to *enter* one's own country.

139 Christopher Staker, 'Jurisdiction' in Malcolm D Evans (ed), *International Law* (5th edn, OUP 2018) 289–90.

140 *Banković and others v Belgium and Others* App no 52207/99 (ECtHR, 12 December 2001) para 73.

141 Grahl-Madsen (n 5) 255; Antonio Fortin, 'The Meaning of Protection in the Refugee Definition' (2000) 12 International Journal of Refugee Law 548 <https://doi.org/10.1093/ijrl/12.4.548>; *Januzi v SSHD* [2006] UKHL 5, [2006] 2 WLR 397 [66].

the State's territory'.[142] In this context, he conceives of 'diplomatic protection' broadly to include consular assistance.[143] He argues that a failure of state protection would be established where

> either the diplomatic or consular authorities refuse to intervene on behalf of nationals of their country when their rights are not respected by the authorities of the foreign country in which they are, or that, owing to well-founded fear of being persecuted, the nationals in question do not want to seek or to accept the protection of their diplomatic or consular authorities.[144]

As explained previously, since 'refugee law is not concerned with assessing state responsibility, and is not retrospective but rather prospective in nature',[145] diplomatic protection, in the sense of the state of origin claiming reparations for an injury of its national from a state responsible for this injury, is not the type of protection envisaged by the Refugee Convention.

This leaves the question of whether consular assistance constitutes effective protection against harm experienced outside the country of origin. Consular functions include rendering (immediate) help and assistance,[146] as well as 'issuing passports and travel documents to nationals of the sending State'.[147] Thus, in theory, a trafficked person could seek assistance from his or her state of origin's consulate, bringing him or herself within the home state's jurisdiction for the purpose of protection from harm. In this context, it is conceivable that a person at risk of harm outside the country of origin would be unable to avail themselves of the consular protection of her country – for example, due to a lack of consular relations between the country of origin and the host state[148] – or would be unwilling to do so. This unwillingness might stem from the fact that, on a practical level, availing oneself of consular assistance implies obtaining help in returning to the country of origin.[149] Assuming a trafficked person is able to approach their country of origin's consulate in order to be issued with a passport which would, in theory, allow him or her to travel back to that country, he or she may not wish to return for fear of being trafficked

142 Fortin (n 141) 564; emphasis added.

143 Indeed, the two are sometimes confused and may partially overlap. See Annemarieke Künzli, 'Exercising Diplomatic Protection: The Fine Line between Litigation, Demarches and Consular Assistance' (2006) 66 Zeitschrift für ausländisches öffentliches Recht und Völkerrecht 321.

144 Fortin (n 141) 565.

145 Hathaway and Foster (n 5) 301. On why it is unnecessary to establish state responsibility for persecution, see Goodwin-Gill and McAdam (n 11) 77.

146 Vienna Convention on Consular Relations (adopted 24 April 1963, entered into force 19 March 1967) 596 UNTS 261 (VCCR) art 5(e).

147 ibid art 5(d).

148 Grahl-Madsen (n 5) 256.

149 Kälin (n 25) 428. See also Grahl-Madsen (n 5) 257. See further Goodwin-Gill and McAdam (n 11) 70.

again. As such, as Fortin suggests, the trafficked person would not accept the protection of the consular authorities. This interpretation, however, would not solve the question what, precisely, the state of origin can do to counter the risk of re-trafficking. Thus, availability of internal state protection would still have to be discussed, albeit in the context of the 'well-founded fear' enquiry.

In summary, where harm is experienced outside the country of origin, approaching the concept of protection in the *refugee* definition as diplomatic or consular protection is unsatisfactory. The next section explores how harm taking place outside the country of origin and state protection being provided within that country can be reconciled with the requirement that the state of origin must have jurisdiction over the individual in question, without resorting to the 'external' consular protection option.

4.3.3 Sequential Harms and the Cumulative Nature of Persecution

What emerges from the preceding discussion is that the state of origin can only protect an individual as long as that individual is within the state's jurisdictional domain. This section considers the sequential nature of harm experienced in the context of trafficking and draws on the cumulative nature of persecution to argue that a state's failure to protect an individual while he or she is still within its territory leads to that individual experiencing additional harm outside the country of origin.

As explained earlier, reception and reintegration measures are seen as a type of state protection against re-trafficking. Thus, protection against socio-economic deprivation plays a major role in trafficking-based asylum claims. While the way the state protection enquiry is approached in UK and German case law is reductive and unsatisfactory, in theory, focusing on socio-economic deprivation in this context makes sense because socio-economic deprivation, which, in turn, is caused by vulnerabilities, may lead to re-trafficking. Thus, although socio-economic deprivation is not normally a reason for refugee status in itself,[150] in the trafficking context, protecting against it is seen to also protect against re-trafficking.

This finding is the starting point for developing an alternative approach to state protection against re-trafficking and irregular re-migration, which takes individual experiences into account and therefore focuses on effectiveness of protection, while resolving the doctrinal difficulties posed by the fact that much of the harm experienced by trafficked persons and irregularised migrants takes place outside the country of origin. The proposed approach is based on the cumulative nature of persecution. According to the Qualification Regulation, an act of persecution can be 'an accumulation of various measures'.[151] Likewise, Foster notes that a 'risk of "being persecuted" [is assessed] on the basis of an accumulation of all harm feared, even if some elements of harm would not individually be considered sufficiently serious to amount of

150 UNHCR Handbook (n 27) para 62.
151 Qualification Regulation (n 5) art 9(1)(b).

[sic] persecution'.[152] Particularly in case of asylum claims based on socio-economic deprivation, 'a fear of being persecuted may be established by an accumulation of a number of less serious violations'.[153] Significantly, socio-economic harm can also be found to be persecutory when 'combined with more "traditional" (i.e. civil and political) forms of persecution'.[154] This should not detract from the fact that, under certain circumstances, socio-economic deprivation in itself can form the basis of an asylum claim.[155] Rather, the cumulative nature of persecution is important where socio-economic deprivation in the country of origin simply does not reach the threshold of serious harm.

Based on the preceding discussion, I propose that socio-economic deprivation experienced in the country of origin, which, in itself, does not amount to serious harm, can 'anchor' serious harm experienced *outside* the country of origin (as the result of leaving that country, in order to escape socio-economic deprivation) for the purpose of establishing a failure of state protection. Risk of re-trafficking can be inferred from risk of socio-economic deprivation (caused by intersecting vulnerabilities). The relevant risk in the trafficking context, then, is one of persecution, because the harm experienced is sequential and cumulative. The harm experienced outside the country of origin is likely to entail violations of civil and political rights and thus more easily satisfies the serious harm threshold. Meanwhile, socio-economic deprivation provides the 'jurisdictional anchor' in the country of origin. A failure to protect against the (lesser) harm in the country of origin leads to additional (more severe) harm outside the country. This allows for an understanding of persecution under which the state of origin's failure to protect against harm experienced in its territory results in additional harm experienced outside the country. As explained in Chapter 3, as a consequence of escaping socio-economic harm, individuals experience other types of serious harm. Thus, a failure to protect against the former results in the latter. This requires considering risks which may not materialise imminently on return to the country of origin, but only after some time has elapsed and arrangements for re-trafficking have been made. As Foster *et al.* demonstrate with regard to establishing future risk in the context of armed conflict, 'while a fear of persecution must be current, the ill-treatment feared may occur in the present or the future. The test is whether it is reasonably foreseeable, which necessarily embodies a degree of speculation'.[156] As explained in

152 Foster (n 95) 93.
153 ibid 104.
154 ibid 132. See also Kate Jastram, 'Economic Harm as a Basis for Refugee Status and the Application of Human Rights Law to the Interpretation of Economic Persecution' in James C Simeon (ed), *Critical Issues in International Refugee Law* (CUP 2010) 154.
155 Foster (n 95) 132; Mariana Ferolla Vallandro do Valle, 'Fleeing Deprivation: Deducing *Non-Refoulement* Obligations from Economic, Social and Cultural Rights' (2024) 36(4) International Journal of Refugee Law 353 <https://doi.org/10.1093/ijrl/eeae036>.
156 Michelle Foster and others, '"Time" in Refugee Status Determination in Australia and the United Kingdom: A Clear and Present Danger from Armed Conflict?' (2022) 34(2) International Journal of Refugee Law 163, 177 <https://doi.org/10.1093/ijrl/eeac033>.

Chapter 3, a risk of re-trafficking is foreseeable as long as vulnerabilities are present.

This line of reasoning can be applied beyond the trafficking context and to the situation of irregularised migrants. It should be possible to take harm that will take place outside the country of origin into account during refugee status determination for asylum seekers who have no well-founded fear of persecution in their country of origin but whose country of origin is unable to protect them against (lesser) harms, which will, in turn, trigger their re-migration by compelling them to leave and confront harms outside the country of origin.

Effective protection against re-trafficking and irregular re-migration, then, would entail guaranteeing individuals' socio-economic rights in a manner which takes account of their individual vulnerabilities and obviates the need for seeking economic security through re-trafficking or irregular re-migration. Thus, the state protection enquiry cannot be reduced to the question of availability of financial reintegration assistance but must address all the intersecting vulnerabilities resulting in socio-economic deprivation. As such, the level at which protection can be considered effective should not be measured with reference to the question of whether socio-economic rights are guaranteed in the country of origin generally, since economic, social and cultural rights are subject to progressive realisation.[157] Likewise, effective protection should not be measured by reference to the (high) level of socio-economic rights guaranteed to nationals of the country of destination generally, or against the (low) level of such rights foreseen for asylum seekers.[158] Rather, what constitutes effective protection will depend on the vulnerabilities of the individual protection seeker. If the state of origin can address (the cumulative effects of) an individual's mental health issues, stigmatisation, etc. and the resulting socio-economic deprivation, state protection will be established. If, however, one or several vulnerabilities cannot be effectively addressed through reception and reintegration measures, and thus the risk of re-trafficking or irregular re-migration remains, there will be a failure of state protection.

This constitutes a high threshold for effective state protection, which many countries of origin are unlikely to be able to meet. As a result, courts in countries of destination may be reluctant to accept this argument. Indeed, in the context of cases dealing with a risk of destitution under Article 3 ECHR,[159] and also in cases dealing with the availability of an IPA,[160] courts have returned applicants to face extreme poverty. However, what distinguishes the present argument

157 International Covenant on Economic, Social and Cultural Rights (adopted 16 December 1966, entered into force 3 January 1976) 993 UNTS 3 (ICESCR) art 2(1).

158 See, for example, C-179/11 *Cimande and GISTI* [2012] ECLI:EU:C:2012:594; C-79/13 *Saciri and Others* [2014] ECLI:EU:C:2014:103,

159 For example, *SSHD v Said* [2016] EWCA Civ 442, [2016] 5 WLUK 88.

160 For example, *Januzi* (n 141).

from cases in which protection was refused despite a risk of destitution is the fact that socio-economic deprivation (caused by a range of vulnerabilities) is material to the risk of re-trafficking and irregular re-migration, and thus to the question of persecution. Failure on the part of the country of origin to provide effective protection against socio-economic deprivation not only leads to poverty but may also lead to violations of civil and political rights as a consequence. Courts must take this into account when making their assessment.

4.4 Conclusion

The criminal law concepts of 'trafficking' and 'smuggling' suggest that trafficked persons suffer harm, while smuggled persons – and, by extension, irregularised migrants – do not. This chapter has shown that not only do persons undertaking dangerous migratory journeys, too, suffer serious harm, but also that this harm may amount to persecution where states of origin fail to offer protection. Indeed, both groups are likely to experience serious harm outside the country of origin where they are re-trafficked or re-migrate irregularly.

In this context, this chapter has argued that the concept of persecution in the Refugee Convention is not limited to experiences in the territory of the country of origin. This argument is based on the fact that trafficked persons and irregularised migrants experience sequential and cumulative harms. First, they experience harm in the country of origin, which, in itself, will likely not amount to persecution for the purpose of refugee law. This type of harm is caused by a set of vulnerability indicators which exacerbate one another and ultimately converge to impact a person's livelihood options, resulting in socio-economic deprivation. Second, where the first type of harm remains unaddressed, trafficked persons and irregularised migrants will exercise agency and attempt to respond to this harm themselves by re-migrating irregularly. In this process, they will experience violations of civil and political rights. The non-state actors inflicting this second type of harm are not limited territorially in the same way as state actors seeking to protect against it. Thus, in order to offer effective state protection, countries of origin must protect against the first type of harm, addressing the intersecting vulnerabilities causing socio-economic deprivation.

Where they are unable or unwilling to do so, both types of harm, cumulatively, will amount to persecution for the purpose of refugee law. Having identified vulnerabilities as relevant indicators for risk of re-trafficking, courts ought to return to these risk factors when assessing availability of state protection, asking whether countries of origin are able (and willing) to effectively counter returnees' vulnerabilities and thus reduce or eliminate the risk of re-trafficking and irregular re-migration.

Thus, irregularised migrants are able to meet not only the well-founded fear element of the *refugee* definition, as established in Chapter 3, but also the definition's persecution element. Yet the *refugee* definition also requires that persecution be for reasons of a Refugee Convention ground. Thus, the next chapter examines how nexus is established in trafficking-based asylum claims and whether irregularised migrants, too, can meet the final element of the *refugee* definition and should, therefore, be able to claim refugee status.

References

AM and BM (Trafficked Women) Albania CG [2010] UKUT 80 (IAC)

Asylgesetz (AsylG) 2 September 2008 (BGBl. I S. 1798) (Asylum Act)

Aydin v Turkey App no 57/1996/676/866 (ECtHR, 25 September 1997)

AZ (Trafficked Women) Thailand CG [2010] UKUT 118 (IAC)

Banković and Others v Belgium and Others App no 52207/99 (ECtHR, 12 December 2001)

Bayerischer Verwaltungsgerichtshof, 8 ZB 18.31141, 09.08.2018

Behrman S, 'Refugee Law as a Means of Control' (2019) 32(1) Journal of Refugee Studies 43 <https://doi.org/10.1093/jrs/fey016>

Border Violence Monitoring Network, *The Black Book of Pushbacks*, vols I and II (2020) <https://left.eu/issues/publications/black-book-of-pushbacks-volumes-i-ii/> accessed 9 September 2021

BT v SSHD [2019] UKUT (IAC) PA/07306/2017

C-79/13 *Saciri and Others* [2014] ECLI:EU:C:2014:103

C-175/08, C-176/08, C-178/08 and C-179/08 *Abdulla and Others* [2010] ECLI:EU:C:2010:105

C-179/11 *Cimande and GISTI* [2012] ECLI:EU:C:2012:594

Cantor DJ, 'Defining Refugees: Persecution, Surrogacy and the Human Rights Paradigm' in Bruce Burson and David James Cantor (eds), *Human Rights and the Refugee Definition: Comparative Legal Practice and Theory* (Brill 2016)

Carlier J-Y, 'The Geneva Refugee Definition and the "Theory of the Three Scales"' in Frances Nicholson and Patrick Twomey (eds), *Refugee Rights and Realities: Evolving International Concepts and Regimes* (CUP 1999)

Chetail V, 'Are Refugee Rights Human Rights? An Unorthodox Questioning of the Relations between Refugee Law and Human Rights Law' in Ruth Rubio-Marín (ed), *Human Rights and Immigration* (OUP 2014)

Chimni BS, *International Refugee Law: A Reader* (Sage 2000)

Crépin M, *Persecution, International Refugee Law and Refugees: A Feminist Approach* (Routledge 2020)

Cyprus v Turkey App no 25781/94 (ECtHR, 10 May 2001)

Deutsche Welle, 'Land Migration in Africa Twice as Deadly as Mediterranean, says UNHCR' (3 November 2019) <www.dw.com/en/land-migration-in-africa-twice-as-deadly-as-mediterranean-says-unhcr/a-51096086> accessed 1 May 2020

Dimitriadi A, 'The Interrelationship between Trafficking and Irregular Migration' in Sergio Carrera and Elspeth Guild (eds), *Irregular Migration, Trafficking and Smuggling of Human Beings: Policy Dilemmas in the EU* (CEPS 2016) <www.ceps.eu/wp-content/uploads/2016/02/Irregular%20Migration,%20Trafficking%20and%20SmugglingwithCovers.pdf> accessed 18 August 2022

DK v SSHD [2024] UKUT (IAC) UI-2023-003379

Dorevitch A and Michelle Foster, 'Obstacles on the Road to Protection: Assessing the Treatment of Sex-Trafficking Victims under Australia's Migration and Refugee Law' (2008) 9(1) Melbourne Journal of International Law 140

Dowd R, 'Dissecting Discrimination in Refugee Law: An Analysis of its Meaning and Its Cumulative Effect' (2011) 23(1) International Journal of Refugee Law 28 <https://doi.org/10.1093/ijrl/eeq043>

Dugard J, 'Diplomatic Protection' in James Crawford and others (eds), *The Law of International Responsibility* (OUP 2010)
EK (Article 4 ECHR- Anti-Trafficking Convention) Tanzania v SSHD [2013] UKUT 00313 (IAC)
ES (s82 NIA 2002, Negative NRM) [2018] UKUT 335 (IAC)
European Convention for the Protection of Human Rights and Fundamental Freedoms Rights, as amended (adopted 4 November 1950, entered into force 3 September 1953) CETS No 005 (ECHR)
Ferolla Vallandro do Valle M, 'Fleeing Deprivation: Deducing *Non-Refoulement* Obligations from Economic, Social and Cultural Rights' (2024) 36(4) International Journal of Refugee Law 353 <https://doi.org/10.1093/ijrl/eeae036>
FK v SSHD [2015] UKUT (IAC) AA/08453/2014
Fortin A, 'The Meaning of Protection in the Refugee Definition' (2000) 12 International Journal of Refugee Law 548 <https://doi.org/10.1093/ijrl/12.4.548>
Foster M, *International Refugee Law and Socio-Economic Rights: Refuge from Deprivation* (CUP 2007)
Foster M and others, '"Time" in Refugee Status Determination in Australia and the United Kingdom: A Clear and Present Danger from Armed Conflict?' (2022) 34(2) International Journal of Refugee Law 163 <https://doi.org/10.1093/ijrl/eeac033>
Giuffré M, *The Readmission of Asylum Seekers under International Law* (Hart Publishing 2020)
Goodwin-Gill GS and Jane McAdam, *The Refugee in International Law* (4th edn, OUP 2021)
Grahl-Madsen A, *The Status of Refugees in International Law*, vol I (A W Sijthoff 1966)
Greek Case App nos 3321/67, 3322/67, 3323/67, 3344/67 (European Commission of Human Rights, 5 November 1969)
Grundler M, 'The Locus of Persecution Reconsidered: Risk of Re-Trafficking, Cumulative Harm and Failure of State Protection' (2023) 35(4) International Journal of Refugee Law 441 <https://doi.org/10.1093/ijrl/eeae016>
Guild E, 'Asymmetrical Sovereignty and the Refugee: Diplomatic Assurances and the Failure of Due Process, *Agiza v. Sweden* and *Alzery v. Sweden*' in James C Simeon (ed), *Critical Issues in International Refugee Law* (CUP 2010)
Hailbronner K and Daniel Thym (eds), *EU Immigration and Asylum Law: A Commentary* (2nd edn, Beck, Hart, Nomos 2016)
Hathaway JC and Michelle Foster, *The Law of Refugee Status* (2nd edn, CUP 2014)
Hathaway JC and Hugo Storey, 'What is the Meaning of State Protection in Refugee Law? A Debate' (2016) 28(3) International Journal of Refugee Law 480 <https://doi.org/10.1093/ijrl/eew053>
HC v SSHD [2021] UKUT (IAC) PA/05060/2019
HD (Trafficked Women) Nigeria CG [2016] UKUT 00454 (IAC)
HG v SSHD [2019] UKUT (IAC) PA/10947/2018
Horvath v SSHD [2000] UKHL 37, [2000] Imm AR 552
Human Rights Committee, *Lopez Burgos v Uruguay*, Comm 52/1979 (29 July 1981)
Human Rights Committee, *Vidal Martins v Uruguay*, Comm 57/1979 (23 March 1982)
HVT v SSHD [2018] UKUT (IAC) PA/03104/2017
Immigration and Refugee Board of Canada, 'Eritrea: Situation of People Returning to the Country after They either Spent Time Abroad, Claimed Refugee Status, or Were Seeking Asylum (September 2014–June 2015)' (2015) <www.refworld.org/docid/577b6d024.html> accessed 3 June 2020

Inayatullah N, 'Beyond the Sovereignty Dilemma: Quasi-States as Social Construct' in Thomas J Biersteker and Cynthia Weber (eds), *State Sovereignty as Social Construct* (CUP 2011)

International Covenant on Civil and Political Rights (adopted 16 December 1966, entered into force 23 March 1976) 999 UNTS 171 (ICCPR)

International Covenant on Economic, Social and Cultural Rights (adopted 16 December 1966, entered into force 3 January 1976) 993 UNTS 3 (ICESCR)

International Criminal Court, 'Statement to the United Nations Security Council on the Situation in Libya, Pursuant to UNSCR 1970 (2011)' (8 May 2019) <www.icc-cpi.int/Pages/item.aspx?name=180508-otp-statement-libya-UNSC> accessed 3 October 2020

Ireland v The United Kingdom App no 5310/71 (ECtHR, 13 December 1977)

Januzi v SSHD [2006] UKHL 5, [2006] 2 WLR 397

Jastram K, 'Economic Harm as a Basis for Refugee Status and the Application of Human Rights Law to the Interpretation of Economic Persecution' in James C Simeon (ed), *Critical Issues in International Refugee Law* (CUP 2010)

JV v SSHD [2024] UKUT (IAC) UI-2024-001176

Kälin W, 'Non-State Agents of Persecution and the Inability of the State to Protect' (2001) 15 Georgetown Immigration Law Journal 415

Kelly E, 'Journeys of Jeopardy: A Review of Research on Trafficking in Women and Children in Europe' (2002) IOM <https://publications.iom.int/system/files/pdf/mrs_11_2002.pdf> accessed 29 April 2020

Künzli A, 'Exercising Diplomatic Protection: The Fine Line Between Litigation, Demarches and Consular Assistance' (2006) 66 Zeitschrift für ausländisches öffentliches Recht und Völkerrecht 321

Kuosmanen J, 'What's So Special about Persecution?' (2014) 17 Ethical Theory and Moral Practice 129 <https://doi.org/10.1007/s10677-013-9425-4>

Lehmann JM, *'Protection' in European Union Asylum Law: International and European Law Requirements for Assessing Available Protection as a Criterion for Refugee and Subsidiary Status* (Brill 2020)

LTD v SSHD [2015] UKUT (IAC) AA/13630/2011

Markard N, *Kriegsflüchtlinge: Gewalt gegen Zivilpersonen in bewaffneten Konflikten als Herausforderung für das Flüchtlingsrecht und den subsidiären Schutz* (Mohr Siebeck 2012)

MD v SSHD [2021] UKUT (IAC) PA/12142/2019

Moreno-Lax V, *Accessing Asylum in Europe: Extraterritorial Border Controls and Refugee Rights under EU Law* (OUP 2017)

Moreno-Lax V, 'Intersectionality, Forced Migration, and the Jus-Generation of the Right to Flee: Theorising a Composite Entitlement to Leave to Escape Irreversible Harm' in Başak Çalı, Ledi Bianku and Iulia Motoc (eds), *Migration and the European Convention on Human Rights* (OUP 2021)

MP (Trafficking – Sufficiency of Protection) Romania [2005] UKIAT 00086

MS (Pakistan) v SSHD [2020] UKSC 9, [2020] Imm AR 967

MSF, 'Violence, Vulnerability and Migration: Trapped at the Gates of Europe - a Report on the Situation of Sub-Saharan Migrants in an Irregular Situation in Morocco' (2013) <www.msf.org/violence-vulnerability-and-migration-trapped-gates-europe> accessed 2 May 2020

Nationality and Borders Act 2022

Noll G, 'Diplomatic Assurances and the Silence of Human Rights Law' (2006) 7(1) Melbourne Journal of International Law 104

NX v SSHD [2014] UKUT (IAC) AA/01621/2013

OHCHR, 'Desperate and Dangerous: Report on the Human Rights Situation of Migrants and Refugees in Libya' (2018) <https://reliefweb.int/report/libya/

desperate-and-dangerous-report-human-rights-situation-migrants-and-refugees-libya>
OHCHR, 'Report of the Special Rapporteur on Torture and Other Cruel, Inhuman or Degrading Treatment or Punishment' (26 February 2018) A/HRC/37/50
O'Sullivan M, 'Acting the Part: Can Non-State Entities Provide Protection Under International Refugee Law?' (2012) 24(1) International Journal of Refugee Law 85 <https://doi.org/10.1093/ijrl/ees001>
Paposhvili v Belgium App no 41738/10 (ECtHR, 13 December 2016)
Peers S and others (eds), *EU Immigration and Asylum Law (Text and Commentary): Volume 3: EU Asylum Law* (2nd Revised edn, Brill 2015)
PG v SSHD [2022] UKUT (IAC) PA/00229/2020
PO (Trafficked Women) Nigeria CG [2009] UKAIT 00046
Price M, 'Persecution Complex: Justifying Asylum Law's Preference for Persecuted People' (2006) 47 Harvard International Law Journal 413
Regulation (EU) 2024/1347 of the European Parliament and of the Council of 14 May 2024 on Standards for the Qualification of Third-Country Nationals or Stateless Persons as Beneficiaries of International Protection, for a Uniform Status for Refugees or for Persons Eligible for Subsidiary Protection and for the Content of the Protection Granted, Amending Council Directive 2003/109/EC and Repealing Directive 2011/95/EU of the European Parliament and of the Council [2024] OJ L 2024/1347 (Qualification Regulation)
Rempell S, 'Defining Persecution' (2013) 1 Utah Law Review 283
Saito K, 'International Protection for Trafficked Persons and Those who Fear Being Trafficked' (2007) UNHCR Research Paper No 149 <www.unhcr.org/sites/default/files/legacy-pdf/476652742.pdf> accessed 2 February 2019
Sanchez G, *Human Smuggling and Border Crossings* (Routledge 2015)
Sanderson S, 'Left to Die: How Algeria Deports Migrants to Niger' (*INFOMIGRANTS*, 5 May 2019) <www.infomigrants.net/en/post/16148/left-to-die-how-algeria-deports-migrants-to-niger> accessed 1 May 2020
Schultz J, *The Internal Protection Alternative in Refugee Law: Treaty Basis and Scope of Application under the 1951 Convention Relating to the Status of Refugees and Its 1967 Protocol* (Brill Nijhoff 2019)
Smyth C, 'The Human Rights Approach to "Persecution" and Its Child Rights Discontents' (2021) 33(2) International Journal of Refugee Law 238 <https://doi.org/10.1093/ijrl/eeab039>
Squire V and others, *Crossing the Mediterranean Sea by Boat: Mapping and Documenting Migratory Journeys and Experiences* (University of Warwick 2017) <https://warwick.ac.uk/fac/soc/pais/research/projects/crossingthemed/ctm_final_report_4may2017.pdf> accessed 6 August 2021
SSHD v Said [2016] EWCA Civ 442, [2016] 5 WLUK 88
Stahlmann F, 'Erfahrungen und Perspektiven Abgeschobener Afghanen im Kontext Aktueller Politischer und Wirtschaftlicher Entwicklungen Afghanistans' (*Diakonie Deutschland, Brot für die Welt, Diakonie Hessen*, June 2021) <www.fluechtlingsrat-mv.de/wp-content/uploads/2021/06/AFG_Monitoring-Studie_FINAL.pdf> accessed 28 August 2024
Staker C, 'Jurisdiction' in Malcolm D Evans (ed), *International Law* (5th edn, OUP 2018)
Stevens D, 'What Do We Mean by Protection' (2013) 20 International Journal on Minority & Group Rights 233 <http://doi.org/10.1163/15718115-02002005>
Storey H, 'What Constitutes Persecution? Towards a Working Definition' (2014) 26(2) International Journal of Refugee Law 272 <https://doi.org/10.1093/ijrl/eeu017>
Stoyanova V, *Human Trafficking and Slavery Reconsidered: Conceptual Limits and States' Positive Obligations in European Law* (CUP 2017)

Stoyanova V, 'The Right to Leave Any Country and the Interplay between Jurisdiction and Proportionality in Human Rights Law' (2020) 32(3) International Journal of Refugee Law 403 <https://doi.org/10.1093/ijrl/eeaa030>
TAN v SSHD [2023] UKUT (IAC) UI-2022-003801
TD and AD (Trafficked Women) CG [2016] UKUT 92
TSN v SSHD [2019] UKUT (IAC) PA/07665/2017
TT (Vietnam) [2019] EWCA Civ 248, [2019] 2 WLUK 401
TVP v SSHD [2018] UKUT (IAC) PA/02997/2018
Tyrer v UK App no 5856/72 (ECtHR, 25 April 1978)
UNGA, 'Unlawful Death of Refugees and Migrants' (15 August 2017) A/72/335
UNHCR, 'Desperate Journeys: Refugees and Migrants Entering and Crossing Europe via the Mediterranean and Western Balkans Routes' (February 2017) <www.unhcr.org/uk/news/updates/2017/2/58b449f54/desperate-journeys-refugees-migrants-entering-crossing-europe-via-mediterranean.html> accessed 11 September 2022
UNHCR, 'Guidelines on International Protection: The Application of Article 1A(2) of the 1951 Convention and/or 1967 Protocol Relating to the Status of Refugees to Victims of Trafficking and Persons at Risk of Being Trafficked' (2006) HCR/GIP/06/07 (UNHCR Trafficking Guidelines)
UNHCR, 'Handbook on Procedures and Criteria for Determining Refugee Status and Guidelines on International Protection under the 1951 Convention and the 1967 Protocol Relating to the Status of Refugees' (1979, reissued 2019) HCR/1P/4/ENG/REV.4 (UNHCR Handbook)
UNHCR, 'On this Journey, No One Cares if You Live or Die: Abuse, Protection and Justice Along Routes between East and West Africa and Africa's Mediterranean Coast: A Route-based Perspective on Key Risks', vol 2 (March 2024) <www.unhcr.org/media/journey-no-one-cares-if-you-live-or-die-abuse-protection-and-justice-along-routes-between-1> accessed 19 August 2024
UNHCR, 'UNHCR Note on Diplomatic Assurances and International Refugee Protection' (2006) <www.refworld.org/policy/legalguidance/unhcr/2006/en/40015> accessed 13 May 2021
United Nations, 'Draft Articles on Diplomatic Protection' (2006) <https://legal.un.org/ilc/texts/instruments/english/draft_articles/9_8_2006.pdf> accessed 12 May 2021
UNODC, 'Global Study on Smuggling of Migrants 2018' (2018) <www.unodc.org/documents/data-and-analysis/glosom/GLOSOM_2018_web_small.pdf> accessed 5 June 2020
VD (Trafficking) Albania CG [2004] UKIAT 00115
VG Aachen, 2 K 2224/15.A, 28.12.2017
VG Aachen, 2 K 2514/21 A, 06.06.2023
VG Aachen, 2 K 2521/18.A, 10.11.2020
VG Aachen, 8 K 1220/02.A, 21.01.2004
VG Augsburg, Au 7 K 12.30184, 18.09.2012
VG Augsburg, Au 7 K 17.30060, 13.12.2017
VG Cottbus, 9 K 1516/18.A, 11.01.2021
VG Düsseldorf, 27 K 2264/18.A, 15.12.2020
VG Magdeburg, 6 A 40/19, 28.01.2020
VG München, M 10 K 16.30286, 17.11.2016
VG München, M 11 K 06.51323, 11.09.2007
VG München, M 13 K 21.30776, 21.06.2022
VG München, M 23 K 11.30389, 30.09.2013
VG Regensburg, 15 K 21.31190, 16.12.2021
VG Regensburg, RO 15 K 20.30871, 26.04.2021
VG Stuttgart, A 7 K 1405/12, 16.05.2014

VG Würzburg, W 8 K 20 31251, 20.05.2022

Vienna Convention on Consular Relations (adopted 24 April 1963, entered into force 19 March 1967) 596 UNTS 261 (VCCR)

Wilsher D, 'Between Martyrdom and Silence: Dissent, Duress, and Persecution as the Suppression of Human Rights under the Refugee Convention' (2021) 33(1) International Journal of Refugee Law 28 <https://doi.org/10.1093/ijrl/eeab025>

Women's Refugee Commission, '"More Than One Million Pains": Sexual Violence Against Men and Boys on the Central Mediterranean Route to Italy' (March 2019) <www.womensrefugeecommission.org/wp-content/uploads/2020/04/Libya-Italy-Report-03-2019.pdf> accessed 19 September 2020

X v Finland App no 34806/04 (ECtHR, 3 July 2012)

Zambelli P, 'Knowing Persecution When We See It: Non-State Actors and the Measure of State Protection' (2020) 32(1) International Journal of Refugee Law 28 <https://doi.org/10.1093/ijrl/eeaa001>

5 The Nexus to Refugee Convention Grounds

A Return to 'Route Causes'

5.1 Introduction

Having established that irregular re-migration entails a risk of persecution, to determine whether irregularised migrants can claim refugee status, a final question is whether they can meet the Refugee Convention's nexus requirement. The Refugee Convention specifies that a refugee's well-founded fear of being persecuted must be 'for reasons of' (at least) one of the five Convention grounds race, religion, nationality, political opinion and membership of a particular social group (PSG).[1]

Although, as Lehman argues, the nexus requirement constitutes an 'insurmountable hurdle' for some asylum seekers – for example, for those fleeing the indiscriminate effects of armed conflict or natural disasters – it has 'witnessed a gradual evolution through the relatively flexible concept of particular social group' and therefore 'accommodates . . . claims not anticipated at the time of drafting [the Refugee Convention]'.[2] With respect to the trafficking context, Jayasinghe and Baglay, in examining Australian and Canadian case law, argue that where the Refugee Convention has failed to protect trafficked persons, this has been due to problems in establishing a nexus to Convention grounds, particularly due to problems in relation to establishing membership of a PSG.[3] Magugliani has shown that this is a particular problem for male trafficked persons.[4] With trafficked persons facing obstacles in relation to the nexus requirement, it would seem that their claims may be of limited use for establishing

1 Convention Relating to the Status of Refugees (adopted 28 July 1951, entered into force 22 April 1954) 189 UNTS 137 (Refugee Convention) art 1A(2).

2 Julian M Lehman, 'At the Crossroads: The 1951 Geneva Convention Today' in Satvinder Singh Juss (ed), *Research Handbook on International Refugee Law* (Edward Elgar Publishing 2019) 5.

3 Udara Jayasinghe and Sasha Baglay, 'Protecting Victims of Human Trafficking within a "Non-Refoulement" Framework: Is Complementary Protection an Effective Alternative in Canada and Australia?' (2011) 23(3) International Journal of Refugee Law 489 <https://doi.org/10.1093/ijrl/eer022>.

4 Noemi Magugliani, 'Trafficked Adult Males as (Un)Gendered Protection Seekers: Between Presumption of Invulnerability and Exclusion from Membership of a Particular Social Group'

DOI: 10.4324/9781032664644-5

nexus for irregularised migrants' claims by analogy. As such, rather than using trafficked persons' claims as a template, this chapter, while exploring how nexus is established in trafficking-based asylum claims, will propose a novel approach to fulfilling this requirement, which can be applied to both trafficked persons and irregularised migrants. To do so, the chapter returns to the 'route causes' of irregular re-migration discussed in Chapter 3. Having identified route *causes* of irregular re-migration, it is pertinent to examine whether these can be framed in terms of nexus grounds and establish the necessary connection to persecution.

First, however, the chapter examines the nexus element of the *refugee* definition, including the nature of the link between persecution and the Convention grounds, as well as those grounds themselves in Section 2. The section pays particular attention to the 'predicament approach'[5] to establishing nexus and to the Convention ground 'membership of a PSG', both of which will be of relevance later in the chapter.

Section 3 then explores how nexus is established in trafficking-based asylum claims. In UK and German case law, the only Convention ground relied upon is 'membership of a PSG', and the two main PSGs identified are the PSG 'women' and the PSG 'trafficked persons'. The section deals with both of these in turn and also considers the utility of a PSG 'men' in trafficking-based asylum claims, as well as the tendency to frame PSGs narrowly. In addition, the section explores the 'innate characteristics' and the 'social perception' test in the context of these different PSGs, arguing that the latter can be met through trafficked persons' own actions and behaviours. Finally, although the actual nexus element is rarely discussed in the available case law, the section briefly examines this issue, clarifying different scenarios in which the link is made out and showing that courts, at times, employ a predicament approach to establish nexus.

Section 4 builds on the findings from Section 3 in considering the PSG 'smuggled persons' or 'irregular migrants' as an equivalent of the PSG 'trafficked persons', showing that these PSGs can meet the 'innate characteristics' and 'social perception' tests. However, the section argues that the PSG 'persons in vulnerable situations', as well as the Convention ground 'nationality', better satisfies the nexus requirement for both trafficked persons and irregularised migrants. Thus, in examining the PSG 'persons in vulnerable situations', the section links the predicament of having to re-migrate irregularly to vulnerability indicators discussed in the context of establishing a risk of irregular re-migration. Finally, the section continues the analysis of the relevance of vulnerability indicators for the nexus enquiry by returning to the role of

---

(2022) 34(3–4) International Journal of Refugee Law 353 <https://doi.org/10.1093/ijrl/eeac030>.

5 Michelle Foster, *International Refugee Law and Socio-Economic Rights: Refuge from Deprivation* (CUP 2007) 277.

the global visa regime and linking irregular re-migration to the Convention ground 'nationality'.

The chapter concludes by highlighting the interconnected nature of the elements of the *refugee* definition. In particular, it argues that the nexus element can be inferred from the well-founded fear enquiry by examining whether the reasons identified in the context of the future risk analysis can be conceived of in terms of nexus grounds. More specifically, the vulnerability reasoning employed in earlier chapters informs the relevant PSGs identified in this chapter and helps satisfy the nexus requirement.

5.2 The Nexus to Refugee Convention Grounds

The *refugee* definition requires the persecution feared to be 'for reasons of' one or several Convention grounds, all of which are considered to constitute 'protected characteristics'.[6] As Dauvergne puts it, 'nexus in refugee law functions as a limiting principle: it ensures that not all those at risk of being persecuted fall within the [refugee] definition, only those whose risk is discriminatory in a way that links directly to human rights principles'.[7] The nexus requirement has raised many complex questions, such as whether the persecutor and the persecuted can share a protected characteristic; the question of whether nexus can be established where only some, rather than all, persons possessing the protected characteristic are at risk; and the question of whether persecution can be 'for reasons of' that characteristic even though the relevant group is not a minority.[8] Hathaway and Foster demonstrate that none of these considerations pose an obstacle to establishing nexus. They explain that '[t]he key function of the "for reasons of" clause is to establish a link between a risk of being persecuted and one of the Convention grounds'.[9] This section gives a brief overview, both of the nature of this 'link' and of the five Convention grounds, in order to lay the groundwork for the discussion in the remainder of the chapter.

5.2.1 *The Nexus 'Link'*

Hathaway and Foster describe the nexus element as 'a causal relationship between the risk of being persecuted and the protected ground',[10] thus invoking the language of causation. Nevertheless, they emphasise that a 'but for'

6 James C Hathaway and Michelle Foster, *The Law of Refugee Status* (2nd edn, CUP 2014) 365.

7 Catherine Dauvergne, 'Women in Refugee Jurisprudence' in Cathryn Costello, Michelle Foster and Jane McAdam (eds), *The Oxford Handbook of International Refugee Law* (OUP 2021) 739.

8 For a detailed discussion of these and additional questions, see Hathaway and Foster (n 6) 363–67.

9 ibid 363.

10 ibid 364.

or a 'sole cause' test of causation is not appropriate to establish the existence of this link and instead argue in favour of a '"contributing cause" test', under which 'it is sufficient if the Convention reason or ground accounts in part or is a contributing factor in creating the risk of being persecuted'.[11] This approach was echoed by the House of Lords in *Fornah*, observing that the 'ground on which the claimant relies need not be the only or even the primary reason for the apprehended persecution. It is enough that the ground relied on is an effective reason'.[12] Meanwhile, Goodwin-Gill and McAdam do not use the language of causation but argue that all that is required is 'a link'.[13] This is similar to EU law, which merely requires 'a connection' between acts of and reasons for persecution.[14] This, according to Peers *et al.*, means that 'a strict "causal link"' is not required under EU law.[15] Generally, but particularly in the context of seeking to establish nexus in the context of irregular re-migration, it is important to note that the claimant's allegedly 'unreasonable' conduct does not sever the (causal) connection; what matters is that some connection exists.[16]

The next question, then, is what exactly the Convention ground must be connected to in order to establish nexus. Hathaway and Foster explain that the 'causal connection', as they term it, has been interpreted as meaning that the 'Convention ground must be linked to the intention of the persecutor [or] to the intention of . . . the state withholding protection; or . . . simply to the applicant's predicament of being persecuted'.[17] Under each of these approaches, different degrees of importance are attached to the question of persecutory intent. While persecutory intent 'may be sufficient to establish a claim to refugee status, it cannot be considered a *necessary* condition'.[18] Both 'legislative or organizational intent' on the part of the state of origin[19] and personal motives of non-state actors are difficult to establish, and doing so shifts

11 ibid 387–90.
12 *K v SSHD, Fornah v SSHD* [2006] UKHL 46, [2006] 3 WLR 733 [17].
13 Guy S Goodwin-Gill and Jane McAdam, *The Refugee in International Law* (4th edn, OUP 2021) 80.
14 Regulation (EU) 2024/1347 of the European Parliament and of the Council of 14 May 2024 on Standards for the Qualification of Third-Country Nationals or Stateless Persons as Beneficiaries of International Protection, for a Uniform Status for Refugees or for Persons Eligible for Subsidiary Protection and for the Content of the Protection Granted, Amending Council Directive 2003/109/EC and Repealing Directive 2011/95/EU of the European Parliament and of the Council [2024] OJ L 2024/1347 (Qualification Regulation) art 9(3).
15 Steve Peers and others (eds), *EU Immigration and Asylum Law (Text and Commentary): Second Revised Edition: Volume 3: EU Asylum Law* (Brill 2015) 110.
16 Michelle Foster, 'Causation in Context: Interpreting the Nexus Clause in the Refugee Convention' (2002) 23(2) Michigan Journal of International Law 265, 295.
17 Hathaway and Foster (n 6) 367.
18 Goodwin-Gill and McAdam (n 13) 79; see also Hathaway and Foster (n 6) 368.
19 Goodwin-Gill and McAdam (n 13) 79; see also Hathaway and Foster (n 6) 368.

attention away from the more relevant 'wider societal context of discrimination and oppression'.[20] According to Hathaway and Foster, these problems have been mitigated to an extent by recognising that 'nexus is established where *either* of the two constituent elements of [being persecuted] – the risk of harm *or* the failure of state protection – is linked to a Convention ground'.[21] If 'the state is unwilling to protect for a Convention reason', nexus is established.[22] This, however, still implies intention, as the state must be unwilling rather than unable to protect.[23] The 'predicament approach', on the other hand, does not require showing intent by the persecutor or the state but focuses 'on the reason for the exposure to the risk'.[24] Under the predicament approach, the nexus requirement is satisfied if 'the applicant's Convention ground status puts him or her at a disproportionately high risk of the relevant harm feared'.[25] Foster argues that this approach

> allows for a more realistic assessment of the wider context of a person's fear of being persecuted, admitting of the possibility that, where the predicament is the result of widespread discrimination against a group on a ground protected by the Refugee Convention, refugee status will be established.[26]

Goodwin-Gill and McAdam agree that 'the governing criterion [for refugee protection] remains that of a serious possibility of persecution, not proof of intent to harm on the part of the persecutor'.[27]

As explained later, while UK and German courts do rely on persecutory intent to establish nexus in some cases, they also apply a predicament approach in trafficking-based asylum claims. The predicament approach will also be particularly useful for establishing nexus in irregularised migrants' asylum claims.

5.2.2 The Convention Grounds

In what follows, we will see that the most common way of establishing nexus in the trafficking context is by way of the ground 'membership of a PSG'. Jayasinghe and Baglay note that this is also the case in Australian and Canadian jurisprudence, 'although the identification of a social group in the context of human trafficking has not always been straightforward'.[28] The same may be

20 Hathaway and Foster (n 6) 371–72.
21 ibid 373.
22 ibid 374.
23 ibid 376.
24 ibid 378.
25 Foster (n 5) 277.
26 ibid 283.
27 Goodwin-Gill and McAdam (n 13) 81.
28 Jayasinghe and Baglay (n 3) 500.

said for UK and German jurisprudence. Before examining the Convention ground 'membership of a PSG' in more detail, it is important to acknowledge that the other Convention grounds may also be relevant, not only in the trafficking context, but also in the context of irregular migration.

According to both EU and UK law, the Convention ground 'race' includes 'considerations of colour, descent, or membership of a particular ethnic group'.[29] The United Nations High Commissioner for Refugees (UNHCR) Trafficking Guidelines note that an individual may be targeted for trafficking based on 'market demands for a particular race'.[30] Regarding the risk of irregular re-migration, it is conceivable that ethnic discrimination contributes to and exacerbates other vulnerabilities. Individuals may also be targeted for ill-treatment during the migratory journey based on their race. For example, there are reports of smugglers transporting migrants by boat, 'separating passengers according to race and locking Africans below deck', as well as accounts of 'different races being split up, with the lighter-skinned appearing to receive marginally better treatment'.[31] It is also worth noting that the Convention ground 'nationality' is often 'linked to the notion of race',[32] as it includes 'membership of a group determined by its cultural, ethnic, or linguistic identity', but can also mean 'citizenship'.[33] This ground, and particularly the 'citizenship' meaning, is discussed in more detail in Section 5.4.2 later on.

Under EU and UK law, the Convention ground 'religion' includes 'the holding of theistic, non-theistic and atheistic beliefs, the participation in, or abstention from, formal worship . . .'.[34] UNHCR notes that individuals may be targeted for trafficking based on a perceived (lack of) religious belief.[35] Likewise, it is possible that religious discrimination contributes to and exacerbates other vulnerabilities. Further, having, or being perceived as having, a particular religion may lead to individuals being targeted for harm during the migratory journey.

'Political opinion' constitutes 'the holding of an opinion, thought or belief on a matter related to the potential actors of persecution . . . and to their

29 Qualification Regulation (n 14) art 10(1)(a); Nationality and Borders Act 2022, s 33(1)(a).

30 UNHCR, 'Guidelines on International Protection: The Application of Article 1A(2) of the 1951 Convention and/or 1967 Protocol Relating to the Status of Refugees to Victims of Trafficking and Persons at Risk of Being Trafficked' (2006) HCR/GIP/06/07 (UNHCR Trafficking Guidelines) para 34.

31 Lizzie Dearden, 'The Darker Your Skin – the Further Down You Go: The Hierarchical System Aboard Italy's Migrant Boats That Governs Who Lives and Who Dies' (*The Independent*, 22 April 2015) <www.independent.co.uk/news/world/europe/the-paler-your-skin-the-higher-up-you-go-the-hierarchical-system-aboard-italys-migrant-boats-that-10193130.html> accessed 1 May 2020.

32 Hathaway and Foster (n 6) 397.

33 Qualification Regulation (n 14) art 10(1)(c).

34 ibid art 10(1)(b); Nationality and Borders Act 2022, s 33(1)(b).

35 UNHCR Trafficking Guidelines (n 30) para 35.

policies or methods'.[36] Again, individuals may be targeted for trafficking based on their political opinion,[37] while discrimination on grounds of political opinion may contribute to and exacerbate other vulnerabilities or cause irregular migrants to be targeted for harm during dangerous journeys.

Finally, 'membership of a PSG' has not been given as straightforward an explanation as the other nexus grounds in EU and UK law. Indeed, this ground has generated a lot of debate and commentary, and since it will play a prominent role in this chapter, it is pertinent to briefly outline some of the relevant issues around this Convention ground.

A PSG 'cannot be defined solely by reference to the well-founded fear of being persecuted'.[38] In practice, this means that the fact of, for example, fearing irregular re-migration does not make individuals members of a PSG, as this would result in circular reasoning, to the effect that any group of people fearing persecution would automatically come within the scope of a PSG, 'render[ing] the nexus clause superfluous'.[39] However, it should be noted that a past experience of persecution can be considered an innate characteristic,[40] while being targeted for persecution can give rise to differential social perception.[41]

The 'innate characteristics' and the 'social perception' tests are commonly used to establish whether a certain group can be said to constitute a PSG. The former test requires that members of the group share innate or unchangeable characteristic,[42] while the latter requires that members of the group be perceived as different from the rest of society in the country of origin.[43] EU and UK law requires that both tests are satisfied at the same time,[44] giving rise to a two-tier test which has been criticised as being too restrictive.[45] Indeed, the House of Lords in *Fornah* rejected the idea that both the 'social perception' and the 'innate characteristic' test must be met.[46] Further, in more recent

36 Qualification Regulation (n 14) art 10(1)(e); Nationality and Borders Act 2022, s 33(1)(d).
37 UNHCR Trafficking Guidelines (n 30) para 40.
38 Hathaway and Foster (n 6) 425.
39 ibid 424.
40 Such as the fact of having been trafficked. See Section 5.3.2, which follows.
41 Goodwin-Gill and McAdam (n 13) 106; see, for example, VG Regensburg, RN 5 K 16.30603, 19.10.2016, pp 6–7; discussed in Section 5.3.2.
42 Hathaway and Foster (n 6) 426.
43 ibid 428.
44 Qualification Regulation (n 14) art 10(1)(d); Nationality and Borders Act 2022, s 33(2).
45 Goodwin-Gill and McAdam (n 13) 118, n 393; Hathaway and Foster (n 6) 429; Peers and others (n 15) 113; Nora Markard, *Kriegsflüchtlinge: Gewalt gegen Zivilpersonen in bewaffneten Konflikten als Herausforderung für das Flüchtlingsrecht und den subsidiären Schutz* (Mohr Siebeck 2012) 263; Kay Hailbronner and Daniel Thym (eds), *EU Immigration and Asylum Law: A Commentary* (2nd edn, Beck, Hart, Nomos 2016) 1188; Christel Querton, 'The Interpretation of the Convention Ground of "Membership of a Particular Social Group" in the Context of Gender-Related Claims for Asylum: A Critical Analysis of the Tribunal's Approach in the UK' (*Refugee Law Initiative*, 2012) <http://sas-space.sas.ac.uk/4690/5/RLI_Working_Paper_No.3.pdf> accessed 13 February 2021.
46 *K and Fornah* (n 12) [16].

judgments, the UT has favoured an alternative rather than a cumulative test.[47] Nevertheless, as of 2022, UK law requires both tests to be satisfied,[48] while German law, following EU law, requires the same.[49] While this poses an obstacle to many claimants, this chapter will show that trafficked persons and irregularised migrants should be able to meet both the 'protected characteristics' and the 'social perception' tests as members of the PSG 'trafficked persons' or the PSG 'persons in vulnerable situations'.

5.3 Establishing Nexus in Trafficking-Based Asylum Claims

This section explores how UK and German courts approach the nexus element for claimants who fear re-trafficking. It is worth noting that most judgments discussed in the following subsections focus only on identifying a relevant Convention ground rather than discussing the connection between this ground and the persecution feared. In all cases, the Convention ground relied on is 'membership of a PSG', and only two main PSGs are identified – the PSG 'women' and the PSG 'trafficked persons'. This section explores both PSGs in turn while evaluating whether, and under which circumstances, reliance on these, in fact, satisfies the nexus element.

5.3.1 The PSG 'Women'

The majority of asylum claims discussed in this book were brought by female applicants, which goes some way towards explaining why the PSG 'women', or variations thereof, constitutes one possibility of establishing nexus in UK and German case law. Jayasinghe and Baglay note that in Australian and Canadian trafficking-based asylum claims, too, 'certain subsets of women or children have been identified to constitute particular social groups',[50] while Magugliani shows that trafficked women are more easily recognised as members of a PSG than trafficked men.[51]

Before discussing gender-based PSGs in some detail, it should be noted that even though a number of trafficking-based asylum claims discussed in what follows were made by claimants who were minors at the time of trafficking but adults at the time of the appeal,[52] the PSG 'children' is not discussed

47 *DH (Particular Social Group: Mental Health) Afghanistan* [2020] UKUT 223 (IAC), [2020] 6 WLUK 523 [50]; *EMAP (Gang violence, Convention Reason) (CG)* [2022] UKUT (IAC) 00335. This approach was endorsed in the trafficking context in *SSHD v NAMT* [2023] UKUT (IAC) UI-2023–002124 [12].

48 Nationality and Borders Act 2022, s33(2)–(4).

49 Asylgesetz (AsylG) 2 September 2008 (BGBl. I S. 1798) (Asylum Act) s 3b(4).

50 Jayasinghe and Baglay (n 3) 501.

51 Magugliani (n 4).

52 *JO (internal relocation – no risk of re-trafficking) Nigeria* [2004] UKIAT 00251; *AM and BM (Trafficked women) Albania* CG [2010] UKUT 80 (IAC); *SHL (Tracing obligation/*

in the relevant case law. Instead, age is seen as contributing to a trafficked person's vulnerability[53] rather than being considered in the context of the nexus element. Nevertheless, it should be noted that children may be targeted for trafficking because of their age[54] and that children can form a PSG.[55] However, since the present discussion is guided by the contents of the case law and because it is not within the scope of this book to cover all PSGs or other nexus grounds relevant to the trafficking context in detail, I will not discuss the PSG 'children' further here; instead, the focus of this section is the PSG 'women' – a nexus ground discussed in the case law – as well as the PSG 'men', which, although not mentioned in the case law, is relevant to the discussion in raising the question of whether gender-based PSGs plausibly establish a connection to risk in the trafficking context. The focus here on 'women' and 'men' is not intended to detract from the fact that transgender individuals, and, indeed, other members of the lesbian, gay, bisexual, transgender, intersex, queer and/or questioning and asexual (LGBTIQA+) community, may be at risk of trafficking, often for reasons of their gender or sexual identity.[56] Rather, this section seeks to unpack the assumption that where persons are at risk of re-trafficking, this is because they are (cis) women and that, conversely, male (and transgender) claimants are unable to establish a nexus to Convention grounds.

Interestingly, there are only three judgments amongst the case laws in which the applicant was found to belong simply to the PSG 'women'. First, a 2005 judgment by the administrative court (AC) Würzburg which concerned a woman trafficked for sexual exploitation and fearing re-trafficking and reprisals from her traffickers. In identifying the relevant PSG, the court argued that trafficking is connected to a woman's gender, age, sex, economic and social standing and, in particular, 'sexual use' for economic purposes.[57] Second, a 2022 judgment by the AC Berlin which concerned a Guinean woman trafficked for sexual exploitation by members of the military who was granted refugee status because she feared renewed sexualised violence and trafficking.[58]

Trafficking) Afghanistan v SSHD [2013] UKUT 00312 (IAC); *HD (Trafficked women) Nigeria CG* [2016] UKUT 00454 (IAC); *BA v SSHD* [2014] UKUT (IAC) AA/03923/2013; *TAN v SSHD* [2016] UKUT (IAC) AA/05644/2014; *FK v SSHD* [2015] UKUT (IAC) AA/08453/2014; *PQ v SSHD* [2017] UKUT (IAC) PA/01480/2015; *TVP v SSHD* [2018] UKUT (IAC) PA/02997/2018; VG Aachen, 3 K 12/07, 08.05.2007; VG München, M 23 K 11.30389, 30.09.2013; VG Würzburg, W 2 K 14.30213, 17.11.2015.

53 *AM and BM* (n 52) [182]; *HD* (n 52) [169]; 3 K 12/07 (n 52); M 23 K 11.30389 (n 52).

54 OHCHR, 'Fact Sheet No 36: Human Rights and Human Trafficking' (2014) 7 <www.ohchr.org/en/publications/fact-sheets/fact-sheet-no-36-human-rights-and-human-trafficking> accessed 29 October 2024. See also Convention on the Rights of the Child (adopted 20 November 1989, entered into force 2 September 1990) 1577 UNTS 3 (CRC) art 35.

55 Foster (n 5) 329; Jason Pobjoy, *The Child in International Refugee Law* (CUP 2017) 177–78.

56 Lynly S Egyes, 'Borders and Intersections: The Unique Vulnerabilities of LGBTQ Immigrants to Trafficking' in Erin C Heil and Andrea J Nichols (eds), *Broadening the Scope of Human Trafficking Research* (Carolina Academic Press 2019).

57 VG Würzburg, W 8 K 04.30919, 19.09.2005, p 6.

58 VG Berlin, 31 K 305/20 A, 17.08.2022.

The AC Berlin noted that rape, trafficking in women, sexual exploitation and forced prostitution are typical expressions of male dominance and claims to power, furthered by patriarchal social structures, so that the PSG 'women' explains why there is a link to a Convention ground. Third, a 2024 judgment by the AC Göttingen concerning a Zambian woman who was trafficked to France for labour exploitation and then to Germany for sexual exploitation.[59] The court referred to the Court of Justice of the European Union's (CJEU) judgment in *WS*,[60] noting that women can form a PSG simply because they face (sexual) violence due to their gender.

Thus, there is an assumption that the fact of being a woman explains why an individual is at risk of trafficking for sexual exploitation. This is likely true to an extent. Since women are more likely to be trafficked for sexual exploitation, while men are more likely to be trafficked for labour exploitation,[61] it can be assumed that 'demand' for trafficking women exists at all times. Nevertheless, women are also trafficked for labour, and men for sexual exploitation.[62] This means that both women and men may be targeted for trafficking based on their gender, so that the PSG 'women' alone cannot explain why both men and women are at risk of trafficking for diverse reasons.

Indeed, if 'women' can form a PSG, 'men' should be able to do so as well. Indeed, in the UK case of *SB*, the tribunal endorsed the view that '[i]t is possible for a particular social group involving men to be gender-based'.[63] However, the tribunal went on to state that, in such a case, 'discrimination in the wider sense must be shown to exist as an identifying characteristic of the particular social group'.[64] If discrimination of the relevant group is indeed necessary to meet the social perception test, 'men' are unlikely to be recognised as a PSG (at least if both the 'social perception' and the 'innate characteristics' tests are required to be met).

59 VG Göttingen, 3 A 135/21, 03.04.2024.

60 C-621/21 *WS* [2024] ECLI:EU:C:2024:47, where the Court held that 'women, as a whole, may be regarded as belonging to a "particular social group". . . where it is established that, in their country of origin, they are, on account of their gender, exposed to physical or mental violence, including sexual violence and domestic violence' (para 57).

61 UNODC, 'Global Report on Trafficking in Persons 2024' 20 <www.unodc.org/documents/data-and-analysis/glotip/2024/GLOTIP2024_BOOK.pdf> accessed 16 December 2024. However, it should be noted that it is questionable whether a distinction between sexual and labour exploitation is appropriate, since sex work is also a form of labour where it is conducted 'outside any relationship of subordination concerning the choice of that activity, working conditions and conditions of remuneration; under that person's own responsibility; and in return for remuneration paid to that person directly and in full' (C-268/99 *Jany and Others* [2001] ECLI:EU:C:2001:616, para 71). On the other hand, as opposed to other forms of forced labour, sexual exploitation impacts the right to physical integrity.

62 UNODC (n 61) 10; see also *FK* (n 52) for a case of male sex trafficking.

63 *SB (PSG – Protection Regulations – Reg 6) Moldova CG* [2008] UKAIT 00002 [53].

64 ibid.

The tribunal in *SB* also found, however, that

> where the members of a social group share a common background which is an immutable characteristic and which they cannot change (for example, the sharing of a common past experience) or they ought not to be required to change, it may be that such common background defines the group by giving it a distinct identity in the society in question.[65]

Insofar as gender can be considered 'immutable',[66] it is a characteristic that cannot be changed, and both women and men are likely to form a recognisable group in society. The tribunal in *SB* did not resolve the question of whether 'men' can form a PSG. However, if it is sufficient that male gender, as a common background, gives men a distinct identity in society, all that men have to prove to establish membership of a PSG is that they, too, are perceived as different by surrounding society, albeit in a different way than women. Indeed, men are often perceived as breadwinners and as responsible for providing for and defending their family. With regard to migrant men, Donaldson and Howson note that 'men's responsibility as the breadwinners or key providers for the family household is a very strong part of their sense of self and masculinity regardless of nationality, education, family background and experience'.[67] In particular:

> (but not only) . . . those [men] from parts of Africa and the Pacific . . . are explicitly expected to be the guides and protectors of women and children, and to be responsible not only for their own families, but also for and to the wider community.[68]

Shankley makes similar observations with regard to Polish migrant men in Britain and details how pressure to fulfil expectations associated with traditional gender roles increases their vulnerability to labour exploitation.[69] If 'men', like 'women', can form a PSG, both PSGs serve to establish a link to re-trafficking since there will be demand for both genders as (sex) workers, and patriarchal

65 ibid.

66 As Hailbronner and Thym note, gender 'is not static or innate but acquires socially and culturally constructed meaning over time'. See Hailbronner and Thym (n 45) 1180. However, this meaning can be considered immutable for a certain cultural context at a particular moment in time with regard to those (perceived as) belonging to a particular gender.

67 Mike Donaldson and Richard Howson, 'Men, Migration and Hegemonic Masculinity' in Mike Donaldson and others (eds), *Migrant Men: Critical Studies of Masculinities and the Migration Experience* (Routledge 2009) 212.

68 ibid 213.

69 William Shankley, 'Gender, Modern Slavery and Labour Exploitation: Experiences of Male Polish Migrants in England' (2023) 49(5) Journal of Ethnic and Migration Studies 1274 <https://doi.org/10.1080/1369183X.2021.2000853>.

social structures explain why both men and women may find themselves in the predicament of having to submit to trafficking. In the case law, however, the PSG 'men' is not discussed.

What the case law does discuss, however, are 'subsets' of the PSG 'women'.[70] Jayasinghe and Baglay note that such subsets of the group are often 'tied to victims' particular vulnerabilities' and include the PSGs 'single women, widows, divorced women [and] illiterate women'.[71] Foster, meanwhile, observes that there is a general tendency to frame the PSG 'women' narrowly due to 'implicit floodgates concerns'.[72] A similar tendency can also be observed in UK and German case law. Thus, in the UK case of *AZ*, the UT found that the applicant belonged to the PSG 'young females who have been victims of trafficking for sexual exploitation'[73] since 'the shared past experience of being trafficked for sexual exploitation amounts to a common, immutable characteristic'.[74] In *AM and BM*, the relevant PSG identified was 'trafficked women from Albania',[75] with the tribunal noting that members of this group 'share . . . a characteristic by which they would become known in the wider society'.[76]

A number of German judgments also favour a narrow PSG, such as 'single women who were affected by trafficking and have freed themselves of it'.[77] The AC Cologne has proposed the PSG 'women returning to Nigeria, who have been victims of trafficking in the form of prostitution'.[78] Meanwhile, the AC Stuttgart settled on the PSG 'women who are victims of trafficking and return from Europe to Nigeria'.[79] Similarly, the AC Würzburg accepted that 'women returning to Nigeria who have been victims of trafficking and have freed themselves of it' form a PSG.[80]

In these narrow PSGs, it is not so much the applicants' (female) gender which links to the persecution feared but the fact of having been trafficked previously. Thus, simply the PSG 'trafficked women' could have explained why these applicants were at risk of re-trafficking, rather than the narrower versions of this group. Indeed, the idea that it is necessary to identify a narrow PSG to

70 Jayasinghe and Baglay (n 3) 501.
71 ibid; emphasis added.
72 Michelle Foster, 'Why We Are Not There Yet: The Particular Challenge of "Particular Social Group"' in Efrat Arbel, Catherine Dauvergne and Jenni Millbank (eds), *Gender in Refugee Law: From the Margins to the Centre* (Routledge 2014) 19.
73 *AZ (Trafficked Women) Thailand CG* [2010] UKUT 118 (IAC) [140].
74 ibid [141].
75 *AM and BM* (n 52) [Headnote f].
76 ibid [165].
77 VG Augsburg, Au 7 K 16.31586, 21.07.2017, p 5; see also VG Stuttgart, A 7 K 1405/12, 16.05.2014; VG Wiesbaden, 3 K 1465/09.WI.A, 14.03.2011; W 2 K 14.30213 (n 52).
78 VG Köln, 2 K 5595/18.A, 28.05.2019.
79 VG Stuttgart, A 1 K 8819/18, 5770443, 16.11.2020.
80 VG Würzburg, W 8 K 20 31251, 20.05.2022 [30].

establish nexus is flawed. In fact, the size of the group is irrelevant.[81] As the AC Berlin has noted, it is precisely not necessary to identify a sub-group of (trafficked) women to establish a PSG.[82]

While framing PSGs narrowly is not necessary and, in fact, is problematic, because this can exclude claimants who do not fit the exact description of recognised groups, the narrow PSGs discussed in the preceding text take a first step in the direction of identifying the previous trafficking experience as the main reason behind the risk of re-trafficking, focusing on the experiences of the individual trafficked persons. As the next section will show, this realisation is better expressed through the (broad and gender-neutral) PSG 'trafficked persons'.

5.3.2 The PSG 'Trafficked Persons'

In the trafficking context, besides relying on the PSG 'women' and variations thereof, an alternative, and more widely used, approach to establishing nexus is the PSG 'trafficked persons' (and variations thereof). Köhler argues that the status of 'trafficked person' falls under the non-discrimination provision in Article 14 of the European Convention on Human Rights (ECHR) under 'other status', since the experience of having been trafficked cannot be reversed, and thus, this status cannot be discarded.[83] Following a similar line of reasoning, in case law from Australia and Canada, 'victims of trafficking may be considered a "particular social group" due to the immutability of their experience of having been trafficked'.[84] However, in UK and German case law, demands that, in addition, the social perception test must be met have led to some debate as to whether a similar approach may be taken.

In early trafficking-based asylum claims, such as the 2004 case of *JO*, it was asserted that 'trafficked women do not qualify as a PSG, since what defines them is essentially the fact of persecution'.[85] Similarly, in the 2005 case of *MP*, it was found that '"people who have been trafficked" falls foul of the principle that the group must exist independently of the persecution it fears. Such a group is defined by no more than the persecutory element of trafficking'.[86] However, in 2008, the tribunal in *SB* stated:

> [F]ormer victims of trafficking and former victims of trafficking for sexual exploitation are capable of being members of a particular social

81 Hathaway and Foster (n 6) 367.
82 31 K 305/20 A (n 58) p 21.
83 Christine Köhler, *Opferschutz im Bereich des Menschenhandels* (Duncker & Humblot 2016) 162–63.
84 Jayasinghe and Baglay (n 3) 501–2.
85 *JO* (n 52) [18].
86 *MP (Trafficking – Sufficiency of Protection) Romania* [2005] UKIAT 00086 [95].

> group because of their shared common background or past experience of having been trafficked.

The tribunal argued that the use of the word 'former' made it clear that such a PSG exists 'independently of the feared persecution'.[87] Similarly, in *AZ*, the UT found that 'the shared past experience of being trafficked for sexual exploitation amounts to a common, immutable characteristic'.[88]

It is interesting to compare *SB*, a 2008 case, with German case law from around the same time. Thus, in a 2007 judgment by the AC Munich, it was found that being a sex worker is not an immutable characteristic.[89] This judgment, however, can be considered to be an outlier. Indeed, generally, German courts recognise the trafficking experience as an immutable characteristic. For example, in a 2018 judgment by the AC Würzburg, a Nigerian woman trafficked for sex work and forced labour was found to be a member of a PSG since the fact of having been trafficked was seen as constituting an immutable background.[90] This was also confirmed by the AC Stuttgart in 2020,[91] the AC Hannover in 2021,[92] as well as the AC Düsseldorf[93] and the AC Wiesbaden in 2022.[94]

Thus, while it is generally accepted that the fact of having been trafficked constitutes an immutable characteristic, trafficked persons have struggled to meet the social perception test. In *SB*, the tribunal stated that

> in order for 'former victims of trafficking' or 'former victims of trafficking for sexual exploitation' to be members of a particular social group, the group in question must have a distinct identity in the society in question.[95]

The social perception test poses a particular hurdle to persons trafficked for labour exploitation, and therefore to men, who are more likely to be trafficked for this purpose than mere sexual exploitation.[96] It is important to note that, as the tribunal in *SB* explained, the PSG 'trafficked persons' is gender-neutral. As the tribunal put it,

> individuals may be trafficked for the purposes of sexual exploitation as well as for other purposes (such as for labour and for begging) and

87 *SB* (n 63) [56]–[57].
88 *AZ* (n 73) [141].
89 VG München, M 24 K 07.50603, 06.11.2007, p 6.
90 VG Würzburg, W 10 K 18.31682, 21.12.2018 [29].
91 A 1 K 8819/18, 5770443 (n 79).
92 VG Hannover, 10 A 6353/18, 09.09.2021.
93 VG Düsseldorf, 27 K 3867/19.A, 12.12.2022 [23].
94 VG Wiesbaden, 3 K 264/19.WI.A, 08.06.2022, p 9.
95 *SB* (n 63) [56].
96 UNODC (n 61) 10.

given, further, that there is evidence that men have also been trafficked, although on a smaller scale . . . 'former victims of trafficking' and 'former victims of trafficking for sexual exploitation', are not necessarily gender-based, nor do they have any gender-based features to narrow the group.[97]

The tribunal then explained that trafficked persons' being stigmatised as sex workers serves as evidence of them being perceived as different from surrounding society.[98] Later cases confirm that not only women, but also men trafficked for sexual exploitation can establish membership of a PSG based on the stigma attached to this.[99] However, the tribunal in *SB* did 'not consider that . . . individuals who have been trafficked for the purposes of labour, or begging, are perceived differently by the surrounding society'.[100]

The same view is reflected in some later cases, for example, in the 2018 case of *TVP*, an appeal by a Vietnamese man (a minor at the time of trafficking) who had been trafficked to China, Russia, France and finally to the UK for forced labour.[101] The UT determined that the applicant was vulnerable, particularly due to his 'mental fragility', and had 'little doubt that he would find it difficult to integrate within the community and would readily be perceived as an outsider and therefore somebody who would be an obvious target to be retrafficked'.[102] Nevertheless, the tribunal concluded that those trafficked for forced labour would not be perceived as different by surrounding society, and thus the applicant was granted subsidiary protection.[103] In a factually similar case from 2017, the tribunal also 'had difficulty in immediately identifying the relevant PSG'.[104]

On the other hand, in the 2019 case of *HQB*, a Vietnamese man trafficked for forced labour was granted refugee status as a member of the PSG 'victim[s] of trafficking'.[105] The tribunal noted that the 'perception of being different arises in the minds of those who know about the history [of having been trafficked], such as people-smugglers surveying a list of debtors as they look for people to exploit'.[106] Further, in the 2024 case of *DK*, which concerned an Albanian man who was forced to work in a cannabis factory and

97 *SB* (n 63) [54].
98 ibid [105].
99 *HVT v SSHD* [2018] UKUT (IAC) PA/03104/2017 [29]; *TAN* (n 52) [59].
100 *SB* (n 63) [93].
101 *TVP* (n 52).
102 ibid [61].
103 ibid [54]–[56].
104 *PQ* (n 52) [12]. See also *AN v SSHD* [2017] UKUT (IAC) PA/04137/2016; *AB v SSHD* [2018] UKUT (IAC) AA/10878/2015; *SSHD v ES* [2023] UKUT (IAC) UI-2023-000934.
105 *HQB v SSHD* [2019] UKUT (IAC) PA/10410/2018 [23].
106 ibid [22].

sexually abused and exploited in Albania, the tribunal relied on the PSG 'male VOT[s]', that is, male victims of trafficking.[107] The tribunal found that male trafficked persons can meet the immutable characteristics test, 'namely the experience of being trafficked',[108] as well as the social perception test, seeing as 'there is a stigmatisation that male VOT face if their trafficking comes to light which would make them appear "weak" and "powerless"'.[109]

In German case law, the social perception test has also caused difficulties, even for persons trafficked for sexual exploitation. Thus, a 2007 judgment by the AC Munich found that sex workers were not perceived as different from surrounding society.[110] In 2022, the AC Düsseldorf argued that the fact that someone has been trafficked for sexual exploitation is not perceivable from the outside on return to the country of origin.[111] Also in 2022, the AC Wiesbaden found that women trafficked for sexual exploitation are not perceived as different from surrounding society and therefore do not form a PSG,[112] with the AC Sigmaringen making the same argument in 2023.[113]

On the other hand, a 2011 judgment by the AC Wiesbaden found that 'former victims of trafficking who have freed themselves of it (and have testified against the traffickers) and are returning to Nigeria' constitute a PSG, with the differential social perception being evident from the discrimination they experience from their family and society generally.[114] The AC Stuttgart agreed with this reasoning in 2014,[115] and in 2016, the AC Regensburg made the same argument with regard to a Nigerian woman trafficked for sex work.[116] The AC Würzburg in 2018[117] and AC Magdeburg in 2020 followed the same approach.[118] Similarly, in 2021, the AC Hannover argued that the differential social perception arises out of discrimination and ostracism experienced by persons who were trafficked for sexual exploitation.[119]

Thus, the social perception test has, at times, posed a hurdle, especially for persons trafficked for labour exploitation, but also for those trafficked for sexual exploitation. However, along with the case of *DK*, which is particularly useful for illustrating why men trafficked for labour exploitation may also be perceived as different from surrounding society, the judgment in *AM and BM* may have solved this problem. In this case, the UT, relying on the judgment

107 *DK v SSHD* [2024] UKUT (IAC) UI-2023-003379 [23].
108 ibid.
109 ibid [28].
110 VG München, M 24 K 07.50603, 06.11.2007, p 6.
111 27 K 3867/19.A (n 93) [24].
112 3 K 264/19.WI.A (n 94) pp 9–10.
113 VG Sigmaringen, A 7 K 4913-20, 15.02.2023 [41].
114 3 K 1465/09.WI.A (n 77) p 12.
115 A 7 K 1405/12 (n 77) p 12.
116 RN 5 K 16.30603 (n 41) p 7.
117 W 10 K 18.31682 (n 90) [29].
118 AC Magdeburg, 6 A 40/19, 28.01.2020 [31].
119 10 A 6353/18 (n 92) p 8.

in *SB*, found that 'victims of trafficking in Albania'[120] or 'trafficked women from Albania'[121] can form a PSG. The tribunal found that the main issue in this context was, again, the social perception test but argued that it will be met if trafficked women availing themselves of the protection of shelters for trafficked persons thereby make themselves recognisable to traffickers, but also to society generally: 'The fact that they had been trafficked would be an obvious inference that would be drawn by the wider population if they went to a shelter and where [sic] in that shelter for some time'.[122]

Thus, *AM and BM* opens up the argument that trafficked persons may set themselves apart from surrounding society by their own actions or behaviour. Juss argues that '[t]he "social perception" requirement looks dangerously like a tool for rejecting potential asylum-seekers', since '[a trafficking] victim may have come to the UK as a young minor many years ago, she may have grown up, and she may have changed her appearance' and '[s]he would not be known in that way to anybody else'[123] on return to her country of origin. Yet *AM and BM* suggests that, even if a returned trafficked person no longer knows anyone in the country of origin, he or she may be perceived as different from surrounding society based on his or her actions and behaviour. Relevant actions and behaviour setting an individual apart from surrounding society may be linked back to that individual's vulnerabilities. For example, trafficked persons may be perceived as different due to their mental health difficulties and due to the action of availing themselves of reception facilities and reintegration assistance and – as suggested in *DK* – the stigma they experience if their trafficking experience thereby comes to light. I will return to this proposition in Section 5.4.1.

In summary, the case law suggests that, in principle, 'trafficked persons', whether male or female, whether trafficked for sexual or labour exploitation, can form a PSG. The next question, then, is whether the persecution they fear is 'for reasons of' their status as a former trafficked person. Curiously, this question is rarely discussed in the case law. In *SB*, the UT, in discussing 'causation', merely notes that

> anyone who is at a heightened risk of ill-treatment which is shown to be at least *related* to the individual's past experience of having been trafficked constitutes harm for a Geneva Convention reason provided that the individual is a member of a social group which is defined independently of the feared act of future persecution [sic].[124]

120 *AM and BM* (n 52) [166].
121 ibid [Headnote f].
122 ibid [165].
123 Satvinder S Juss, 'Recognizing Refugee Status for Victims of Trafficking and the Myth of Progress' (2015) 34(2) Refugee Survey Quarterly 107, 118 <https://doi.org/10.1093/rsq/hdv003>.
124 *SB* (n 63) [111]; emphasis in original.

Based on this, and by returning to the findings from Chapter 3, we can see how membership of the PSG 'trafficked persons' links to risk of re-trafficking. The tribunal in *SB* adopts a predicament approach in requiring a 'heightened risk of ill-treatment . . . related to the individual's past experience of having been trafficked'. As explained in Chapter 3, a prior trafficking experience leads to consequential vulnerabilities and therefore explains why an individual will be vulnerable to being re-trafficked. Thus, to return to Foster's conceptualisation of the predicament approach, 'the applicant's Convention ground status [being a 'trafficked person'] puts him or her at a disproportionately high risk of the relevant harm feared', that is, re-trafficking.[125] Foster notes:

> [A] key way in which the predicament approach has begun to be implemented in practice is displayed in cases in which decision-makers focus on the factors that led to or contributed to the person's vulnerability to the relevant harm feared, concluding that if those factors can be related to a Convention ground (most commonly membership of a particular social group) then nexus is established.[126]

A useful example for this is an Italian case identified by Magugliani in which the relevant PSG is narrowed with reference to vulnerability indicators to the PSG 'trafficked men "lacking significant family networks, uneducated, unemployed and homeless, who are easy prey for criminal groups"'.[127] Even though UK and German courts do not explicitly return to trafficked persons' vulnerabilities in the same way, they do recognise that a prior trafficking experience is an immutable characteristic and may set people apart from surrounding society, which ultimately explains why there is a risk of re-trafficking.

In the next section, I will develop this line of reasoning further by returning to irregularised migrants' vulnerabilities, or the 'route causes' of irregular re-migration, examining whether these can be related to Convention grounds.

5.4 Establishing Nexus for Irregularised Migrants: A Link to Vulnerability

While the PSG 'trafficked persons' explains trafficked persons' predicament of being at a disproportionately high risk of re-trafficking, this PSG is of no use for those with no prior experience of having been trafficked. Nevertheless, irregularised migrants may be able to meet the nexus requirement by relying on the PSG '(previously) smuggled persons' or '(past) irregular migrants' as an equivalent to the PSG 'trafficked persons'. Like the trafficking experience, the irregular migration experience cannot be changed and, as such, constitutes

125 Foster (n 5) 277.
126 ibid 283.
127 Magugliani (n 4) 359.

an immutable characteristic. Meanwhile, the social perception test can be met through stigma experienced by irregularised migrants, or through their own actions and behaviour resulting from the migration experience. As in the trafficking context, the PSG refers to the past experience of irregular migration and is, therefore, independent of the persecution feared. Just like how the 'status' of 'trafficked person' implies consequential vulnerabilities which explain their predicament of being at risk of re-trafficking, irregularised migrants may have the same vulnerabilities which account for their predicament of being at risk of irregular re-migration.

However, neither the PSG 'trafficked persons' nor the PSG 'irregular migrants' makes explicit what lies at the heart of both groups' predicament: their vulnerabilities. Thus, in this section, I propose that by returning to the vulnerability enquiry from the future risk analysis, it is possible to identify a PSG which explains both trafficked persons' and irregularised migrants' predicament. The PSG in question is 'persons in vulnerable situations', which, as explained in what follows, meets the innate characteristics test and the social perception test and exists independently of the persecution feared. In addition, taking into account both groups' 'migratory vulnerability',[128] the Convention ground 'nationality' is also relevant because, when interpreted as 'citizenship', it explains why an individual is unable to travel legally and safely. Together, these two Convention grounds explain why irregularised migrants are at a disproportionately high risk of irregular re-migration.

5.4.1 The PSG 'Persons in Vulnerable Situations'

As explained in Chapter 3, 'vulnerability' is a vague concept, and calling an individual 'vulnerable' can have essentialising and disempowering effects. Thus, to avoid designating irregularised migrants as 'vulnerable', in this section I explore the PSG 'persons in vulnerable situations',[129] which seeks to convey that it is not the individual who *is* vulnerable but his or her circumstances which *render* him or her vulnerable. Despite the general vagueness of the vulnerability concept, Chapter 3 has shown that, in the context of re-trafficking and irregular re-migration, the concept is filled with a particular meaning,

128 Moritz Baumgärtel, 'Facing the Challenge of Migratory Vulnerability in the European Court of Human Rights' (2020) 38(1) Netherlands Quarterly of Human Rights 12, 13 <https://doi.org/10.1177/0924051919898127>.

129 This phrase is borrowed from OHCHR guidance, which explains that 'migrants are not inherently vulnerable, nor do they lack resilience and agency. Rather, vulnerability to human rights violations is the result of multiple and intersecting forms of discrimination, inequality and structural and societal dynamics that lead to diminished and unequal levels of power and enjoyment of rights'. See OHCHR, 'Principles and Guidelines, Supported by Practical Guidance, on the Human Rights Protection of Migrants in Vulnerable Situations' (2018) 5–6 <www.ohchr.org/sites/default/files/Documents/Issues/Migration/PrinciplesAndGuidelines.pdf> accessed 29 October 2024.

namely, the presence and interplay of a range of vulnerability indicators, such as mental health issues and stigma, leading to socio-economic deprivation. Theoretically, some of these vulnerability indicators could constitute PSGs in their own right. For example, with regard to mental health issues, Foster shows that 'illness and disability may constitute a PSG'.[130] She also argues that 'it is clear that the poor can properly be considered a PSG, such that if being poor makes one vulnerable to persecutory types of harm, whether socio-economic or not'.[131]

Nevertheless, the PSG 'persons in vulnerable situations' better captures the fact that susceptibility to persecution stems from a range of intersecting vulnerabilities rather than a single factor. As such, 'persons in vulnerable situations' are different from those who are 'merely' (mentally) ill or 'merely' poor. Yet because the vulnerability analysis requires an individualised assessment, and since every individual will be vulnerable in slightly different ways, it may be argued that the PSG 'persons in vulnerable situations' is antithetical to the individualised notion of vulnerability. However, the fact that vulnerability indicators may differ for different individuals does not preclude the finding that there is a group of persons who are vulnerable in similar ways, with this vulnerability producing similar effects.

As a PSG, 'persons in vulnerable situations' must share an immutable characteristic and/or must be perceived as different from surrounding society. In this context, the social perception test is more easily satisfied than the immutable characteristics test. Many of the relevant vulnerability indicators will lead to differential social perception, including having 'illegitimate' children, being stigmatised, lacking family support or having mental health issues (which lead a person to behaving differently). In addition, as explained in *AM and BM*, attempts to access (government) assistance for returnees can mark a person out as different. While in the trafficking context this can include accessing shelters, in the context of irregular migration and return generally, it is conceivable that individuals will reveal that they are in a vulnerable situation by attempting to access other forms of return and reintegration assistance.

The question of immutability or innateness, however, is more difficult to answer. On the one hand, according to Fineman, vulnerability is universal[132] and, as Mackenzie *et al.* put it, thus 'inherent in human embodiment'.[133] On the other hand, individual vulnerability indicators, such as mental health issues or stigma, are not immutable, as they may improve or fade over time. However, in *DH*, which concerned (the immutability of) a mental health condition

130 Foster (n 5) 322; see also *DH* (n 47) [102].

131 Foster ibid 310.

132 Martha Albertson Fineman, 'The Vulnerable Subject: Anchoring Equality in the Human Condition' (2008) 20(1) Yale Journal of Law and Feminism 9, 10.

133 Catriona Mackenzie, Wendy Rogers and Susan Dodds, 'Introduction: What Is Vulnerability, and Why Does It Matter for Moral Theory?' in Catriona Mackenzie, Wendy Rogers and Susan Dodds (eds), *Vulnerability: New Essays in Ethics and Feminist Philosophy* (OUP 2014) 4.

as the basis for establishing a PSG, the UT noted that '[t]he PSG assessment must be made at the date of the hearing'.[134] The same finding has been made in relation to the PSG 'children' and the question of immutability of age.[135] Thus, as long as vulnerabilities are present at the time of refugee status determination (RSD), they should be considered to be immutable.

Further, something the vulnerability indicators have in common is that they are brought about or exacerbated by the migration experience itself. Thus, it is possible to understand vulnerability as immutable insofar as it is related to a migration experience, which – as accepted in the trafficking context – is an experience that cannot be changed. It should also be noted that in order to claim that a characteristic is not immutable, 'disassociation [from said characteristic] or ability to change, . . . must logically be a present option, not one that is merely possible on an abstract or theoretical level'.[136] Persons in vulnerable situation cannot simply disassociate themselves from their vulnerability indicators.

Importantly, the PSG 'persons in vulnerable situations' exists independently of the persecution feared. It might be argued that 'vulnerable' is only a different way of saying 'at risk of' and that, therefore, relying on vulnerability is a way of defining a PSG with reference to the harm feared. For example, a political activist may be said to be vulnerable to state reprisals, or a person fleeing armed conflict may be thought of as vulnerable to indiscriminate violence. However, when the term *vulnerability* is understood to refer to specific vulnerability indicators and their interplay and effects, it becomes clear that it refers to something concrete which is external to the persecution feared. It is not these vulnerabilities which irregularised migrants fear but their effects: irregular re-migration and the harm experienced in this context. As the UT clarified in *HD*, '[i]t is not the poverty, destitution or vulnerability itself which is the basis of the claim, but the harm that ensues from that namely the exploitation'.[137] Thus, the PSG 'persons in vulnerable situations' exists independently of the risk of irregular re-migration.

Interestingly, a UK case suggests that 'persons in vulnerable situations' could indeed be accepted as a relevant PSG. The 2014 case of *BA* concerned an appellant who was 11 years old when he was trafficked from Ghana to the UK to work in a brothel but who was an adult at the time of the appeal. Counsel for the appellant suggested that their client may belong to the PSG 'young and vulnerable people with no family support'.[138] This is effectively a version of

134 *DH* (n 47) [36i]; see also Foster (n 5) 329–31; Pobjoy (n 55) 177–78.
135 Foster (n 5) 331; see also Pobjoy (n 55) 178.
136 Foster ibid 308.
137 *HD* (n 52) [171].
138 *BA* (n 52) [12].

the PSG 'persons in vulnerable situations', which also mentions age and lack of family support as vulnerability indicators. However, the tribunal was

> not satisfied that . . . it is enough to say that a finding that a person is 'young and vulnerable with no family support', inevitably leads to the conclusion he will also then be at risk of persecution. The evidence must show this.[139]

The tribunal found that evidence to this effect had not been presented and dismissed the appeal. Nevertheless, where such evidence can be adduced, the PSG should be made out.

If 'persons in vulnerable situations' can form a PSG, this PSG is particularly suitable for establishing a nexus to harm experienced during irregular re-migration because it links the predicament of having to re-migrate irregularly to the vulnerable situation irregularised migrants find themselves in in the country of origin. This includes structural vulnerabilities, which explain why a person is at risk not only of migration but also of *irregular* migration. Thus, the next subsection returns to the role of the global visa regime and examines whether it is possible to establish a connection between risk of irregular re-migration and the Convention ground nationality.

5.4.2 The Convention Ground Nationality

As explained in previous chapters, states of destination contribute to the predicament of applicants who fear irregular re-migration through the imposition of visa requirements and extraterritorial border controls. In this context, nationality – in the sense of *citizenship* – is a key determinant of where an individual is able to travel to legally and safely. States distinguish between different non-citizens on grounds of nationality, allowing some nationalities visa-free access to their territory while requiring others to hold visas. Though factors such as wealth, levels of education and qualification impact a person's ability to obtain such visas,[140] generally, 'the global visa regime hierarchizes mobility' according to national origin.[141] There are, of course, exceptions to this general rule,[142] which, however, apply to only a small proportion of nationals of

139 ibid [45].

140 Thomas Spijkerboer, 'The Global Mobility Infrastructure: Reconceptualising the Externalisation of Migration Control' (2018) 20 European Journal of Migration and Law 452, 457 <https://doi.org/10.1163/15718166-12340038>.

141 Noora A Lori, 'Statelessness, "In-Between" Statuses, and Precarious Citizenship' in Ayelet Shachar, Rainer Bauböck, Irene Bloemraad and Maarten Vink (eds), *The Oxford Handbook of Citizenship* (OUP 2017) 752.

142 Moreno-Lax explains that in the EU context, 'holders of local border traffic (LBT) cards' as well as school pupils residing in an EU member state and 'travelling in the context of a

a country who require visas. Thus, since '[s]election through visa is primarily based on nationality',[143] it is worth examining the relevance of the Convention ground nationality for establishing a nexus between harm experienced as a result of irregular migration and the restrictions imposed by the global visa regime. Relying on the predicament approach and recalling that to establish a nexus it is enough that there is some link or that the Convention ground in question is a contributing cause, this section examines whether irregularised migrants' predicament is for reasons of their nationality and the travel restrictions attached to it.

As mentioned earlier, the Convention ground nationality is usually defined as being '[c]losely linked to the notion of race'.[144] However, I propose that in line with the Vienna Convention on the Law of Treaties (VCLT), nationality should be given its ordinary meaning,[145] that is, citizenship. This is not to suggest that nationality-based visa discrimination is not interconnected with racial discrimination. As van Houtum notes, the very terms 'blacklist' and 'whitelist', originally used by EU policymakers to denote nationalities who do and do not need visas, respectively, themselves have racial connotations.[146] He also notes that 'there are a significantly high number of Muslim states' as well as developing countries on the blacklist.[147] Nevertheless, those excluded are identified on the basis of citizenship rather than skin colour or religion.

Grahl-Madsen states that '"[n]ationality" may mean citizenship (nationality in a formal sense, *Staatsangehörigkeit*)',[148] and both EU and UK law also support this, stating that 'the concept of nationality shall not be confined to *citizenship* or lack thereof'.[149] The Refugee Convention itself also supports the

school excursion taking place within Schengen territory' are exempt from visa requirements, even if they are of a nationality normally required to obtain a visa. Further, 'holders of diplomatic and other official passports', 'civilian air/sea crew', 'holders of *laissez-passer* issued by international organizations', as well as 'members of the armed forces travelling on NATO business' may be exempted from visa requirements. There are also exemptions from airport transit visas. See Violeta Moreno-Lax, *Accessing Asylum in Europe: Extraterritorial Border Controls and Refugee Rights under EU Law* (OUP 2017) 100–3.

143 Spijkerboer (n 140) 457. See also Elspeth Guild, 'Moving the Borders of Europe: Inaugural Lecture' (2001) Faculteit der Rechtsgeleerdheid, KU Nijmegen 69 <https://cmr.jur.ru.nl/cmr/docs/oratie.eg.pdf> accessed 20 July 2021. See further Jane McAdam, 'Visas' in Peter Cane and Joanne Conaghan (eds), *The New Oxford Companion to Law* (OUP 2008) 1225–26.

144 Hathaway and Foster (n 6) 397.

145 Vienna Convention on the Law of Treaties (adopted 23 May 1969, entered into force on 27 January 1980) 1155 UNTS 331 (VCLT) art 31(1).

146 Henk van Houtum, 'Human Blacklisting: The Global Apartheid of the EU's External Border Regime' (2010) 28(6) Environment and Planning D: Society and Space 957, 964 <https://doi.org/10.1068/d1909>.

147 ibid.

148 Atle Grahl-Madsen, *The Status of Refugees in International Law*, vol I (A W Sijthoff 1966) 218.

149 Qualification Regulation (n 14) art 10(c); emphasis added. Nationality and Borders Act 2022, s 33(1)(c).

reading of nationality as citizenship by stating in Article 1A(2) that '[i]n the case of a person who has more than one nationality, the term "the country of his nationality" shall mean each of the countries of which he is a national', that is, a citizen. Articles 1C and 1E of the Refugee Convention similarly support the reading of *nationality* as citizenship.

Interpreting *nationality* as citizenship in the context of the nexus enquiry is unproblematic insofar as it does not affect the validity of the claim that 'each of the [Convention] grounds "describes persecution aimed at an immutable characteristic: a characteristic that either is beyond the power of an individual to change or . . . ought not be required to be changed"'.[150] Citizenship may be described as an immutable characteristic as it is arbitrarily assigned through the 'accident of birth'[151] and is difficult to change – only 'three percent of the global population' change their citizenship during their lifetime.[152]

Nevertheless, in refugee law, interpreting *nationality* as citizenship is, in practice, limited to cases of denationalised or stateless persons, or persons persecuted due to former citizenship and (perceived) allegiances related to this.[153] Outside of these examples, interpreting nationality as citizenship has largely been dismissed. This is based, for example, on the opinion that it is unlikely that 'a state would choose to persecute its own citizens merely by reason of their status as citizens',[154] or that the 'reference to persecution for reasons of nationality is somewhat odd, given the absurdity of a State persecuting its own nationals on account of their membership of the body politic'.[155] These objections to interpreting *nationality* as citizenship, however, assume that the state is the persecutor and that there is an intention to persecute. Utilising the predicament approach makes it possible to focus on the question of why irregularised migrants are at a disproportionately high risk of having to undertake a dangerous journey. Besides irregularised migrants' vulnerabilities discussed earlier, their citizenship contributes to their predicament of irregular migration since visa requirements and carrier sanctions prevent regular travel to countries of destination. Even though there are more and less privileged groups of persons of the same nationality when it comes to visa requirements,[156] nationality plays an important role in the process. While

150 USBIA, *Acosta*, 1985; quoted in Hathaway and Foster (n 6) 426.
151 Ayelet Shachar, *The Birthright Lottery: Citizenship and Global Inequality* (Harvard UP 2009) 4.
152 ibid 11.
153 Hathaway and Foster (n 6) 397f.
154 ibid 397.
155 Goodwin-Gill and McAdam (n 13) 99.
156 This is not only due to exemptions from visa requirements which apply to certain groups based on, for example, occupation. There are also differences in the ability to obtain a visa, which depends on criteria such as socio-economic status, but also on the category of visa applied for, as well as the EU member state representation applied to and domestic member state policies regarding visa exemptions. See Elspeth Guild, 'When Even Machiavelli's Prince Needs a Visa: Migration, Euro-Mediterranean Relations and Intercultural Dialogue' (2010) 15(3) European Foreign Affairs Review 367 <https://doi.org/10.54648/eerr2010026>.

the debate as to whether distinctions made on grounds of citizenship in the immigration context amount to discriminatory treatment is ongoing,[157] for the purpose of the nexus analysis, it is clear that that a person's citizenship at least contributes to the predicament of irregular re-migration.

In sum, a person's citizenship determines the mode and conditions of travel and thus contributes to harm experienced during the journey. This qualifies as 'a link', and thus, it should be possible to consider the Convention ground nationality in claims based on a fear of irregular re-migration. In combination with membership of the PSG 'persons in vulnerable situations', the Convention ground nationality explains why individuals are at a disproportionately high risk of irregular re-migration.

5.5 Conclusion

The Refugee Convention requires that persecution be 'for reasons of' at least one of the five Convention grounds. Having examined the underlying reasons for irregular re-migration in detail in Chapter 3, this chapter returned to the relevant findings and considered whether these reasons can be conceived of in terms of nexus grounds. As Foster has noted, 'there is a certain element of artificiality in analysing the various elements of the Refugee Convention definition separately'.[158] This is particularly true with regard to the well-founded fear enquiry on the one hand and the nexus enquiry on the other. Having identified 'route *causes*' of irregular re-migration, it makes sense to consider whether these can explain the ('causal') connection to Refugee Convention grounds. In other words, the vulnerabilities resulting from, and causing, dangerous journeys can be thought of in terms of indicators of future risk, while persons experiencing these vulnerabilities can be conceived of as a PSG for the purpose of the nexus enquiry.

Indeed, vulnerabilities are, implicitly, already being considered during the nexus enquiry in trafficking-based asylum claims. The PSG 'trafficked persons' is related to the past trafficking experience, and therefore to both the vulnerabilities which led to the initial trafficking and the consequential vulnerabilities brought about by this experience. Based on this, this chapter has made explicit the relevance of the vulnerability analysis for the nexus enquiry and explored

157 Ryszard Cholewinski, 'Borders and Discrimination in the European Union' (*ILPA*, 2002) <www.migpolgroup.com/_old/wp-content/uploads/2016/10/152.bordersandDiscrimination_exec_summary_01.02.pdf> accessed 7 November 2019; Marten den Heijer, 'Visas and Non-discrimination' (2018) 20(4) European Journal of Migration and Law 470 <https://doi.org/10.1163/15718166-12340039>; Spijkerboer (n 140); Maja Grundler, '"Treatment Accorded to Aliens Generally": Article 7(1) of the 1951 Refugee Convention as a Basis for Visa-Free Access to States Parties' Territory? An Examination of the Prohibition of Nationality Discrimination in the Refugee Convention' (2021) 33(3) International Journal of Refugee Law 469 <https://doi.org/10.1093/ijrl/eeac003>.

158 Foster (n 72) 25.

two Convention grounds which explain the predicament of both trafficked persons and irregularised migrants.

First, the PSG 'persons in vulnerable situations' explicitly relies on the vulnerability analysis. At the time of RSD, an individual's vulnerabilities constitute immutable characteristics, and they are likely to cause that individual to be perceived as different from surrounding society. Since vulnerabilities are reasons for exposure to irregular re-migration and re-trafficking, they exist independently of the persecution feared.

Second, the Convention ground nationality provides a more complete picture of the real reasons for persecution experienced in the context of irregular re-migration. Nationality, or citizenship, is a type of situational vulnerability (or, indeed, a pathogenic vulnerability, as suggested in Chapter 3), which impacts an individual's ability to travel legally and safely. The persecution experienced during irregular re-migration is 'for reasons of' a person's nationality insofar as this nationality forces them to travel (or stay) irregularly.

Thus, the nexus analysis ties in organically with the future risk analysis, particularly when focusing on the applicant's predicament, rather than on persecutory intent. Indeed, the predicament approach is particularly compatible with vulnerability or 'route causes' reasoning, since both focus on the reasons for exposure to harm. This also means that not only can the future risk analysis inform the nexus enquiry, but *vice versa*.

As mentioned earlier, it is common to use adjectives and descriptions to narrow PSGs. These adjectives may give insight into what makes a particular claimant 'vulnerable' to harm in a particular situation. Indeed, with regard to adjectives used to qualify the PSG 'children', Pobjoy notes that the adjectives used 'explain . . . the reasons why the child will be exposed to a risk of being persecuted'.[159] Adjectives used to narrow down the PSG 'women', identified by Jayasinghe and Baglay in the trafficking context, such as 'single', 'divorced', and 'illiterate',[160] signal a lack of family support and education, respectively, and clearly explain why these claimants are at risk. As Foster notes, where a PSG is narrowed, this is

> often by reference to issues that truly belong to a different element of the refugee definition such as well-founded fear (for example vulnerability), persecution ('risk of circumcision', 'subjected to, or threatened by, stove burnings'), and/or failure of state protection ('incapable of securing effective protection from the police').[161]

Foster shows that this is problematic where it leads to the group being defined by reference to the persecution feared.[162] However, this problem is most likely

159 Jason Pobjoy, 'Refugee Children' in Cathryn Costello, Michelle Foster and Jane McAdam (eds), *The Oxford Handbook of International Refugee Law* (OUP 2021) 752.
160 Jayasinghe and Baglay (n 3) 501.
161 Foster (n 72) 30–31.
162 ibid 31.

to arise where direct reference to persecution is made. References to vulnerability, on the other hand, may inform the well-founded fear enquiry, and conversely, risk factors identified in the context of the well-founded fear assessment may inform the nexus enquiry.

In conclusion, as members of the PSG 'persons in vulnerable situations' and as persons whose nationality contributes to the risk of undertaking dangerous journeys, irregularised migrants can establish a nexus between the risk of irregular re-migration and Refugee Convention grounds. Thus, they can meet the third, and final, element of the *refugee* definition.

References

AB v SSHD [2018] UKUT (IAC) AA/10878/2015

AM and BM (Trafficked Women) Albania CG [2010] UKUT 80 (IAC)

AN v SSHD [2017] UKUT (IAC) PA/04137/2016

Asylgesetz (AsylG) 2 September 2008 (BGBl. I S. 1798) (Asylum Act)

AZ (Trafficked Women) Thailand CG [2010] UKUT 118 (IAC)

BA v SSHD [2014] UKUT (IAC) AA/03923/2013

Baumgärtel M, 'Facing the Challenge of Migratory Vulnerability in the European Court of Human Rights' (2020) 38(1) Netherlands Quarterly of Human Rights 12 <https://doi.org/10.1177/0924051919898127>

C-268/99 *Jany and Others* [2001] ECLI:EU:C:2001:616

C-621/21 *WS* [2024] ECLI:EU:C:2024:47

Cholewinski R, *Borders and Discrimination in the European Union* (*ILPA*, 2002) <www.migpolgroup.com/_old/wp-content/uploads/2016/10/152.bordersand-Discrimination_exec_summary_01.02.pdf> accessed 7 November 2019

Convention on the Rights of the Child (adopted 20 November 1989, entered into force 2 September 1990) 1577 UNTS 3 (CRC)

Convention Relating to the Status of Refugees (adopted 28 July 1951, entered into force 22 April 1954) 189 UNTS 137 (Refugee Convention)

Dauvergne C, 'Women in Refugee Jurisprudence' in Cathryn Costello, Michelle Foster and Jane McAdam (eds), *The Oxford Handbook of International Refugee Law* (OUP 2021)

Dearden L, 'The Darker Your Skin - the Further Down You Go: The Hierarchical System Aboard Italy's Migrant Boats that Governs who Lives and Who Dies' (*The Independent*, 22 April 2015) <www.independent.co.uk/news/world/europe/the-paler-your-skin-the-higher-up-you-go-the-hierarchical-system-aboard-italys-migrant-boats-that-10193130.html> accessed 1 May 2020

Den Heijer M, 'Visas and Non-Discrimination' (2018) 20(4) European Journal of Migration and Law 470 <https://doi.org/10.1163/15718166-12340039>

DH (Particular Social Group: Mental Health) Afghanistan [2020] UKUT 223 (IAC), [2020] 6 WLUK 523

DK v SSHD [2024] UKUT (IAC) UI-2023-003379

Donaldson M and Richard Howson, 'Men, Migration and Hegemonic Masculinity' in Mike Donaldson and others (eds), *Migrant Men: Critical Studies of Masculinities and the Migration Experience* (Routledge 2009)

Egyes LS, 'Borders and Intersections: The Unique Vulnerabilities of LGBTQ Immigrants to Trafficking' in Erin C Heil and Andrea J Nichols (eds), *Broadening the Scope of Human Trafficking Research* (Carolina Academic Press 2019)

EMAP (Gang Violence, Convention Reason) (CG) [2022] UKUT (IAC) 00335

Fineman MA, 'The Vulnerable Subject: Anchoring Equality in the Human Condition' (2008) 20(1) Yale Journal of Law and Feminism 9

FK v SSHD [2015] UKUT (IAC) AA/08453/2014

Foster M, 'Causation in Context: Interpreting the Nexus Clause in the Refugee Convention' (2002) 23(2) Michigan Journal of International Law 265

Foster M, *International Refugee Law and Socio-Economic Rights: Refuge from Deprivation* (CUP 2007)

Foster M, 'Why We are Not There Yet: The Particular Challenge of "Particular Social Group"' in Efrat Arbel, Catherine Dauvergne and Jenni Millbank (eds), *Gender in Refugee Law: From the Margins to the Centre* (Routledge 2014)

Goodwin-Gill GS and Jane McAdam, *The Refugee in International Law* (4th edn, OUP 2021)

Grahl-Madsen A, *The Status of Refugees in International Law*, vol I (A W Sijthoff 1966)

Grundler M, '"Treatment Accorded to Aliens Generally": Article 7(1) of the 1951 Refugee Convention as a Basis for Visa-Free Access to States Parties' Territory? An Examination of the Prohibition of Nationality Discrimination in the Refugee Convention' (2021) 33(3) International Journal of Refugee Law 469 <https://doi.org/10.1093/ijrl/eeac003>

Guild E, 'Moving the Borders of Europe: Inaugural Lecture' (Faculteit der Rechtsgeleerdheid, KU Nijmegen 2001) <https://cmr.jur.ru.nl/cmr/docs/oratie.eg.pdf> accessed 20 July 2021

Guild E, 'When Even Machiavelli's Prince Needs a Visa: Migration, Euro-Mediterranean Relations and Intercultural Dialogue' (2010) 15(3) European Foreign Affairs Review 367 <https://doi.org/10.54648/eerr2010026>

Hailbronner K and Daniel Thym (eds), *EU Immigration and Asylum Law: A Commentary* (2nd edn, Beck, Hart, Nomos 2016)

Hathaway JC and Michelle Foster, *The Law of Refugee Status* (2nd edn, CUP 2014)

HD (Trafficked Women) Nigeria CG [2016] UKUT 00454 (IAC)

HQB v SSHD [2019] UKUT (IAC) PA/10410/2018

HVT v SSHD [2018] UKUT (IAC) PA/03104/2017

Jayasinghe U and Sasha Baglay, 'Protecting Victims of Human Trafficking within a "Non-Refoulement" Framework: Is Complementary Protection an Effective Alternative in Canada and Australia?' (2011) 23(3) International Journal of Refugee Law 489 <https://doi.org/10.1093/ijrl/eer022>

JO (Internal Relocation – No Risk of Re-Trafficking) Nigeria [2004] UKIAT 00251

Juss SS, 'Recognizing Refugee Status for Victims of Trafficking and the Myth of Progress' (2015) 34(2) Refugee Survey Quarterly 107 <https://doi.org/10.1093/rsq/hdv003>

K v SSHD, Fornah v SSHD [2006] UKHL 46, [2006] 3 WLR 733

Köhler C, *Opferschutz im Bereich des Menschenhandels* (Duncker & Humblot 2016)

Lehman JM, 'At the Crossroads: The 1951 Geneva Convention Today' in Satvinder Singh Juss (ed), *Research Handbook on International Refugee Law* (Edward Elgar 2019)

Lori NA, 'Statelessness, "In-Between" Statuses, and Precarious Citizenship' in Ayelet Shachar and others (eds), *The Oxford Handbook of Citizenship* (OUP 2017)

Mackenzie C, Wendy Rogers and Susan Dodds, 'Introduction: What is Vulnerability, and Why Does It Matter for Moral Theory?' in Catriona Mackenzie, Wendy Rogers and Susan Dodds (eds), *Vulnerability: New Essays in Ethics and Feminist Philosophy* (OUP 2014)

Magugliani N, 'Trafficked Adult Males as (Un)Gendered Protection Seekers: Between Presumption of Invulnerability and Exclusion from Membership of a Particular Social Group' (2022) 34(3–4) International Journal of Refugee Law 353 <https://doi.org/10.1093/ijrl/eeac030>

Markard N, *Kriegsflüchtlinge: Gewalt gegen Zivilpersonen in bewaffneten Konflikten als Herausforderung für das Flüchtlingsrecht und den subsidiären Schutz* (Mohr Siebeck 2012)

McAdam J, 'Visas' in Peter Cane and Joanne Conaghan (eds), *The New Oxford Companion to Law* (OUP 2008)

Moreno-Lax V, *Accessing Asylum in Europe: Extraterritorial Border Controls and Refugee Rights under EU Law* (OUP 2017)

MP (Trafficking – Sufficiency of Protection) Romania [2005] UKIAT 00086

Nationality and Borders Act 2022

OHCHR, 'Fact Sheet No 36: Human Rights and Human Trafficking' (2014) <www.ohchr.org/en/publications/fact-sheets/fact-sheet-no-36-human-rights-and-human-trafficking> accessed 29 October 2024

OHCHR, 'Principles and Guidelines, Supported by Practical Guidance, on the Human Rights Protection of Migrants in Vulnerable Situations' (2018) <www.ohchr.org/sites/default/files/Documents/Issues/Migration/PrinciplesAndGuidelines.pdf> accessed 29 October 2024

Peers S and others (eds), *EU Immigration and Asylum Law (Text and Commentary): Volume 3: EU Asylum Law* (2nd Revised edn, Brill 2015)

Pobjoy J, *The Child in International Refugee Law* (CUP 2017)

Pobjoy J, 'Refugee Children' in Cathryn Costello, Michelle Foster and Jane McAdam (eds), *The Oxford Handbook of International Refugee Law* (OUP 2021)

PQ v SSHD [2017] UKUT (IAC) PA/01480/2015

Querton C, 'The Interpretation of the Convention Ground of "Membership of a Particular Social Group" in the Context of Gender-Related Claims for Asylum: A Critical Analysis of the Tribunal's Approach in the UK' (*Refugee Law Initiative*, 2012) <http://sas-space.sas.ac.uk/4690/5/RLI_Working_Paper_No.3.pdf> accessed 13 February 2021

Regulation (EU) 2024/1347 of the European Parliament and of the Council of 14 May 2024 on Standards for the Qualification of Third-Country Nationals or Stateless Persons as Beneficiaries of International Protection, for a Uniform Status for Refugees or for Persons Eligible for Subsidiary Protection and for the Content of the Protection Granted, Amending Council Directive 2003/109/EC and Repealing Directive 2011/95/EU of the European Parliament and of the Council [2024] OJ L 2024/1347 (Qualification Regulation)

SB (PSG - Protection Regulations – Reg 6) Moldova CG [2008] UKAIT 00002

Shachar A, *The Birthright Lottery: Citizenship and Global Inequality* (Harvard UP 2009)

Shankley W, 'Gender, Modern Slavery and Labour Exploitation: Experiences of Male Polish Migrants in England' (2023) 49(5) Journal of Ethnic and Migration Studies 1274 <https://doi.org/10.1080/1369183X.2021.2000853>

SHL (Tracing Obligation/Trafficking) Afghanistan v SSHD [2013] UKUT 00312 (IAC)

Spijkerboer T, 'The Global Mobility Infrastructure: Reconceptualising the Externalisation of Migration Control' (2018) 20 European Journal of Migration and Law 452 <https://doi.org/10.1163/15718166-12340038>

SSHD v ES [2023] UKUT (IAC) UI-2023-000934

SSHD v NAMT [2023] UKUT (IAC) UI-2023-002124

TAN v SSHD [2016] UKUT (IAC) AA/05644/2014

TVP v SSHD [2018] UKUT (IAC) PA/02997/2018

UNHCR, 'Guidelines on International Protection: The Application of Article 1A(2) of the 1951 Convention and/or 1967 Protocol Relating to the Status of Refugees to Victims of Trafficking and Persons at Risk of Being Trafficked' (2006) HCR/GIP/06/07 (UNHCR Trafficking Guidelines)

UNODC, 'Global Report on Trafficking in Persons 2024' <www.unodc.org/documents/data-and-analysis/glotip/2024/GLOTIP2024_BOOK.pdf> accessed 16 December 2024

Van Houtum H, 'Human Blacklisting: The Global Apartheid of the EU's External Border Regime' (2010) 28(6) Environment and Planning D: Society and Space 957 <https://doi.org/10.1068/d1909>
VG Aachen, 3 K 12/07, 08.05.2007
VG Augsburg, Au 7 K 16.31586, 21.07.2017
VG Berlin, 31 K 305/20 A, 17.08.2022
VG Düsseldorf, 27 K 3867/19.A, 12.12.2022
VG Göttingen, 3 A 135/21, 03.04.2024
VG Hannover, 10 A 6353/18, 09.09.2021
VG Köln, 2 K 5595/18.A, 28.05.2019
VG Magdeburg, 6 A 40/19, 28.01.2020
VG München, M 13 K 21.30776, 21.06.2022
VG München, M 23 K 11.30389, 30.09.2013
VG München, M 24 K 07.50603, 06.11.2007
VG Regensburg, RN 5 K 16.30603, 19.10.2016
VG Sigmaringen, A 7 K 4913-20, 15.02.2023
VG Stuttgart, A 1 K 8819/18, 5770443, 16.11.2020
VG Stuttgart, A 7 K 1405/12, 16.05.2014
VG Wiesbaden, 3 K 264/19.WI.A, 08.06.2022
VG Wiesbaden, 3 K 1465/09.WI.A, 14.03.2011
VG Würzburg, W 2 K 14.30213, 17.11.2015
VG Würzburg, W 8 K 04.30919, 19.09.2005
VG Würzburg, W 8 K 20 31251, 20.05.2022
VG Würzburg, W 10 K 18.31682, 21.12.2018
Vienna Convention on the Law of Treaties (adopted 23 May 1969, entered into force on 27 January 1980) 1155 UNTS 331 (VCLT)

6 From Complementary Protection to Refugee Status? Finding Irregularised Migrants in Existing Case Law

6.1 Introduction

Having shown in the previous chapters how irregularised migrants may be able to meet the *refugee* definition, in this chapter, I consider evidence for the fact that individuals who could benefit from the argument I make in this book already submit protection claims. These claims are not based on a risk of irregular re-migration and do not focus on the Refugee Convention but succeed under complementary protection regimes because the applicants fear destitution or obstacles to integration in their countries of origin. Thus, these cases are based on socio-economic deprivation and an inability to reintegrate – factors familiar from trafficking-based asylum claims and relevant to establishing a risk of irregular re-migration. As such, it is pertinent to explore whether the claimants in these cases could be reconceptualised as irregularised migrants and their claims resolved under the Refugee Convention rather than under complementary protection regimes.[1]

Complementary protection is protection against *refoulement*, derived from human rights treaties, which complement the Refugee Convention by protecting those who cannot meet the *refugee* definition, or those who are excluded from it.[2] Complementary protection in the UK and Germany derives from the European Convention on Human Rights (ECHR), EU law through its subsidiary protection status (and the UK equivalent called 'humanitarian protection'), as well as a range of provisions in domestic law, described in more detail in the passages that follow.

As such, complementary protection is an important tool ensuring that persons who are not eligible for refugee status can nevertheless obtain protection. At the same time, refugee status is the most beneficial protection status available and should therefore be considered first. As opposed to most instruments

1 It should be noted that, under certain circumstances, denial of socio-economic rights may afford individuals refugee status. See Michelle Foster, *International Refugee Law and Socio-Economic Rights: Refuge from Deprivation* (CUP 2007) 353.

2 Jane McAdam, 'Complementary Protection' in Cathryn Costello, Michelle Foster and Jane McAdam (eds), *The Oxford Handbook of International Refugee Law* (OUP 2021).

DOI: 10.4324/9781032664644-6

complementary forms of protection are derived from, the Refugee Convention 'confers a range of civil and political and socio-economic rights on those recognized as refugees'[3] and thus provides the most comprehensive form of protection. While some complementary forms of protection do come with a catalogue of rights, for example, in case of subsidiary protection status under EU law, there are a number of important differences.[4]

There are cases in both UK and German case law of persons who are granted complementary protection because they possess certain characteristics reminiscent of the vulnerability indicators courts rely on to establish a risk of re-trafficking. Since, as this book has shown, these vulnerabilities are also indicators for a risk of irregular re-migration, this chapter considers whether the relevant claimants can be reconceptualised as refugees. The chapter posits that these claimants may be irregularised migrants 'hidden' in existing case law, and that by shifting the focus of the protection enquiry to the assessment of a risk of irregular re-migration, they may be found to be eligible for refugee status rather than complementary protection. Thus, it is not the aim of this chapter to examine the reasoning in, and coherence of, the complementary protection case law itself. The chapter does point out some questions raised by the case law, most notably the question of establishing a violation of Article 3 ECHR in 'destitution' cases – which is approached very differently in UK case law on the one hand and German case law on the other.[5] Rather than analysing the complementary protection case law itself, I use it to point out that the claimants in the relevant cases are 'vulnerable' in similar ways as irregularised migrants and examine the implications of this for their protection claims.

The chapter begins by considering UK complementary protection case law on 'very significant obstacles to integration' and the risk of destitution in Section 2. Section 3 examines German complementary protection cases on destitution. In both sections, I show that eligibility for complementary protection is established based on factors very similar to the vulnerability indicators

3 Foster (n 1). For a detailed discussion of these rights, see James C Hathaway, *The Rights of Refugees under International Law* (2nd edn, CUP 2021).

4 Differences between refugee status and subsidiary protection status include durations of validity of residence permits and eligibility for social welfare. See Steve Peers and others (eds), *EU Immigration and Asylum Law (Text and Commentary): Second Revised Edition: Volume 3: EU Asylum Law* (Brill 2015) 75. In addition, the EU Family Reunification Directive – and its favourable provisions foreseen for refugees – does not apply to beneficiaries of subsidiary protection. See Council Directive 2003/86/EC of 22 September 2003 on the Right to Family Reunification [2003] OJ L 251 (Family Reunification Directive) art 3(2)(c). See also Minos Mouzourakis, 'Refugee Rights Subsiding? Europe's Two-Tier Protection Regime and Its Effect on the Rights of Beneficiaries (*ECRE*, 2016) 15–23 <www.refworld.org/reference/regionalreport/ecre/2016/en/116217> accessed 21 July 2021; see further McAdam (n 2) 670–71.

5 For a human rights–based definition of *destitution* and a discussion of how this concept can be distinguished from (extreme) poverty, see Luke Graham, *International Human Rights Law and Destitution: An Economic, Social and Cultural Rights Perspective* (Routledge 2022).

relied on in the analysis of the risk of re-trafficking. At the same time, additional factors for finding a risk of destitution or very significant obstacles to integration are mentioned in the case law, and I argue that, therefore, these cases can inform the analysis of a risk of re-trafficking/irregular re-migration by revealing additional vulnerability indicators. German case law further reveals that, at times, trafficked persons' protection claims are reduced to a risk of destitution, without considering the relevance of vulnerability indicators for the risk of re-trafficking. Similarly, in some 'destitution' cases, risk of trafficking is mentioned, but not investigated.

The chapter concludes that there may be irregularised migrants 'hidden' in complementary protection case law and that these claimants may be eligible for refugee status based on a risk of (re-)trafficking or irregular re-migration. The conclusion emphasises that individuals unable to meet the high threshold of a level of destitution infringing human rights or 'very significant' obstacles to integration, who are therefore refused protection, may nevertheless be able to show that the factors underlying their claim are material to the risk of (re-)trafficking or irregular re-migration, and thus to the question of persecution.

6.2 Vulnerability Indicators in UK Complementary Protection Case Law

Applicants not eligible for refugee status in the UK may be able to claim different types of complementary protection: humanitarian protection, which is equivalent to subsidiary protection under EU law;[6] protection from removal under human rights law (most commonly under Article 3 or 8 ECHR);[7] or leave to remain outside the Immigration Rules.[8]

It is not the purpose of this section to go into detail regarding these different routes to non-removal but to highlight two strands of case law in which eligibility for complementary protection is established based on factors very similar to the vulnerability indicators relied on in the analysis of the risk of re-trafficking. These two strands of case law are, first, the 'very significant obstacles to integration' test, which forms part of the investigation into an applicant's permission to stay on the basis of their private life under Article 8 ECHR, and, second, the Article 3 ECHR test, as to a risk of torture or inhuman or degrading treatment, applied to the risk of destitution in the country of origin.

6 Immigration Rules (HC 395), Rules 339C-339CA.

7 Nationality, Immigration and Asylum Act 2002, s 84(1)(c) and s 84(2).

8 Home Office, 'Leave Outside the Immigration Rules' (29 August 2023) Version 3.0 <https://assets.publishing.service.gov.uk/media/64eef28f13ae1500116e3013/Leave_outside_the_Immigration_Rules.pdf> accessed 22 July 2024.

6.2.1 *'Very Significant Obstacles to Integration' as a Reason for Non-Removal*

The UK's Immigration Rules contain a clause which will prevent applicants (who have been continuously resident in the UK for less than 20 years) from being removed where 'there would be very significant obstacles to the applicant's integration into the country where they would have to live if required to leave the UK'.[9] It is pertinent to investigate this provision in some detail, seeing as it was established in Chapter 3 that factors constituting obstacles to reintegration can also be considered as vulnerabilities to re-trafficking and, indeed, to irregular re-migration.

The 'very significant obstacles to integration' provision is set out in detail in the relevant caseworker guidance, which explains that 'the private life that an individual has established in the UK is not relevant when . . . considering whether there are very serious obstacles to integration into the country of return'.[10] As such, the 'very significant obstacles to integration' test deals only with the applicant's potential experiences in the country of return. According to the guidance:

> A very significant obstacle [to integrating into the country of return] may arise where the applicant would be at a real risk of prosecution or significant harassment or discrimination as a result of their sexual or political orientation or faith or gender, or where their rights and freedoms would otherwise be so severely restricted as to affect their fundamental rights.[11]

Other relevant factors include, but are not limited to, 'the applicant's cultural ties and familiarity with the country of return',[12] 'the proportion of the person's life spent in that country' and 'the quality of any relationships with family or friends in the country of return'.[13]

As such, there are at least some factors considered to form very significant obstacles to integration which are also vulnerability indicators for the risk of re-trafficking/irregular re-migration. Harassment and discrimination are very similar to stigmatisation; lack of family support is relevant in both contexts. Interestingly, the caseworker guidance states explicitly that lack of

9 Immigration Rules (n 6) Appendix Private Life, para PL 5.1(b); through para PL 6.1, the Rules exclude applicants whose asylum claims have been declared inadmissible from benefitting from this provision.

10 Home Office, 'Private Life: Version 2.0' (18 May 2023) <www.gov.uk/government/publications/private-life-caseworker-guidance> accessed 23 April 2024.

11 ibid 21.

12 ibid.

13 ibid 22.

employment opportunities, another vulnerability indicator for re-trafficking/ irregular re-migration, is not considered to form an obstacle to integration.[14]

However, it is important to note that the factors cited in the caseworker guidance are not exhaustive, and indeed, the courts have expanded the factors which must be considered when assessing whether there are very significant obstacles to integration. Thus, in *Kamara*, the Court of Appeal stated:

> The idea of 'integration' calls for a broad evaluative judgment to be made as to whether the individual will be enough of an insider in terms of understanding how life in the society in that other country is carried on and a capacity to participate in it, so as to have a reasonable opportunity to be accepted there, to be able to operate on a day-to-day basis in that society and to build up within a reasonable time a variety of human relationships to give substance to the individual's private or family life.[15]

Thus, this judgment suggests that other issues, such as lack of employment opportunities and (mental) health, may, in fact, play a role in the assessment, seeing as they affect an individual's ability to participate in life in the country of return and to function there on a day-to-day basis. It should be noted that *Kamara* concerned a so-called 'foreign criminal'. Under the Nationality, Immigration and Asylum Act 2002, there is an exception to the general rule that 'foreign criminals' sentenced to four years' imprisonment or more must be deported, stating that this does not apply where the individual in question has been lawfully resident in the UK for most of their life and is socially and culturally integrated in the UK and where there would be very significant obstacles to their integration into the country to which they are proposed to be deported.[16]

However, there is no suggestion that the phrase 'very significant obstacles to integration' has a different meaning for so-called foreign criminals on the one hand and applicants who have not committed a crime on the other.[17] This is demonstrated, for example, by the case of *Parveen*, which concerned an applicant who had overstayed a spouse visa and which cites *Kamara* in examining the meaning of 'very significant obstacles to integration'. In this case, Underhill LJ commented on the high threshold of 'very significant' obstacles to integration, stating:

> It is fair enough to observe that the words 'very significant' connote an 'elevated' threshold, and I have no difficulty with the observation that the test will not be met by 'mere inconvenience or upheaval'. But I am

14 ibid 23.

15 *Kamara v SSHD* [2016] EWCA Civ 813, [2016] 8 WLUK 174 [14].

16 Nationality, Immigration and Asylum Act 2002, s 117C(4).

17 *Wright v SSHD* [2024] UKUT (IAC) UI-2023-005380 [13].

> not sure that saying that 'mere' hardship or difficulty or hurdles, even if multiplied, will not 'generally' suffice adds anything of substance. The task of the Secretary of State, or the Tribunal, in any given case is simply to assess the obstacles to integration relied on, whether characterised as hardship or difficulty or anything else, and to decide whether they regard them as 'very significant'.[18]

Thus, the judgment suggests that all relevant factors must be assessed in the round and cumulatively.

Indeed, higher courts have taken into account additional factors when assessing whether an individual faces very significant obstacles to integration. Thus, in *Lowe*, the Court of Appeal accepted that 'lack of financial support for basic necessities' (coupled with lack of family support and lack of experience of living independently) would constitute such an obstacle.[19] Further, it appears uncontroversial that mental health issues form a very significant obstacle to integration, according to the Supreme Court in *SC (Jamaica)*.[20]

At the tribunal level, there is a wealth of case law dealing with very significant obstacles to integration. Despite the large number of these cases, only relatively few of them result in non-removal of the applicant. While it is not within the scope of this chapter to conduct a comprehensive analysis of all cases, it is worth examining a sample of those in which the applicant did successfully resist removal, since they beg the question of whether these applicants may be irregularised migrants 'hidden' in the case law. While there are a number of successful cases where so-called 'foreign criminals' were granted protection from removal based on significant obstacles to integration, the following examples only deal with individuals who are not 'foreign criminals'. This is because most asylum seekers will not have committed any criminal offences, and 'foreign criminals' have to demonstrate additional criteria (lawful residence in the UK for most of their life and social and cultural integration),[21] so that the situations of the two groups are likely to be too different to compare effectively.

Claimants benefitting from complementary protection due to very significant obstacles to integration include women, men and married couples. Thus, in 2016, the Upper Tribunal (UT) in *Kapinga* agreed with a First-Tier Tribunal (FTT) assessment which found that a Tanzanian woman would have very significant obstacles to integration because of her long absence from Tanzania (16 years), lack of family ties and support, mental health and a lack of employment prospects.[22] Also in 2016, in the case of *Bodun*, the UT dismissed the

18 *Parveen v SSHD* [2018] EWCA Civ 932, [2018] 4 WLUK 429 [9].
19 *Lowe v SSHD* [2021] EWCA Civ 62, [2021] 1 WLUK 248 [36].
20 *SC (Jamaica) v SSHD* [2022] UKSC 15, [2022] 6 WLUK 110 [107].
21 Nationality, Immigration and Asylum Act 2002, s 117C(4).
22 *SSHD v Kapinga* [2016] UKUT (IAC) IA/07269/2015.

Secretary of State's appeal against an FTT decision to grant a Nigerian woman protection based on very significant obstacles to integration arising from her long absence from Nigeria (18 years), lack of family support, her mental and physical health conditions and lack of education and employment experience.[23] Similarly, in the 2020 case of *MI*, a Bangladeshi woman succeeded in showing very significant obstacles to integration based on her mental health difficulties, lack of family support and the stigma attached to single women living alone in Bangladesh.[24] In the 2024 case of *Veintimilla*, an Ecuadorian woman was granted complementary protection based on very significant obstacles to integration in the shape of a lack of family support, qualifications and employment prospects, coupled with the general economic and security situation in Ecuador.[25] These women clearly possess vulnerability indicators – specifically (mental) health issues, stigma and lack of family support, education and employment prospects – so that it would be pertinent to consider whether they are at risk of trafficking or irregular re-migration.

Interestingly, even couples who, although clearly 'vulnerable', have each other for support have been granted complementary protection based on very significant obstacles to integration. Thus, in 2016, the UT in *Rakeshkumar and Hetal* agreed with the FTT's assessment that an Indian married couple would face very significant obstacles to integration in India because they both had health conditions and lacked skills, employment experience and family support and would therefore struggle to find work on return.[26] Likewise, in the 2018 case of *HK and JS*, the UT agreed with the FTT's finding that another Indian married couple would face very significant obstacles to integration because of the wife's mental health issues and the stigma resulting from this, the husband's lack of education and employment experience and their lack of family support and resulting inability to care and provide for themselves and their children.[27] Again, there are clear parallels between the applicants' vulnerabilities and those relied on in establishing risk of re-trafficking and irregular re-migration.

Finally, single men, too, have been granted complementary protection because they would encounter very serious obstacles to integrating in their countries of origin. For example, in the 2015 case of *ZY*, the UT dismissed the Secretary of State's appeal against an FTT decision granting an Afghan man complementary protection, finding that he was

> a very vulnerable young man who would face very significant obstacles in terms of integration back into Afghan society given his severe

23 *SSHD v Bodun* [2016] UKUT (IAC) IA/10292/2015.
24 *MI v SSHD* [2020] UKUT (IAC) PA/10163/2018.
25 *Veintimilla v SSHD* [2024] UKUT (IAC) UI-2024–002985.
26 *SSHD v Rakeshkumar and Hetal* [2016] UKUT (IAC) IA/14784/2015 and IA/14788/2015.
27 *SSHD v HK and JS* [2018] UKUT (IAC) HU/13283/2016 and HU/13292/2016.

> learning difficulties, his overall functioning age of 6 years old, his lack of family support given the murder of his father and brother and the death of his mother and his problems being compounded by his PTSD [post-traumatic stress disorder] and his extremely limited ability to access the labour market, housing and social integration as well as any health-care, and his lack of support available to him in Afghanistan.[28]

Not only does the tribunal refer to the applicant as 'vulnerable', but it also mentions mental health issues and lack of employment opportunities, education and (family) support – all vulnerability indicators for the risk of re-trafficking and irregular re-migration.

Similarly, in the 2020 case of *NP*, an Afghan man who entered the UK as a minor and subsequently remained for eight years was found to have very significant obstacles to integration based on a lack of employment opportunities, family support and likely difficulty finding accommodation as a result, as well as a degree of 'westernisation' and resulting problems in navigating life in Afghanistan.[29] Further, in *MZ*, also decided in 2020, the UT agreed with the FTT judge's assessment that there would be very significant obstacles to the integration of a Pakistani man who had lived in the UK since the age of 11 because he suffered from a 'moderate learning disability and schizoaffective disorder and require[d] 24-hour care and supervision', without which he 'would be at risk of exploitation by others', noting also the stigma against mental illness in Pakistan and a lack of family support.[30] In *YT*, another case decided in 2020, an Algerian man was found to have significant obstacles to integration based on his mental health problems and his resulting inability to find work and accommodation.[31] In the 2022 case of *Shah*, the UT found that a Pakistani man would encounter very significant obstacles to integration in Pakistan based on his lack of family ties there, his mental health issues, 'difficulty . . . in accessing accommodation and finding work' and an absence of almost 20 years.[32] In the case of *SS*, also decided in 2022, the UT found that the applicant, also a Pakistani man, would be unable to reintegrate into Pakistani society due to his mental health issues, which would lead to 'stigma and discrimination' and an 'inability to form relationships'.[33] Further, in the 2024 case of *Wright*, a Jamaican man succeeded in showing very significant obstacles to integration due to health issues, which made it difficult for him to work, and a lack of family support.[34]

28 *SSHD v ZY* [2015] UKUT (IAC) IA/18670/2014 [25].
29 *NP v SSHD* [2020] UKUT (IAC) PA/05297/2018.
30 *MZ (Hospital order: whether a 'foreign criminal') Pakistan* [2020] UKUT 00225 (IAC) [16]–[17].
31 *YT v SSHD* [2020] UKUT (IAC) PA/02930/2019.
32 *Shah v SSHD* [2022] UKUT (IAC) HU/02664/2020 [24].
33 *SS v SSHD* [2022] UKUT (IAC) PA/00677/2020 [82]–[83].
34 *Wright* (n 17) [63]–[69].

The aforementioned cases demonstrate that factors which are framed as obstacles to integration are very similar to vulnerability indicators for the risk of re-trafficking/irregular re-migration. In both strands of case law, factors mentioned include lack of education, lack of employment opportunities, lack of family support, stigma and (mental) health issues.

Considering these vulnerability indicators only in the context of complementary protection can lead to an unjust refusal of refugee status. This is demonstrated by the 2020 case of *MS*.[35] This case concerned an Afghan man who feared persecution at the hands of the Taliban in his home area and whose asylum claim before the FTT had only failed due to the alleged availability of an internal protection alternative (IPA). The FTT judge nevertheless granted the applicant complementary protection due to very significant obstacles to integration. The UT, however, found that the factors leading the FTT judge to conclude that the applicant could not be removed due to very significant obstacles to integration – specifically, lack of employment opportunities and family support, and therefore a lack of assistance in obtaining employment, housing and education – were also relevant to the IPA inquiry, thus allowing the appeal on asylum grounds.

This case shows that it is possible to approach the factors considered to pose 'very significant obstacles to integration' as relevant to an asylum claim. As discussed in Chapter 3, vulnerability indicators preclude an IPA because they hinder reintegration in the entire country of origin. Thus, it is not surprising that, conversely, factors which preclude reintegration also preclude an IPA. Importantly, however, the same factors which preclude reintegration and an IPA also indicate a risk of (re-)trafficking or irregular re-migration. As such, the applicants in the aforementioned cases could potentially have claimed refugee status based on such a risk, especially seeing as the standard of proof of 'very significant obstacles' is much higher than the well-founded fear test in refugee law.

Thus, claimants relying on 'very significant obstacles to integration' to resist removal may, in fact, be irregularised migrants because they have (some of) the relevant vulnerability indicators for the risk of re-trafficking/irregular re-migration. At the same time, the 'very significant obstacles' case law can inform the analysis of a risk of re-trafficking/irregular re-migration. One obstacle to integration mentioned in a number of the aforementioned cases is the long period of time spent outside the country of origin and a resulting unfamiliarity with life in that country. As such, a long period of absence – which may result, for example, from a protracted journey and slow asylum procedures – should be taken into account as a vulnerability indicator when considering irregularised migrants' asylum claims.

35 *MS v SSHD* [2020] UKUT (IAC) PA/07803/2016.

6.2.2 *Risk of Destitution as a Reason for Non-Removal*

A second line of UK cases where irregularised migrants may be identified in existing case law concerns applicants claiming that their removal would be contrary to Article 3 ECHR because they face a risk of destitution on return. As discussed in what follows, this line of reasoning is very common in German case law, but much less so in UK case law.

Indeed, UK courts rarely accept that the high threshold of Article 3 ECHR is met where an applicant faces destitution. This is illustrated, for example, by the case of *Said*, decided by the Court of Appeal in 2016.[36] In this case, the applicant argued that he would be destitute upon being returned to Somalia, basing this mainly on his poor mental health, but also issues such as having no family support network in Somalia. However, the Court of Appeal found that although 'his PTSD and depression will make it difficult for him integrate back into life in Somalia and have some impact on his ability to work', '[t]here is no suggestion that he is precluded from working and much to support the finding that he will be able to do so'.[37] Thus, the Court concluded that this case was 'so far removed from the nature of exceptional and compelling circumstances envisaged in the Strasbourg cases as to make it clear that [the applicant's] deportation would not breach article 3 of the [ECHR]'.[38]

Said was decided a couple of months before the European Court of Human Rights' (ECtHR) judgment in *Paposhvili*,[39] which modified the threshold for so-called Article 3 'medical' cases, so that *Said* may well have been decided differently had the Court of Appeal had the benefit of reading the judgment in *Paposhvili*. Mr Paposhvili suffered from leukaemia and other illnesses and claimed that he would be unable to access adequate medical treatment in his country of origin, Georgia.

Prior to *Paposhvili*, in *N v UK*, the ECtHR had decided that in cases where no actor of harm can be identified (i.e. where the harm – in these cases an illness – was 'naturally occurring'), to meet the threshold of Article 3 ECHR, a claimant had to show that they were 'critically ill' and 'close to death'.[40] In *Paposhvili*, however, the ECtHR required that a seriously ill person

> although not at imminent risk of dying, would face a real risk, on account of the absence of appropriate treatment in the receiving country or the lack of access to such treatment, of being exposed to a serious, rapid and irreversible decline in his or her state of health resulting in intense suffering or to a significant reduction in life expectancy.[41]

36 *SSHD v Said* [2016] EWCA Civ 442, [2016] 5 WLUK 88.
37 ibid [19].
38 ibid.
39 *Paposhvili v Belgium* App no 41738/10 (ECtHR, 13 December 2016).
40 *N v The United Kingdom* App no 26565/05 (ECtHR, 27 May 2008); see also *D v The United Kingdom* App no 30240/96 (ECtHR, 2 May 1997).
41 *Paposhvili* (n 39) para 183.

The ECtHR has not had an opportunity to clarify whether this threshold should also be applied to scenarios other than 'medical' cases, such as 'destitution' cases like *Said*. In *Sufi and Elmi*, decided prior to *Paposhvili*, the ECtHR suggested that the higher *N v UK* threshold should apply where an applicant is at risk of harm due to state poverty and lack of resources.[42] In *SHH* – also decided prior to *Paposhvili* – the Court applied this high threshold and rejected the claim of a disabled man who would be returned to dire humanitarian conditions in Afghanistan, citing the availability of family support as a major reason for the requisite threshold not being reached.[43] Notably, in cases concerning return not to the country of origin but to a Council of Europe member state, the Court has had little difficulty finding a violation of Article 3 ECHR where the applicant faced 'a situation of extreme material poverty' in that country,[44] without resorting to the high *N v UK* threshold applied to applicants returned to their country of origin. Due to these and other complexities, the ECtHR has been criticised for a 'lack of a single coherent normative rationale for [its] *non-refoulement* case law'.[45] While the modified *Paposhvili* threshold may help reduce the complexities and discrepancies in the case law, to date, the ECtHR has not applied the *Paposhvili* test to an applicant facing destitution upon return to their country of origin.

The UK UT, however, did just that in 2021. In *Ainte*, which concerned a Somali man who feared extreme material deprivation on return, the tribunal considered whether the claimant would 'be exposed to conditions resulting in intense suffering or to a significant reduction in his life expectancy'.[46] The UT emphasised that 'it is entirely possible that someone returning to Somalia from the UK will find themselves living in conditions that are inhuman and degrading such that would place the UK in breach of its obligations under Article 3'.[47] However, regarding the particular claimant in question, despite his lack of family support in Somalia or from abroad, his long absence from Somalia and the resulting lack of social connections and his mental health issues, the UT found that he was

> a fit and able bodied young man who has proved himself capable of living in Mogadishu in far more challenging circumstances than those he

42 *Sufi and Elmi v The United Kingdom* App nos 8319/07 and 11449/07 (ECtHR, 28 June 2011) para 282.

43 *SHH v The United Kingdom* App no 60367/10 (ECtHR, 29 January 2013) para 93.

44 *MSS v Belgium and Greece* App no 30696/09 (ECtHR, 21 January 2011); *Tarakhel v Switzerland* App no 29217/12 (ECtHR, 4 November 2014).

45 Cathryn Costello, 'The Search for the Outer Edges of *Non-Refoulement* in Europe: Exceptionality and Flagrant Breaches' in Bruce Burson and David J Cantor (eds), *Human Rights and the Refugee Definition* (Brill Nijhoff 2016) 184; see also Margit Ammer and Monika Mayrhofer, 'Cross-Border Disaster Displacement and *Non-Refoulement* under Article 3 of the ECHR: An Analysis of the European Union and Austria' (2023) 35(3) International Journal of Refugee Law 322 <https://doi.org/10.1093/ijrl/eead036>.

46 *Ainte (material deprivation – Art 3 – AM (Zimbabwe)* [2021] UKUT 00203 (IAC) [62].

47 ibid [135].

> faces today. He will be able to find work, albeit that it may be of low quality or low status, and that work will enable him to find and pay for accommodation.[48]

The tribunal dismissed the appeal.

In 2022, a country guidance case on Somalia followed in *OA (Somalia)*, concerning another Somali man fearing, *inter alia*, extreme material deprivation.[49] Again, the UT decided that despite his mental health issues, drug addiction, long absence from Somalia and lack of employment experience, the appellant would have social and clan connections on return, benefit from financial reintegration assistance and, since he had some qualifications, would be able to make a livelihood, dismissing the appeal. The UT also introduced a requirement of imminence regarding the 'intense suffering' feared by a returnee on account of his living conditions on return, stating that it would not suffice for such suffering to manifest 'at some unknown point in the future'.[50] Further, the tribunal stated that such suffering is only likely to arise if 'the returnee would be without any prospect of initial accommodation, support or another base from which to begin to establish themselves'.[51]

As such, despite applying the lower *Paposhvili* threshold, these cases illustrate how difficult it is for an applicant to establish a violation of Article 3 ECHR in destitution cases. Nevertheless, cases in which claimants have successfully argued that their living conditions on return would breach Article 3 ECHR do exist.

Thus, as early as 2011, the UT in *AMM and Others* – which concerned the protection claims of several Somali applicants who were all either granted refugee status or humanitarian protection, though not for reasons of destitution – decided that there was a 'generalised Article 3 risk, which exists by reason of the famine [in southern and central Somalia]'.[52] The UT held that 'the present situation is one of those "very exceptional cases" in which humanitarian conditions trigger Article 3', despite applying the high *N v UK* threshold in this case.[53] Thus, the UT found that anyone affected by the famine, without anything more, would be at risk of harm, contrary to Article 3 ECHR. This, however, is the only UK case in which such a conclusion was ever reached, and in the few other successful 'destitution' cases, applicants had to show that they had particular characteristics making them 'vulnerable' to destitution.

Thus, in 2023, the UT in the case of *RK* allowed the appeal of an Afghan man at risk of destitution on Article 3 ECHR human rights grounds, holding that this risk was established based on the applicant's lack of education,

48 ibid [136].
49 *OA (Somalia) Somalia CG* [2022] UKUT 00033 (IAC).
50 ibid [127].
51 ibid [356j].
52 *AMM and Others v SSHD* [2011] UKUT 00445 (IAC), [2011] 7 WLUK 464 [477]–[490].
53 ibid [480].

qualifications, employment experience and family support in Afghanistan, as well as his learning difficulties, drug addiction and mental health issues.[54] Even with financial reintegration assistance, the tribunal argued, he would not be able to reintegrate sufficiently and he would be unable to find a job.

In *Cardos*, another 2023 case, the Secretary of State unsuccessfully appealed against the decision to grant a Gambian man protection under Article 3 ECHR.[55] The applicant was held to be at risk of destitution based on his mental health, which would likely deteriorate upon return given fewer treatment options there, the stigma resulting from his mental health condition, his lack of family support and the likely difficulties in finding and maintaining employment.

Further, in the 2024 case of *KF*, a Guinean man was granted humanitarian protection due to a risk of 'harm, destitution and exploitation' stemming from an inability to access a national ID card (which is needed to travel and access employment and accommodation), coupled with a lack of family support, education and employment experience.[56] Also in 2024, in *Ismail Mohamoud Ali*, the UT agreed with the FTT's assessment that a Somali man who had no family support in Somalia was at risk of destitution, and therefore entitled to human rights protection, due to his physical and mental health issues and the resulting low prospects of securing employment.[57]

Thus, although few and far between, cases in which persons succeed under Article 3 ECHR (or are granted humanitarian protection) based on a risk of destitution do exist. As with the 'very significant obstacles to integration' cases, factors very similar to the vulnerability indicators from trafficking-based asylum case law inform the analysis in most cases. In particular, lack of education, employment experience and family support, as well as mental health issues and stigma, are considered. Again, this begs the questions whether the applicants could have argued that they are at risk of being trafficked or of re-migrating irregularly.

At the same time, these cases, again, serve to expand the vulnerability analysis for the purpose of establishing a risk of re-trafficking or irregular re-migration. One of the factors informing the analysis under Article 3 ECHR which does not appear in trafficking-based asylum claims is drug addiction. Since this can contribute to destitution and an inability to reintegrate in the country of origin, it should also be taken into account when assessing risk of re-trafficking/irregular re-migration.

54 *RK v SSHD* [2023] UKUT (IAC) UI-2022–006079.
55 *SSHD v Joachim Cardos* [2023] UKUT (IAC) UI-2022–004930.
56 *KF v SSHD* [2024] UKUT (IAC) UI-2023–003705.
57 *SSHD v Ismail Mohamoud Ali* [2024] UKUT (IAC) UI-2024–000166.

6.3 Vulnerability Indicators in German Complementary Protection Case Law

In addition to refugee status[58] and subsidiary protection,[59] German law provides for two types of national complementary protection. Section 60(5) Residence Act prohibits removal constituting a violation of the ECHR,[60] specifically a violation of Article 3 ECHR.[61] Meanwhile, Section 60(7) Residence Act states that 'foreigners are not to be deported to another state in which they face a substantial concrete threat to life and limb or liberty'. As discussed in what follows, both Section 60(5) and Section 60(7) Residence Act have been used to grant protection to persons at risk of destitution.

Tiedemann explains that, in theory, Section 60(7) is 'obsolete' because it does not add anything to Section 60(2), which codifies Article 15 Qualification Regulation.[62] He notes, however, that Section 60(7) nevertheless remains popular with administrative courts (ACs) and, he argues, is seen as 'a way to deny the persons concerned the status they are entitled to under EU law [and the rights attached] without appearing inhumane'.[63] It should be noted, however, that the Court of Justice of the European Union (CJEU) in *M'Bodj* clarified that serious harm for the purpose of Article 15 Qualification Regulation 'must take the form of conduct on the part of a third party and that it cannot therefore simply be the result of general shortcomings in the health system of the country of origin'.[64] By analogy, this is likely to apply to destitution cases, so that Section 60(7) Residence Act may add some protection after all, though, as evident from the cases discussed later, most destitution cases are seen to engage Article 3 ECHR (and therefore Section 60(5) Residence Act) despite the ECtHR's lack of guidance on the issue, discussed earlier.

This section explores German 'destitution' case law and, in Section 6.3.1, shows that, as in UK case law, the relevant cases rely on factors very similar to the vulnerability indicators considered in asylum claims based on a risk of re-trafficking, so that it can be argued that the applicants' risk of being trafficked or re-migrating irregularly should be investigated. At the same time, as shown in Section 6.3.2, some applicants with a prior experience of being trafficked only have their risk of destitution assessed, with courts not considering

58 Gesetz über den Aufenthalt, die Erwerbstätigkeit und die Integration von Ausländern im Bundesgebiet (Aufenthaltsgesetz – AufenthG) 25 February 2008 (BGBl. I S. 162) (Residence Act) s 60(1); Asylgesetz (AsylG) 2 September 2008 (BGBl. I S. 1798) (Asylum Act) s 3(1).

59 Residence Act (n 58) s 60(2); Asylum Act (n 58) s 4(1).

60 Residence Act (n 58) s 60(5).

61 Bundesverwaltungsgericht, 1 B 25.18, 08.08.2018.

62 Paul Tiedemann, 'Die Geschichte des subsidiären Flüchtlingsschutzes' in Paul Tiedemann and Janina Gieseking (eds), *Flüchtlingsrecht in Theorie und Praxis: 5 Jahre Refugee Law Clinic an der Justus-Liebig-Universität Gießen* (Nomos 2014) 118.

63 ibid 119; my translation.

64 C-542/13 *M'Bodj* [2014] ECLI:EU:C:2014:2452, para 35.

the relevance of their findings on destitution for the enquiry into a risk of re-trafficking. Similarly, in some 'destitution' cases, risk of trafficking is mentioned, but not investigated. While this supports my suggestion that these cases should be considered under the Refugee Convention rather than under complementary protection provisions, it also shows that courts may indeed be deliberately denying individuals the (more beneficial) protection status they are entitled to, as Tiedemann suggests.

6.3.1 Risk of Destitution as a Reason for Non-Removal

There is a wealth of case law granting complementary protection to applicants who are at risk of destitution on return to their country of origin.[65] As opposed to UK courts, German courts have no difficulty finding that a risk of destitution engages Article 3 ECHR. As such, most of the cases discussed in this subsection were allowed under Section 60(5) Residence Act. Where a case is allowed instead under Section 60(7) Residence Act, it is not necessarily clear why this is the case, since the reasoning for both provisions is very similar. It is not the purpose of this section to discuss any doctrinal difficulties raised by this lack of clarity; rather, the purpose of the section is to show that, as in UK case law, there are claimants in German case law who may well be able to invoke a risk of trafficking or irregular re-migration since the courts effectively rely on vulnerability indicators to decide eligibility for complementary protection.

In German case law, a wide range of applicants is able to establish an entitlement to complementary protection based on a risk of destitution. One such group are single parents and families where the father would be the sole earner. Thus, in 2014, the Bavarian Higher AC granted Section 60(5) protection to an Afghan single father of two children because he would be unable to provide for them due to a lack of family support and the resulting inability to reconcile caring for the children and working.[66] In 2021, the AC Karlsruhe relied on Section 60(5) Residence Act to grant protection to an Iraqi woman, arguing that she would be destitute on return because although she would be able to find work as a hairdresser, she would be unable to provide for her seven children in the absence of family support.[67] Similarly, in 2022, a Moroccan woman succeeded under the same provision because she had little education, would be unable to work while caring for her five children and had no family support in Morocco.[68] Likewise, in 2024, the AC Munich granted Section 60(5) protection to a Gambian woman who was a single mother to three children

65 German courts tend to use the term *Verelendung*, which can be translated as 'destitution' or 'impoverishment'.
66 Bayerischer Verwaltungsgerichtshof, 13a B 14.30285, 21.11.2014.
67 VG Karlsruhe, A 18 K 5065/18, 02.06.2021.
68 VG Gera, 2 K 968/22 Ge, 05.09.2022.

and who lacked family support, education and employment experience.[69] Also in 2024, the AC Karlsruhe granted the same type of protection to an Indian single mother who had little education and lacked employment experience and family support.[70]

Further, in 2017, the Bavarian Higher AC granted Section 60(5) protection to an Afghan family with two minor children because the father would be unable to find work due to his lack of education and his health (a leg injury) and there would be no family support.[71] Interestingly, the court discusses at some length the inadequacy of financial reintegration assistance for countering the applicants' vulnerability, stating that such assistance cannot replace education and the knowledge needed to make a living.[72] The Federal Administrative Court, however, clarified in 2022 that financial reintegration assistance must be taken into account when considering whether an applicant would become destitute.[73]

In another 2017 decision, the Higher AC Baden-Württemberg granted an Afghan family with minor children protection under Section 60(5) Residence Act due to a risk of destitution, basing this on the father being unable to make a livelihood in the absence of relevant employment experience and education, as well as a lack of social connections in Afghanistan.[74] What is particularly interesting about this decision is that it acknowledges that returnees may face stigma for failing to return financially successful or for having been deported, which is associated with criminality.[75]

Further, in 2022, the AC Bremen found that a Sudanese family would be at risk of destitution and granted them complementary protection under Section 60(5) Residence Act because the father would be unable to earn a livelihood for himself, his wife and their child due to the wife's mental illness, which prevented her from looking after their son, the father's lack of any specialist skills that would give him an advantage on the job market, as well as a lack of a social network.[76] Also in 2022, and similarly, the AC Kassel granted protection under Section 60(5) Residence Act to a Somali man because he and his family would become destitute upon return to Somalia due to the applicant's lack of education, employment experience and a social network in Somalia.[77] Likewise, in 2024, the AC Giessen found that a Nigerian couple with four children were eligible for Section 60(5) protection because the mother suffered from mental health issues which would make it difficult for

69 VG München, M 10 K 23.32418, 31.05.2024.
70 VG Karlsruhe, A 5 K 4693/23, 28.05.2024.
71 Bayerischer Verwaltungsgerichtshof, 13a B 17.30030, 23.03.2017.
72 ibid p 9.
73 Bundesverwaltungsgericht, 1 C 10.21, 21.04.2022.
74 Verwaltungsgerichtshof Baden-Württemberg, A 11 S 1704/17, 03.11.2017.
75 ibid [350].
76 VG Bremen, 2 K 610/19, 23.12.2022.
77 VG Kassel, 4 K 1583/18.KS.A, 30.03.2022.

the father to make a living and look after the children in the absence of family support.[78]

However, not only single parents and families are seen as vulnerable and in need of complementary protection where they face destitution. Single 'able-bodied' (young) men, too, can be protected for the same reasons, despite German courts' reluctance to recognise them as vulnerable in the context of trafficking-based asylum claims, as discussed in Chapter 3.

Thus, in a 2008 decision by the AC Koblenz, an Afghan man was granted protection under Section 60(7) Residence Act because he was at risk of destitution due to a lack of education, employment experience and family support.[79] Similarly, in 2017, the AC Hamburg granted a young Afghan man complementary protection under Section 60(7) Residence Act because, having spent his youth outside Afghanistan, he would not be sufficiently familiar with life in Afghanistan and lacked family connections there, so that he would become destitute.[80] Further, in 2020, the AC Cottbus found that another young Afghan man was at risk of destitution and therefore in need of protection under Section 60(5) Residence Act because, having spent most of his youth in Germany, he would be a 'de facto foreigner' in Afghanistan, he had mental health issues and he lacked employment experience and family support.[81]

Further, and also in 2020, an Afghan man succeeded in showing that he would face treatment contrary to Article 3 ECHR upon return to Afghanistan, so that the Higher AC Bremen granted him protection under Section 60(5) Residence Act.[82] The court considered that even able-bodied young men without dependents would be unable to provide for their basic needs on return to Afghanistan unless they possess particular resilience and assertiveness. The court reasoned that such resilience and assertiveness will be hampered by lack of family support, social connections, financial assets and education; the presence of a disability; belonging to minority ethnic groups which experience discrimination; being a minor; and having spent a long time away from the country of return.

Also in 2020, the Higher AC Baden-Württemberg relied on Section 60(5) Residence Act to grant protection to an able-bodied Afghan man, stating that in the absence of resilience factors, such as a family and social networks, financial and material support from third parties and financial assets, he, and others like him, would be unable to make a livelihood in Afghanistan and become destitute.[83]

78 VG Gießen, 18 K 535/22.GI.A, 04.06.2024.
79 AC Koblenz, 1 K 1013/08.KO, 12.11.2008.
80 VG Hamburg, 10 A 6516/16, 10.01.2017.
81 VG Cottbus, 3 K 633/20.A, 29.05.2020.
82 OVG Bremen, 1 LB 258/20, 22.09.2020.
83 Verwaltungsgerichtshof Baden-Württemberg, A 11 S 2042/20, 17.12.2020.

Similarly, in 2022, the AC Saarland granted Section 60(5) protection to a healthy young Afghan man who was, in principle, 'fit for work' but who would have faced difficulties finding employment – and was therefore at risk of destitution – due to ethnic discrimination, a lack of education, employment experience, family support and any indication of resilience, for example, in the shape of financial assets.[84] Also in 2022, the AC Gelsenkirchen granted Section 60(5) protection to a Somali applicant who the court found would become destitute on return to Somalia due to a lack of education, employment prospects and family support.[85] Similarly, and also in 2022, the AC Bremen decided that a Somali man would be at risk of destitution upon return, granting him Section 60(5) protection because he lacked education, employment experience and a family or social network in Somalia and he belonged to a minority ethnic group which experiences discrimination on the job market.[86]

In another 2022 case, the AC Chemnitz granted protection under Section 60(5) Residence Act to an Ethiopian man of Somali ethnicity, justifying this based on his complete lack of a family or social network in Ethiopia and the resulting inability to find work, which would lead to destitution.[87] A similar argument, with the same outcome in terms of protection, was made by the AC Darmstadt in 2024, citing the applicant's mental health issues and his lack of social connections in Somalia.[88]

Finally, in 2024, the AC Oldenburg granted protection under Section 60(5) to a man from Montenegro based on a risk of destitution due to the discrimination he would encounter on the job market because of his Roma ethnicity, his lack of family support in the country and his mental and physical health issues.[89] The same year, the AC Braunschweig granted the same type of protection to a 59-year-old Somali man who had physical health issues; lacked employment experience, education and family support; and had been absent from Somalia for 15 years, all of which would make it difficult for him to find employment in Somalia.[90]

Based on the foregoing discussion, there is clearly a wealth of case law which bases its assessment of eligibility for complementary protection on the presence of vulnerability indicators which lead to socio-economic deprivation amounting to destitution. Nevertheless, it should be noted that decisions by ACs dealing with similar issues at a similar time are not necessarily consistent. For example, in 2020, the Bavarian Higher AC stated that lack of family support need not be taken into account when considering whether an able-bodied young man from Afghanistan is at risk of treatment contrary to

84 VG Saarland, 5 K 741/20, 23.02.2022.
85 VG Gelsenkirchen, 17a K 2612/18.A, 04.11.2022.
86 VG Bremen, 7 K 2424/21, 29.11.2022.
87 VG Chemnitz, 2 K 322/19.A, 26.08.2022.
88 VG Darmstadt, 3 K 1022/19.DA.A, 31.01.2024.
89 VG Oldenburg, 3 A 710/23, 09.02.2024.
90 VG Braunschweig, 5 A 317/20, 16.08.2024.

Article 3 ECHR upon return.[91] On the other hand, in the same year, the same court stated that when it comes to deciding the same issue with regard to a family with minor children, the mere presence of family members in Afghanistan is not a decisive risk-reducing factor; rather, those family members would have to have an above-average income or assets in order to consider them able to support the returning family.[92] This same reasoning was also used by the AC Minden in 2022, which granted an Afghan man protection under Section 60(5) Residence Act precisely because, although he had family in Afghanistan, they would, in practice, be unable to support him so that he was at risk of destitution.[93]

Despite some inconsistencies in the case law, the aforementioned cases clearly show that factors courts rely on in order to determine whether there is a risk of re-trafficking are also relied on to determine a risk of destitution. These factors include lack of family or social support, education and employment experience, as well as experiencing (mental) health issues, stigma and discrimination. In addition, factors not cited in the context of trafficking-based asylum claims but referred to in the destitution enquiry are having dependents (normally children – and not just 'illegitimate' children, as in the trafficking context), having been absent from the country of origin for a long time (leading to a lack of social connections and understanding of daily life there) and a lack of financial assets and specialist skills. These factors should be taken into account as vulnerability indicators for the risk of re-trafficking/irregular re-migration in the asylum context.

As such, rather than framing the claimants in these cases as individuals at risk of destitution who are in need of complementary protection, it may be possible to reframe them as persons at risk of trafficking or irregular re-migration – irregularised migrants hidden in 'destitution' case law. Interestingly, in the case of the Afghan man who received protection under Section 60(5) Residence Act from the Higher AC Bremen, discussed earlier, the court explicitly acknowledges that persons returned to Afghanistan and becoming destitute there are likely to respond to this by re-migrating irregularly.[94]

6.3.2 Complementary Protection and Risk of Re-Trafficking

Concerningly, German courts also apply the reasoning discussed earlier to persons with a prior trafficking experience. Rather than recognising that the vulnerability indicators relied upon to find a risk of destitution are also indicators for the risk of re-trafficking, German courts sometimes simply grant complementary protection based on the trafficked person's risk of destitution.

91 Bayerischer Verwaltungsgerichtshof, 13a B 19.33510, 06.02.2020.
92 Bayerischer Verwaltungsgerichtshof, 13a B 19.34211, 17.12.2020.
93 VG Minden, 3 K 1476/19.A, 28.01.2022.
94 1 LB 258/20 (n 82) p 19.

What is more, when it comes to persons with no prior trafficking experience, courts, in determining that they are at risk of destitution, mention a possible risk of trafficking but do not pursue this line of enquiry.

Thus, the AC Aachen decided in 2007 that a woman who was a minor at the time of trafficking was entitled to complementary protection under Section 60(7) of the Residence Act.[95] The applicant was promised work as a babysitter in Germany but, upon arrival, was told she would have to become a sex worker. She was found by the police before any sexual exploitation happened, but she feared re-trafficking. The appellant claimed to be from Sierra Leone, but after language analysis, the court proceeded on the assumption that she was from Ghana. It was accepted that, whatever her country of origin, she had suffered severe child- and gender-specific violence and suffered from PTSD. The court then decided that she was entitled to complementary protection, since she had no family support, and thus, also due to her mental health issues, she would be unable to secure a livelihood on return to Ghana. The court briefly mentioned that a lack of livelihood options could cause her to work as a sex worker or to be trafficked again but did not investigate this risk further.

Similarly, in 2012, the AC Aachen granted complementary protection under Section 60(7) Residence Act to a Nigerian woman who, it was found, may have been trafficked to Spain for sex work.[96] The court reasoned that the stigma attached to having worked as a sex worker, the resulting lack of family support upon return and the fact that she had a young child would make it difficult for her to meet her socio-economic needs. The risk of re-trafficking was not considered.

Likewise, a 2014 judgment by the AC Munich granted Section 60(7) Residence Act protection to a Nigerian woman due to a risk of extreme poverty.[97] The appellant was trafficked to Italy for sex work but refused to engage in this and instead worked as a cleaner. She already had one child and was pregnant at the time of the hearing. In deciding the case, the court focused on her socio-economic situation upon return and her inability to secure a livelihood for herself and her children due to her particular circumstances, including lack of education and family support. It only marginally touched on the issue of re-trafficking.

Further, a 2017 judgment by the AC Aachen, again, granted protection under Section 60(7) Residence Act to a trafficked person.[98] In this case, the appellant had left Nigeria due to a fear of Boko Haram, who had burned down her church. However, she had also been trafficked to Italy in 2004. Yet the judgment only dealt with her livelihood options upon return, which would be limited due to her having an 'illegitimate' child and lacking both family support and education, granting her complementary protection.

95 VG Aachen, 3 K 12/07, 08.05.2007.
96 VG Aachen, 2 K 1712/10.A, 24.05.2012.
97 VG München, M 21 K 11.30680, 28.04.2014.
98 VG Aachen, 2 K 2224/15.A, 28.12.2017.

In 2021, the AC Saarland granted protection under Section 60(5) Residence Act to a Nigerian woman who the court found had suffered physically and mentally as a victim of human trafficking, had no family support in Nigeria and would, therefore, be unable to secure a livelihood.[99] Again, the risk of re-trafficking was not discussed.

Finally, in 2022, the AC Düsseldorf granted Section 60(5) protection to a Nigerian woman who feared reprisals from her traffickers.[100] The applicant had a child, lacked family support in Nigeria, as well as education, and had mental health issues. The court mentioned that single women in Nigeria are at risk of trafficking, but made no inquiry into whether the applicant's vulnerabilities would put her at risk on this context, granting her protection due to a risk of destitution instead.

In these cases, even though the applicants were trafficked persons and clearly possessed vulnerability indicators for the risk of re-trafficking, the courts focused only on their risk of destitution. What is more, when it comes to persons with no prior trafficking experience, courts, in determining that they are at risk of destitution, sometimes mention a possible risk of trafficking but then do not pursue this line of enquiry.

Thus, the AC Ansbach, in 2011, granted complementary protection under Section 60(7) Residence Act to a woman from Kosovo.[101] She had several children and had separated from her husband. She and her children were found to be at risk of destitution upon return due to her being a single mother with health issues who lacked any family support. The court mentioned that, due to this destitution, she would be at risk of trafficking, but did not consider the implications of this for her protection claim.

Also in 2011, the AC Würzburg decided the case of a Yezidi woman from Iraq who left the country due to the security situation and due to her ill health.[102] She was granted protection under Section 60(7) Residence Act because she was found to be at risk of destitution upon return due to lack of education and employment experience, as well as a lack of family support. The court mentioned that, as a result, she was also at risk of forced prostitution, but, again, did not enquire into this any further.

Further, in 2015, the AC Aachen decided the case of a Nigerian woman and her child, granting both applicants Section 60(7) protection.[103] The mother had little education and, due to the stigma of being a single woman with a child out of wedlock, would have no family support, so that she would be unable to secure a livelihood in Nigeria. The court mentioned that single

99 VG Saarland, 3 K 1408/20, 01.06.2021.
100 VG Düsseldorf, 27 K 3867/19.A, 12.12.2022.
101 VG Ansbach, AN 14 K 11.30049, 17.05.2011.
102 VG Würzburg, W 4 K 09.30232, 29.07.2011.
103 VG Aachen, 2 K 2738/13.A, 24.08.2015.

women in Nigeria are at risk of prostitution and human trafficking but did not consider whether she might be eligible for refugee status based on this.

Finally, in a 2022 case, the AC Münster found that a Nigerian woman with little education and work experience, no family support and two small children was entitled to complementary protection under Section 60(7) Residence Act because she would face destitution.[104] The court mentioned in passing that single women are at risk of prostitution and trafficking, but did not enquire whether this was the case for this applicant.

In summary, both applicants with a prior trafficking experience and those for whom a risk of being trafficked was mentioned but not investigated were granted complementary protection *inter alia* because they had children; lacked (family) support networks, education and employable skills; would be stigmatised; and had mental health issues, all of which exacerbate existing socio-economic deprivation. These are the same reasons cited for establishing a risk of re-trafficking in cases which result in refugee status. Notably, all applicants in the cases discussed in this subsection are female. It is worth highlighting that although the risk of re-trafficking is not seriously investigated for these applicants, the possibility is raised, which is more than can be said for the male 'destitute' claimants in Section 6.3.1. Nonetheless, while the aforementioned cases mention that destitution (and, by extension, the relevant vulnerability indicators) potentially puts the applicants at risk of trafficking, the case law does not engage with the relevance of these vulnerability indicators for the future risk enquiry under refugee law. As such, there is a danger that courts, as Costello has put it, 'siphon off those who warrant recognition as Convention refugees into [a] lesser status'.[105] Instead, courts should investigate whether the factors relied on to establish a risk of destitution are, in fact, indicators for a risk of (re-)trafficking or irregular re-migration and investigate applicants' eligibility for refugee status, irrespective of the applicant's gender.

6.4 Conclusion

The case law discussed in this chapter shows that it may be possible to identify irregularised migrants in existing complementary protection case law. National practice in both the UK and Germany shows that vulnerability indicators are being taken into account in establishing eligibility for non-removal outside the trafficking context, specifically where applicants are at risk of destitution or have 'very significant obstacles to integration' in their country of origin.

Since the factors relied on to establish eligibility for complementary protection in these contexts are very similar to the vulnerabilities indicating a risk of re-trafficking, these cases raise the question of whether the relevant claimants

104 VG Münster, 5 K 3492/21 A, 22.08.2022.

105 Cathryn Costello, *The Human Rights of Migrants and Refugees in European Law* (OUP 2016) 200.

may be eligible for refugee status based on a risk of (re-)trafficking or irregular re-migration. In this context, it should be kept in mind that applicants may find it easier to establish a risk of (re-)trafficking or irregular re-migration in refugee law than a violation of Article 3 ECHR or 'very significant' obstacles to integration. 'Very significant obstacles' undoubtedly constitutes a higher threshold than the test for well-founded fear or 'reasonable chance', 'real risk' or 'reasonable degree of likelihood' of persecution in refugee law,[106] so that individuals who experience vulnerabilities which constitute obstacles to integration but which are not deemed to be 'very significant' may nevertheless be able to argue that they are at risk of trafficking or irregular re-migration.

While the threshold to establish a well-founded fear in refugee law is similar to the 'substantial grounds'[107] that need to be shown to establish a violation of Article 3 ECHR, socio-economic deprivation plays different roles in a refugee claim based on a risk of re-trafficking or irregular re-migration on the one hand and a human rights claim based on a risk of destitution on the other. In the latter case, the (high) threshold of Article 3 ECHR must be reached, but in the former, socio-economic deprivation, in itself, need not amount to persecution or a violation of Article 3 ECHR.

The relationship between socio-economic deprivation and risk of persecution was illustrated aptly by the UK UT in *HD*.[108] The tribunal, in explaining how future risk of re-trafficking is established, stated that '[i]t is not the poverty, destitution or vulnerability itself which is the basis of the claim, but the harm that ensues from that namely the exploitation'.[109] Thus, there is no need for the 'poverty, destitution or vulnerability' to amount to persecution or a violation of Article 3 ECHR. As such, both applicants whose socio-economic deprivation engages Article 3 ECHR and those whose situation does not but who nevertheless have vulnerability indicators causing socio-economic deprivation may be able to show that they are at risk of (re-)trafficking or irregular re-migration. Vulnerabilities and socio-economic deprivation are material to the risk of re-trafficking and irregular re-migration, and thus to the question of persecution, even if, in themselves, they do not amount to persecution for the purpose of refugee law or serious harm for the purpose of human rights law. Thus, the claimants in *Said*, *Ainte* and *OA (Somalia)* may have been able to establish a risk of irregular re-migration even though they could not reach the

106 *R v SSHD, ex p Sivakumaran* [1987] UKHL 1, [1988] Imm AR 147; Guy S Goodwin-Gill and Jane McAdam, *The Refugee in International Law* (4th edn, OUP 2021) 61–62; James C Hathaway and Michelle Foster, *The Law of Refugee Status* (2nd edn, CUP 2014) 114. In *Parveen*, the Court of Appeal referred to the 'very significant obstacles test' as an '"elevated" threshold' (n 18) [9].

107 See, for example, *Soering v United Kingdom* App no 14038/88 (ECtHR, 7 July 1989) para 91; *Chahal v The United Kingdom* App no 22414/93 (ECtHR, 15 November 1996) para 74; *HLR v France* App no 24573/94 (ECtHR, 29 April 1997) para 34.

108 *HD (Trafficked women) Nigeria CG* [2016] UKUT 00454 (IAC).

109 ibid [171].

threshold of Article 3 ECHR. In this context, it is also worth recalling that, as explained in Chapter 3, a risk of re-trafficking or irregular re-migration is foreseeable as long as vulnerabilities are present, so that imminence of harm is not required. Further, as explained in Chapter 4, any financial reintegration assistance provided by actors other than the country of origin should not be considered in the analysis, as this has the effect of circumventing the requirement that protection must be provided by the state of origin. As such, where relevant vulnerabilities are present, courts ought to assess whether applicants are at risk of being (re-)trafficked or of re-migrating irregularly, whether there is effective state protection against this risk and whether the applicant can establish a nexus to Refugee Convention grounds.

This, however, would require courts to acknowledge the implications of those factors currently considered to inform risk of destitution and obstacles to reintegration for the risk enquiry in refugee law. As German case law shows, this does not yet happen even where there is a past trafficking experience and/or a recognition of a connection between destitution and risk of trafficking. As a result, persons with the relevant vulnerability indicators are granted only complementary protection, rather than having their eligibility for refugee status considered.

It may be argued that this is not much of a problem, seeing as the claimants in question do receive a type of protection. However, as mentioned earlier, refugee protection – as the most beneficial protection status – should be assessed first. In addition, failing to consider eligibility for refugee status also raises doctrinal issues. It is illogical to rely on the same risk factors for different purposes in different contexts. This is especially so because although, as explained in Chapter 3, both male and female individuals may be vulnerable and at risk of re-trafficking or irregular re-migration, male applicants may struggle to get decision-makers to recognise and accept their vulnerability. Courts in both the UK and Germany appear to accept that both male and female applicants may face destitution or obstacles to integration. However, considering vulnerabilities only as indicators for destitution or obstacles to integration perpetuates the failure to recognise that male claimants, too, may be at risk of re-trafficking or irregular re-migration.

Irregularised migrants of all genders who are 'hidden' in complementary protection case law ought to have their claims considered under refugee law where there is any indication that they are 'vulnerable' to re-trafficking or irregular re-migration. Provided that they meet all elements of the *refugee* definition, they should be recognised as refugees.

References

Ainte (Material Deprivation – Art 3 – AM (Zimbabwe) [2021] UKUT 00203 (IAC)

AMM and Others v SSHD [2011] UKUT 00445 (IAC), [2011] 7 WLUK 464

Ammer M and Monika Mayrhofer, 'Cross-Border Disaster Displacement and *Non-Refoulement* under Article 3 of the ECHR: An Analysis of the European Union and Austria' (2023) 35(3) International Journal of Refugee Law 322 <https://doi.org/10.1093/ijrl/eead036>

Asylgesetz (AsylG) 2 September 2008 (BGBl. I S. 1798) (Asylum Act)
Bayerischer Verwaltungsgerichtshof, 13a B 14.30285, 21.11.2014
Bayerischer Verwaltungsgerichtshof, 13a B 17.30030, 23.03.2017
Bayerischer Verwaltungsgerichtshof, 13a B 19.33510, 06.02.2020
Bayerischer Verwaltungsgerichtshof, 13a B 19.34211, 17.12.2020
Bundesverwaltungsgericht, 1 B 25.18, 08.08.2018
Bundesverwaltungsgericht, 1 C 10.21, 21.04.2022
C-542/13 *M'Bodj* [2014] ECLI:EU:C:2014:2452
Chahal v The United Kingdom App no 22414/93 (ECtHR, 15 November 1996)
Costello C, *The Human Rights of Migrants and Refugees in European Law* (OUP 2016)
Costello C, 'The Search for the Outer Edges of *Non-Refoulement* in Europe: Exceptionality and Flagrant Breaches' in Bruce Burson and David J Cantor (eds), *Human Rights and the Refugee Definition* (Brill Nijhoff 2016)
Council Directive 2003/86/EC of 22 September 2003 on the Right to Family Reunification [2003] OJ L 251 (Family Reunification Directive)
D v The United Kingdom App no 30240/96 (ECtHR, 2 May 1997)
Foster M, *International Refugee Law and Socio-Economic Rights: Refuge from Deprivation* (CUP 2007)
Gesetz über den Aufenthalt, die Erwerbstätigkeit und die Integration von Ausländern im Bundesgebiet (Aufenthaltsgesetz - AufenthG) 25 February 2008 (BGBl. I S. 162) (Residence Act)
Goodwin-Gill GS and Jane McAdam, *The Refugee in International Law* (4th edn, OUP 2021)
Graham L, *International Human Rights Law and Destitution: An Economic, Social and Cultural Rights Perspective* (Routledge 2022)
Hathaway JC, *The Rights of Refugees under International Law* (2nd edn, CUP 2021)
Hathaway JC and Michelle Foster, *The Law of Refugee Status* (2nd edn, CUP 2014)
HD (Trafficked Women) Nigeria CG [2016] UKUT 00454 (IAC)
HLR v France App no 24573/94 (ECtHR, 29 April 1997)
Home Office, 'Leave Outside the Immigration Rules' Version 3.0 (29 August 2023) <https://assets.publishing.service.gov.uk/media/64eef28f13ae1500116e3013/Leave_outside_the_Immigration_Rules.pdf> accessed 22 July 2024
Home Office, 'Private Life: Version 2.0' (18 May 2023) <www.gov.uk/government/publications/private-life-caseworker-guidance> accessed 23 April 2024
Immigration Rules (HC 395)
Kamara v SSHD [2016] EWCA Civ 813, [2016] 8 WLUK 174
KF v SSHD [2024] UKUT (IAC) UI-2023-003705
Lowe v SSHD [2021] EWCA Civ 62, [2021] 1 WLUK 248
McAdam J, 'Complementary Protection' in Cathryn Costello, Michelle Foster and Jane McAdam (eds), *The Oxford Handbook of International Refugee Law* (OUP 2021)
MI v SSHD [2020] UKUT (IAC) PA/10163/2018
Mouzourakis M, *Refugee Rights Subsiding? Europe's Two-Tier Protection Regime and Its Effect on the Rights of Beneficiaries* (ECRE 2016) <www.refworld.org/reference/regionalreport/ecre/2016/en/116217> accessed 21 July 2021
MS v SSHD [2020] UKUT (IAC) PA/07803/2016
MSS v Belgium and Greece App no 30696/09 (ECtHR, 21 January 2011)
MZ (Hospital Order: Whether a 'Foreign Criminal') Pakistan [2020] UKUT 00225 (IAC)
N v The United Kingdom App no 26565/05 (ECtHR, 27 May 2008)
Nationality, Immigration and Asylum Act 2002
NP v SSHD [2020] UKUT (IAC) PA/05297/2018
OA (Somalia) Somalia CG [2022] UKUT 00033 (IAC)
OVG Bremen, 1 LB 258/20, 22.09.2020

Paposhvili v Belgium App no 41738/10 (ECtHR, 13 December 2016)
Parveen v SSHD [2018] EWCA Civ 932, [2018] 4 WLUK 429
Peers S and others (eds), *EU Immigration and Asylum Law (Text and Commentary): Volume 3: EU Asylum Law* (2nd Revised edn, Brill 2015)
R v SSHD, ex p Sivakumaran [1987] UKHL 1, [1988] Imm AR 147
RK v SSHD [2023] UKUT (IAC) UI-2022-006079
SC (Jamaica) v SSHD [2022] UKSC 15, [2022] 6 WLUK 110
Shah v SSHD [2022] UKUT (IAC) HU/02664/2020
SHH v The United Kingdom App no 60367/10 (ECtHR, 29 January 2013)
Soering v United Kingdom App no 14038/88 (ECtHR, 7 July 1989)
SS v SSHD [2022] UKUT (IAC) PA/00677/2020
SSHD v Bodun [2016] UKUT (IAC) IA/10292/2015
SSHD v HK and JS [2018] UKUT (IAC) HU/13283/2016 and HU/13292/2016
SSHD v Ismail Mohamoud Ali [2024] UKUT (IAC) UI-2024-000166
SSHD v Joachim Cardos [2023] UKUT (IAC) UI-2022-004930
SSHD v Kapinga [2016] UKUT (IAC) IA/07269/2015
SSHD v Rakeshkumar and Hetal [2016] UKUT (IAC) IA/14784/2015 and IA/14788/2015
SSHD v Said [2016] EWCA Civ 442, [2016] 5 WLUK 88
SSHD v ZY [2015] UKUT (IAC) IA/18670/2014
Sufi and Elmi v The United Kingdom App nos 8319/07 and 11449/07 (ECtHR, 28 June 2011)
Tarakhel v Switzerland App no 29217/12 (ECtHR, 4 November 2014)
Tiedemann P, 'Die Geschichte des subsidiären Flüchtlingsschutzes' in Paul Tiedemann and Janina Gieseking (eds), *Flüchtlingsrecht in Theorie und Praxis: 5 Jahre Refugee Law Clinic an der Justus-Liebig-Universität Gießen* (Nomos 2014)
Veintimilla v SSHD [2024] UKUT (IAC) UI-2024-002985
Verwaltungsgerichtshof Baden-Württemberg, A 11 S 1704/17, 03.11.2017
Verwaltungsgerichtshof Baden-Württemberg, A 11 S 2042/20, 17.12.2020
VG Aachen, 2 K 1712/10.A, 24.05.2012
VG Aachen, 2 K 2224/15.A, 28.12.2017
VG Aachen, 2 K 2738/13.A, 24.08.2015
VG Aachen, 3 K 12/07, 08.05.2007
VG Ansbach, AN 14 K 11.30049, 17.05.2011
VG Braunschweig, 5 A 317/20, 16.08.2024
VG Bremen, 2 K 610/19, 23.12.2022
VG Bremen, 7 K 2424/21, 29.11.2022
VG Chemnitz, 2 K 322/19.A, 26.08.2022
VG Cottbus, 3 K 633/20.A, 29.05.2020
VG Darmstadt, 3 K 1022/19.DA.A, 31.01.2024
VG Düsseldorf, 27 K 3867/19.A, 12.12.2022
VG Gelsenkirchen, 17a K 2612/18.A, 04.11.2022
VG Gera, 2 K 968/22 Ge, 05.09.2022
VG Gießen, 18 K 535/22.GI.A, 04.06.2024
VG Hamburg, 10 A 6516/16, 10.01.2017
VG Karlsruhe, A 5 K 4693/23, 28.05.2024
VG Karlsruhe, A 18 K 5065/18, 02.06.2021
VG Kassel, 4 K 1583/18.KS.A, 30.03.2022
VG Koblenz, 1 K 1013/08.KO, 12.11.2008
VG Minden, 3 K 1476/19.A, 28.01.2022
VG München, M 10 K 23.32418, 31.05.2024
VG München, M 21 K 11.30680, 28.04.2014
VG Münster, 5 K 3492/21 A, 22.08.2022
VG Oldenburg, 3 A 710/23, 09.02.2024

VG Saarland, 3 K 1408/20, 01.06.2021
VG Saarland, 5 K 741/20, 23.02.2022
VG Würzburg, W 4 K 09.30232, 29.07.2011
Wright v SSHD [2024] UKUT (IAC) UI-2023-005380
YT v SSHD [2020] UKUT (IAC) PA/02930/2019

7 Vulnerability to Irregular (Re-)Migration in the Context of Climate Change and Disasters

7.1 Introduction

This chapter considers whether persons who cross international borders due to the effects of climate change and disasters can benefit from the argument made in this book. I use 'climate change and disasters' as a shorthand to signify a context encompassing both sudden-onset disasters and gradual environmental change, focussing on the effects rather than the causes of these phenomena and, therefore, recognising that climate change affects disasters, do not seek to distinguish between the two.[1] The chapter thus considers possible protection claims by persons who have been, *inter alia*, referred to as the 'disaster displaced',[2] 'climate refugees',[3] 'environmental refugees', 'climate-displaced persons' or 'environmentally displaced persons'.[4] Despite some of these labels invoking the concept of 'refugee', the individuals in question have not been able to claim refugee status. Indeed, the United Nations High Commissioner for Refugees (UNHCR) Handbook states that the *refugee* definition 'rules out such persons as victims of famine or natural disaster' while acknowledging that such circumstances 'may not, however, be altogether irrelevant to the process of determining refugee status'.[5]

The aim of this chapter is to show why experiencing disasters, famine and climate change–related harm may have relevance for refugee status

1 cf Jane McAdam, 'Displacement in the Context of Climate Change and Disasters' in Cathryn Costello, Michelle Foster and Jane McAdam (eds), *The Oxford Handbook of International Refugee Law* (OUP 2021) 832–33.
2 ibid 837.
3 Avidan Kent and Simon Behrman, 'Why "Climate Refugees"' in Avidan Kent and Simon Behrman (eds), *Facilitating the Resettlement and Rights of Climate Refugees* (Routledge 2018).
4 Sumudu Anopama Atapattu, 'A New Category of Refugees? "Climate Refugees" and a Gaping Hole in International Law' in Simon Behrman and Avidan Kent (eds), *'Climate Refugees': Beyond the Legal Impasse?* (Routledge 2018).
5 UNHCR, 'Handbook on Procedures and Criteria for Determining Refugee Status and Guidelines on International Protection under the 1951 Convention and the 1967 Protocol Relating to the Status of Refugees' HCR/1P/4/ENG/REV.4 (1979, reissued 2019) (UNHCR Handbook) para 39.

DOI: 10.4324/9781032664644-7

determination (RSD) after all – not necessarily as grounds for protection in themselves but as factors contributing to a risk of irregular re-migration. The chapter suggests a novel and common approach to the protection claims of persons affected by climate change and disasters by reconceptualising them as irregularised migrants and showing that, via this route, they may be recognised as refugees after all.

Reconceptualising persons affected by climate change and disasters as irregularised migrants is possible because, as the case law analysis in this chapter shows, their protection claims frequently revolve around a risk of socio-economic deprivation. Based on the premise that socio-economic deprivation brought about by vulnerabilities creates a risk of irregular re-migration, the chapter therefore explores how such a risk can be established in the context of climate change and disasters. It considers what a risk of irregular re-migration entails in this context, examining, in particular, risks resulting from becoming undocumented in the process of adapting to climate change through migration. As such, and because not all claimants in the case law analysed have previously undertaken dangerous journeys (irregular travel or becoming undocumented in a host country), the chapter analyses the risk of irregular (re-)migration (rather than re-migration). The chapter considers the effects of disasters and individual vulnerabilities on a sliding scale of risk to account for the many different types of climate change–related effects and how, coupled with individual characteristics, these contribute to the risk of (re-)migrating irregularly.

The chapter begins by setting out current approaches to protecting persons affected by climate change and disasters in Section 2. It considers existing legal frameworks, specifically international refugee law and international human rights law, and outlines some of the obstacles to protection claims succeeding under those regimes, but also creative approaches to interpreting refugee law which may afford individuals refugee protection in the future. The section then turns to domestic applications of refugee and human rights law and shows that, under certain circumstances, persons affected by climate change and disasters can obtain human rights protection. Since these claims are largely based on the effects disasters have on the ability to make a livelihood, they raise the question of whether, rather than basing the claim on a risk stemming from disasters and destitution, applicants could argue that they are at risk of irregular (re-)migration.

Section 3 then seeks to answer that question by, first, considering what a risk of irregular (re-)migration entails in the context of migration in response to climate change and disasters. The section considers, in particular, risks stemming from becoming undocumented in the process of adapting to climate change through migration. Second, the section determines how a risk of irregular (re-)migration can be established by considering the effects of disasters and individual vulnerabilities on a sliding scale of risk.

The chapter concludes by explaining how reconceptualising persons affected by climate change and disasters as irregularised migrants addresses the obstacles this group of persons experiences in seeking to claim refugee status.

7.2 Current Approaches to Protecting Persons Affected by Climate Change and Disasters

While it is the aim of this chapter to examine whether the Refugee Convention may apply to persons affected by climate change and disasters, it should be noted that refugee or human rights protection may not necessarily be the best option for those affected. Adaptation strategies obviating the need for migrating, or safe and regular migration options, may effectively address the predicament of those displaced (or at risk of displacement) by disasters.[6] Nevertheless, as evident from the cases discussed in this section, persons affected by climate change and disasters do request international protection.

This section first examines the literature on the intersection of asylum, climate change and disasters, mapping doctrinal obstacles to recognising persons affected by climate change and disasters as refugees or persons eligible for protection under human rights law. It then outlines academic arguments aiming to overcome these obstacles to protection. Next, the section turns to analysing case law to show how far, and under what circumstances, persons affected by climate change and disasters are protected under existing laws. The section shows that both UK and German courts have found such claimants to be eligible for protection under Article 3 of the European Convention on Human Rights (ECHR). Due to the limited number of UK cases on the topic, the analysis is supplemented by case law from New Zealand, which has some of the most developed jurisprudence on asylum claims in the context of climate change and disasters.[7]

7.2.1 International Refugee Law

As McAdam notes, '[t]o date, no refugee claim based on the harmful impacts of climate change has succeeded'.[8] This is due to a number of obstacles those affected by climate change and disasters face when trying to bring themselves within the scope of the Refugee Convention's *refugee* definition. McAdam explains that those affected by climate change and disasters are often displaced internally, rather than crossing international borders, and therefore do not meet the *refugee* definition's alienage requirement.[9] Further, characterising the harm experienced in the context of climate change and disasters as persecution can be difficult, either because the harm experienced does not reach the

6 McAdam (n 1) 846.

7 Jane McAdam, 'The Emerging New Zealand Jurisprudence on Climate Change, Disasters and Displacement' (2015) 3(1) Migration Studies 131 <https://doi.org/10.1093/migration/mnu055>.

8 McAdam (n 1) 837. It is worth noting that regional refugee definitions may be better able to respond to the predicament of persons at risk in the context of climate change and disasters since both the OAU Convention and the Cartagena Declaration protect against a breakdown in public order which may be caused or exacerbated by the disaster context. See ibid 837–38.

9 Jane McAdam, *Climate Change, Forced Migration, and International Law* (OUP 2012) 43.

required threshold of severity and/or because there is no identifiable persecutor.[10] Finally, even if these obstacles can be overcome, it is difficult to establish a nexus to Refugee Convention grounds, seeing as 'the impacts of climate change are largely indiscriminate'.[11]

Despite these obstacles, and despite the UNHCR Handbook stating that 'victims of . . . natural disaster' do not fall within the scope of the *refugee* definition,[12] in other publications, UNHCR acknowledges that 'the impacts of a disaster may create conditions that reinforce or bolster claims for refugee status under the Refugee Convention'.[13] Cantor *et al.* explore in detail how this may play out in practice, listing five non-exhaustive scenarios in which the disaster context may produce international protection needs: (1) disagreements around disaster (responses) leading to individuals involved being harmed; (2) disasters leading 'to a breakdown in law and order or exacerbat[ing] dynamics of conflict, violence or exploitation'; (3) humans intentionally inducing disasters to harm others; (4) state responses to disasters 'produc[ing] or exacerbat[ing] the risk of harm or suffering' of those affected; (5) the disaster itself causing (a risk of) harm and suffering, bearing in mind that vulnerability to such harm is connected to social factors.[14]

Thus, they point out that decision-makers must pay careful attention to the human factors at play in disaster contexts, which can inform the persecution analysis.[15] Further, they emphasise the 'need to consider the varied ways in which Convention reasons contribute to the exposure and vulnerability of a claimant to hazards' by considering any type of discrimination at play.[16] Similarly, Scott argues that 'exposure to climate- and disaster-related harm . . . is . . . the consequence of existing patterns of discrimination and marginalisation that generate unsafe conditions where individuals are exposed and vulnerable to natural hazard events'.[17] Scott has devoted an entire book to elaborating how persons fleeing climate change and disasters may be brought within the scope of the Refugee Convention by following a 'social'- rather than a 'hazard'-focused disaster paradigm.[18] However, such progressive inter-

10 ibid 43–45.
11 ibid 46.
12 UNHCR Handbook (n 5) para 39.
13 Sanjula Weerasinghe, 'In Harm's Way: International Protection in the Context of Nexus Dynamics between Conflict or Violence and Disaster or Climate Change' (*UNHCR*, 2018) 10 <www.unhcr.org/uk/media/no-39-harms-way-international-protection-context-nexus-dynamics-between-conflict-or-violence> accessed 25 July 2024.
14 David Cantor and others, 'International Protection, Disasters and Climate Change' (2024) 36(1–2) International Journal of Refugee Law 176, 183–84 <https://doi.org/10.1093/ijrl/eeae012>.
15 ibid 184.
16 ibid 186.
17 Matthew Scott, *Climate Change, Disasters, and the Refugee Convention* (CUP 2020) 6.
18 ibid.

pretations of refugee law have, to date, not been adopted in practice, so that international refugee law is, currently, not able to effectively respond to the predicament of persons affected by climate change and disasters.

7.2.2 *International and Regional Human Rights Law*

Another potential avenue for protection, then, is human rights law. Human rights law does not limit the personal scope of those eligible for protection by reference to Refugee Convention grounds, and the prohibition of *refoulement* under human rights law is absolute (although certain codified complementary protection regimes do contain exclusion clauses similar to those of the Refugee Convention).[19] Nevertheless, persons affected by climate change and disasters have struggled to obtain human rights protection. Some courts applying the relevant human rights principles have required applicants to show a connection between the harm feared and acts or omissions of the country of origin, have required them to satisfy a higher threshold of severity of harm where such harm is caused predominantly by a lack of resources in the country of origin or have deemed the harm individuals may experience as a result of climate change to be too far removed in time to trigger a present *non-refoulement* duty.[20]

Thus, the United Nations (UN) Human Rights Committee (HRC) in *Teitiota* considered that, in principle,

> the effects of climate change . . . may expose individuals to a violation of their rights under articles 6 [right to life] or 7 [freedom from torture or cruel, inhuman or degrading treatment] of the [International Covenant on Civil and Political Rights (ICCPR)], thereby triggering the *non-refoulement* obligations of sending states.[21]

However, in this particular case, the harm was seen as too far removed to warrant protection at the material time.

Focusing on European human rights law, it is not clear how a *non-refoulement* case based on risk in the context of climate change and disasters would be decided by the European Court of Human Rights (ECtHR). In *Sufi and Elmi*, which concerned two Somali nationals who feared harm on return due to an

19 Jane McAdam, *Complementary Protection in International Refugee Law* (OUP 2007) 21–23; see also Vincent Chetail, 'Moving towards an Integrated Approach of Refugee Law and Human Rights Law' in Cathryn Costello, Michelle Foster and Jane McAdam (eds) *The Oxford Handbook of International Refugee Law* (OUP 2021).

20 McAdam (n 1) 840–42.

21 Human Rights Committee, *Ioane Teitiota v New Zealand*, UN doc CCPR/C/127/D/2728/2016 (24 October 2019) para 9.11.

ongoing armed conflict, the ECtHR considered the impact of environmental factors on the overall security situation. The Court stated:

> If the dire humanitarian conditions in Somalia were solely or even predominantly attributable to poverty or to the State's lack of resources to deal with a naturally occurring phenomenon, such as a drought, the test in *N. v. the United Kingdom* may well have been considered to be the appropriate one.[22]

As explained in Chapter 6, the *N v UK* test requires that, in cases where no actor of harm can be identified (i.e. where the harm is 'naturally occurring'), to meet the threshold of Article 3 ECHR, a claimant has to show that they are 'critically ill' and 'close to death'.[23] In *Sufi and Elmi*, the ECtHR went on to state, however, that 'while drought has contributed to the humanitarian crisis, that crisis is predominantly due to the direct and indirect actions of the parties to the conflict'.[24] Thus, to date, the ECtHR has not considered a case where a disaster is the predominant cause of harm and whether this engages Article 3 ECHR, nor has it had the opportunity to decide whether the modified 'medical cases' threshold in *Paposhvili* should apply in such a scenario.[25] Thus, so far, neither international nor regional human rights law has responded effectively to the predicament of persons affected by climate change and disasters.

7.2.3 Domestic Applications of Refugee and Human Rights Law

Domestic courts, however, have taken environmental factors into account when examining eligibility for protection under Article 3 ECHR, but also under other human rights law provisions and refugee law. As evident from the following analysis, 'the impacts of climate change and disasters do not cause displacement on their own' but 'interact with a range of drivers (economic, social, political) that themselves affect mobility'.[26] Thus, climate change and disasters may interact with and exacerbate harm experienced in other contexts,

22 *Sufi and Elmi v The United Kingdom* App nos 8319/07 and 11449/07 (ECtHR, 28 June 2011) para 282.

23 *N v The United Kingdom* App no 26565/05 (ECtHR, 27 May 2008); see also *D v The United Kingdom* App no 30240/96 (ECtHR, 2 May 1997).

24 *Sufi and Elmi* (n 22) para 282.

25 See the discussion in Chapter 6, Section 2.2; cf Margit Ammer and Monika Mayrhofer, 'Cross-Border Disaster Displacement and *Non-Refoulement* under Article 3 of the ECHR: An Analysis of the European Union and Austria' (2023) 35(3) International Journal of Refugee Law 322 <https://doi.org/10.1093/ijrl/eead036>. The authors argue that it would not be appropriate to apply the 'medical cases' and 'source of harm' approach in the disaster displacement context.

26 McAdam (n 1) 833.

such as armed conflict.[27] In the majority of judgments discussed in this section, however, climate change and disasters interact with socio-economic deprivation.

7.2.3.1 *The UK and New Zealand*

In 2011, the UK Upper Tribunal (UT) in the case of *AMM and Others* decided that there was a 'generalised Article 3 risk, which exists by reason of the famine [in southern and central Somalia]', caused by 'the worst drought there has been for 60 years'.[28] As such, the effects of a drought alone were sufficient to engage Article 3 ECHR, despite the tribunal following *Sufi and Elmi* and applying the high *N v UK* threshold in this case. As mentioned in Chapter 6, none of the applicants in *AMM* relied on this finding, because all of them were either granted refugee status (not because of the effects of drought but because of a risk of persecution on religious grounds at the hands of Al-Shabab) or humanitarian protection (due to a risk of harm during armed conflict).

Nonetheless, the judgment shows that socio-economic deprivation brought about by a disaster – that is, a risk of famine caused by drought – can engage Article 3 ECHR. The UT in *AMM* also noted, however, that the drought and resulting famine were 'likely to be temporary in duration',[29] and indeed, following this 2011 case, no other UK courts or tribunals have found that the Article 3 threshold was met in a disaster context. For example, in *OA (Somalia)* the UT found that '[t]he cumulative impact of extreme weather, drought, conflict, the mass displacement of people into the city, and the fragile security situation presents significant challenges for many returnees, albeit not at the levels documented in *AMM*'.[30] Overall, UK case law on non-removal due to the effects of climate change and disasters is quite sparse.

Other jurisdictions, however, have more extensive jurisprudence in this area. As noted earlier, amongst English-speaking countries, New Zealand has the most developed jurisprudence on asylum claims in the context of climate change and disasters. Given the dearth of UK case law on the subject, New Zealand jurisprudence is examined here to give more depth to the analysis, as well as more breadth – the case law in question largely deals not only with sudden-onset disasters but also considers the effects of slow-onset environmental degradation.

In the year 2000, the New Zealand Refugee Status Appeals Authority (RSAA) dealt with a number of claims by nationals of Tuvalu which were

27 Cantor and others (n 14).
28 *AMM and Others v SSHD* [2011] UKUT 00445 (IAC), [2011] 7 WLUK 464 [477]–[490].
29 ibid [490].
30 *OA (Somalia) Somalia CG* [2022] UKUT 00033 (IAC) [229].

based on 'fears in relation to environmental and economic difficulties'.[31] All these claims dealt with the effects of sea level rise (such as land erosion, lack of drinking water and crop failure) on the applicants' ability to make a livelihood. These cases are relatively sparse on facts, and the discussion is limited to assessing the applicants' claims under the Refugee Convention. All these appeals were dismissed on the basis that '[a]ll Tuvalu citizens face the same environmental problems and economic difficulties living in Tuvalu', which, in the RSAA's view, meant that there was no nexus to Refugee Convention grounds.[32]

Between 2012 and 2023, the New Zealand Immigration and Protection Tribunal (NZIPT), which replaced the RSAA, dealt with a number of claims by nationals of Fiji, Kiribati, Tuvalu and Eritrea. These decisions are more detailed, and in addition to eligibility for refugee status, they also consider whether the applicants are entitled to protection under the ICCPR or the Convention against Torture (CAT), though most of the applicants did not rely on the latter in their appeals.

The first of these cases, the 2012 decision in *BG (Fiji)*, concerned a Fijian man of Banaban ethnicity – an ethic group forcibly relocated to Fiji from Kiribati and Tuvalu in the 1940s – who feared discrimination and socio-economic deprivation due to a lack of employment prospects (partly due to ethnic discrimination) and family support, as well as the effects of a cyclone which had caused crop failure and a lack of drinking water.[33] While the tribunal acknowledged that the 'socio-economic condition of the Banaban community . . . is poor', with high poverty rates, poor housing and limited employment opportunities,[34] it held that the applicant's circumstances did not amount to persecution for the purpose of the Refugee Convention because he was not being denied the right to housing or employment. Nor was there a violation of Article 7 ICCPR, because there was 'no deliberate socio-economic deprivation of the appellant', and therefore no inhuman or degrading *treatment*.[35]

In 2013, the NZIPT heard the case of *AF (Kiribati)*,[36] which would later become known internationally as the *Teitiota* case.[37] Following the dismissal of several domestic appeals, the applicant turned to the UN HRC – unsuccessfully,

31 Refugee Appeal No 72185 [2000] NZRSAA (10 August 2000) [4]; see also Refugee Appeal No 72186 [2000] NZRSAA 336 (10 August 2000); Refugee Appeal Nos 72189–72195 [2000] NZRSAA 355 (17 August 2000); Refugee Appeal Nos 72179–72181 [2000] NZRSAA 385 (31 August 2000); Refugee Appeal No 72313 [2000] NZRSAA 491 (19 October 2000); Refugee Appeal No 72314 [2000] NZRSAA 492 (19 October 2000); Refugee Appeal No 72315 [2000] NZRSAA 493 (19 October 2000); Refugee Appeal No 72316 [2000] NZRSAA 464 (19 October 2000).

32 Refugee Appeal No 72185 (n 31) [16].

33 *BG (Fiji)* [2012] NZIPT 800091.

34 ibid [25].

35 ibid [160].

36 *AF (Kiribati)* [2013] NZIPT 800413.

37 See n 21.

as mentioned earlier. At the NZIPT, the applicant argued that there was a lack of employment opportunities in Kiribati, sea level rise was limiting his access to drinking water and his ability to grow crops, while overpopulation was limiting access to services. Although the NZIPT acknowledged 'the effects of both sudden onset environmental events (storms) and slow-onset processes (sea-level-rise)' on the applicant's living situation,[38] it also found that he and his family would have access to land where growing crops, although difficult, was not impossible. Further, the family was being financially supported by the applicant's brother-in-law, so that they were not, in fact, at risk of serious harm. The tribunal also noted that there was no nexus to Refugee Convention grounds or a violation of the right to life under the ICCPR, since the government of Kiribati was taking steps to address the effects of climate change and because the risk to the applicant was not 'imminent'.[39] It thus dismissed the appeal.

In 2014, the NZIPT heard the case of *AC (Tuvalu)*, which concerned a family claiming to be 'in danger of being arbitrarily deprived of their lives or in danger of being subjected to cruel treatment if returned to Tuvalu because of the effects of climate change in Tuvalu'.[40] The family father, though educated and trained as a teacher, feared being unable to find work, and the family was worried about access to food and water due to environmental degradation. However, there was

> no evidence before the Tribunal to establish that, if returned to Tuvalu, the appellants' lives would be so precarious as a result of any act or omission by the state that they are in danger of being arbitrarily deprived of their lives.[41]

The tribunal found that even if the father could not find work as a teacher, he had the skills to find other work. Further, the government of Tuvalu was taking steps to combat the effects of climate change and to ensure continued access to food and water. Again, the appeal was dismissed.

In the 2015 case of *AF (Tuvalu)*, the NZIPT considered the claim of a Tuvaluan man who had come to New Zealand aged 13 on a visitor visa with his mother and who, rather than attending school, had worked casual jobs, later married a New Zealand citizen, had two children, and who had been sentenced to a prison term and deportation due to several criminal convictions.[42] He claimed asylum because he feared not being able to find work in Tuvalu due to his criminal convictions and lack of education and because he would

38 *AF (Kiribati)* (n 36) [39].
39 ibid [89].
40 *AC (Tuvalu)* [2014] NZIPT 800517–520 [3].
41 ibid [100].
42 *AF (Tuvalu)* [2015] NZIPT 800859.

not have access to safe drinking water. The tribunal found that the applicant was not at risk of persecution, because he would not be denied the right to work. Even if he could not find employment, he could resort to subsistence living, with the tribunal stating that the 'hardship that entails (including hardship caused by climate change) will not be as a result of any action (including inaction) by the state'[43] and therefore not amount to a violation of Article 7 ICCPR. The tribunal made the same argument with regard to access to water and held that there was also no nexus to Refugee Convention grounds. The appeal was dismissed.

In *AI (Tuvalu)*, decided by the NZIPT in 2017, the appeals of a Tuvaluan couple were also dismissed.[44] The applicants claimed

> to be at risk of serious harm due to the adverse effects of climate change on Tuvalu [in particular access to drinking water] and that they would not be able to obtain employment due to the general lack of employment opportunities in Tuvalu.[45]

As in previous cases, the tribunal found that the applicants would have access to safe water (they had purchased water from the government before), and since both applicants had 'a history of work in Tuvalu in a range of areas including construction, fishing, retail and cleaning',[46] they would be able to find employment again. Their claims failed under the Refugee Convention because there was no nexus to Convention grounds, the harm feared was not sufficiently serious and the government of Tuvalu was taking steps to address the effects of climate change.

Also in 2017, the tribunal heard – and dismissed – the appeal of a family of four in *AJ (Tuvalu)*.[47] The husband and children were citizens of Tuvalu, while the wife was a citizen of Fiji. The applicants sought protection due to the 'effects [of climate change] on life and livelihoods because of rising sea levels and associated environmental processes and events', 'extreme financial hardship' and lack of access to clean water.[48] The tribunal accepted 'that returning to Tuvalu will pose challenges for the appellants both socioeconomically and in terms of the negative environmental impacts of climate change'.[49] However, there was 'no basis for finding that any harm they do face as a result of the adverse impacts of climate change has any nexus whatsoever to any one of the five Convention grounds'.[50] Nor did this constitute a violation of the ICCPR

43 ibid [71].
44 *AI (Tuvalu)* [2017] NZIPT 801093–094.
45 ibid [2].
46 ibid [57].
47 *AJ (Tuvalu)* [2017] NZIPT 801120–123.
48 ibid [2].
49 ibid [33].
50 ibid [35].

in the tribunal's view, because the state of Tuvalu was not preventing the applicants from accessing employment and was taking steps to protect its citizens from the effects of climate change.

In 2022, the case of *AW (Kiribati)* resulted in the same outcome.[51] This case concerned a male citizen of Kiribati who, inter alia, feared socio-economic deprivation and the effects of climate change. The applicant was in his mid-50s, and although he had in the past worked as a fisherman and owned a boat, he had sold the boat when moving to New Zealand and now had no funds to purchase another one. He believed that he would be destitute, as the compulsory retirement age in Kiribati was 55 and he would only become entitled to a state pension at the age of 60. The tribunal, however, considered that he would be able to claim unemployment benefits in the meantime (although it did admit that 'the eligibility criteria are unclear')[52] and that he would be supported by his family (although it accepted that he was 'estranged from extended family').[53] Further, although the fact that 'the appellant will in Kiribati be exposed to the adverse impacts of climate change [was] accepted',[54] the tribunal then found that there was 'no direct evidence to establish that his land has been eroded to a point of no utility'[55] (though neither was there any evidence that it had not). More generally, it noted that the Kiribati government was undertaking adaptation and disaster risk reduction measures so that there was, at the time of the determination, no risk of serious harm to the applicant.

Finally, in the 2023 case of *AC (Eritrea)*, the NZIPT did grant protection under the ICCPR to applicants who, *inter alia*, feared the effects of climate change.[56] This case concerned an elderly Eritrean couple who feared poverty as a result of a combination of the general conditions in Eritrea – ongoing armed conflict and the effects of climate change – and their individual vulnerabilities, specifically their age, lack of employment opportunities and lack of family and community support. The tribunal accepted that 'the risk of the appellants returning to abject poverty, even starvation, is further heightened by climate change',[57] noting that the Eritrean 'government has taken actions . . . which deny villagers their socio-economic necessities'.[58] This finding sets the case apart from the cases discussed earlier, in which the tribunal does not accept state responsibility for the harm feared by the applicants.

The New Zealand jurisprudence shows that, especially in more recent cases, the tribunal does recognise the potentially harmful effects of climate change and disasters. These harmful effects are considered to exacerbate existing

51 *AW (Kiribati)* [2022] NZIPT 802085.
52 ibid [91].
53 ibid [92].
54 ibid [116].
55 ibid [117].
56 *AC (Eritrea)* [2023] NZIPT 802201–202.
57 ibid [144].
58 ibid [147].

socio-economic deprivation, yet most protection claims framed around these issues fail for a number of reasons. Some claims fail because the harm feared is not deemed to be sufficiently serious – either due to mitigating factors, like availability of family support, which have the potential to reduce risk immediately, or due to climate change adaptation strategies, which are expected to have a risk-reducing effect in the future. Thus, although some decisions require 'imminence' of harm, the assessment seems to have moved away from this requirement. Indeed, the tribunal in *AW (Kiribati)* criticised the use of the imminence concept as an 'unwelcome development'.[59] Instead, the NZIPT appears to broadly agree with Anderson *et al.*, who note that 'if a threat is likely to manifest very soon, it may be easier for an individual to argue that he or she faces a real chance of being harmed, since there may be less opportunity for mitigating factors to intervene'.[60] However, the tribunal appears to place considerable weight on the possibility of such mitigating factors having an effect. As such, cases in which harm is not seen as (presently) serious enough to warrant protection turn on questions of fact, and as evident from *AW (Kiribati)*, there may be a degree of speculation involved in establishing those facts.

Other cases, however, turn on questions of law. In particular, doctrinal obstacles to protection for persons fearing the effects of climate change and disasters are a lack of attribution of the harm feared to the state and an inability to establish a nexus to Refugee Convention grounds. Only is one case – *AC (Eritrea)* – did the tribunal accept that the state of origin would be responsible for the harm the applicants feared.

In sum, the New Zealand cases follow a very different approach to the UK case of *AMM*, in which the effects of a drought alone were sufficiently serious to engage Article 3 ECHR and no attribution of the resulting harm to the state was required to find a breach (nor a nexus to Convention grounds, seeing as the analysis was conducted under human rights law). Before considering the implications of New Zealand and UK jurisprudence for an enquiry into a risk of irregular (re-)migration, the next subsection examines German case law on protection claims in the context of climate change and disasters, which follows a similar line of reasoning as UK jurisprudence.

59 *AW (Kiribati)* (n 51) [102]. For a critique of the imminence concept in the determination of risk, see Michelle Foster and Jane McAdam, 'Analysis of "Imminence" in International Protection Claims: *Teitiota v New Zealand* and beyond' (2022) 71(4) International & Comparative Law Quarterly 975 <https://doi.org/10.1017/S0020589322000367>. See also Adrienne Anderson and others, 'A Well-Founded Fear of Being Persecuted . . . but When?' (2020) 42(2) Sydney Law Review 155; see further Adrienne Anderson and others, 'Imminence in Refugee and Human Rights Law: A Misplaced Notion for International Protection' (2019) 68 International and Comparative Law Quarterly 111 <https://doi.org/10.1017/S0020589318000398>.

60 Anderson and others, 'Imminence in Refugee and Human Rights Law' (n 59) 139.

7.2.3.2 Germany

In the German-speaking world, too, courts take environmental factors into account when examining eligibility for protection under Article 3 ECHR. Ammer and Mayrhofer show that Austrian courts consider 'the impacts of disasters (particularly droughts, floods, and earthquakes). . . in the legal reasonings relating to subsidiary protection' under EU law, which the courts interpret as synonymous with Article 3 ECHR and (contrary to the jurisprudence of the Court of Justice of the European Union (CJEU)) as not requiring an actor to whom the serious harm can be attributed.[61] In particular, the authors identify 'several decisions where personal circumstances in light of the strained supply situation caused by the drought [in Somalia] reached the article 3 ECHR threshold since the livelihood of the complainant was not regarded as secure upon return'.[62]

This reasoning is very similar to German courts' approach to destitution cases discussed in the previous chapter; what is more, Austrian courts take into account similar vulnerability indicators in this context, such as availability of clan or family support, health, wealth, caring responsibilities, and length of absence from the country of origin.[63] Indeed, German courts, too, take both environmental factors and (the effects of) disasters and individual vulnerabilities into account in their jurisprudence on Article 3 ECHR. As Schloss shows in respect of a number of administrative court (AC) decisions, the impact of disasters, alongside applicants' personal circumstances, is considered in deciding whether an individual is entitled to protection under Section 60(5) Residence Act, that is, Article 3 ECHR.[64] As such, in German case law, complementary protection is available for some claimants who fear the effects of climate change and disasters. This section discusses a range of judgments to show that these claims are framed similarly to the destitution cases discussed in the previous chapter but add considerations of environmental factors and disasters to the analysis.

In some cases, these factors are mentioned only in passing. Thus, in a 2020 case decided by the Bavarian Higher AC, an Afghan man was granted protection under Section 60(5) Residence Act because he was at risk of destitution based on a lack of family support, which would make it difficult for him to earn a sufficient livelihood for himself, his wife and his children, with the court mentioning in passing that the 2018 drought in Afghanistan had exacerbated food

61 Ammer and Mayrhofer (n 25) 339.

62 ibid 340.

63 ibid 342–43.

64 Camilla Schloss, 'The Role of Environmental Disasters in Asylum Cases: Do German Courts Take Disasters into Account?' in Simon Behrman und Avidan Kent (eds), *Climate Refugees: Global, Local, and Critical Approaches* (CUP 2022). For a discussion of the German complementary protection regime, see Chapter 6, Section 3.

insecurity and lack of access to drinking water.[65] Similarly, in a 2022 case, the AC Saarland granted complementary protection under Section 60(5) Residence Act to an Afghan man who was at risk of destitution based on a lack of family support, education and employment experience.[66] The court mentioned that 'climatic influences' had exacerbated the difficult socio-economic situation in Afghanistan, in particular, floods and droughts. In 2023, the Higher AC Berlin-Brandenburg granted Section 60(5) protection to a Somali man who had left the country 10 years earlier, had no family support in Somalia and lacked education and employment experience, all of which would make it difficult for him to make a livelihood on return, given the overall economic situation which had been exacerbated by the worst drought in decades.[67] Similarly, in 2024, the AC Cologne granted the same type of protection to a Somali man, noting that Somalia was experiencing the worst drought in over 40 years, accompanied by famine, so that the applicant, who had no family or social ties in Somalia and lacked education and employment experience, was likely to become destitute.[68]

In other cases, however, environmental factors and disasters are discussed in more detail and seen as factors contributing directly to the risk of destitution. Thus, in 2021, AC Lüneburg granted a Sudanese man protection under Section 60(5) Residence Act because he would face inhuman treatment due to heavy floods in Sudan.[69] Noting that the 2020 floods had exacerbated the food insecurity and poverty of Sudanese people, the court considered that the question of whether an individual could secure a livelihood in these circumstances would depend on the existence of family support and professional qualifications. The applicant in question lacked family ties and education. He did have some employment experience, and the court found that he would be able to look for employment as an agricultural day labourer. However, due to the effects of the floods, he would not be able to find any work in practice. In another case decided the same year, the AC Lüneburg made the same decision in respect of another Sudanese man, noting that he, too, lacked education and would therefore only be able to work as an agricultural day labourer, which, again, would be difficult because of the floods.[70] Even though this applicant had family in Sudan, the court found that they would not be able to financially support him and granted him protection under Section 60(5) Residence Act. Similarly, in 2022, the AC Berlin found that an Afghan man was at risk of destitution, and therefore entitled to protection under Section 60(5) Residence Act, because he lacked financial resources, family support, education and the

65 Bayerischer Verwaltungsgerichtshof, 13a B 20.30347, 29.10.2020.
66 VG Saarland, 5 K 741/20, 23.02.2022.
67 OVG Berlin-Brandenburg, OVG 4 B 8/22, 30.11.2023.
68 VG Köln, 8 K 4355/18 A, 29.02.2024.
69 VG Lüneburg, 6 A 7/20, 22.02.2021.
70 VG Lüneburg, 6 A 350/19, 10.06.2021.

means to make a livelihood because, although he could potentially return to his family home, which included farmland, this had effectively become unusable due to an ongoing drought.[71]

In still other cases, environmental factors and disasters themselves are cited as the main reason for the socio-economic deprivation feared. Thus, the AC Hannover in 2020,[72] and also the AC Leipzig in 2021,[73] granted Section 60(5) Residence Act protection to Sudanese men who were at risk of destitution because of the floods in Sudan. As opposed to the Sudanese applicants in the cases decided by the AC Lüneburg, the applicants in these two cases had no particular vulnerabilities which would prevent them from earning a livelihood. On the contrary, both the AC Hannover and the AC Leipzig found that, in principle, the applicant in each case would be able to make a livelihood on return to Sudan since, as a healthy young man, he would be able to reintegrate and find work. The applicant in the case decided by the AC Leipzig, additionally, had an uncle in Sudan who would be able to support him. The reason the applicants were nevertheless granted complementary protection was that, in the courts' assessment, they would be unable to find work and make a livelihood due to the severity of the effects of the 2020 Sudan floods. Drawing on a range of media reports, the courts explained that the floods had destroyed infrastructure and farmland, killed people and cattle and led to food insecurity, lack of access to drinking water and the outbreak of illnesses. As such, the courts found that the applicants could not be expected to return. The AC Hannover granted a Sudanese man the same type of protection for the same reasons in another 2020 case[74] and made the same decision for the same reasons in respect of a Sudanese woman in 2021.[75]

Further, in a 2023 case, the AC Munich granted complementary protection under Section 60(5) Residence Act to a Somali man by referring to Somalia experiencing a historic drought, which had exacerbated existing food insecurity, so that the applicant, his wife and their two young children would face treatment contrary to Article 3 ECHR on return.[76] This case is similar to the UK case of *AMM* in that it was the risk of socio-economic deprivation, that is, food insecurity brought about by a drought, which formed the basis of the claim.

These cases clearly show that disasters, either by themselves or in combination with certain vulnerabilities, can cause socio-economic deprivation of sufficient severity to meet the Article 3 ECHR threshold. Like the claimants in the 'destitution' cases in the previous chapter, the applicants in these cases are,

71 VG Berlin, 20 K 666.17 A, 24.03.2022.
72 VG Hannover, 5 A 2783/17, 30.09.2020.
73 VG Leipzig, 7 K 153/18.A, 28.04.2021.
74 VG Hannover, 5 A 11015/17, 29.10.2020.
75 VG Hannover, 5 A 8988/17, 04.01.2021.
76 VG München, M 11 K 19.30060, 04.10.2023.

therefore, eligible for complementary protection. However, as in the destitution cases, the question remains whether they could, instead, claim refugee status if they are reconceptualised as irregularised migrants. The next section seeks to answer that question.

7.3 Persons Affected by Climate Change and Disasters as Irregularised Migrants

From the discussion of UK, New Zealand and German case law two different types of disaster displacement scenarios emerge: first, a situation in which a (sudden-onset) disaster is severe and ongoing, so that the harm resulting from it is deemed to be serious enough to warrant protection; second, a situation where (slow-onset) environmental degradation or the effects of (sudden-onset) disasters are present but not in themselves sufficient to warrant protection. In the latter case, applicants' vulnerabilities are deemed to heighten their risk of exposure to harm. In both types of scenario, the relevant harm does not stem mainly from the disaster itself but from the socio-economic deprivation it may bring about. In neither scenario is this harm seen as engaging states' responsibilities under the Refugee Convention.

This section seeks to consider how persons affected by climate change and disasters may nevertheless be reconceptualised as refugees. It draws on the findings in previous chapters of this book to argue that persons affected by climate change and disasters may, in fact, be irregularised migrants whose claims should be considered under the Refugee Convention. To show why this may be the case, the section considers, first, what harm individuals affected by climate change and disasters may be said to be at risk of.

As with other irregularised migrants, such harm may stem from experiences during dangerous migratory journeys. However, seeing as citizens of a number of (island) states affected by climate change are comparatively privileged in their mobility, not all persons moving due to the effects of climate change and disasters are at risk of *travelling* irregularly. The first subsection therefore considers both irregular *travel* and irregular *status* as sources of harm.

Second, the section examines how the relevant risk can be established, drawing on a mechanism EU law employs to establish risk in the conflict displacement context – the *Elgafaji* sliding scale. This model of risk assessment is useful because it shows that the effects of climate change and disasters can lead to a high risk of destitution, and therefore a high probability of irregular (re-)migration. At the same time, in situations where some individuals can still make a livelihood despite the effects of climate change and disasters, the sliding scale model allows for taking individual circumstances – or vulnerabilities – into account in establishing whether individuals' socio-economic deprivation is likely to become so severe as to put them at risk of (re-)migrating irregularly.

Despite this section's focus on the risk of irregular (re-)migration, it does not intend to suggest that refugee status can never be granted based on the effects of climate change and disasters themselves; rather, the section aims to complement existing suggestions for progressive interpretations of international law, such as Scott's,[77] which would make such protection more widely available.

7.3.1 *Harm Experienced as a Consequence of Climate Change and Disasters: Irregular Travel and Irregular Status*

It is clear from the case law discussed earlier that the claimants in each case do not fear climate change and disasters as such but rather their effects. Specifically, rather than, for example, being killed or injured during disasters, they fear a lack of an adequate standard of living, encompassing a lack of access to drinking water and access to livelihoods. In short, they fear socio-economic deprivation or destitution. As the NZIPT in *AW (Kiribati)* notes, 'climate change exacerbates pre-existing development-related drivers of poverty and contributes to poor general socio-economic conditions'.[78] This approach chimes with McAdam's observation that 'the impacts of climate change and disasters do not cause displacement on their own. Rather, they interact with a range of drivers (economic, social, political) that themselves affect mobility'.[79]

With the relevant claims framed effectively as destitution cases, it is not surprising that relatively few of them succeed. As discussed in the previous chapter, socio-economic deprivation will amount to a violation of Article 3 ECHR only in exceptional cases, though some courts more easily accept that the required threshold has been reached than others. However, given that, as discussed in previous chapters, socio-economic deprivation – caused by a range of vulnerabilities – is also an indicator for the risk of (re-)trafficking and irregular (re-)migration, individuals affected by climate change and disasters may be able to reframe their claims to argue that these are the relevant risks which should be assessed.

It is, of course, conceivable that as disasters become more frequent and more extreme, individuals will be at real risk of serious harm immediately caused by a disaster, such as being killed or injured. Nevertheless, since such a scenario does not currently seem to be made out on the facts of the relevant cases, it is worth considering whether persons affected by climate change and disasters can argue that they are at risk of irregular (re-)migration or (re-)trafficking based on socio-economic deprivation exacerbated by the effects of climate change and disasters. Indeed, there is evidence for the fact that the link between, at least, trafficking and climate change is already being considered by courts. For example, courts in Italy have taken 'climate vulnerability' into

77 Scott (n 17).
78 *AW (Kiribati)* (n 51) [71].
79 McAdam (n 1) 833.

account when assessing the risk of re-trafficking.[80] Similarly, in *AC (Tuvalu)*, the NZIPT, while discussing what constitutes cruel treatment in the context of disasters, notes that 'the increased vulnerability of persons displaced in the wake of natural disasters increases the risk of them being subjected to cruel treatment (for example, being trafficked) by non-state actors'.[81]

When considering whether the applicants in the aforementioned cases may be at risk of trafficking or irregular (re-)migration, it is important to note a significant difference between UK and German case law on the one hand and New Zealand case law on the other: the fact that most of the applicants in the New Zealand cases are citizens of island states who are relatively privileged in their mobility. Thus, even if they can be said to be vulnerable to irregular (re-)migration (a question discussed in Section 7.3.2), they may nevertheless not be at risk in the same way as the claimants in UK and German case law.

The individuals in the UK and German cases discussed earlier were citizens of Afghanistan, Somalia and Sudan. All these nationalities have few options for safe and regular travel and, therefore, travel irregularly and are at risk of harm in this context.[82] In contrast, citizens of Tuvalu and Kiribati (and, indeed, other island sates, like Antigua and Barbuda, the Bahamas, Barbados, Brunei, Dominica, Grenada, the Marshall Islands, Mauritius, Micronesia, Palau, Saint Kitts and Nevis, Saint Lucia, Saint Vincent and the Grenadines, Samoa, the Seychelles, the Solomon Islands, Tonga and Trinidad and Tobago) are able to travel visa-free to a range of destinations, including countries in the Global North.[83] Citizens of Fiji are not quite as privileged in their movement but do

80 Jane McAdam and Chiara Scissa, 'How Domestic Courts Are Using International Refugee Law and Human Rights Law in the Context of Climate Change and Disasters' (*EJIL:Talk!* 22 November 2024) <www.ejiltalk.org/how-domestic-courts-are-using-international-refugee-law-and-human-rights-law-in-the-context-of-climate-change-and-disasters/> accessed 25 November 2024.

81 *AC (Tuvalu)* (n 40) [83]. Indeed, the effects of climate change exacerbate vulnerability to trafficking. See UNODC, 'Global Report on Trafficking in Persons 2024' 80–83 <www.unodc.org/documents/data-and-analysis/glotip/2024/GLOTIP2024_BOOK.pdf> accessed 16 December 2024.

82 UNHCR, 'Desperate Journeys: Refugees and Migrants Arriving in Europe and at Europe's Borders January – December 2018' (2019) <https://data.unhcr.org/en/documents/details/67712> accessed 16 August 2024.

83 Kiribati, Tuvalu and the remaining countries listed here are on the EU's travel 'whitelist': Regulation (EU) 2018/1806 of the European Parliament and of the Council of 14 November 2018 Listing the Third Countries Whose Nationals Must Be in Possession of Visas When Crossing the External Borders and Those Whose Nationals Are Exempt from That Requirement [2018] OJ L 303 (Visa Regulation) Annex II. It should be noted that citizens of all those countries will have to obtain an electronic travel authorisation once the ETIAS Regulation is implemented. See Regulation (EU) 2018/1240 of the European Parliament and of the Council of 12 September 2018 Establishing a European Travel Information and Authorisation System (ETIAS) and Amending Regulations (EU) No 1077/2011, (EU) No 515/2014, (EU) 2016/399, (EU) 2016/1624 and (EU) 2017/2226 (ETIAS Regulation). Under this Regulation, a travel authorisation can be denied if the traveller 'poses a security, illegal immigration or high epidemic risk' (art 1), so that under those circumstances, even theoretically visa-exempt individuals would be denied boarding by carriers (art 45).

have the option to travel to Ireland visa-free, a Global North country.[84] In addition, citizens of certain Pacific Island nations have access to a range of short- and long-term regular migration schemes offered by the United States, Australia and New Zealand.[85]

As such, it is less likely that these individuals would travel irregularly and experience harm in the process. In fact, many of the applicants in the case law discussed earlier came to New Zealand regularly, for example, as tourists or on work visas. The applicant in *AF (Tuvalu)*, for example, came to New Zealand on a visitor visa in 2003 and stayed unlawfully until 2010.[86] Likewise, the applicants in *AI (Tuvalu)* came on visitor visas which expired, rendering their stay unlawful.[87]

As such, these applicants were, initially, regular migrants. As McAdam notes, for persons from island states like Kiribati and Tuvalu, 'movement is likely to be pre-emptive and planned in response to slow-onset changes'.[88] Indeed, migration – whether internal or across borders – is an adaptation strategy for climate change, although not all affected individuals and communities are willing and able to exercise this option.[89] Yet how suitable international migration is to escape the harmful effects of climate change and disasters depends on the security of status a migrant holds in their host country, as well as the accompanying security of residence and protection from return. Thus, when it comes to assessing whether citizens of the aforementioned island states can be said to be at risk of irregular (re-)migration despite their ability to travel to many destinations regularly, it is important to keep in mind that being able to enter a country visa-free does not imply being able to settle and work there in the long term. Indeed, many Pacific Islanders who move regularly to countries like Australia and New Zealand overstay their visitor or seasonal worker visas and become undocumented.[90]

Against this background, it is important to reiterate what a risk of irregular (re-)migration means exactly. As explained in Chapter 3, I conceive of the

84 The Travelscope website visualises visa data for all nationalities, including Fiji. See <www.markuslerner.com/travelscope/> accessed 16 August 2024. It should be noted, however, that this data is taken from Wikipedia and may therefore not be entirely accurate.

85 Jillian Ash and Jillian Campbell, 'Climate Change and Migration: The Case of the Pacific Islands and Australia' (2016) 36(1) The Journal of Pacific Studies 53.

86 *AF (Tuvalu)* (n 42) [5] and [10].

87 *AI (Tuvalu)* (n 44) [25].

88 Jane McAdam, 'Swimming against the Tide: Why Climate Change Displacement Treaty Is Not the Answer' (2011) 23(1) International Journal of Refugee Law 2, 8 <https://doi.org/10.1093/ijrl/eeq045>.

89 Celia McMichael, Carol Farbotko, Karen E McNamara, 'Climate-Migration Responses in the Pacific Region' in Cecilia Menjívar, Marie Ruiz and Immanuel Ness (eds), *The Oxford Handbook of Migration Crises* (OUP 2018).

90 Makiko Nishitani and Helen Lee, 'Becoming 'Overstayers': The Coloniality of Citizenship and the Resilience of Pacific Farm Workers' in Victoria Stead and Jon Altman (eds), *Labour Lines and Colonial Power: Indigenous and Pacific Islander Labour Mobility in Australia* (ANU Press 2019).

dangerous route in broad terms to include experiences of irregularity in countries of transit and destination (such as being undocumented while working), so that individuals who have migrated regularly and, for example, overstayed a visa and experienced the adverse effects of irregularity can be included in the analysis.

This becomes particularly relevant where claimants who are unlikely to *travel* irregularly *stay* in host states irregularly because they fear the effects of climate change and disasters in their home nations. For such individuals, a risk of irregular (re-)migration can still be considered as the basis for a protection claim, even where the risk would manifest in a host state rather than during a journey. This is because people with irregular status are 'disproportionately exposed to discrimination, exclusion, abuse and exploitation'.[91] This includes an increased risk of becoming a victim of crime (including crimes such as sexual abuse and violent assault) due to a reluctance to report such crimes, given that contact with state authorities can lead to deportation.[92] It also includes a risk of exploitative working practices and forced labour.[93] Indeed, there is also a strong connection between being undocumented and the risk of being trafficked,[94] so that a risk of trafficking becomes relevant in this context once again.

In summary, persons affected by climate change and disasters may be at risk or irregular (re-)migration. This risk can manifest as harm experienced during irregular travel, where the individuals in question lack regular migration options (including where such options become closed to them as a result of having previously overstayed visas). It can also manifest as harm experienced in host states after arrival – whether the individual entered regularly or irregularly – where no regular migration status can be obtained or is lost. To determine how this risk of irregular (re-)migration can be established, the next

91 Sarah Spencer and Anna Triandafyllidou, 'Irregular Migration' in Peter Scholten (ed), *Introduction to Migration Studies: An Interactive Guide to the Literatures on Migration and Diversity* (Springer 2022) 195.

92 Nicola Delvino, 'Safe Reporting of Crime: Research Highlights and Learnings for the EU Victims Strategy' (*COMPAS*, 2020) 2 <www.compas.ox.ac.uk/wp-content/uploads/Safe-reporting-project-Research-Highlights-and-Learnings-for-the-EU-Victims-Strategy-Final.pdf> accessed 13 August 2024.

93 Peter Dwyer and others, 'Socio-Legal Status and Experiences of Forced Labour among Asylum Seekers and Refugees in the UK' (2016) 32(3) Journal of International and Comparative Social Policy 182 <https://doi.org/10.1080/21699763.2016.1175961>; Anna Triandafyllidou and Laura Bartolini, 'Irregular Migration and Irregular Work: A Chicken and Egg Dilemma' in Sarah Spencer and Anna Triandafyllidou (eds), *Migrants with Irregular Status in Europe: Evolving Conceptual and Policy Challenges* (Springer 2020). See also Nishitani and Lee (n 90).

94 Fiona David, Katharine Bryant and Jacqueline Joudo Larsen, 'Migrants and Their Vulnerability to Trafficking, Modern Slavery and Forced Labour' (*International Organization for Migration*, 2019) 38 <https://publications.iom.int/system/files/pdf/migrants_and_their_vulnerability.pdf> accessed 13 August 2024.

subsection considers the effects of disasters and individual vulnerabilities on a sliding scale.

7.3.2 Vulnerability to Irregular (Re-)Migration in the Disaster Context: A Sliding Scale of Risk

In previous chapters, we have seen that a risk of irregular (re-)migration can be established through certain vulnerability indicators. In the cases discussed earlier, such vulnerabilities – or, indeed, a lack thereof – can also be found. Indeed, another major difference between UK and German case law on the one hand, and New Zealand jurisprudence on the other, is that applicants in the former are more obviously 'vulnerable' than those in the latter. Claimants in the UK and German cases either possess relevant vulnerability indicators, such as a lack of financial resources, family support, employment experience and education, or the disaster context causes such an extreme risk of destitution that even 'non-vulnerable' applicants are unable to make a livelihood.

In the New Zealand cases, only the applicants in *AC (Eritrea)* are explicitly found to be 'vulnerable elderly persons' due to their age, lack of employment opportunities and lack of family and community support, coupled with the effects of climate change.[95] In the other judgments, the tribunal does mention a lack of employment opportunities in most cases,[96] as well as a lack of education in some.[97] However, these vulnerabilities appear to be countered by 'resilience factors', such as employment experience, access to financial support, availability of family support and access to land. This, of course, does not necessarily mean that no other vulnerability indicators were present for the applicants in the case law discussed earlier; it is possible that these factors were simply not deemed relevant and therefore omitted from the discussion. For example, as established in the previous chapter, a long absence from the country of origin is a vulnerability indicator, and some of the claimants in the New Zealand cases discussed earlier had been absent from their state of origin for long periods of time. The applicants in *AC (Tuvalu)* had been absent for seven years,[98] the applicant in *AF (Tuvalu)* had been absent for 12[99] and the applicant in *AW (Kiribati)* for 14.[100]

95 *AC (Eritrea)* (n 56) [127].
96 Refugee Appeal No 72185 (n 31) [9]; Refugee Appeal Nos 72189–72195 (n 31) [8]; Refugee Appeal Nos 72179–72181 (n 31) [9]; Refugee Appeal No 72313 (n 31) [9]; *BG (Fiji)* (n 33) [25]; *AF (Kiribati)* (n 36) [13]; *AC (Tuvalu)* (n 40) [100]; *AF (Tuvalu)* (n 42) [16]; *AI (Tuvalu)* (n 44) [2]; *AJ (Tuvalu)* (n 47) [19].
97 Refugee Appeal Nos 72189–72195 (n 31) [8]; Refugee Appeal Nos 72179–72181 (n 31) [9]; Refugee Appeal No 72313 (n 31) [9]; *BG (Fiji)* (n 33) [25]; *AF (Tuvalu)* (n 42) [16].
98 *AC (Tuvalu)* (n 40) [21].
99 *AF (Tuvalu)* (n 42) [5].
100 *AW (Kiribati)* (n 51) [37].

Further, it is possible that vulnerabilities are present but not, or not sufficiently, acknowledged. The case of *AW (Kiribati)*, for example, seems to have failed largely due to speculation as to the applicant's lack of vulnerability. The tribunal's reasoning as to the availability of unemployment benefits, access to land and family support is not backed up by any evidence. Overall, it is certainly conceivable that there will be future claimants who lack family support, education, employment opportunities; have mental health issues; etc. As established, vulnerability indicators are relevant for assessing the risk of irregular (re-)migration and, therefore, courts and tribunals should pay particular attention to the presence of any vulnerabilities.

Yet as mentioned already, UK and German case law shows that even persons without any individual vulnerability indicators can be at risk of destitution in disaster contexts due to the severe and ongoing nature of the disaster in question. While, as discussed in Chapter 3, the 'route causes' of irregular (re-)migration include structural factors, such as environmental degradation,[101] this raises the question of how to assess a risk of irregular (re-)migration in disaster contexts (or, indeed, other contexts causing an extreme risk of destitution).

To answer this question, it is helpful to remember that whereas in the case law discussed earlier the effects of climate change and disasters – specifically socio-economic deprivation – are the basis of the protection claim, in a claim based on a risk of irregular (re-)migration, the harm feared encompasses violations of civil and political rights, either during irregular travel or in host countries (see Section 7.3.1. above), as well as socio-economic deprivation (caused by the disaster context and/or intersecting vulnerabilities). In this context, it is important to keep in mind that, as established in Chapter 6, there is no need to find that the socio-economic deprivation causing irregular (re-)migration must be so severe as to amount to a violation of human rights in itself.

As such, a high likelihood of destitution implies a high probability of irregular (re-)migration. To illustrate how this observation might be translated into an effective risk assessment against the background of destitution caused by the effects of climate change and disasters, I propose adapting the 'sliding scale' model of risk,[102] a method of risk assessment from the context of subsidiary protection under EU law, to the context of refugee law.

The sliding scale model of risk was introduced to assess risk of harm during armed conflict. EU law makes special provision for those fleeing armed conflict under Article 15(c) Qualification Regulation, which provides for subsidiary

101 David Ingram, *World Crisis and Underdevelopment: A Critical Theory of Poverty, Agency, and Coercion* (CUP 2018) 127; cf Chapter 3, Section 3.4.3.

102 C-465/07 *Elgafaji, Opinion of AG Maduro* [2008] ECLI:EU:C:2008:479; cf Evangelia (Lilian) Tsourdi, 'What Protection for Persons Fleeing Indiscriminate Violence? The Impact of the European Courts on the EU Subsidiary Protection Regime' in David James Cantor and Jean-François Durieux (eds), *Refuge from Inhumanity? War Refugees and International Humanitarian Law* (Brill Nijhoff 2014) 277.

protection for persons who do not meet the *refugee* definition but face a 'serious and individual threat to a civilian's life or person by reason of indiscriminate violence in situations of international or internal armed conflict'.[103] In interpreting the meaning of Article 15(c) (of the Qualification *Directive*, as it was then), the CJEU in *Elgafaji* held that since it covers situations of indiscriminate violence, this 'implies that it may extend to people irrespective of their personal circumstances'.[104] This will be the case where any individual will be at risk of harm because 'the degree of indiscriminate violence . . . reaches such a high level' that 'a civilian . . . would [be at risk] solely on account of his presence on the territory' where the conflict is taking place.[105] At the same time, the court explained that 'the more the applicant is able to show that he is specifically affected by reason of factors particular to his personal circumstances, the lower the level of indiscriminate violence required for him to be eligible for subsidiary protection'.[106]

Thus, risk will be present on either end of the sliding scale; however, what is needed where the violence during armed conflict is of lower intensity is individualisation, that is, a person's individual characteristics exposing them to the risk. At the same time, 'if a risk is likely to affect the applicant at personal level, there is no obligation to demonstrate any specific "singling out" in her regard of the measures or circumstances concerned'.[107] Thus, the *Elgafaji* sliding scale is not about severity of harm; it is about *exposure* to harm, that is, probability.

Adapting the *Elgafaji* sliding scale to the disaster context can therefore inform the determination of risk of irregular (re-)migration. At one end of the scale, the situation in the country of origin in itself is such that anyone present in that country will be exposed to harm. In *Elgafaji*, the relevant situation was one of a high level of indiscriminate violence during armed conflict. However, a high risk of exposure to harm could also be caused by severe disaster or famine. The sliding scale test says nothing about the nature of such harm;[108] however, judging from the earlier case law, destitution might be a relevant type of

103 Regulation (EU) 2024/1347 of the European Parliament and of the Council of 14 May 2024 on Standards for the Qualification of Third-Country Nationals or Stateless Persons as Beneficiaries of International Protection, for a Uniform Status for Refugees or for Persons Eligible for Subsidiary Protection and for the Content of the Protection Granted, Amending Council Directive 2003/109/EC and Repealing Directive 2011/95/EU of the European Parliament and of the Council [2024] OJ L, 2024/1347 (Qualification Regulation) art 15(c).

104 C-465/07 *Elgafaji* [2009] ECLI:EU:C:2009:94, para 34.

105 ibid para 35.

106 ibid para 39.

107 Violeta Moreno-Lax, 'Of Autonomy, Autarky, Purposiveness and Fragmentation: The Relationship between EU Asylum Law and International Humanitarian Law' in David James Cantor and Jean-François Durieux (eds), *Refuge from Inhumanity? War Refugees and International Humanitarian Law* (Brill Nijhoff 2014) 339.

108 Jean-Francois Durieux, 'Of War, Flows, Laws and Flaws: A Reply to Hugo Storey' (2012) 31(3) Refugee Survey Quarterly 161, 173 <https://doi.org/10.1093/rsq/hds012>.

harm in this context. As such, in the event of a severe disaster, the likelihood of destitution, and therefore the probability of irregular (re-)migration, is high.

At the other end of the scale, the situation in the country of origin in itself is *not* such that anyone present in that country will be exposed to harm. However, an applicant's personal characteristics may contribute to this individual being exposed to harm nonetheless. In *Elgafaji*, the relevant situation was one of a low level of indiscriminate violence during armed conflict. Individual circumstances taken into account when assessing risk of exposure to harm in this context could be the location of the applicant's home (where this is close to places which may become targets) or the applicant's job, such as being a journalist or a doctor.[109] As evident from the case law discussed earlier (and in previous chapters), individual vulnerabilities heighten the likelihood of experiencing socio-economic deprivation, with climate change and disasters increasing this likelihood further. As such, in the event of slow-onset climate change or less severe disasters, the likelihood of destitution is increased by individual vulnerabilities. Cumulatively, these factors can lead to a high probability of irregular (re-)migration.

Based on this, it is worth considering that there may also be vulnerability indicators specific to the climate change and disaster context. For example, climate change causes or contributes to a range of physical and mental health conditions in Pacific Island states – ranging from PTSD and anxiety to physical injuries sustained during disasters.[110] Vice versa, disabilities make individuals more vulnerable to the effects of climate change. This was demonstrated in the 2022 case of *AV (Tuvalu)*, in which the NZIPT heard a humanitarian appeal against deportation by a 55-year-old man from Tuvalu.[111] Although this was not an appeal against the refusal of an asylum claim, the NZIPT briefly considered the circumstances the applicant would face if returned to Tuvalu, noting that 'as a deaf and mute person, the appellant is inherently going to be more vulnerable to natural hazards'.[112] Thus, each applicant's situation must be assessed on its individual facts, and any relevant vulnerabilities which may contribute to a risk of irregular (re-)migration must be taken into account.

Considering vulnerability to irregular (re-)migration in the disaster context on a sliding scale of risk accounts for the many different types of climate change–related effects and disasters and how these influence decisions to (re-)migrate, while taking account of individuals' personal characteristics.

109 UNHCR, 'Safe at Last? Law and Practice in Selected EU Member States with Respect to Asylum-Seekers Fleeing Indiscriminate Violence' (2011) 53 <www.refworld.org/reference/regionalreport/unhcr/2011/en/80324> accessed 16 June 2024.

110 John Connell, 'Climate Change and Health: A Security Challenge in the Pacific Islands' Policy Brief No 166 (*Toda Peace Institute*, 2023) <https://toda.org/assets/files/resources/policy-briefs/t-pb-166_climate-change-and-health_connell.pdf> accessed 14 August 2024.

111 *AV (Tulvalu)* [2022] NZIPT 505532.

112 ibid [26].

Climate change and disasters contribute to socio-economic deprivation, and thus to a risk of irregular (re-)migration.

7.4 Conclusion

Reconceptualising persons affected by climate change and disasters as irregularised migrants addresses the obstacles this group of persons experiences in seeking to claim refugee status. Basing the assessment on a risk of irregular (re-)migration resolves the problems claimants fleeing the effects of climate change and disaster face in their protection claims.

First, persons at risk of irregular (re-)migration are at risk of persecution due to the cumulative harm experienced in the country of origin (socio-economic deprivation) and outside it (violations of civil and political rights) and due to the country of origin's failure to protect against the former, causing the latter to materialise. Thus, it can no longer be claimed that the harm feared is not sufficiently serious. In this context, there is no need to find that the socio-economic deprivation experienced is severe enough as to amount to a violation of human rights in itself; it is enough that, combined with the harm experienced outside the country of origin, socio-economic deprivation amounts to serious harm.

Further, persons at risk of irregular (re-)migration can establish a failure of state protection by arguing that the country of origin's failure to protect against socio-economic deprivation in the country of origin leads to experiencing serious harm outside that country. Non-state actors are responsible for this harm, so that it can no longer be argued that there is no identifiable persecutor.[113] Further, rather than speculating as to the effects of governments' climate change adaptation strategies, the state protection enquiry can focus on the question of whether, at the time of RSD, countries of origin are effectively addressing individuals' vulnerabilities in a way which obviates their need for seeking economic security through irregular (re-)migration.

Second, shifting the assessment to the risk of irregular (re-)migration addresses the 'imminence' problem. The enquiry into a well-founded fear of irregular (re-)migration will assess whether, presently, climate change and disasters, coupled with individual vulnerabilities, would render making a livelihood in the country of origin so difficult as to leave the individual no choice but to (re-)migrate irregularly. As explained in Chapter 3, there is no requirement

113 According to a UNHCR study, 'criminal gangs are perceived as the main perpetrators [of harm experienced during irregular migration] followed by armed groups, smugglers, State entities, other migrants, people from local communities and family members'. See UNHCR, 'On This Journey, No One Cares If You Live Or Die: Abuse, Protection and Justice along Routes between East and West Africa and Africa's Mediterranean Coast: A Route-based Perspective on Key Risks' vol 2 (March 2024) 43 <www.unhcr.org/media/journey-no-one-cares-if-you-live-or-die-abuse-protection-and-justice-along-routes-between-1> accessed 19 August 2024.

that (re-)migration happen immediately upon return to the country of origin; as long as vulnerabilities are present, the risk of irregular (re-)migration is foreseeable.

Finally, the shift towards an assessment of the risk of irregular (re-)migration means that claimants may be able to establish a nexus to Refugee Convention grounds. As suggested in Chapter 5, they can do so by arguing that they are 'persons in vulnerable situations', or by invoking the Convention ground nationality. Indeed, the analysis in this chapter shows that both of these ways of establishing nexus are relevant in the context of claims based on a risk of irregular (re-)migration brought by persons affected by climate change and disasters. Individuals at the end of the sliding scale where risk is established by taking into account individual vulnerabilities will be able to argue that they are 'persons in vulnerable situations' as long as their vulnerabilities set them apart from surrounding society and/or constitute immutable characteristics. However, persons at the other end of the sliding scale, where risk of socio-economic deprivation, and therefore of irregular (re-)migration, is high for anyone present in the territory will not be able to rely on the same argument. Such individuals may be able to argue that they share an immutable characteristic by relying on a previous experience of having undertaken dangerous journeys or their experience, and resulting vulnerability, of being impacted by climate change and disasters. However, if they do not have any individual vulnerabilities – as was the case for the claimants in the cases decided by the AC Hannover, AC Leipzig and AC Munich,[114] discussed earlier – they will not be able to show that they would be perceived as different from surrounding society. Indeed, the applicants in these cases seemed to have no vulnerability indicators. This is why the Convention ground nationality has particular relevance for these 'non-vulnerable' applicants. The applicants in these cases were nationals of Sudan and Somalia – countries whose nationals cannot easily travel regularly.[115] Thus, for persons at risk of irregular travel, but also for those at risk of harm in host countries having overstayed visas, this Convention ground explains that these applicants are at risk because, based on their citizenship, they are excluded from safe and regular migration options.

As in all protection claims, for persons affected by climate change and disasters seeking to argue that they are at risk of irregular (re-)migration, much depends on questions of fact, in particular, on questions around vulnerability and (in)ability to travel regularly. If the facts of a case indicate that an individual is at risk of irregular (re-)migration, lacks state protection against this and can establish a nexus to Refugee Convention ground, then that person is a refugee.

114 5 A 2783/17 (n 72); 7 K 153/18.A (n 73); 5 A 8988/17 (n 75); M 11 K 19.30060 (n 76). See Section 7.2.3.2 earlier.

115 Somalia and Sudan are on the EU's visa 'blacklist'. See Visa Regulation (n 83) Annex I; cf Travelscope Website (n 84).

References

AC (Eritrea) [2023] NZIPT 802201-202
AC (Tuvalu) [2014] NZIPT 800517-520
AF (Kiribati) [2013] NZIPT 800413
AF (Tuvalu) [2015] NZIPT 800859
AI (Tuvalu) [2017] NZIPT 801093-094
AJ (Tuvalu) [2017] NZIPT 801120-123
AMM and Others v SSHD [2011] UKUT 00445 (IAC), [2011] 7 WLUK 464
Ammer M and Monika Mayrhofer, 'Cross-Border Disaster Displacement and *Non-Refoulement* under Article 3 of the ECHR: An Analysis of the European Union and Austria' (2023) 35(3) International Journal of Refugee Law 322 <https://doi.org/10.1093/ijrl/eead036>
Anderson A and others, 'Imminence in Refugee and Human Rights Law: A Misplaced Notion for International Protection' (2019) 68 International and Comparative Law Quarterly 111 <https://doi.org/10.1017/S0020589318000398>
Anderson A and others, 'A Well-Founded Fear of Being Persecuted . . . But When?' (2020) 42(2) Sydney Law Review 155
Ash J and Jillian Campbell, 'Climate Change and Migration: The Case of the Pacific Islands and Australia' (2016) 36(1) The Journal of Pacific Studies 53
Atapattu SA, 'A New Category of Refugees? "Climate Refugees" and a Gaping Hole in International Law' in Simon Behrman and Avidan Kent (eds), *'Climate Refugees': Beyond the Legal Impasse?* (Routledge 2018)
AV (Tulvalu) [2022] NZIPT 505532
AW (Kiribati) [2022] NZIPT 802085
Bayerischer Verwaltungsgerichtshof, 13a B 20.30347, 29.10.2020
BG (Fiji) [2012] NZIPT 800091
C-465/07 *Elgafaji* [2009] ECLI:EU:C:2009:94
C-465/07 *Elgafaji, Opinion of AG Maduro* [2008] ECLI:EU:C:2008:479
Cantor D and others, 'International Protection, Disasters and Climate Change' (2024) 36(1–2) International Journal of Refugee Law 176 <https://doi.org/10.1093/ijrl/eeae012>
Chetail V, 'Moving Towards an Integrated Approach of Refugee Law and Human Rights Law' in Cathryn Costello, Michelle Foster and Jane McAdam (eds), *The Oxford Handbook of International Refugee Law* (OUP 2021)
Connell J, 'Climate Change and Health: A Security Challenge in the Pacific Islands' Policy Brief No. 166 (*Toda Peace Institute,* 2023) <https://toda.org/assets/files/resources/policy-briefs/t-pb-166_climate-change-and-health_connell.pdf> accessed 14 August 2024
D v The United Kingdom App no 30240/96 (ECtHR, 2 May 1997)
David F, Katharine Bryant and Jacqueline Joudo Larsen, 'Migrants and their Vulnerability to Trafficking, Modern Slavery and Forced Labour' (*International Organization for Migration*, 2019) <https://publications.iom.int/system/files/pdf/migrants_and_their_vulnerability.pdf> accessed 13 August 2024
Delvino N, 'Safe Reporting of Crime: Research Highlights and Learnings for the EU Victims Strategy' (*COMPAS*, 2020) <www.compas.ox.ac.uk/wp-content/uploads/Safe-reporting-project-Research-Highlights-and-Learnings-for-the-EU-Victims-Strategy-Final.pdf> accessed 13 August 2024
Durieux J-F, 'Of War, Flows, Laws and Flaws: A Reply to Hugo Storey' (2012) 31(3) Refugee Survey Quarterly 161 <https://doi.org/10.1093/rsq/hds012>
Dwyer P and others, 'Socio-Legal Status and Experiences of Forced Labour Among Asylum Seekers and Refugees in the UK' (2016) 32(3) Journal of International and Comparative Social Policy 182 <https://doi.org/10.1080/21699763.2016.1175961>

Foster M and Jane McAdam, 'Analysis of "Imminence" in International Protection Claims: *Teitiota v New Zealand* and Beyond' (2022) 71(4) International & Comparative Law Quarterly 975 <https://doi.org/10.1017/S0020589322000367>
Human Rights Committee, *Ioane Teitiota v New Zealand*, UN doc CCPR/C/127/D/2728/2016 (24 October 2019)
Ingram D, *World Crisis and Underdevelopment: A Critical Theory of Poverty, Agency, and Coercion* (CUP 2018)
Kent A and Simon Behrman, 'Why "Climate Refugees"' in Avidan Kent and Simon Behrman (eds), *Facilitating the Resettlement and Rights of Climate Refugees* (Routledge 2018)
McAdam J, *Climate Change, Forced Migration, and International Law* (OUP 2012)
McAdam J, *Complementary Protection in International Refugee Law* (OUP 2007)
McAdam J, 'Displacement in the Context of Climate Change and Disasters' in Cathryn Costello, Michelle Foster and Jane McAdam (eds), *The Oxford Handbook of International Refugee Law* (OUP 2021)
McAdam J, 'The Emerging New Zealand Jurisprudence on Climate Change, Disasters and Displacement' (2015) 3(1) Migration Studies 131 <https://doi.org/10.1093/migration/mnu055>
McAdam J, 'Swimming against the Tide: Why Climate Change Displacement Treaty Is Not the Answer' (2011) 23(1) International Journal of Refugee Law 2 <https://doi.org/10.1093/ijrl/eeq045>
McAdam J and Chiara Scissa, 'How Domestic Courts Are Using International Refugee Law and Human Rights Law in the Context of Climate Change and Disasters' (*EJIL:Talk!*, 22 November 2024) <www.ejiltalk.org/how-domestic-courts-are-using-international-refugee-law-and-human-rights-law-in-the-context-of-climate-change-and-disasters/> accessed 25 November 2024
McMichael C, Carol Farbotko and Karen E McNamara, 'Climate-Migration Responses in the Pacific Region' in Cecilia Menjívar, Marie Ruiz and Immanuel Ness (eds), *The Oxford Handbook of Migration Crises* (OUP 2018)
Moreno-Lax V, 'Of Autonomy, Autarky, Purposiveness and Fragmentation: The Relationship between EU Asylum Law and International Humanitarian Law' in David James Cantor and Jean-François Durieux (eds), *Refuge from Inhumanity? War Refugees and International Humanitarian Law* (Brill Nijhoff 2014)
N v The United Kingdom App no 26565/05 (ECtHR, 27 May 2008)
Nishitani M and Helen Lee, 'Becoming "Overstayers": The Coloniality of Citizenship and the Resilience of Pacific Farm Workers' in Victoria Stead and Jon Altman (eds), *Labour Lines and Colonial Power: Indigenous and Pacific Islander Labour Mobility in Australia* (ANU Press 2019)
OA (Somalia) Somalia CG [2022] UKUT 00033 (IAC)
OVG Berlin-Brandenburg, OVG 4 B 8/22, 30.11.2023
Refugee Appeal No 72185 [2000] NZRSAA (10 August 2000)
Refugee Appeal No 72186 [2000] NZRSAA 336 (10 August 2000)
Refugee Appeal No 72313 [2000] NZRSAA 491 (19 October 2000)
Refugee Appeal No 72314 [2000] NZRSAA 492 (19 October 2000)
Refugee Appeal No 72315 [2000] NZRSAA 493 (19 October 2000)
Refugee Appeal No 72316 [2000] NZRSAA 464 (19 October 2000)
Refugee Appeal Nos 72179–72181 [2000] NZRSAA 385 (31 August 2000)
Refugee Appeal Nos 72189–72195 [2000] NZRSAA 355 (17 August 2000)
Regulation (EU) 2018/1240 of the European Parliament and of the Council of 12 September 2018 Establishing a European Travel Information and Authorisation System (ETIAS) and Amending Regulations (EU) No 1077/2011, (EU) No 515/2014, (EU) 2016/399, (EU) 2016/1624 and (EU) 2017/2226 (ETIAS Regulation)

Regulation (EU) 2018/1806 of the European Parliament and of the Council of 14 November 2018 Listing the Third Countries Whose Nationals Must Be in Possession of Visas When Crossing the External Borders and Those Whose Nationals Are Exempt from That Requirement [2018] OJ L 303 (Visa Regulation)

Regulation (EU) 2024/1347 of the European Parliament and of the Council of 14 May 2024 on Standards for the Qualification of Third-Country Nationals or Stateless Persons as Beneficiaries of International Protection, for a Uniform Status for Refugees or for Persons Eligible for Subsidiary Protection and for the Content of the Protection Granted, Amending Council Directive 2003/109/EC and Repealing Directive 2011/95/EU of the European Parliament and of the Council [2024] OJ L 2024/1347 (Qualification Regulation)

Schloss C, 'The Role of Environmental Disasters in Asylum Cases: Do German Courts Take Disasters into Account?' in Simon Behrman and Avidan Kent (eds), *Climate Refugees: Global, Local, and Critical Approaches* (CUP 2022)

Scott M, *Climate Change, Disasters, and the Refugee Convention* (CUP 2020)

Spencer S and Anna Triandafyllidou, 'Irregular Migration' in Peter Scholten (ed), *Introduction to Migration Studies: An Interactive Guide to the Literatures on Migration and Diversity* (Springer 2022)

Sufi and Elmi v The United Kingdom App nos 8319/07 and 11449/07 (ECtHR, 28 June 2011)

Travelscope Website <www.markuslerner.com/travelscope/> accessed 16 August 2024

Triandafyllidou A and Laura Bartolini, 'Irregular Migration and Irregular Work: A Chicken and Egg Dilemma' in Sarah Spencer and Anna Triandafyllidou (eds), *Migrants with Irregular Status in Europe: Evolving Conceptual and Policy Challenges* (Springer 2020)

Tsourdi E, 'What Protection for Persons Fleeing Indiscriminate Violence? The Impact of the European Courts on the EU Subsidiary Protection Regime' in David James Cantor and Jean-François Durieux (eds), *Refuge from Inhumanity? War Refugees and International Humanitarian Law* (Brill Nijhoff 2014)

UNHCR, 'Desperate Journeys: Refugees and Migrants Arriving in Europe and at Europe's Borders January – December 2018' (2019) <https://data.unhcr.org/en/documents/details/67712> accessed 16 August 2024

UNHCR, 'Handbook on Procedures and Criteria for Determining Refugee Status and Guidelines on International Protection Under the 1951 Convention and the 1967 Protocol Relating to the Status of Refugees' (1979, reissued 2019) HCR/1P/4/ENG/REV.4 (UNHCR Handbook)

UNHCR, 'On this Journey, No One Cares if You Live or Die: Abuse, Protection and Justice Along Routes between East and West Africa and Africa's Mediterranean Coast: A Route-based Perspective on Key Risks', vol 2 (March 2024) <www.unhcr.org/media/journey-no-one-cares-if-you-live-or-die-abuse-protection-and-justice-along-routes-between-1> accessed 19 August 2024

UNHCR, 'Safe at Last? Law and Practice in Selected EU Member States with Respect to Asylum-Seekers Fleeing Indiscriminate Violence' (2011) <www.refworld.org/reference/regionalreport/unhcr/2011/en/80324> accessed 16 June 2024

UNODC, 'Global Report on Trafficking in Persons 2024' <www.unodc.org/documents/data-and-analysis/glotip/2024/GLOTIP2024_BOOK.pdf> accessed 16 December 2024

VG Berlin, 20 K 666.17 A, 24.03.2022

VG Hannover, 5 A 2783/17, 30.09.2020

VG Hannover, 5 A 8988/17, 04.01.2021

VG Hannover, 5 A 11015/17, 29.10.2020

VG Köln, 8 K 4355/18 A, 29.02.2024

VG Leipzig, 7 K 153/18.A, 28.04.2021
VG Lüneburg, 6 A 7/20, 22.02.2021
VG Lüneburg, 6 A 350/19, 10.06.2021
VG München, M 11 K 19.30060, 04.10.2023
VG Saarland, 5 K 741/20, 23.02.2022
Weerasinghe S, 'In Harm's Way: International Protection in the Context of Nexus Dynamics between Conflict or Violence and Disaster or Climate Change' (*UNHCR*, 2018) <www.unhcr.org/uk/media/no-39-harms-way-international-protection-context-nexus-dynamics-between-conflict-or-violence> accessed 25 July 2024

8 Conclusion

Protection From Dangerous Migratory Journeys

8.1 Irregular Migration, Refugee Status and the Law

This book has proposed a novel approach to the phenomenon of irregular migration by arguing that it ought to be treated as a protection issue. Persons who undertake dangerous migratory journeys are at risk of serious human rights violations. Thus, this book has investigated the protection needs of irregularised migrants – people who undertake dangerous migratory journeys due to a lack of legal migration pathways, who are unable to obtain refugee protection based on harm feared in their country of origin and who, if returned, may re-migrate irregularly.

In the process, the book has examined the relationship between irregular migration, refugee status and the law. It has shown that irregular (re-)migration is a risk which may warrant refugee status and that the law is therefore able to respond to the protection needs of irregularised migrants. In doing so, the book has contributed new ideas and knowledge on the scope of the *refugee* definition, refugee law doctrine, vulnerability theory, migration theories and migration policy. This chapter summarises the book's main contributions.

It begins by outlining how the analysis of trafficking-based asylum claims and the drawing of analogies to irregularised migrants lead to the latter being reconceptualised as refugees. The rigorous analysis of case law conducted in this book has not only provided new insights into the causes and consequences of irregular re-migration but has also shown how a better understanding of these leads to new outcomes in refugee law. First, the analysis shows that rather than constituting a 'voluntary' choice, irregular re-migration is a risk certain individuals, and especially those with previous experiences of irregular migration, are exposed to. Second, it demonstrates that harm experienced during irregular re-migration can be conceptualised as persecution and that this concept is not limited to the territory of the country of origin. Finally, it explains that as members of the particular social group (PSG) 'persons in vulnerable situations' and as persons whose nationality contributes to the risk of undertaking dangerous journeys, irregularised migrants can establish a nexus between the risk of irregular re-migration and Refugee Convention grounds.

DOI: 10.4324/9781032664644-8

In order to make the argument that irregularised migrants can meet the refugee definition, this book has developed refugee law doctrine and added to both vulnerability theory and migration theories. This chapter shows that the book develops refugee law doctrine by proposing a novel approach to the scope of the concept of persecution, by contributing new insights on the Convention ground 'membership of a PSG' and the Convention ground 'nationality' and by exploring the *refugee* definition's relationship with vulnerability theory. Thus, the book has argued that persecution is not limited to the territory of the country of origin. This is a novel idea which allows refugee law to respond to new and emerging refugee situations by considering the interplay of different types of harm as well as new geographical and temporal contexts in which such harm is inflicted. The book has also contributed to debates around establishing a nexus to Refugee Convention grounds by introducing the PSG 'persons in vulnerable situations' and by exploring the relevance of the Convention ground 'nationality' when given its ordinary meaning of 'citizenship'. These considerations are informed by vulnerability theory, and the book has explored the *refugee* definition's relationship with vulnerability theory in detail. In doing so, the book has developed a technique for conducting a holistic assessment of a protection claim based on an understanding of how vulnerability permeates and connects the elements of the *refugee* definition. The book not only utilises but also develops vulnerability theory, introducing the concept of 'consequential vulnerability', which explains why particular past experiences expose individuals to an increased risk of going through the same experience again in the future. An understanding of consequential vulnerability, in turn, informs migration theory and forms part of the concept of 'route causes' of irregular re-migration developed in this book.

Following the discussion of the book's doctrinal and theoretical contributions, this chapter shows that these considerations, and the resulting progressive interpretation of refugee law, have practical implications in broadening the scope of the *refugee* definition. Thus, the chapter recaps who may benefit from the argument made in this book. Persons currently receiving complementary protection due to 'very significant obstacles to integration' in the country of origin or based on a risk of destitution may, in fact, be irregularised migrants, and thus refugees. Similarly, persons affected by climate change and disasters may be reconceptualised as irregularised migrants in need of refugee protection. The chapter then considers criticism in the shape of floodgate concerns and possible negative policy consequences of making the argument that (some) irregularised migrants are, in fact, refugees. Based on this, the chapter then considers the argument's implications for migration policy, showing that conceiving of irregularised migrants as refugees implies a need for a shift away from states' restrictive border control measures.

8.2 Refugee Status for Irregularised Migrants

The dangers inherent in irregular migration are, reluctantly, recognised by states. The international law framework on trafficking and smuggling admits that *some* irregular migrants, that is, trafficked persons, experience harm and are therefore in need of protection. This is also accepted in refugee law, where a future risk of re-trafficking can form the basis for refugee status.

This book has used trafficked persons' protection claims as a starting point for investigating irregularised migrants' protection needs. Chapter 2 compared the experiences of trafficked persons, who are described in international law as forced migrants in need of protection, with those of smuggled persons, who in international law are seen as voluntary migrants without protection needs. This comparison showed that both groups' experiences are very similar in terms of their migration motivations, the migratory routes they take and, crucially, the serious human rights violations they experience during dangerous journeys. While not all irregularised migrants will have been smuggled, questioning the reasons for distinguishing between trafficked and smuggled persons, despite their clearly very similar experiences, is the first step in using trafficked persons' asylum claims as a 'template' for the protection claims of irregularised migrants.

The book analysed trafficked persons' asylum claims and their implications for irregularised migrants in Chapters 3 to 5. Chapter 3 showed that the risk of re-trafficking is mirrored by a risk of irregular re-migration. It demonstrated that the risk of re-trafficking is established through vulnerability indicators which apply not only to trafficked persons but also to individuals with no prior experience of trafficking, and especially to persons who have previously undertaken dangerous migratory journeys. Relevant vulnerability indicators – derived from an analysis of trafficked persons' asylum claims, but also those of other similarly 'vulnerable' individuals – include age; poverty; lack of employment opportunities and experience, education, specialist skills and financial assets; having no family or other support networks in the country of origin or experiencing pressure from the family to earn money; having (mental) health issues; experiencing stigmatisation; having 'illegitimate' children or other dependants; a long period of absence from the country of origin; and drug addiction. Some of these are what I term 'consequential vulnerabilities', brought about by experiences during dangerous migratory journeys. This book has highlighted the importance of previous dangerous journeys for the future risk analysis. It has argued that to understand the risk of irregular re-migration, it is necessary to consider 'route causes' of irregular re-migration: those vulnerabilities which cause an individual to undertake a dangerous journey in the first place, those which are caused by this dangerous journey, as well as their interplay. As such, structural factors – or situational vulnerabilities – like conflict, environmental degradation and restrictions on regular movement, must also be considered. The interplay of these intersecting vulnerabilities makes it difficult for an individual to reintegrate and to earn a livelihood in the country of origin, and irregular re-migration is a response addressing the resulting socio-economic deprivation. Although economic reasons play an important role in the future risk analysis, irregular re-migration is not 'voluntary' but a risk individuals are exposed to due to their vulnerabilities. As such, 'vulnerable' irregularised migrants can be said to have a well-founded fear of irregular re-migration.

Irregular re-migration can be described as a risk because it entails serious harm, such as physical and sexual violence, torture, deprivation of liberty and forced labour. Yet this harm materialises largely outside the country of origin, during the journey, in countries of transit and destination. Chapter 4 investigated whether irregularised migrants' experiences can, nevertheless, be classified as persecution for the purpose of refugee law. While the fact that the majority of the relevant harm trafficked persons experience takes place outside the country of origin is not seen as an obstacle to their protection claims, it does pose doctrinal difficulties. I suggested that to overcome these, harm experienced during re-trafficking and irregular re-migration should be thought of as sequential and cumulative. While still in the country of origin, trafficked persons and irregularised migrants experience socio-economic deprivation (brought about by intersecting vulnerabilities), which, on its own, is unlikely to amount to persecution. However, cumulatively with the serious human rights violations experienced outside the country of origin, socio-economic deprivation will reach the required severity of harm to amount to persecution, while explaining why there is a failure of state protection. In order to protect against the serious harm experienced outside its territory, a state of origin would have to protect individuals against the socio-economic deprivation experienced in its territory by addressing their individual vulnerabilities and their interplay. Thus, irregularised migrants, whose state of origin is unable to protect them in this manner and who are therefore at risk of both socio-economic deprivation in the country of origin and serious human rights violations outside that country, can be said to be at risk of being persecuted.

Individuals with a well-founded fear of irregular re-migration will only be eligible for refugee status if they can show that there is a connection between the persecution feared and one of the five Refugee Convention grounds. Chapter 5 considered how the nexus link might be made out. Returning to the vulnerability analysis, I proposed that the PSG 'persons in vulnerable situations' explains why 'vulnerable' irregularised migrants are at a disproportionately high risk of re-migrating irregularly. Since it is individuals' vulnerabilities and their interplay and effects which put them at risk of re-migrating irregularly, it is logical to return to these reasons in the nexus enquiry. 'Persons in vulnerable situations' constitute a PSG because they are likely to be perceived as different from surrounding society due to their characteristics and/or behaviour. They also share immutable characteristics: their vulnerability and the prior migration experience. In addition to this PSG, the Convention ground nationality is relevant to establishing nexus. 'Nationality' can be interpreted as 'citizenship', and citizenship, as a determining factor of international mobility, explains why an individual is at a disproportionately high risk of undertaking dangerous migratory journeys. Thus, irregularised migrants can show that their fear of irregular re-migration is for reasons of these Convention grounds.

In summary, not only will many irregularised migrants be able to establish a future risk of irregular re-migration, but in addition, experiences during dangerous journeys are likely to amount to persecution, and this risk of persecution can be linked to Refugee Convention grounds. Even though they are unable to obtain refugee status based on harm feared in their country of origin alone, where irregularised migrants can meet (the three main elements of) the *refugee* definition as described earlier, they are refugees for the purpose of the Refugee Convention.

8.3 Doctrinal and Theoretical Contributions

To make the preceding argument, this book has developed refugee law doctrine by proposing a novel approach to the scope of the concept of persecution, by contributing new insights on the Convention ground 'membership of a PSG' and the Convention ground 'nationality' and by exploring the relationship of the *refugee* definition with vulnerability theory. In doing so, the book has also added to vulnerability theory and to migration theories.

This book has developed the concept of 'persecution' by arguing that its cumulative nature allows it to encompass temporally sequential harms experienced in different locations, including outside the country of origin. As long as some harm is experienced in the country of origin and that country fails to provide protection against it, there is a 'jurisdictional anchor' for the additional harm taking place outside the country of origin and experienced as a result of the failure of state protection. Arguing that persecution for the purpose of the Refugee Convention is not limited to the territory of the country of origin is a novel claim with major implications for refugee law doctrine. Questioning the idea that the locus of persecution is solely the country of origin opens up the possibility of examining the protection needs of persons who, although not at risk of persecution in their country of origin, may be exposed to persecution outside that country. Through this understanding of persecution, the Refugee Convention is able to respond to new and emerging refugee situations, by considering the interplay of not only different types of harm but also new geographical and temporal contexts in which such harm is inflicted.

This book has also developed both the Convention grounds 'membership of a PSG' and 'nationality'. The insights this book contributes by introducing the PSG 'persons in vulnerable situations' are discussed in what follows in the context of its contribution to developing the relationship between refugee law and vulnerability theory. Regarding the Convention ground 'nationality', the book's contribution lies in creating an enhanced understanding of this Convention ground's relevance when given its ordinary meaning of 'citizenship'. A person's *citizenship* determines whether they can travel legally and safely and informs the security of status a migrant holds in their host country, including security of residence and protection from return. Thus, in addition to situations of denationalisation, statelessness and persecution due to former citizenship, an individual's nationality is relevant in the nexus enquiry where it contributes to the predicament of having to undertake dangerous migratory journeys. This approach to the Convention ground 'nationality' thus allows for establishing a link between the persecution experienced during dangerous journeys and the immutable characteristic of 'citizenship'.

These considerations on the Convention ground 'nationality' are informed by vulnerability theory, since a person's nationality can be said to constitute a situational vulnerability exposing them to harm in the context of irregular migration. This book has drawn on vulnerability theory to make its arguments and has developed the relationship between refugee law and the vulnerability concept. In doing so, it has highlighted the interconnected nature of the elements of the *refugee* definition, with the vulnerability analysis informing the future risk analysis, the state protection enquiry and the nexus question. Thus, vulnerability theory informs the future risk analysis because it illustrates how different layers of vulnerability converge to create the requisite risk. Inherent, situational, and consequential vulnerabilities, brought about by a prior experience of being persecuted, interact to constrain an individual's choices, thus explaining why that individual might be at risk in the future. As such, the vulnerability concept advances the well-founded fear analysis by developing a better understanding of the relevance of past persecution for the future risk enquiry. Instead of conducting this enquiry solely based on the likelihood of persecutors re-targeting the applicant, the vulnerability analysis shifts the focus onto the effects past experiences of persecution have had on the applicant and the resulting increased risk of experiencing harm in the future.

Further, vulnerabilities identified in the context of the future risk analysis also inform the state protection enquiry. Having identified what factors put a person at risk of irregular re-migration, these must be considered when it comes to the question of availability of protection. Importantly, the vulnerability analysis highlights the individual circumstances which the country of origin would have to address in order to offer effective protection to a particular person. Addressing only the immediate effects of these vulnerabilities, that is, socio-economic deprivation, for example through financial reintegration assistance, would not constitute effective protection since such an approach fails to consider the complexity of different vulnerabilities and how they interact. Instead, to provide effective protection against irregular re-migration, states of origin would have to address (the cumulative effects of) each person's individual vulnerabilities.

Finally, the vulnerability concept also informs the nexus enquiry. This book has shown that the PSG 'persons in vulnerable situations' links the predicament of having to re-migrate irregularly to the vulnerable situation irregularised migrants find themselves in in the country of origin. Introducing this PSG provides insights into the nexus question by highlighting the interconnected nature of the different elements of the *refugee* definition. It shows that vulnerabilities not only inform the future risk and the state protection enquires but can also be framed in terms of nexus grounds to explain why a risk of persecution exists. At the same time, adjectives used to narrow down PSGs may give hints as to why an individual is vulnerable to a particular type of harm, thereby informing the future risk and state protection enquiries. Thus, relying on the PSG 'persons in vulnerable situations' demonstrates how the vulnerability concept allows for connecting the individual elements of the *refugee* definition and for analysing it both methodically and holistically.

In addition to utilising vulnerability theory to develop a refugee law doctrine, the book develops vulnerability theory itself. It does so by introducing the concept of 'consequential vulnerability', which serves to explain why individuals who have been through a particular experience – in the present context irregular migration – are at an increased risk of going through that experience again. Thus, the concept contributes a new category to existing frameworks of vulnerability,[1] highlighting the importance of taking into account past experiences when considering exposure to future harm.

An understanding of consequential vulnerability, in turn, informs migration theory and forms part of the concept of 'route causes' of irregular re-migration developed in this book. In order to understand why individuals re-migrate irregularly, it is necessary to consider those individuals' inherent and situational vulnerabilities, but also their experiences during previous dangerous journeys, which cause them to develop additional, consequential vulnerabilities. Thus, the 'route causes' approach adds to existing migration theories by explaining, first of all, that irregular re-migration is not 'voluntary' but a response to vulnerabilities. Further, 'route causes' theory explains why irregular migration is a continuous phenomenon, that is, why a previous experience of migrating irregularly increases the likelihood of irregular re-migration after return to the country of origin.

In summary, the arguments advanced in this book develop vulnerability theory and add to migration theories. Most importantly, however, they have implications for refugee law doctrine by allowing for novel and more nuanced approaches to refugee law concepts. This, in turn, has the effect of broadening the scope of the *refugee* definition. The next section considers the practical implications of the argument advanced in this book, by explaining which claimants may benefit from this argument and engages with possible criticism of expanding the *refugee* definition.

8.4 Practical Implications: Expanding the Refugee Definition

Arguing that (certain) irregularised migrants must be considered to be refugees expands the *refugee* definition to include persons previously thought to fall outside its scope. Individuals who submit protection claims but are only granted complementary forms of protection may benefit from the argument advanced in this book and thus show that they are, in fact, refugees.

1 In particular, it builds on and contributes to theories developed by Fineman and Mackenzie and others: See Martha Albertson Fineman, 'The Vulnerable Subject: Anchoring Equality in the Human Condition' (2008) 20(1) Yale Journal of Law and Feminism 9; Martha Albertson Fineman, 'Equality, Autonomy, and the Vulnerable Subject in Law and Politics' in Martha Albertson Fineman and Anna Grear (eds), *Vulnerability: Reflections on a New Ethical Foundation for Law and Politics* (Routledge 2016); Catriona Mackenzie, Wendy Rogers and Susan Dodds, 'Introduction: What Is Vulnerability, and Why Does It Matter for Moral Theory?' in Catriona Mackenzie, Wendy Rogers and Susan Dodds (eds), *Vulnerability: New Essays in Ethics and Feminist Philosophy* (OUP 2014).

Chapter 6 showed that where individuals' claims for complementary protection succeed because of 'very significant obstacles to integration' or due to a risk of destitution, courts effectively rely on vulnerability indicators to explain why an individual needs protection. As such, it would be pertinent to consider whether the relevant factors indicate a risk of trafficking or irregular re-migration and, if so, whether the claimant in question is entitled to refugee status. Importantly, even persons whose complementary protection claims do not succeed (because they cannot meet the high threshold of 'very significant' obstacles to integration or show that the socio-economic deprivation they would experience will amount to a breach of human rights) may still be able to show that they are at risk of trafficking or irregular re-migration, since their vulnerabilities (and their effects) indicating such a risk need not amount to a violation of human rights in themselves.

Indeed, reframing claimants who currently either receive only complementary protection or no protection at all as irregularised migrants may extend refugee status to persons who normally experience obstacles in claiming refugee protection. Thus, Chapter 7 showed that individuals affected by climate change and disasters may benefit from the argument made in this book. Climate change and disasters lead to socio-economic deprivation, and the chapter proposed considering the risk of irregular (re-)migration in the disaster context on a sliding scale. Doing so accounts for the fact that the effects of climate change and disasters can be so severe as to cause anyone present in the territory to be exposed to socio-economic deprivation, and thus to a high likelihood of irregular re-migration. It also accounts for the fact that were the effects of climate change and disasters are less severe, individual vulnerabilities heighten the risk of socio-economic deprivation and thus the likelihood of irregular (re-)migration. A similar argument may be made for other displacement contexts leading to socio-economic deprivation and exacerbating individual vulnerabilities, such as the context of armed conflict.[2]

In sum, the argument advanced in this book may be applicable to a range of individuals who are not currently thought to be in need of refugee protection. Although, in this book, I have developed my argument mostly with the help of UK and German case law, which situates the enquiry in the EU and European legal context, my argument is applicable beyond the regional setting and to other signatory states to the Refugee Convention where irregularised migrants arrive. Of course, the usual caveats to inclusion under the *refugee* definition apply in this context. Thus, claimants may be subject to the Refugee Convention's exclusion clauses, or their protection claims may fail due to credibility issues. Nevertheless, the argument advanced in this book, if accepted and applied in practice, is likely to lead to a number of persons who would normally be considered to be 'migrants' being reclassified as 'refugees',

2 Persons fleeing armed conflict may, however, be eligible for refugee status for reasons unrelated to the risk of irregular re-migration. See, for example, Christel Querton, *Conflict Refugees: European Union Law and Practice* (CUP 2023).

thus challenging or, rather, dissolving, what Hamlin calls the 'migrant/refugee binary'.[3] Since, as Hamlin explains, this binary is based on a number of assumptions around protection needs and voluntariness of movement, which the analysis in this book has refuted, disengaging from these binary categories and the assumptions that come with them ought to be seen as a positive step. Yet interpreting the *refugee* definition to include irregularised migrants within its scope is likely to meet with some resistance.

Even though it has been argued that 'refugees are migrants' because both are equally impacted by migration control measures, while questioning the notion that only refugees are in need of protection,[4] it has not outright been suggested, as I have, that (certain) migrants must be considered to be refugees. Although it has been recognised that 'insisting on a migrant/refugee dichotomy leads many to believe that refugees need protection while migrants do not', protection for migrants is envisaged as a matter of human rights law rather than refugee protection.[5]

This is, in part, because refugee status is viewed as a 'scare resource'.[6] As Haddad explains, a 'wide definition of who falls into the category "refugee" increases the potential burden on the host state'.[7] While Juss, for example, has argued that 'there is no logical or necessary distinction to be made between political and economic migrants' as '[b]oth are forced to leave their homelands in search of a better life',[8] others argue that such a position does not take into account the capacities of the refugee protection regime. Steinbock, for example, is concerned that a liberal interpretation of refugee law 'would make millions of people potential refugees'.[9]

Foster shows that the 'difficulty with [such a] floodgates argument is that it is clearly not a legal argument'.[10] Thus, having shown why and how irregularised migrants can be brought within the scope of refugee law, I take the position that those who meet the *refugee* definition must be granted refugee status,

3 Rebecca Hamlin, *Crossing: How We Label and React to People on the Move* (Stanford UP 2021) 9.
4 RefMig, 'Refugees are Migrants: Refugee Mobility, Recognition and Rights' (2021) <www.refmig.org> accessed 1 October 2024.
5 Idil Atak and Francois Crépau, 'Refugees as Migrants' in Cathryn Costello, Michelle Foster and Jane McAdam (eds), *The Oxford Handbook of International Refugee Law* (OUP 2021) 136.
6 David A Martin, 'The Refugee Concept: On Definitions, Politics, and the Careful Use of a Scarce Resource' in Howard Adelman (ed), *Refugee Policy: Canada and the United States* (Centre for Refugee Studies, York University 1991) 36.
7 Emma Haddad, 'Who is (Not) a Refugee?' (2004) EUI Working Paper SPS No 2004/6 <https://cadmus.eui.eu/server/api/core/bitstreams/b59a79ab-f0e7-5968-bc2f-609322fd134f/content> accessed 19 September 2024, 5.
8 Satvinder S Juss, 'Free Movement and the World Order' (2004) 16(3) International Journal of Refugee Law 289, 306 <https://doi.org/10.1093/ijrl/16.3.289>.
9 Daniel J Steinbock, 'Interpreting the Refugee Definition' (1998) 19 Immigration and Nationality Law Review 137, 186.
10 Michelle Foster, *International Refugee Law and Socio-Economic Rights: Refuge from Deprivation* (CUP 2007) 344.

rather than artificially circumscribing groups of beneficiaries based on policy concerns. Otherwise, refugee law becomes meaningless. As Haddad points out, a 'narrow [*refugee*] definition . . . runs the risk of denying protection and assistance to individuals in need'.[11] Legally speaking, it is irrelevant how many individuals have such protection needs. As Grahl-Madsen puts it, '[o]nce a person is subjected to a measure of such gravity that we consider it "persecution", that person is "persecuted" in the sense of the Convention, irrespective of how many others are subjected to the same or similar measures'.[12]

In defending her own approach to broadening the *refugee* definition based on violations of socio-economic rights, Foster aptly counters floodgate concerns by explaining that not every person who could potentially benefit from a broad interpretation of the *refugee* definition will, in fact, seek protection in the Global North, nor will every person who does seek protection ultimately satisfy the *refugee* definition.[13] The same is true with regard to irregularised migrants.

Yet Foster also recognises that where a legal argument extending refugee status to new groups is accepted, states may respond by making asylum legislation more restrictive or by further increasing their border control measures to prevent asylum seekers from reaching their territory.[14] Thus, my argument, if accepted, could have the opposite effect of what it intends to do in increasing the dangers protection seekers are exposed to during dangerous journeys. Nevertheless, I agree with Foster that against the background of states' restrictive immigration policies, 'the only remaining feasible site for contestation remains rights-based litigation'.[15] As such, I subscribe to the view that 'a scholarship that reifies untenable migrant/refugee divisions risks being implicated in the normalisation of seemingly objective, value-neutral, and technocratic labels, and thus risks becoming complicit in the disciplining of migration'.[16] Thus, instead of shying away from expansive interpretations of refugee law in fear of a policy backlash, I want to outline how my argument can challenge states' border control policies.

8.5 Policy Implications: Challenging States' Border Control Prerogative

By virtue of having implications for refugee law doctrine, the argument advanced in this book also has implications for states' approach to irregularised

11 Haddad (n 7) 5.

12 Atle Grahl-Madsen, *The Status of Refugees in International Law*, vol I (A W Sijthoff 1966) 213.

13 Foster (n 10) 344–45.

14 ibid 346–47.

15 ibid 348; see also Helen Duffy, *Strategic Human Rights Litigation: Understanding and Maximising Impact* (Bloomsbury 2018) 5 and 77–80.

16 Maurice Stierl, 'Do No Harm? The Impact of Policy on Migration Scholarship' (2022) 40(5) Environment and Planning C: Politics and Space 1083, 1090 <https://doi.org/10.1177/2399654420965567>.

migrants and their protection claims, and, ultimately, states' border control measures. States view migration as governable, and irregular migration as a contravention of their immigration rules. They approach irregular migration in a simplistic manner, relying on reductive migration law and policy categories. Yet this book has shown that in order to implement their obligations under the Refugee Convention, states must look beyond migration law and policy categories and their underlying assumptions and approach irregular re-migration as a protection issue.

Based on the main finding of this book – that irregularised migrants who are able to meet all elements of the Refugee Convention's *refugee* definition, as described earlier, ought to be recognised as refugees – states will have to consider their own role in creating irregularised migrants' protection needs. The phenomenon of irregular re-migration is underexplored, both in migration theories and in law and policy. Indeed, currently, both refugee law and migration policy ignore the effects of dangerous journeys. Although in trafficking-based asylum claims, individuals' experiences *en route* are taken into consideration, the relevant enquiry is neither linked explicitly to states' border control practices nor employed beyond the trafficking context. In this book, I have emphasised the importance of considering the effects of dangerous migratory journeys, arguing that the risk of irregular re-migration is heightened for those who have experienced a previous dangerous journey. I have also highlighted the role an individual's nationality (i.e. citizenship), and the corresponding ability to travel legally and safely, plays in this context.

Importantly, it is states in the Global North that create the conditions under which irregularised migrants move and experience harm. Indeed, by adopting nationality-based travel restrictions and other extraterritorial border control measures, and thus forcing irregular migrants onto dangerous routes, states contribute to and exacerbate migrants' vulnerability to irregular re-migration. Even though 'deterrence is largely ineffective',[17] it continues to be practised, causing people to risk more and more dangerous migratory routes. As a result, states perpetuate, rather than prevent, irregular migration. In short, states contribute to creating irregularised migrants' protection needs. While it may seem counterintuitive for irregularised migrants to seek protection from future dangerous journeys in the very countries which create irregular migration through their border control policies, it is not unusual or unheard of for states to protect persons whose predicament they have played a part in creating. For example, individuals from Iraq who have worked with Western forces, organisations or companies have been granted refugee status in those Western states.[18]

17 Vicki Squire and others, *Reclaiming Migration: Voices from Europe's 'Migrant Crisis'* (Manchester UP 2021) 74.

18 See, for example, *BA (Returns to Baghdad) Iraq* CG [2017] UKUT 18 (IAC) [107]. See also *NS (Iraq: perceived collaborator: relocation) Iraq* CG [2007] UKAIT 00046.

The fact that states contribute to irregularised migrants' predicament has interesting implications for these states' migration control policies. In fact, the finding that (certain) irregularised migrants are refugees turns the logic of migration control on its head. Treating irregular re-migration as a risk shows that by seeking to deter migrants and forcing them onto dangerous routes, states create a category of claimant entitled to refugee status not exceptionally, based on experiences in the claimant's country of origin, but (potentially) as a rule, because of harm experienced during a (future) dangerous journey. Unless states cease to attempt to exclude irregular migrants through extraterritorial border controls, they will have to include (certain) irregularised migrants as refugees.

References

Atak I and Francois Crépau, 'Refugees as Migrants' in Cathryn Costello, Michelle Foster and Jane McAdam (eds), *The Oxford Handbook of International Refugee Law* (OUP 2021)

BA (Returns to Baghdad) Iraq CG [2017] UKUT 18 (IAC)

Duffy H, *Strategic Human Rights Litigation: Understanding and Maximising Impact* (Bloomsbury 2018)

Fineman MA, 'Equality, Autonomy, and the Vulnerable Subject in Law and Politics' in Martha Albertson Fineman and Anna Grear (eds), *Vulnerability: Reflections on a New Ethical Foundation for Law and Politics* (Routledge 2016)

Fineman MA, 'The Vulnerable Subject: Anchoring Equality in the Human Condition' (2008) 20(1) Yale Journal of Law and Feminism 9

Foster M, *International Refugee Law and Socio-Economic Rights: Refuge from Deprivation* (CUP 2007)

Grahl-Madsen A, *The Status of Refugees in International Law*, vol I (A W Sijthoff 1966)

Haddad E, 'Who is (Not) a Refugee?' (2004) EUI Working Paper SPS No 2004/6 <https://cadmus.eui.eu/server/api/core/bitstreams/b59a79ab-f0e7-5968-bc2f-609322fd134f/content> accessed 19 September 2024

Hamlin R, *Crossing: How We Label and React to People on the Move* (Stanford UP 2021)

Juss SS, 'Free Movement and the World Order' (2004) 16(3) International Journal of Refugee Law 289 <https://doi.org/10.1093/ijrl/16.3.289>

Mackenzie C, Wendy Rogers and Susan Dodds, 'Introduction: What is Vulnerability, and Why Does It Matter for Moral Theory?' in Catriona Mackenzie, Wendy Rogers and Susan Dodds (eds), *Vulnerability: New Essays in Ethics and Feminist Philosophy* (OUP 2014)

Martin DA, 'The Refugee Concept: On Definitions, Politics, and the Careful Use of a Scarce Resource' in Howard Adelman (ed), *Refugee Policy: Canada and the United States* (Centre for Refugee Studies, York University 1991)

Querton C, *Conflict Refugees: European Union Law and Practice* (CUP 2023)

RefMig, 'Refugees are Migrants: Refugee Mobility, Recognition and Rights' (2021) <www.refmig.org> accessed 1 October 2024

Squire V and others, *Reclaiming Migration: Voices from Europe's 'Migrant Crisis'* (Manchester UP 2021)

Steinbock DJ, 'Interpreting the Refugee Definition' (1998) 19 Immigration and Nationality Law Review 137

Stierl M, 'Do No Harm? The Impact of Policy on Migration Scholarship' (2022) 40(5) Environment and Planning C: Politics and Space 1083 <https://doi.org/10.1177/2399654420965567>

Index

FSC
www.fsc.org
MIX
Papier | Fördert gute Waldnutzung
FSC® C083411

Kolibri 360 GmbH
Ferdinand-Jühlke-Straße 7
99095 Erfurt, Deutschland
produktsicherheit@kolibri360.de